WALL STREET

WALL STREET

*How It Works
and for Whom*

———◆———

DOUG HENWOOD

V

VERSO
London • New York

First published by Verso 1997
This paperback edition 1998
© Copyright Doug Henwood 1998
All rights reserved

Verso
UK: 6 Meard Street, London W1V 3HR
USA: 180 Varick Street, New York NY 10014-4606

Verso is the imprint of New Left Books

ISBN 0-86091-670-7

British Library Cataloguing in Publication Data
A catalogue record for this book is available from the British Library.

Library of Congress Cataloging-in-Publication Data
A catalog record for this book is available from the Library of Congress.

Designed and typeset by LBO Graphics, New York
Printed and bound in the United States of America

The credit system, which has its focal point in the allegedly national banks and the big money-lenders and usurers that surround them, is one enormous centralization and gives this class of parasites a fabulous power not only to decimate the industrial capitalists periodically but also to interfere in actual production in the most dangerous manner— and this crew know nothing of production and have nothing at all to do with it.

— Marx, *Capital,* vol. 3, chap. 33

I'm not a parasite. I'm an investor.

— Lyonya Gulubkov, described by the *New York Times* as "a bumbling Russian Everyman" responding to "Soviet-style" taunts in an ad for the fraudulent MMM investment scheme which collapsed in 1994

Contents

Acknowledgments

Though one name usually appears on the cover, a book is a far more collaborative project than that. I've enjoyed splendid research assistance from (in chronological order) Michael Tremonte, who gathered most of the material found in the bibliography; Kim Phillips; Lisa Westberg; Josh Mason, who assembled lots of last-minute articles and numbers; Adria Scharf; and Shana Siegel. Thanks to Jean Bratton for reading the proofs. Thanks too to all the sources, named and unnamed. For all the faults of American society, I've long been amazed at its openness; both public- and private-sector sources are almost always happy to help an author out. Thanks as well to my cyber-colleagues in two computer networks, the Progressive Economists Network and Post-Keynesian Thought (for information on both, visit http://csf.colorado.edu), and to my real-life friends Patrick Bond, Bob Fitch, Dan Lazare, John Liscio, Bob Pollin, and Gregg Wirth. Deep expressions of gratitude are also due to three editors: Ben Sonnenberg of *Grand Street* and Victor Navasky of *The Nation,* who gave me a public forum when my newsletter was young and little more than a vanity operation, and Colin Robinson of Verso, who not only offered me a book contract when I was even more obscure than I am now, but who also put up with my endless delays in getting this thing done.

Thanks, along with love, to my parents, Harold and Victorine Henwood, for a lifetime of support of every kind, and to Christine Bratton, my companion and partner in life and in many aspects of work as well. Chris has not only spent a decade reading and improving my prose, but she put up with me as I wrote this book. For years, I thought that authors' expressions of gratitude for indulgence from intimates were mere boilerplate, but when I think back on what a cranky, preoccupied monster I was for nearly six years (not to mention the brief paperback relapse), I now realize just how deeply felt they were. I'll say once again that life would be unimaginable without her.

Introduction

It's rare that someone should develop an obsession with Wall Street without sharing its driving passion, the accumulation of money. It would probably take years of psychoanalysis to untangle that contradiction, not to mention others too sensitive to name here.

No doubt that contradictory obsession has early roots, but its most potent adult influence was probably my first job out of college, at a small brokerage firm in downtown Manhattan. The firm had been started by a former Bell Labs physicist, who wanted to use his quantitative skills to analyze and trade a then-new instrument known as listed options. The refugee physicist was considerably ahead of his time; few people understood options in 1975, and fewer still were interested in using the kinds of high-tech trading strategies that would later sweep Wall Street.

My title was secretary to the chairman, which meant not only that I typed his letters, but also that I got his lunch and went out to buy him new socks when he'd left his old ones in a massage parlor. And I studied the place like an anthropologist, absorbing the mentality and culture of money. It was fascinating in its own way, but it also struck me as utterly cynical and empty, a profound waste of human effort.

One morning, riding the elevator up to work, I noticed a cop standing next to me, a gun on his hip. I realized in an instant that all the sophisticated machinations that went on upstairs and around the whole Wall Street neighborhood rested ultimately on force. Financial power, too, grows out of the barrel of a gun. Of course a serious analysis of the political economy of finance has to delve into all those sophisticated machinations, but the image of that gun should be kept firmly in mind.

On what is loosely called the left, such as it is these days, two unhappy attitudes towards modern finance prevail — one, the everything's-changed-

and-capital-no-longer-matters school, and two, a stance of uninformed condemnation. An example of the first is this silly but representative eruption from Jean Baudrillard (1993, pp. 10–11, 33):

> Marx simply did not foresee that it would be possible for capital, in the face of the imminent threat to its existence, to transpoliticize itself, as it were: to launch itself into an orbit beyond the relations of production and political contradictions, to make itself autonomous in a free-floating, ecstatic and haphazard form, and thus to totalize the world in its own image. Capital (if it may still be so called) has barred the way of political economy and the law of value; it is in this sense that it has successfully escaped its own end. Henceforward it can function independently of its own former aims, and absolutely without reference to any aims whatsoever.... Money is now the only genuine artificial satellite. A pure artifact, it enjoys a truly astral mobility; and it is instantly convertible. Money has now found its proper place, a place far more wondrous than the stock exchange: the orbit in which it rises and sets like some artificial sun.

This isn't that surprising from a writer who can declare the Gulf War a media event. But it displays an understanding of finance apparently derived from capital's own publicists, like George Gilder, who celebrate the obsolescence of matter and the transcendence of all the old hostile relations of production. Cybertopians and other immaterialists are lost in a second- or even third-order fetishism, unable to decode the relations of power behind the disembodied ecstasies of computerized trading.

And, on the other hand, lefties of all sorts — liberal, populist, and socialist — who haven't succumbed to vulgar postmodernism have continued the long tradition of beating up on finance, denouncing it as a stinkpot of parasitism, irrelevance, malignancy, and corruption, without providing much detail beyond that. Many critics denounce "speculation" as a waste of social resources, without making any connections between it and the supposedly more fundamental world of "production." Sociologists who study power structures write portentously of "the banks," but their evidence is often vague and obsolete (see, for example, Glasberg 1989b, a piece written at the end of one of the great financial manias of all time that nonetheless relies heavily on evidence from the 1970s). It's as if such people stopped thinking and collecting evidence 20 or even 60 years ago.

This book is an attempt to get down and dirty with how modern American finance works and how it's connected to the real world. It's a system that seems overwhelming at times — almost sublime in its complexity and power, reminiscent of Fredric Jameson's (1991, pp. 39–44) reading of John Portman's Bonaventure Hotel, at once packed and empty, a spatial analogue of our disorientation as subjects in the dizzy world of modern multinational capitalism. (It seems especially dizzying as I write this in early 1998, with the U.S. stock market at or near its highest levels of valuation in 125 years, and the broad public the most deeply involved it's been in decades, and maybe ever.) As an antidote to that sense of disorientation, Jameson suggested the need for "cognitive mapping," critical expositions of that vertiginous world that remind us that despite its vast scope, it is the product of human intelligence and society, comprehensible with a little effort, and maybe even transformable with a little more.

In a soundbite, the U.S. financial system performs dismally at its advertised task, that of efficiently directing society's savings towards their optimal investment pursuits. The system is stupefyingly expensive, gives terrible signals for the allocation of capital, and has surprisingly little to do with real investment. Most money managers can barely match market averages — and there's evidence that active trading reduces performance rather than improving it — yet they still haul in big fees, and their brokers, big commissions (Lakonishok, Shleifer, and Vishny 1992). Over the long haul, almost all corporate capital expenditures are internally financed, through profits and depreciation allowances. And instead of promoting investment, the U.S. financial system seems to do quite the opposite; U.S. investment levels rank towards the bottom of the First World (OECD) countries, and are below what even quite orthodox economists — like Darrel Cohen, Kevin Hassett, and Jim Kennedy (1995) of the Federal Reserve — term "optimal" levels. *Real* investment, not buying shares in a mutual fund.

Take, for example, the stock market, which is probably the centerpiece of the whole enterprise.[1] What does it do? Both civilians and professional apologists would probably answer by saying that it raises capital for investment. In fact it doesn't. Between 1981 and 1997, U.S. nonfinancial corporations retired $813 billion more in stock than they issued, thanks to takeovers and buybacks. Of course, some individual firms did issue stock to raise money, but surprisingly little of that went to investment either. A *Wall Street Journal* article on 1996's dizzying pace of stock issuance (McGeehan 1996) named overseas privatizations (some of which, like Deutsche Telekom, spilled into U.S. markets) "and the continuing restructuring of U.S. corporations" as the driving forces behind the torrent of new paper. In other words, even the new-issues market has more to do with the arrangement and rearrangement of ownership patterns than it does with raising fresh capital — a point I'll return to throughout this book.

But most of the trading in the stock market is of existing shares, not newly issued ones. New issues in 1997 totaled $100 billion, a record — but that's about a week's trading volume on the New York Stock Exchange.[2]

One thing the financial markets do very well, however, is concentrate wealth. Government debt, for example, can be thought of as a means for upward redistribution of income, from ordinary taxpayers to rich bondholders. Instead of taxing rich people, governments borrow from them, and pay them interest for the privilege. Consumer credit also enriches the rich; people suffering stagnant wages who use the VISA card to make ends meet only fatten the wallets of their creditors with each monthly payment. Nonfinancial corporations pay their stockholders billions in annual dividends rather than reinvesting them in the business. It's no wonder, then, that wealth has congealed so spectacularly at the top. Chapter 2 offers detailed numbers; for the purposes of this introduction, however, a couple of gee-whiz factoids will do. Leaving aside the principal residence, the richest ½% of the U.S. population claims a larger share of national wealth than the bottom 90%, and the richest 10% account for over three-quarters of the total. And with that wealth comes extraordinary social power — the power to buy politicians, pundits, and professors, and to dictate both public and corporate policy.

That power, the subject of Chapter 6, is something economists often ignore. With the vast increase of government debt since the Reagan experiment began has come an increasing political power of "the markets," which typically means cuts in social programs in the name of fiscal probity. Less visibly, the increased prominence of institutional investors, particularly pension funds, in the stock market has increased rentier power over corporate policy. Though globalization and technology have gotten most of the blame for the recent wave of downsizings, the prime culprits are really portfolio managers demanding higher stock prices — a demand that translates into layoffs and investment cutbacks. This growth in stockholder influence has come despite the fact that outside shareholders serve no useful social purpose; they trade on emotion and perceptions of emotion, and know nothing of the businesses whose management they're increasingly directing. They're walking arguments for worker ownership.

This book concentrates almost entirely on American markets. That's not only for reasons of the author's nationality, but also because the U.S. (and British) financial system, with the central role it accords to loosely regu-

lated stock and bond markets, has been spreading around the globe. Henry
Kaufman (1994) called this "the 'Americanization' of global finance." The
World Bank and its comrades in the development establishment have urged
a stock-market-driven model of finance and corporate control on its client
countries in the Third World and the former socialist world, and the En-
glish-language business press is full of stories on how the Germans and
Japanese are coming to their senses, or have to if they know what's good
for them, and junk their stodgy old regulated, bank-centered systems for a
Wall Street/City of London model. And all evidence is that they are, though
never quickly enough for the editorialists.

Also, the international financial markets, which Japanese and German
investors participate in, resemble the Anglo-Saxon system in all their loose-
ness and speed. Finally, the stock market has become a kind of economic
ideal in the minds of neoliberal reformers everywhere: every market,
whether for airline tickets or human labor, has been or is being restructured to resemble the constantly fluid world of Wall Street, in which prices
float freely and arrangements are as impermanent as possible. For these
reasons, a study of the U.S. financial markets, particularly the stock market, could be of interest to an audience beyond those specifically curious
about the American way of financial life.

This book inhabits a strange world between journalism and scholarship: the first three chapters in particular look at the empirical realities of
the financial markets — the instruments traded and the agents doing the
trading — and then the fourth and fifth chapters look at some of the things
economists have said about finance over the past two centuries. I hope
that I've managed to bring the two normally separate worlds together in
an illuminating way, but of course the risk is that I'll only succeed at alien-
ating both the popular and the academic audience. It's worth the risk.
Most financial journalism is innocent of any theoretical and historical perspective, and academic work — mainstream and radical — is often indifferent to daily practice.

I must confess that I am not a "trained" economist. For someone not
initiated into the priesthood, several years spent exploring the professional
literature can be a traumatic experience. One of the finest glosses on that
experience came long ago from, of all people, H.L. Mencken, in his essay
"The Dismal Science": "The amateur of such things must be content to
wrestle with the professors, seeking the violet of human interest beneath
the avalanche of their graceless parts of speech. A hard business, I daresay,
to one not practiced, and to its hardness there is added the disquiet of a

doubt." That doubt, Mencken wrote — after conceding that in things economic he was about as orthodox as they come — was inspired by the fact that the discipline

> hits the employers of the professors where they live. It deals, not with ideas that affect those employers only occasionally or only indirectly or only as ideas, but with ideas that have an imminent and continuous influence upon their personal welfare and security, and that affect profoundly the very foundations of that social and economic structure upon which their whole existence is based. It is, in brief, the science of the ways and means whereby they have come to such estate, and maintain themselves in such estate, that they are able to hire and boss professors.

Apostates, Mencken argued, were far more unwelcome in the field than in others of less material consequence (like, say, literary studies).

There are few subspecialties of economics where this is truer than in finance. The bulk of the finance literature consists of painfully fine-grained studies designed for the owners and managers of money capital. Important matters, like whether the financial markets serve their advertised purpose of allocating social capital effectively, are studied with an infrequency surprising only to someone unfamiliar with Mencken's Law.

But the violet of interests is no longer hidden behind graceless parts of speech alone; mathematics is now the preferred disguise. The dismal science now flatters itself with delusions of rigor — an elaborate statistical apparatus built on the weakest of foundations, isolated from the other social sciences, not to mention the broader culture, and totally dead to the asking of any fundamental questions about the goals of either the discipline or the organization of economic life itself.

I do ask, and I hope answer, lots of those difficult questions, but I also want to take on the dismal scientists on their own terms. For many nonspecialist readers, this may seem like heavy going. I've tried, wherever possible, to isolate the heavily technical bits and plaster appropriately cautionary headlines on the dangerous sections. But too much writing these days, and not only on the left, consists of anecdote, narrative, moralizing, and exhortation. Even though both the financial markets and the discipline of economics have penetrated so deeply and broadly into much of social life, these institutions remain largely immune to critical examination. The next 300 pages undertake that examination, and perhaps in more detail than some readers might like, but I don't ever want to lose sight of this simple fact: behind the abstraction known as "the markets" lurks a set of institutions designed to maximize the wealth and power of the most privileged group of people in the world, the creditor–rentier class of the First World and their junior partners in the Third.

I've committed at least two commercial sins in writing this book — one, the omission of practical investment advice, and two, going lightly on scandal-mongering and naming of rotten apples. As penance for the first, I'll offer this bit of advice: forget about beating the market; it can be done, but those who can do it are rare. And for the second: pointing to rotten apples implies that the rest of the barrel is pure and refreshing. My point is that the entire batch of apples is pretty poor nourishment. By this I don't mean to imply that everyone who works in finance is devious, corrupt, or merely rapacious. There are many fine people who underwrite, analyze, trade, and sell securities; some of them are my friends and neighbors. Their personal characteristics have nothing to do with what follows. That's the point of a systemic analysis — to take apart the institutions that are larger than the personalities who inhabit them. *Charitable*

Between the publication of the hardcover edition of this book and the paperback, the U.S. stock market rose almost without interruption, to truly extraordinary levels of valuation, the highest since modern records begin in 1871. In the past, high valuations have been associated with nasty subsequent declines, but it's always possible this is a new era, a Nirvana of capital, in which the old rules don't apply. If Social Security is privatized, it could constitute an official stock price support mechanism.

Households — presumably mostly in the upper half of the income distribution — plunged into stocks (through the medium of mutual funds) in a way not seen in 30, or maybe 70, years. At the same time, households — presumably poorer ones than the mutual fund buyers — have also continued to go deeper into debt, and with record debt levels matched by record bankruptcy filings. The more a society polarizes, the more people on the bottom borrow from those on the top.

When I started this book, the prestige of Anglo-American stock-market-centered capitalism was a lot lower than it was when I finished it. I say a few kind things about Japanese and Germanic systems of corporate finance, ownership, and governance that would have been taken as semi-respectable in 1992. In 1998, it is deeply against the grain (though not as against the grain as saying kind things about Marx). But I'll stick to my position. The stagnation of Europe has a lot less to do with rigid structures and pampered citizens than it does with fiscal and monetary austerity dictated by the Maastricht project of unification. To blame Japan's problems on overregulation is to ignore that the 1980s bubble was the product of deregulation and a speculative mania. Isn't enthusiasm about the American Way in 1998 a bit reminiscent of that about Japan ten years earlier?

Coming after Japan's extended slump, the collapse of the Southeast Asian economies in 1997 was a great booster shot for American triumphalism. Quickly forgetting the extraordinary growth performance that led up to it — which, together with Japan's is without precedent in the history of capitalism, sustained rates of growth two to three times what Britain and the U.S. experienced during their rise to wealth — Alan Greenspan, editorialists, and professors of economics have pronounced this the final word on economic policy.

It's not clear why the weakest U.S. expansion in decades should be taken as vindication of the American Way. Growth between the recession's trough in 1991 and the last quarter of 1997 was the slowest of any post-World War II business cycle. Despite the mighty stock market, investment levels are only middling, and productivity growth, modest. From the hype, you'd also think the U.S. was leaving its major rivals in the dust, but comparisons of per capita GDP growth rates don't bear this out. At the end of 1997, the U.S. was tied with France at second in the growth league, behind Canada, and just tenths of a point ahead of the major European countries. Step back a bit, and the U.S. sags badly. For the 1989–95 period, when the U.S. was stuck in a credit crunch and a sputtering recovery, it was at the bottom of the G7 growth league, along with Canada and the U.K. Between 1979 and 1988, there's no contest, with the U.S. tying France for the worst numbers in the G-7. Comparisons with the pre-crisis Asian tigers are hardly worth making.

It may be as capitalisms mature, financial surpluses break the bounds of regulated systems, and force an American-style loosening of the bonds. So all these questions of comparative capitalisms may be academic; it may be the destiny of Japan and Western Europe to become more like the U.S. Certainly that's one of the likely effects of European monetary union. But if that's the case, then the debate shouldn't turn on what "works better" in some sort of engineering sense.

And moving beyond this technocratic terrain, to say a U.S.-style system "works better" doesn't say what it's better at. The November 22, 1997, issue of the *Financial Times* had three stories above its fold: two on the crises in Asia, and one headlined "Reform may push US poor into squalor." According to the last, a survey by the U.S. Conference of Mayors reported that "huge numbers" of poor Americans could face utter ruin when welfare "reform" takes full effect in 1999. That prospect, surely a social disaster of great magnitude, is not defined by official lexicographers as either a disgrace or a crisis.

The planned immiseration of the American poor has a lot to do with the subject of this book. U.S. financial and ownership relations, which are fragmented, abstract, and manic, seem deeply connected to other social mechanisms — partly as causes, partly as effects — that make this such a voracious, atomized, polarized, turbulent, often violent culture, one that insists each of us be in competition with every other. If this is success, then the U.S. model is a great success. It may even be partly duplicable in countries interested in a fresh lifestyle strategy.

After several hundred pages of diagnosis, readers have a right to expect a prescription for cure at the end. I've tried to fulfill that, but the final chapter is short and mainly suggestive. I could get high-minded and say that the reason for that is that a transformative agenda is worth a book in itself, which is true enough. But another reason is that financial reforms are no easy or isolated matter. Money is at the heart of what capitalism is all about, and reforms in the monetary sphere alone won't cut much ice. If you find the hypertrophy of finance to be appallingly wasteful and destructive then you're making a judgment on capitalism itself. That's not very chic these days, but if I thought that this cultural pathology would persist forever, then I wouldn't have written this book.

Doug Henwood
(dhenwood@panix.com)
New York, April 1998

textual note   *Almost all the figures in this edition have been updated since the hardcover; major exceptions are those used for illustrative purposes only. Aside from correcting a few typos and egregious anachronisms, the text is unchanged.*

notes

1. In many ways, credit markets are more important, but they don't enjoy the same attention from the broad public, nor do they inspire the same lusts that stocks do.

2. Despite the prominence of the stock market, daily trading volume in U.S. Treasury securities is over four times that of the NYSE — about $225 billion in federal paper in early 1998, compared with $50 billion in stocks.

1 Instruments

In February 1998, $1.4 trillion a day crossed the wire connecting the world's major banks. That figure — which captures most of the world's financial action with the U.S. dollar on at least one side of the trade — was a mere $600 billion around the time of the 1987 stock market crash. After that inconsequential cataclysm, daily volume resumed its mighty rise, passing $800 billion in 1989, and $1 trillion in 1993 (Grant 1995, 1996). It is a prodigious number: an amount equal to a year's U.S. gross domestic product (GDP) turns over in a week, and total world product in about a month.

Where does it all come from, and where does it go? Open the *Wall Street Journal* or the business section of a major metropolitan daily, and you get a clue. Every day, they publish an overwhelming array of price quotes — thousands upon thousands — for stocks, bonds, currencies, commodities, options, futures, options on futures, indexes, options on indexes, mutual funds.... If you own a hundred shares of Iomega, or you're short wheat for April delivery, then you have no problem deciding what they all mean — your money is at stake. But do all these prices, with acres of type and graphics devoted to analyzing and charting their often fevered movements in loving detail, have any meaning beyond the narrowly mercenary? Is the movement of the Dow, reported in about 30 seconds on every evening network newscast, of interest to anyone besides the half of the population that owns stocks, or the 1% of the population that owns them in meaningful quantity? And do these price gyrations have any relation to the other news reported in the paper or on TV — to the fate of corporations, to the real standard of living, to our public lives?

Figuring that out has to start with a picture of the elements of this financial universe — the instruments and institutions that construct the claims that people make on each other over time and space. These claims are denominated in money, the stuff that economists study, but economists forget that money is a form of social power. One of the persistent delusions of conventional theory is that money is "neutral," a lubricant with no influence of its own, one that merely simplifies transactions in an economy based on the exchange of goods.[1] In a barter economy, the seller of wheat would have to find a personal buyer; in a money economy, the wheatholder can sell for money, and let the system take care of the rest.

Money is a richer phenomenon than that explanation allows; it is one of our fundamental principles of social organization. Ownership is represented through monetary claims, and the exchange of those claims in the financial markets amounts to the social construction of ownership.

Over the last decade or so, these "markets" — usually conveniently referred to as an anonymous external force, as pervasive and inevitable as gravity — have grown enormously. It's a cliché of the daily press that the markets are now more powerful than governments, that the daily votes cast by the bond and currency markets are more important than elections, legislatures, and public budgets. The cliché contains a partial truth: these markets are tremendously powerful. But they are social institutions, instruments of power, that derive their power in part from the sense of powerless awe they inspire among non-initiates. Say "the markets won't like" a minimum wage increase or a public jobs program, and critical scrutiny often evaporates, like wishes crushed by the unfriendly voice of God.

While modern financial markets seem sublimely complex, they're essentially composed of several basic instruments and institutional participants. Most of the instruments, despite their apparent novelty, are quite old, their age measured better in centuries than decades.

What are these markets, and who populates them?

stocks

To many people, the stock market is Wall Street, and the New York Stock Exchange (NYSE) is the stock market. A recent edition of Paul Samuelson's warhorse economics text even described the exchange as the "hub" of capitalism, with no further explanation. Geography reinforces this perception; the NYSE stands at the intersection of Broad and Wall, at the spiritual epicenter of Manhattan's financial district. But in fact, stock market trading volume is dwarfed by trading in bonds and foreign exchange, and the NYSE itself accounts for a declining share of stock market volume.

These mere facts aside, there is some justification in giving the stock market the prominence it enjoys in the popular mind. But one notion that must be quickly dismissed is the idea that the market raises lots of capital for real investment.[2] Corporations typically sell large blocks of stock when they go from private (a small circle of family or otherwise tight owners) or state hands (in a privatization) to "public" hands. It goes without saying that a very narrow segment of the public is involved. Afterwards, public firms rarely issue significant amounts of stock, and new flotations are but a blip in the chart of corporate cash flows. Since the early 1980s, thanks to buyouts and buybacks, more stock was retired than newly floated, transactions that were mostly funded through heavy borrowing.

But just because the stock market plays a very minor role in raising investment finance doesn't mean it's a sideshow. Shares of stock represent ownership claims on an economy's real productive assets, and claims as well to a portion of the present and future profits generated by those assets. Though managers of public corporations enjoy partial autonomy — just how much is a matter of dispute — they are the hired agents of the stockholders, and ultimately answerable to them. In moments of crisis, stockholders can intervene directly in the running of their corporation; in more normal times, pleasing investors, which means pushing up the stock price, is a prime managerial concern. Failures to please are punished by a chronically low stock price, a condition that can be an invitation to a takeover. In mainstream theory, this is how the market disciplines managers; that it doesn't work very well is one of the themes of this book.

Stock comes in many flavors. Most prevalent — 98% of the market value of the NYSE, almost all the Nasdaq — is common stock. Common stockholders have the last claim on a corporation's income and assets; though firms will occasionally stretch to meet a dividend, dividends are normally paid after interest owed to creditors — making common stockholders "residual claimants" in legal jargon. After debtholders but ahead of common stockholders are holders of preferred stock, who must be paid all dividends due them before owners of the common stock can get a penny. In a bankruptcy, common stockholders are often wiped out; creditors and holders of the preferred get paid off first. Common's allure is that if a corporation does well, creditors and preferred stockholders can be easily satisfied, and the excess juice all goes to the stockholders.

evolution from a founding principle

Today's stock markets have their roots, as do many institutions of modern finance, in medieval Italy, though unlike the more sophisticated early Italian financial institutions, their early stock markets were pretty rudimentary.

Modern versions took shape first in Amsterdam in the 17th century and then in London in the 18th, with the growth of government debt and corporate shares. Free-market ideology to the contrary, the role of government debt in the development of finance can't be exaggerated; while American practice treats stock and government bond markets as being as distinct as church and state, in Britain, where church and state aren't so separate either, people still call public debt certificates government stock.

In the early 17th century, the Dutch and English East India Companies issued shares to the public to fund their early imperial enterprises (another state link to the development of finance); in return, investors were granted a share of the profits in the form of dividends. But since the investors didn't want to wed themselves irrevocably to these companies without any possibility of divorce, the share certificates were made freely transferable. As R.C. Michie (1992) puts it, "what was being established were markets to claims to future income" — fictitious capital, in Marx's famous phrase: not real capital, but claims on capital. This enables a whole class to own an economy's productive assets, rather than being bound to a specific property as they once were.

The transformation of a future stream of dividend or interest payments into an easily tradeable capital asset is the founding principle of all financial markets. While the future payment stream of a bond is usually fixed, and barring default fairly certain, dividends and the profits on which they are based are largely unpredictable. In most cases, they can be expected to grow over time with the rest of the economy, but not always. Figuring out the likelihood and speed of that growth is what much of the stock game is all about.

Amsterdam's early market was quite loosely organized; brokers and their clients simply congregated around the pillars of the exchange building and did deals. There was no formal organization designed to police conduct and offer some guarantee against default until 1787. The first formally organized exchange was established in Paris in 1724. The revolution, however, so disturbed trading — war isn't always good for business — that London stepped into the breach.

The opening of the London Stock Exchange in 1802 marked the real beginning of recognizably modern stock exchanges, with regular trading and a fixed, self-regulating membership. New York's stock exchange was founded 10 years before London's (by 24 brokers meeting under a buttonwood tree at what is now 68 Wall Street), but the New York market would take a back seat to London until fairly late in the 19th century. Paris would return to prominence some decades later as the major exchange for trading continental European shares (not just French ones), but it would never again match London as a financial center.

What government debts and state-licensed monopolies were to the financial markets of the 18th century, railroad shares and bonds were to the 19th — claims on wealth that proliferated wildly and provided rich raw material for trading. British railway shares grew from £48 million in 1848 to £1.3 billion in 1913; over the same period, U.S. railway stocks grew from $318 million to $19.8 billion. Also over the same period, the London exchange saw a tremendous increase in trading of foreign shares — a reminder that in spite of today's talk about the globalization of finance, finance has long been as transnational as politics and technology allowed.

Modern American stock markets came of age in the late 19th and early 20th centuries, simultaneously with the emergence of modern corporations, with dispersed owners and professional managers. The stock market was central to the establishment of these new institutions in the first place, as small firms were combined into giants, and it quickly became essential to settling matters around their subsequent ownership. Late 19th century promoters also thought of the market as a way to ease the burden on small producers who were being displaced or enveloped by corporatization: modest stock holdings were a compensation for the loss of real capital ownership (Livingston 1986).

After World War I, there was an attempt to restore the borderless order of the decades before the conflict, but the attempt never really took. Though the U.S. enjoyed a tremendous boom during the 1920s, Europe wasn't so lucky; Britain suffered chronically high unemployment, and Germany was a wreck. When the U.S. boom ended with the 1929 crash, and the world entered depression, the loose financial markets of the 1920s were indicted as prime suspects. Many European markets were shut or sharply restricted, and the New Deal brought the U.S. market under tight regulation.[3]

Stock markets and financial gunslinging in general remained under heavy suspicion until well after end of World War II; policy and habit conspired to keep stock and other financial markets sleepy for decades. New York Stock Exchange trading volume for all of 1950 totaled 525 million shares, equal to about two average days' trading in 1993, and a vigorous day in 1996. By the end of the 1950s, however, the market was beginning to shake off this torpor; volume took off in the 1960s, plateaued in the 1970s, and then exploded during the 1980s (New York Stock Exchange 1994, pp. 100, 101).

As this is written, stock markets in general are enjoying a period of high prices and high prestige, and not only in the First World.[4] Encouraged by official institutions like the World Bank and International Monetary Fund (IMF), Third World stock markets have flourished as targets for First World investors, bored with the prospects of their own mature home markets. Despite their growth in the last decade, they remain quite small, however, and it doesn't take much Northern money to drive up prices ten- or a hundred-fold — nor does it take much to generate a panic exit and a stunning collapse in prices.

taxonomy

While just about every country in the world now has a stock market, their size and importance vary greatly. One easy way of making this point is by grouping national financial systems into bank-centered and stock-market-centered ones. In the former, stock markets tend to be small in size and importance; not only do banks, rather than the stock and bond markets, provide most corporate finance, they own a great deal of corporate stock as well. Germany is the classic example of a bank-centered system, with a market capitalization (measured relative to GDP) a quarter the level of the U.S. and a fifth that of the U.K. Most of the continental European countries tend towards Germanic levels of market capitalization, while other English-speaking countries tend toward Anglo-American ones.

With the wave of free-market "reforms" of the last 15 years has come a tremendous growth in stock markets in what is alternately called the "developing" or Third World; in financial jargon, their stock markets are usually called the "emerging" markets (though at moments like the 1994–95 Mexican crisis, wits call them submerging markets). On balance, the "emerging" markets remain quite small, even after all this growth; in 1996, the markets followed by the International Finance Corporation, the World Bank's in-house investment bank, accounted for just 11% of world stock market capitalization, half their 21% share of global GDP. Still, within that group, there are considerable variations, with Chile and South Africa showing market caps that would put them in the Anglo-American league, and China barely on the radar screen, at least in 1996. Yet despite the relative size of some of these markets, they remain tiny on a world scale; an influx of what would seem like pocket change to investors in New York or London could easily buy up the entire Philippine or Argentine stock market. The small size, when combined with the limited number of stocks traded, make the emerging markets extraordinarily volatile.

stock market capitalization, 1996

	percent of GDP	millions of US$	percent of world
emerging			
Malaysia	310	307,179	1.5
South Africa	191	241,571	1.2
Taiwan	105	273,608	1.4
Philippines	96	80,649	0.4
Chile	89	65,940	0.3
Thailand	54	99,828	0.5
Indonesia	40	91,106	0.5
India	34	122,605	0.6
Mexico	32	106,540	0.5
Brazil	29	216,990	1.1
Korea	29	138,817	0.7
Argentina	15	44,769	0.2
China	14	113,755	0.6
developed			
Hong Kong	290	449,381	2.2
Singapore	160	150,215	0.7
U.K.	152	1,740,246	8.6
Switzerland	137	402,104	2.0
U.S.	116	8,484,433	42.0
Sweden	99	247,217	1.2
Netherlands	97	378,721	1.9
Canada	84	486,268	2.4
Australia	79	311,968	1.5
Japan	67	3,088,850	15.3
Spain	42	242,779	1.2
France	38	591,123	2.9
Germany	29	670,997	3.3
Italy	21	258,160	1.3
totals			
emerging	37	2,225,957	11.0
developed	81	17,951,705	89.0
world	72	20,177,662	100.0

The terms "emerging" and "developed" are in common use, though one could write a book on that choice of words alone. Markets shown accounted for 86% of "emerging" markets and 98% of developed markets. Between 1994 and 1996, world market capitalization grew more than three times as fast as GDP (33% vs. 11%). Source: International Finance Corporation, *Emerging Stock Markets Factbook 1995, 1997*.

In the predominantly English-speaking countries, stock markets are also essential mechanisms for regulating how corporations are owned and run. (This market style is sometimes called Anglo-Saxon, despite the presence of many non-Anglo-Saxons in their populations. Anglo-American is a less problematic label.) Nearly anyone with sufficient cash or credit can enter the open market and buy a controlling interest in a publicly traded corporation.[5] In Germanic countries, however, controlling interests are typically in the hands of large banks, and it's practically impossible for firms to be bought and sold on the open market. With increased foreign investment by German firms, and their listings on foreign stock exchanges, their model appears to be taking on a more Anglo-Saxon cast.

Japan is an anomaly. While the stock market looks Anglo-American in its size, controlling interests are typically held by banks and close business partners like suppliers and customers, making it nearly impossible for uninvited actors to buy up a Japanese firm.

technical details

In the U.S., stocks and other securities are traded in two kinds of institutional environments: organized exchanges and over-the-counter (OTC). In exchange trading, orders to buy or sell are transmitted from customers to a central trading floor which, despite computerization, is still populated by specialized human traders who shout and gesticulate at each other to consummate deals. With OTC trading, there is no central floor — just a virtual exchange made up of networked computers.

The largest U.S. exchange is the New York Stock Exchange, which despite its relentless loss of market share to OTC trading, is still the home of the shares of most large American corporations — over 2,300 firms in all — as well as the U.S. trading for major foreign firms. To be listed on the NYSE, firms must meet several criteria: a record of consecutive profitability at least three years long, tangible assets and a total market value of $18 million or more, a minimum of 1.1 million shares outstanding, and at least 2,000 shareholders (NYSE 1994, p. 31). While these standards may not sound too rigorous, they rule out most U.S. corporations.

A customer buying a stock traded on the NYSE, whether an individual trading 10 shares or a money manager trading 100,000, transmits an order to his or her broker. The broker transmits the order to the firm's trading desk, which passes it on to the NYSE floor. (To trade on the floor, the firm must be a member of the exchange.) The order can be filled in one of two ways. Small, simple orders are filled through the NYSE's SuperDot computer system; bigger orders are filled by human brokers cutting deals on the exchange floor.

At the heart of the NYSE is its specialist system. Specialists are inhabitants of the exchange floor who are assigned to make markets in specified stocks; they're annointed in this role by a board elected by exchange member. Though their role isn't especially obscure, their names usually are; unlike brokers and portfolio managers, there are no celebrity specialists. They have several tasks, for which they are handsomely rewarded. Specialists maintain "the book," once literally a paper record but now a computerized registry, containing price and quantity information on current bids (offers to buy) and asks (offers to sell) for the stocks assigned to them. Customer orders may be placed either at the market or at a limit — that is, either at prevailing prices or at a specific price. Limit orders can be placed at prices far away from the prevailing price; investors may want to sell shares they own if they hit a certain price, either to limit losses or lock in profits. When the market price hits the limit, the customer's order is executed by the specialist.

In unusual cases where specialists are unable to find a willing buyer for an eager seller, or vice versa, usually because of a ferocious buying or selling stampede, they are supposed to step in and satisfy the order, using stock from their own inventory or money from their own pockets. Some discretion is allowed here; specialists aren't supposed to bankrupt themselves to maintain "a fair and orderly market," as their brief is usually phrased. But they do seem to smooth out the gyrations in moderately extreme markets.

Specialists make a good deal of money in this role. Their books offer them insights into patterns of supply and demand that are offered to no other market players, and they know when it's better to meet orders from their own resources or by matching public customers' orders. Market students often scrutinize published data on specialists' positions for insights into what the supposedly smart money is doing.[6]

In over-the-counter trading, there is no central auction market. Customers still transmit orders to brokers, but instead of going to the corner of Broad and Wall, the order is presented by phone or computer network to other brokers, called market makers, who specialize in trading certain stocks. A market maker, according to the Securities Exchange Act of 1934, is "any dealer who holds himself out...as being willing to buy and sell security for his own account on a regular or continuous basis." To do that, a market maker publishes, either on paper or on computer screens, bid and offer price quotations, and, in the words of the Securities and Exchange Commission regulation, "is ready, willing, and able to effect transactions in reasonable quantities at his quote prices with other brokers and dealers" (quoted in Watson 1992).

At the organizational peak is the National Association of Securities Dealers (NASD) and its automated quotation system (Nasdaq), which provides live computer quotes of stock trades to brokers around the world. The National Market System (NMS), a subset of Nasdaq universe, is the trading home of the biggest OTC stocks, like Microsoft and Intel. Many of the NMS companies could trade on the NYSE, but for various reasons they choose not to have their stocks listed there. But despite the sprinkling of giants, listing requirements for the NMS are significantly looser than the NYSE's: if a firm is profitable, it needs tangible assets of at least $4 million and a market value of at least $3 million; if the firm is unprofitable, it needs to hit values of $12 million and $15 million respectively. In most cases, it needs only 400 public shareholders.

Traveling down the foodchain, you pass the Nasdaq stocks that aren't part of the national system; these tend to be relatively obscure companies whose stocks are somewhat thinly traded; a listing on the Nasdaq SmallCap (small capitalization) market requires only $4 million in assets, a market value of $1 million, and 300 public shareholders. But these look like blue chips compared to stocks outside the Nasdaq system — like those that trade on the so-called pink sheets, a price list distributed daily to brokers on pink paper containing price quotes for stocks that trade essentially by appointment only, with as few as one market-maker. By contrast, the big NMS stocks can have as many as 30 or more market-makers, with the average Nasdaq stock having around 10.

In 1994, the Nasdaq came under heavy criticism in the academic and popular press for unfair trading practices, notably wide spreads between bid and ask prices (Christie and Schultz 1994). That is, in comparison to NYSE trading, buyers of stock paid high prices, and sellers received low prices, with the dealers pocketing the difference. In particular, suspiciously few Nasdaq quotes were for odd-eighths of a point and too many for even quarters — like 10 1/4 instead of 10 1/8 or 10 3/8 — a rounding that, of course, favored the dealer. The academics concluded, modestly, that this raised "the question of whether Nasdaq dealers implicitly collude to maintain wide spreads." These spreads mysteriously narrowed the moment preliminary findings were published in the press (Christie et al. 1994).

The American Stock Exchange drew marketing blood by pointing out that no major broker — the Nasdaq's market-makers — lists its stock on the Nasdaq. If it's so wonderful for investors and listed companies alike, why do those who know its workings best not share in its wonders? But academic studies and popular reporting (Steiner and Salwen 1992) have also shown that specialists often don't publicize attractive bids and offers, preferring to reserve the sweetest deals for themselves.

In August 1996, the Securities and Exchange Commission decided that Nasdaq dealers had, in the words of the *Los Angeles Times*, "colluded to boost profits by harming customers" (Paltrow 1996). The National Association of Securities Dealers agreed (without admitting to wrongdoing) to revamp its trading systems to prevent such abuses in the future. In releasing its decision, the SEC also released tapes of conversations among dealers, including exchanges such as this:

> Trader 1: "I bought 10 at ⅛, and don't print it [report it] for, for a few minutes, 'cause I told the guy I'm just making a sale out of the blue."
> Trader 2: "I'll, I'll print after the bell."
> Trader 1: "Thanks, bud."

•

> Trader 3: "What can I do for you?"
> Trader 4: "Can you go ¼ bid for me?"
> Trader 3: "Yeah, sure."
> Trader 4: "I sold you two (200 shares) at ¼. Just go up there, OK?"
> Trader 3: "I'm goosing it, cuz."
> Trader 2: "Thank you."

Whatever the relative virtues of the systems, there's no question that the NYSE is losing share to the Nasdaq. In 1980, the Nasdaq traded 54% as many shares on the average day as the NYSE; in 1994, Nasdaq share volume was over 101% of the NYSE's. Since NYSE stocks are, on average, more expensive than the Nasdaq's, share volume overstates things a bit, but the trend is visible there, too; in 1980, the money value of shares traded on the Nasdaq was 17% of the NYSE's; in 1994, it was 56% ($1.4 trillion vs. $2.5 trillion). Still, the NYSE is hardly dying; the dollar volume of its trading grew more than sixfold between 1980 and 1994 — though the Nasdaq's grew more than twentyfold (U.S. Bureau of the Census 1994, pp. 528–9).

Of decreasing significance in the stock world is the NYSE's neighbor several blocks to the west, the American Stock Exchange (Amex). Once the home of small growth companies, the Amex is now a mere flyspeck. Few stocks of any significance are traded there, and trading volume was a mere $36 billion in 1990. Amex volume fell from 10% of the Nasdaq's in 1984 to 6% in 1994 (NASD 1995).

In an effort to boost its shabby image, the Amex has been tightening listing standards, after scandal struck its Emerging Company Marketplace (ECM) shortly after its March 1992 opening. The ECM was touted by then Amex-president James Jones — a former Oklahoma congressman who left the Amex to become U.S. ambassador to Mexico, where he served during the Mexican crisis of 1994 and 1995 — as home to the "kind of companies that will grow and make this country great." Unfortunately for Jones and the Amex, the companies did little but embarrass the exchange. Of the 22 companies, over half went public through the shell company route — that is, a firm with no actual business operations sells stock as a "blind pool" to investors (i.e., a pig in a poke) and then acquires a small operating company with the proceeds of the stock sale. That method allows the initial owners of the shell to evade the scrutiny of the Securities and Exchange Commission and its normal registration and disclosure requirements. But that was only the beginning of the ECM's malodorous life. Several weeks later, it emerged that one of the ECM 22, a maker of flame retardants, was controlled by an admitted inside trader and stock manipulator who was also a convicted arsonist. And another ECM company was run by someone who'd previously been sued by the SEC for various misdeeds; the legal trail was covered by the fact that her bad record was run up when her name was John Huminik, before the intervention of hormones, scalpel, and a legal writ had turned her into Eleanor Schuler (U.S. General Accounting Office 1994b; Norris 1995).

Stock performance is usually summarized by indexes. Most exchanges around the world publish their own indexes, which are not directly comparable with each other. To address the comparability problem, the *Financial Times* and Morgan Stanley Capital International offer standardized international indexes, covering countries and regions; and the International Finance Corporation, the World Bank's in-house investment bank, publishes indexes for the "emerging" markets.

In the U.S., the Dow Jones Industrial Average, an average of 30 blue-chip industrial stocks, is the most famous of averages, but it is far from representative of the whole market. A broader blue-chip index is the Standard & Poor's 500, an index of 500 industrial, service, and financial stocks; it's the most widely used measure for grading the performance of money managers. S&P publishes scores of sectoral indexes, and they and other firms produce indexes to measure big stocks, small stocks, medium stocks, and even moral stocks (those that are appropriate for "socially respon-sible" investment).

bonds and other credits

Despite the greater public visibility of stock markets, the financial heart of capitalism is in the credit markets, a term covering loans arranged through a variety of instruments and institutions, from simple bank loans to com-plex bond products. As Marx (1981, p. 596) put it, "interest-bearing capital [is] the mother of every insane form"; debts, mere promises to pay, are nonetheless transformed into commodities in the eyes of creditors. This capitalization of promised incomes enables nearly everything, from an industrial plant to an unspoiled wilderness to a human life, to be modeled as a quasi-credit, whose value today is the value of its future earnings stream — profits or wilderness services or wages, adjusted for value over time using prevailing interest rates and maybe an estimate of risk.

Marx entered that passage from a meditation on the strangeness of gov-ernment debt, a place "where a negative quantity appears as capital" — no asset behind it other than a government's promise to pay. But state debt is far from uniquely insubstantial. Unlike stock, most bonds — loans that can easily be traded on the markets — give you no claim of owner-ship on a firm's capital assets. Though sometimes a pledge of collateral is involved (as in so-called mortgage bonds), most are secured by the borrower's promise and the lender's faith in that promise. The bond's value at any moment is the future stream of interest payments that the borrower promises to pay, with the return of principal at the bond's maturity.

Sexy variations are plentiful — floating rate bonds, whose interest is adjusted periodically; inflation-linked bonds, which guarantee a fixed rate above the inflation rate; zero-coupons, which are sold at a big discount to face value, pay no interest during their life, and are closed out with the payment of the full face value at maturity. Whatever the kink, while cor-porations can cut or skip dividend payments to shareholders, suffering only a blow to the stock price, missing a bond interest payment is likely to result in bankruptcy, or fevered negotiations to avoid bankruptcy.

A large, liquid market in government debt with a central bank at its core is the base of modern financial systems. Central banks manage their domestic money supply through the purchase and sale of official paper, and historically government borrowers have usually been at the vanguard of the development of a national financial system. In a panic, money floods out of stocks and private bonds and into government securities, especially short-term ones. Practically speaking, interest rates on public debts act as a benchmark for the rest of the credit system; interest rates for borrowers other than a central government — state and local governments, households, corporations — are usually set in reference to government rates at the same maturity. Markets in general seem to need benchmarks like this; during the early 1990s, when trading in Latin American bonds was highly fashionable, Mexico served as the benchmark, with interest rates quoted as so much over Mexico, the market's blue chip.

Public paper is a nice mechanism for profit making and income redistribution. It provides rich underwriting and trading profits for investment bankers and interest income for individual and institutional rentiers, courtesy of nonrich taxpayers. Wall Street, despite its ideological fealty to balanced budgets, has made a fortune distributing and trading the Reagan–Bush–early Clinton deficits. This experience has been reproduced on a smaller scale in many other parts of the world, as government debt/GDP ratios more or less doubled between 1980 and the early 1990s (Goldstein et al. 1994, p. 35). If the U.S. budget deficit stays close to zero for years, Wall Street will have to make some very sharp adjustments, though bonds could acquire a scarcity value.

Government debt not only promotes the development of a central national capital market, it promotes the development of a world capital market as well. Short-term paper like treasury bills — places that investors can park short-term cash — is important for a currency's admission to world markets; the yen has remained a highly provincial currency, accounting for only 6.7% of the trade among the six biggest economies and 8.6% of official foreign reserves transactions, in part because yen holders lack a deep treasury bill market.[7] Central banks also deal in their own and other governments' paper in their often vain attempts to manage their currencies. Institutions like the World Bank led the way in internationalizing the credit markets, raising funds in one currency, transforming them into another for temporary storage, and often lending in yet another.

Public debt is a powerful way of assuring that the state remains safely in capital's hands. The higher a government's debts, the more it must please its bankers. Should bankers grow displeased, they will refuse to roll over old debts or to extend new financing on any but the most punishing terms (if at all). The explosion of federal debt in the 1980s vastly increased the power of creditors to demand austere fiscal and monetary policies to dampen the U.S. economy as it recovered, hesitantly at first but then with increasing vigor, from the 1989–92 slowdown. Bill Clinton quickly learned their power, when he had to abandon his tepid stimulus program in 1993 and turn himself into an "Eisenhower Republican," to satisfy what he called "a bunch of fucking bond traders" (Woodward 1994).

That explosion of federal debt was prodigious. At the end of 1952, outstanding debt of the U.S. Treasury totaled 61% of GDP. That figure fell steadily for the next 20 years, bottoming out at 23% in 1974; it rose a bit in the late 1970s, to around 25% in 1980, and then headed straight upwards to 49% in 1994, then drifting town to 47% in 1997. Growth in agency debt — mortgage agencies like Fannie Mae and Freddie Mac, the student loan agency Sallie Mae,[8] and the Resolution Trust Corp., which funded the savings and loan bailout — was even more dramatic. Virtually invisible at under 1% of GDP in 1952, it rose slowly to just under 5% in 1970; doubled to nearly 10% by 1980; more than doubled again to 25% in 1990; and hit 35% with no sign of a pause by the end of 1997.

With the growth in Treasury debt came a torrent of trading not only in the bonds themselves, but also in associated "products," as Wall Street marketers call them, like futures, options, repos, and swaps. This confirms the accuracy of another of Marx's (1977, p. 919) observations:

> The public debt becomes one of the most powerful levers of primitive accumulation. As with the stroke of an enchanter's wand, it endows unproductive money with the power of creation and thus turns it into capital, without forcing it to expose itself to the troubles and risks inseparable from its employment in industry or even in usury. The state's creditors actually give nothing away, for the sum lent is transformed into public bonds, easily negotiable, which go on functioning in their hands just as so much hard cash would. But furthermore, and quite apart from the class of idle *rentiers* thus created, the improvised wealth of the financiers who play the role of middlemen between the government and the nation, and the tax-farmers, merchants and private manufacturers, for whom a good part of every national loan performs the service of a capital fallen from heaven, apart from all these people, the national debt has given rise to joint-stock companies, to dealings in negotiable effects of all kinds, and to speculation: in a word, it has given rise to stock-exchange gambling and the modern bankocracy.

trading Treasuries

The market in U.S. government bonds is the biggest financial market in the world. At the center of the market are 38 major investment and commercial banks who are certified as primary dealers by the Federal Reserve

Bank of New York — the choice inner circle with which the Fed conducts its official monetary business. At the end of 1992, according to a New York Fed survey, total daily trading volume averaged $400–550 billion, or over $100 trillion a year. Traders turned over an amount equal to a year's GDP in about three weeks. Of the total, $40–50 billion (9%) was among primary dealers; $50–60 (11%) was among primary dealers and their customers; $45–115 billion (20%) was among nonprimary dealers; and $250–300 billion (55%) consisted of "financing transactions," deals that use U.S. Treasury paper as collateral.[9] It's largely a family romance among financiers.

A bit surprisingly, in this era of globalized finance, only about 4% of that trading was done in London and another 1% in Tokyo — meaning that 95% of the market was in the U.S., mainly New York. But the London and Tokyo action is enough to assure that there's a round-the-clock market from 8 o'clock in the Tokyo Monday morning to 5 PM on the New York Friday. Though some firms organize trading locally, the global houses run a single portfolio in all three centers. For traders in global firms, the trading day begins in Tokyo; they "pass the book" at about 4 or 5 in the afternoon Tokyo time to London, where it is 7 or 8 in the morning, and pass it westwards at 1 PM to New York, where it is 8 in the morning. The trading day ends when New York closes.

Treasury debt falls into three categories — bills, with maturities running from three months to one year; notes, one year to 10; and bonds, over 10. Most trading occurs in the two- to seven-year range. Shown on p. 26 are three "yield curves," plots of interest rates at various maturities. Normally the yield curve slopes gently upward, with interest rates rising as maturities lengthen. The reason for this is pretty simple — the longer a maturity, the more possibility there is for something to go wrong (inflation, financial panic, war), so investors require a sweeter return to tempt them into parting with their money. It's rare, however, that a bondholder would actually hold it to maturity; holding periods of weeks and hours are more common than years. The Bank for International Settlements (Benzie 1992, p. 43) estimated that the average holding period for U.S. Treasury bonds and notes was just one month, with a similar figure prevailing in Japan, Germany, and Britain. The average holding period for a Treasury bill was three weeks, ten weeks short of the shortest-lived T-bill.

Except in times of crisis or hyperinflation, short-term interest rates are generally under the control of the central bank. In the U.S., the benchmark short-term interest rate is federal funds, which is what banks charge each other for overnight loans of reserves.[10] If the Fed wants to repress the economy by forcing interest rates higher and restricting the available supply of credit, it will drain reserves from the banking system by selling part of its inventory of Treasury securities. Unlike a private sale of securities, which would keep the money sloshing within the financial system, a sale to the Fed means that the dollars leave it. This forces the price of reserves — fed funds — upwards. To stimulate, the Fed buys securities using money created out of thin air; this increases the supply of reserves, which nudges down the funds rate.

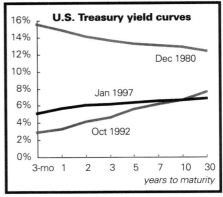

Long-term rates, however, are not so easily analyzed nor controlled. Most of the time they move with the short-term rates dictated by the central bank, but in odd times they don't. In the early 1980s, the curve was negative, as Volcker's Fed drove rates up to record levels to kill inflation; in the early 1990s, it was quite steep, and Greenspan's Fed forced rates down to keep the financial system from imploding. It's likely that investors assumed that both extremes were not sustainable, and that short rates would return to more "normal" levels, which is why the longer end of the curve never got so carried away.

munis

Federal government bonds aren't the only kind, of course. Cities and states sell tax-exempt municipal bonds, which help retired dentists to shelter income and local governments to build sewers and subsidize shopping malls in the name of "industrial development." The muni bond market is smaller than the U.S. Treasury market — at the end of 1997, state and local governments had $1.1 trillion in debt outstanding, compared to $3.8 trillion for the Treasury and another $2.7 trillion for government-related financial institutions — and trading is usually sleepy and uninteresting. But it can be lucrative for practitioners. Underwriting firms — the big investment and commercial banks — contribute mightily to the campaigns of local treasurers and comptrollers. Since so many give, it's hard to see how the local officials can decide among smooth Wall Streeters bearing gifts. Despite some attempts to rein in this essentially legal form of graft, it's almost certain to continue (Taylor 1995). The nexus of bond dealers who raise money for local governments, real estate developers and construction contractors who profit from the capital expenditures so financed, the lawyers who service all sides, and the politicians supported by the rest of the gang are common structures of urban and regional power in the U.S. They assure that the budget will be full of subsidies and tax breaks to developers and contractors, that fresh land will be developed often at the expense of existing settlements, and that in a crunch welfare and other public services will be cut but debt service will continue to flow.

It was long held by the courts that interest on municipal debt could not be taxed for Constitutional reasons, but a 1988 Supreme Court decision changed that. The indulgence has been excused on the grounds that it lowers the borrowing costs for cities and states; from a bondholder's point of view, a 6% tax-free interest rate is as good as an 8–9% taxable one, assuming an income tax rate of around 30%.[11] But a closer look reveals a nice subsidy to the rich at the expense of the U.S. Treasury. The exemption of municipal bond interest costs the federal government just over $20 billion a year (U.S. Office of Management and Budget 1995, p. 42). Former New York State Comptroller Edward Regan (1996) estimated that about two-thirds of the subsidy goes to state and local governments, and one-third to wealthy bondholders. Regan concluded, "If you're not in high [tax] brackets and don't own these bonds, you lose every time your state or local government borrows," since the municipal subsidy means higher federal taxes (or reduced federal services) for the non-bondholder.

corporations and the erosion of commitment

Corporate bonds are the last major type. The market is large — at $3.3 trillion in 1997, starting to approach the U.S. Treasury market in size — but doesn't trade anywhere near as frenetically, and hasn't made much news since the junk bond boom and bust of the 1980s. Annual turnover amounts to only a few days' worth of Treasury action.

While nonfinancial corporate bond debt has grown impressively — from an amount equal to 13% of GDP in 1980 to 18% in 1997 — financial firms were busier issuers, rising from 3% of GDP to 17% over the same period. Much of this was accounted for by the growth in asset-backed securities (ABS) — credit card receivables and mortgages packaged into bonds and sold on the markets rather than remaining with the banks originating the loans). Nonexistent in 1983, ABS issuers' bonds outstanding were worth 9% of GDP in 1997. Such securitization has shifted risk from banks to the institutional investors who buy asset-backed bonds, and has created vast new pots of money to fund the consumer credit boom.

In most cases, only the best corporations are granted access to bond markets — ones whose condition is fairly widely known, and easily analyzed. This is especially true of the short-term corporate debt called commercial paper (CP) — the unsecured debt of large firms, which is secured only on their promise and reputation. The development of the CP market has been a blow to banks, which used to have a lock on these blue-chip customers. CP and securitization have replaced "relationship" banking — long-term associations between firms and their bankers — with "transactions" banking, in which all that matters is the beauty of the deal.

Small, obscure firms are rarely granted access to the bond market. A memorable exception was the junk moment of the 1980s, when the most improbable adventures were financed, and interest was often paid not in real cash, but in a fistful of new bonds. The market collapsed in 1989, languished for years before enjoying a vigorous recovery into the late 1990s, though nothing like its heyday a decade earlier. There's evidence that the collapse of the junk market was good for banks, who picked up some junk-class borrowers, who pay high interest rates — high enough, presumably, to absorb the occasional default.

derivatives

This once-obscure word became famous in 1994, when after five years of indulgent policies, the Federal Reserve began hiking interest rates, causing derivatives to blow up all over. Putatively sophisticated giant corporations, who thought they were limiting risk through exotic instruments crafted by Wall Street, found themselves losing millions instead. Orange County, California, lost millions on derivatives, and filed for bankruptcy rather than tax its rich citizens enough to make good on their debts,[12] and a small army of Wall Street hotdogs were either badly wounded or driven (at least temporarily) out of business. To avoid embarrassment and possible runs, several prominent mutual fund companies had to subsidize derivatives losses in bond and money-market funds.

People heard and said bad things about derivatives without too clear a sense of what they are. The word refers to a broad class of securities — though securities seems too tangible a word for some of them — whose prices are derived from the prices of other securities or even things. They range from established and standardized instruments like futures and options, which are very visibly traded on exchanges, to custom-made things like swaps, collars, and swaptions.

As with most basic financial instruments, derivatives are quite old. A 1688 treatise on the workings of the Amsterdam Stock Exchange described techniques very much like modern futures and options. Organized futures trading of agricultural commodities arose in Chicago the mid-19th century; the modern futures contracts in corn and wheat began trading in 1859. Options on futures traded in Chicago in the 1920s, until the New Dealers snuffed them as part of the general war on speculation, identified as a prime suspect in causing the Great Depression (Merton 1992; Newberry 1992; U.S. Commodity Futures Trading Commission 1995).

mechanics of futures and options

Futures markets exist in a range of real and financial commodities; options are traded on individual stocks, stock indexes, and futures contracts.[13] A futures contract is an agreement made by its buyer to take delivery of a specific commodity on a specific date, and by its seller to make delivery. Options contracts give buyers the right to buy or sell a particular asset either on a particular date (European option) or at any time from when the option contract is opened until its expiration date (American option). Options to buy are called calls, and options to sell, puts. An essential difference is that someone who holds a futures contract on its expiration date must take delivery of the underlying commodity, while the holder of an option need not. In practice, however, almost all futures contracts are closed out before their maturity date; less than 1% of annual trading ends up being consummated in possession-taking.

Some examples might put flesh on these definitions. A single futures contract in wheat covers 5,000 bushels. People who buy July wheat contracts in April agree that should they still hold the contracts come July, they will take possession of the wheat at the contract's stated price. (If wheat actually changes hands, it's typically in the form of warehouse receipts, not railcars full of grain.) Should the price have risen, then that will look like a good deal; if it's fallen, it will look bad.

April sellers of July wheat, however, agree to the reverse — that they will deliver the wheat come July. As with most financial markets, sellers need not actually own the commodity they sell. Farmers may indeed sell their crops forward in the futures markets. But your average speculator has no wheat to sell; he or she is simply hoping the price will drop. A sale made by someone who doesn't own the underlying asset — and this applies to bonds and stocks as well as wheat — is selling it "short," on the anticipation of buying it back at a lower price, or, in a pinch, buying it in the open market at whatever price prevails and delivering the goods.[14] Short-selling exposes the practitioner to enormous risks: when you buy something — go long, in the jargon — your loss is limited to what you paid for it; when you go short, however, your losses are potentially without limit. In theory, brokers are supposed to be sure their clients have the credit rating to justify short-selling, though things don't always work out by the book.

Options are similar. On April 18, 1995, the July wheat contract closed at $3.5175 per bushel for a contract covering 5,000 bushels, or $17,587.50 per contract. The typical player would have to put up 5% margin — a good faith cash deposit with the broker, who treats the other 95% as a loan, on which interest is charged — or $880. An option to buy that July contract at $3.50 a bushel, called a 350, closed the same day at 12.5¢ per bushel, or $625 for the full 5,000 bushels. The option to buy it at $3.60 — a 360 — closed at 8.75¢, or $437.50 for the whole contract. Should wheat climb in price, the option prices would increase also — generally point for point with the 350 option (since it's so close to the target, or "strike" price), and less than point for point with the 360 (since it's away from the target, or "out of the money"). Rights to sell the wheat at 350 — puts — closed at 10.75¢/bushel; the 360 puts closed at 16.5¢. Since the 360 puts give their owner the right to sell at a price above the current market, they're called "in the money." In general, calls are mirror images of puts; calls rise in price as their underlying asset rises; puts fall in price. The principles are the same for a stock option. A single "IBM July 90 call" gives the buyer the right to buy 100 shares (a "round lot") of IBM at $90 a share; an "IBM July 90 put" gives its buyer the right to sell IBM at 90.

The price of an option is generally a reflection of market interest rates, the time to maturity, the closeness of the price of the underlying asset to its strike price, and that underlying asset's historical price volatility. Higher interest rates, a longer time to maturity, and greater volatility tend to raise prices. In the 1970s, Fischer Black and Myron Scholes developed an options pricing formula that has become a classic; it's been tinkered with over the years, but their fundamental technique remains canonical.

from 1,300% returns to the sidewalk

Put- and call-buying is fairly simple. Things do get more complicated, much more complicated. An owner of 100 shares of IBM can sell a call against those shares; should the price rise, he or she would have to buy back the call at a loss — the loss being partly offset by the (paper) rise in the value of the underlying shares — or run the risk of having the stock "called away" by the fortunate buyer of the call. People with losing positions usually close them out at a loss before their maturity date; actual orders to deliver, or exercises, are fairly rare.

Plungers can also sell calls without owning the underlying asset; this is called "going naked." The naked call seller runs a risk far greater than mere embarrassment; as with any short sale, the losses are theoretically limitless. Someone who shorts a stock at 90, or sells a 90 call when the underlying stock is trading at 90, runs the risk that a sharp runup in the stock, whether because of a mania or a takeover, could force the price to 150 or higher.

And things get more complicated still. Complex combinations of futures and options positions are common. In options: short both calls and puts, on the hope that the underlying asset will go nowhere; long both calls and puts, on the hope that it will take off dramatically in one direction or another, it matters not which; long and short calls in strange combinations of maturity and prices; long an asset and short calls for twice the quantity of the underlying asset (a way of going short but hedging one's bets); long an asset and short half the quantity of calls (a way of going long but hedging one's bets). In futures: long crude oil and short gasoline, on the hope that the spread between raw and refined products will narrow; short crude and long gasoline, on the reverse hope (so-called crack spreads); long soybeans and short soy oil; long Treasury bills and short Treasury bonds, or long Eurodollar deposits and short Treasury bills — both on the hope that interest rate spreads will change in one's favor.

But it's not just speculation alone that could motivate complex positions like this. Consider the manufacturer of cooking oil; it buys grains and sells oil made from that grain — in financial terms, it goes long the raw product and short the refined. But the timing doesn't always work in unison; it could buy the grain today, only to find the price of oil collapsing tomorrow. Using futures, it could lock today's price spread for business it will do several months down the road. That would insulate it from the effects of any price changes, whether favorable or unfavorable.

All these strategies, simple purchases or sales or complex combinations of both, can be motivated either by gut instinct or complex mathematical models, by the desire to limit exposure or to bet the house, by routine business decisions of interested parties or speculative interests of players who couldn't tell soybeans from seed corn. But whatever the motivation or strategy, it's usually estimated that 80–90% of nonprofessional futures and options traders lose money.

Norm Zadeh, a money manager and savant based in Beverly Hills who used to run an option-trading competition, said that some of his winners were literally "sleeping on grates" a year or two after their victories. Some would rack up 1,300% returns, take out ads, attract clients, and then lose all their money and then some.

Longer-lived winners are either commercial interests or professionals like floor traders and brokers. Most nonprofessionals have no idea what they're doing and often lose their shirts. Pros speak mockingly of people who buy calls just because they think a stock is going to go up; the amateurs neglect to determine whether the call is under- or overpriced according to theoretical computer models, or neglect to limit their risks through the use of complex hybrid structures.

standardize, centralize

As complex as this is, most of it is transparent to the participant.[15] Customers submit orders to their brokers, who transmit them to the exchange floor. The floor is populated by employees of the big brokerage houses who are the medium for these orders, as well as by independent traders, known as locals, who trade for their own accounts. While there must be a buyer for every seller, the exchanges take care of the details of matching the two parties. This task is simplified by the fact that the contracts are so highly standardized. Standardization and centralization were the key to the development of modern futures exchanges, which have changed little (except for the replacement of paper by computers) since the turn of the century when formal clearinghouses replaced informal "rings" of traders (Williams 1986, p. 5). Clearinghouses offer standardized contracts and a painless (to the traders) matching of buyers and sellers, in place of custom deals that once were made among individual ring members.

The modern exchange and clearinghouse system didn't emerge fully formed. Informal trading arrangements, not merely within rings that knew each other, but among rings and individuals who had no great familiarity with each other, ballooned in complexity. The Chicago Board of Trade (CBOT) at first only offered a forum for individual traders, a central location for firms' clerks. Before the CBOT clearinghouse was formed, clerks would run about with warehouse receipts, exchanging titles to goods on behalf of their employers. In hectic moments, firms would pass receipts along to other firms, sometimes a chain as long as 10 or 25 firms, without any written record; firms would often receive receipts for contracts they never made. With the clearinghouse, a single clerk could examine all the trading lists simultaneously, and arrange transfer of the traded goods.

Options evolved a bit more slowly. Calls and puts on stocks have been traded for a long time, but the trading was fairly thin. Deals had to be nearly custom-made; buyers and sellers had to be matched specifically, which kept trading slow and markets illiquid. However, the Chicago Board Options Exchange, a spinoff of the CBOT, began trading listed options — standardized contracts settled at a clearinghouse — in the mid-1970s. After a slowish start, trading exploded: from no contracts (aside from a few custom deals) in 1970, to 97 million in 1980, to 202 million in 1992.[16]

Clearinghouses are at the heart of the process. Every day, firms submit a list of their trades to the clearinghouse — buying wheat, selling bonds — and the clearinghouse checks and reconciles the filings. Then the clearinghouse either pays or bills the member, depending on the net monetary value of the day's trades. The important feature of the modern system is that settlement is typically in cash; the economic point is that a futures contract is a way of turning a thing promptly into money — and money of a form that can be transformed into scores of other assets. With futures, a bushel of wheat can almost instantly be traded for its equivalent in cash, which then can be turned into oil, Treasury bonds, or a lobster dinner.

While outright market manipulation — corners and such — is rare today, minor offenses are common and certain kinds of insider action are perfectly legal. When the major grain companies negotiated the sale of wheat to the USSR in the 1970s, they didn't announce the deal publicly for a week or so. In the meanwhile, they loaded up on futures, a practice euphemistically known as "anticipatory hedging." Or when floor traders get big orders from customers, orders big enough to move prices significantly in one direction or another, they will frequently wink at a buddy, who then makes the appropriate trade just before the big order is placed. The conspirators can split the profit later by arranging dummy trades.

But in the big picture, these are fairly minor events; the populist claim that the futures markets rig prices in a major way — heard at one time from heartland farmers, and now mainly from Third World commodity exporters — has little basis in fact. The creation of futures markets usually undermines cartels, rather than reinforcing them. Major commodity price trends are the result of the interplay of supply and demand around the cost of production, a dull explanation, but fundamentally true. Third World commodity exporters face chronic problems of oversupply that aren't caused by the gnomes of Chicago.

bespoke derivatives

This section is for readers who want to get some idea of what really complex derivatives are about; those who don't care are advised to skip a few pages for a discussion of the point of all this inventiveness.

Players who find the off-the-rack derivatives that trade on exchanges too common can always turn to custom-tailored instruments. The lack of standardization makes them untradeable, but the possibilities are limited only by imagination and the number of willing partners. As with exchange-traded derivatives, the custom kind — also called over-the-counter (OTC) — can serve as a hedge or a bet, or even both at once.

Details of custom derivatives may be more than many readers want to know, but they do involve the full richness of financial imagination. Swaps were pioneered in the late 1970s, but the first deal to attract wide attention was a currency swap between IBM and the World Bank in 1981, and the first interest rate swap was one involving the Student Loan Marketing Association (Sallie Mae), a U.S.-government-sponsored vendor of student loans (Abken 1991).[17] Unlike exchange-traded derivatives, swaps don't really involve a claim on an underlying asset; in most cases, the partners in the swap, called counterparties, swap two sets of cash flows, cash flows that are usually thrown off by positions in other securities (bond interest, stock dividends, etc.).

That sounds terribly abstract; maybe a bit more detail about so-called "plain vanilla" swaps will make it clearer. In a currency swap, the two counterparties exchange specific amounts of two different currencies, which are repaid over time according to a fixed schedule which reflects the payment of interest and amortization of principal. Essentially, the counterparties are lending each other currencies and paying back the loan over time. The interest rates charged can be either both fixed, or both floating, or one fixed and one floating.

In an interest rate swap, the counterparties exchange payments based on some underlying principal amount (called the "notional" amount). One set of payments could be at floating rates (that is, adjusted with changes in market rates) and the other fixed, or both could be at floating rates, but tied to different market rates.

This still sounds very abstract. The evolution of the currency swap from its 1970s ancestor, the parallel loan agreement, may make things clearer. Imagine that a U.S. firm would like to borrow German marks, for use by a German subsidiary, and a German firm would like to borrow dollars, for complementary reasons. Both the German and the U.S. firms could issue bonds in their domestic markets in similar amounts, swap the principal, leaving the U.S. firm paying mark-denominated interest and the German, dollar interest. In effect, each has borrowed in the other's capital markets — something they might otherwise have been unable to do because of legal restrictions or the lack of name recognition. The problem with such agreements was that if one party defaulted, the other was still on the hook for principal and interest. Currency swaps take care of this by stipulating that a default by one party means the end of the agreement; this limits risk only to the difference between the two interest streams, not the full face value of principal and interest.

And here's an example of an interest rate swap (Abken 1991). Say a bank issues a one-month certificate of deposit, and then invests the proceeds in a two-year note whose interest payments are tied to the London Interbank Offered Rate (LIBOR, the rate banks charge each other in the London-based Euromarkets). The CD will mature well before the note, and the rate the bank might have to pay the CD holder may not move in lockstep with LIBOR. Should the two interest rates march to their own drummers, the bank could find itself losing money on the two-sided transaction. To protect itself, the bank could visit its swap dealer, and work out a LIBOR–CD swap. The bank would pay the dealer the LIBOR interest rate on the underlying principal, and the dealer would pay some CD-linked index rate (minus a fee, of course). The swap dealer could either be acting on its own account, hoping to make money on the fee and maybe some clever trading, or it could be acting on behalf of a customer with complementary needs. The principal amount never changes hands, however, only the interest payments do. That's why the underlying principal is referred to as the "notional" amount.

An old-fashioned banker might also argue that funding a two-year investment by a series of 24 monthly loans is a dumb thing to do, and the swap is a fancy way of getting around that; why not issue a two-year CD to fund a two-year investment? But interest rates on two-year CDs may not be very favorable, and it may be that the bank will come out ahead with the swap. If all goes well, of course.

These are only the simplest examples; intensely more complex deals can be arranged. Swaps can be combined with options in order to limit swings in floating rate payments. Say two parties enter an interest rate swap that begins with neither having to exchange money; both the fixed and floating rate are the same, at 8%, say. But a month later, when it's time to adjust the rates on the floating half of the deal, market rates have risen to 10%. That means the payer of the floating rate would have to hand over to the counterparty 2% of the underlying notional principal. Should rates rise dramatically, the deal could get very expensive. Prudence might lead the payer of the unpredictable rate to buy a "cap" — an option that limits the maximum floating rate to a fixed level, say 9% in our example. The seller of the cap, however, has to pay any amount above 9%.

Further complications are immediately possible: the cap seller will no doubt want to hedge somehow, and the floating-rate payer might want to offset the cost of buying the cap by selling a "floor," the mirror image of the cap. By selling a floor, the floating-rate payer limits any gains from a fall in market interest rates. A cap and floor together create an interest rate "collar" — the establishment of upper and lower bounds on a floating rate. The final word in the exotic vocabulary is "swaption," an option to enter into a swap, for those who are shy about making commitments. After all this maneuvering, it looks suspiciously like a Rube Goldberg version of a fixed interest rate, but participants are adamant that all the complexity is worth it — with the bankers who sell the instruments the most adamant of all.

OTC derivatives began their stunning takeoff in the middle 1980s, paralleling the rise in trading of their exchange-traded cousins. But where much of the rise in exchange-traded instruments was simply a matter of Europe and Japan catching up with U.S. financial futures markets, OTC growth was mainly the proliferation of new instruments worldwide. In 1986, notional principal in interest rate swaps was $400 billion, with another $100 billion in currency swaps outstanding; at the end of 1990, the figures were $2.3 trillion and $578 billion, respectively, to which had been added another $561 billion in caps, floors, collars, and swaptions; in 1997, notional principal on interest rate swaps totaled $22.1 trillion, and currency swaps, $1.5 trillion (Bank for International Settlements 1998).

The biggest users of currency swaps once were nonfinancial corporations — the multinationals that dominate world trade, who borrow and do business in scores of currencies around the world. But financial institutions have been steadily increasing their use, with 40% of notional principal outstanding, a bit ahead of nonfinancial firms, with governments a distant third. Financial institutions dominate the market for interest rate swaps; after all, interest-bearing paper is the basic commodity they deal in. Corporations accounted for just 23% and governments, 6%. The U.S. share of swap markets is surprisingly small — less than a third of interest rate swaps and quarter of the currency kind — and the dollar's share has been shrinking steadily, from 79% of interest rate swaps in 1987 to 30% in 1996, with the yen and the European currencies rising dramatically. No doubt European and Asian economic integration is at work here, though the merger of Continental countries into the euro will change everything.

Moves are already underway to trade standardized swaps on exchanges, or develop clearinghouses for OTC swaps, but it's not clear that this will work; needs may be too personal, and counterparties may not want to expose themselves to the scrutiny of taking public positions.

the point of it all

Having inspected the machinery, the question arises — what's the point? Isn't this all just a fanciful overlay, somewhere between irrelevant and malignant, on "real" activity? One answer might be that derivatives markets are simply the commodity form raised to a higher level of abstraction: the commodity is a thing whose purpose in life is to be sold and transformed into money; once transformed into money, financial markets develop so that money itself might be deployed profitably. A related answer would be that the purveyors of derivatives have a great incentive to invent new products: profits are always highest on newborn instruments, though this advantage quickly deteriorates as competitors mimic the product.

But those explanations are too crude for sophisticates. In polite discourse, derivatives are often justified by resort to parables about farmers and millers. The farmer sells wheat forward to lock in a harvest price while it's still in the ground, and the miller buys forward to guard against unpleasant price spikes. In both cases, potential gains — a fall in price for the miller, a rise for the farmer — are surrendered in advance to avoid potential losses. This is the "insurance" theory of futures markets. There's also a liquidity theory — that the farmer sells today to boost cash flow, since money today always feels better than the hope of money tomorrow.

This model is clean, and it even allows for speculators. Speculators, who want to gamble on movement in prices — up or down, the bigger the better — are good for a market, because they can stand on the other side of a trade, thereby bringing depth and liquidity to a market. Derivatives markets serve the social function of shifting risk from the hedger to the speculator, presumably increasing the happiness of both.

The rural cast of characters gives the model a homey appeal, but real life is different. First, agricultural futures aren't representative of the actual trading world. Trading in financial futures (stocks, bonds, and currencies) accounts for almost 70% of the total; energy products, another 12%; and metals, 4%; ag commodities are only 15%. The sole producer of Treasury bonds is the U.S. government, but it has no presence in the futures markets in its paper; the major players are the big financial institutions who trade it. They use futures markets to speculate for their own profit, or to hedge positions taken when buying or holding instruments for customers or their own inventory. The farmer and the miller are strangers to the wonderworld of Treasury debt.

But the homily hardly applies even where they aren't strangers, in the classic agricultural markets. A 1977 survey (cited in Shiller 1993, p. 101) found only 6% of farmers bought or sold any futures; even in the biggest size class, no more than 13% did. But the trading farmers were mainly speculating, not classically hedging: two in three were trading in crops other than those they were growing, and three in four bought contracts rather than selling them, as the homey myth tells it. (Farmers may be well positioned to speculate in their own crops; they have "inside" info on their markets that may be unknown to Chicago traders or to lawyers speculating from Dallas.) Roughly a fifth of wheat sales in the same 1977 survey were done on a forward basis — though many of these forward sales occurred after price spikes, meaning that farmers were locking in what they thought were to be "high" prices. A true hedger wouldn't change strategy based on a market judgment.

To be fair, futures markets *are* dominated by commercial interests, not outsiders. Grain buyers buy heavily in the futures markets, as do bond dealers and oil refiners. According to Steve Briese (personal communication), editor of the Minneapolis-based futures newsletter *The Bullish Review,* commercial interests account for about 60–70% of the open contracts in major commodity and financial futures markets. Small speculators account for 20–30%, and big speculators for around 10%.[18] But commercial interests, be they farmers or bond dealers, can speculate just like anyone else.

Even apparently cautious derivatives users — multinational corporations (MNCs) who have to cope with volatility in interest rate and foreign exchange markets that interfere with their real-world businesses — can disguise adventure as prudence. Nonfinancial firms are heavy users of derivatives; two-thirds of large U.S. corporations used derivatives regularly in 1993, according to a survey by the industry newsletter *Swaps Monitor* (Hansell 1994), with Ford reporting a notional value of its positions as $45 billion; GE, $27 billion; GM, $25 billion; and IBM, $18 billion.

Nonfinancial corporations are often "selective" hedgers, which means they don't hedge when they think they hold a winning hand. *Finance & Treasury* (1993), a newsletter for corporate treasurers, demanded of its readers: "Time to confess: are you trading for profit or aren't you? If the answer is yes, then why not own up to it?" In a 1992 survey, *F&T* found that under 10% of MNCs described their treasuries as running for-profit operations; the official line is that they existed to manage risk. Yet only 13% required 100% hedging routinely; by *not* hedging, the firm was consciously taking on risk — risk that it could only justify as an attempt at profit. The newsletter offers the example of a U.S. MNC, which borrowed in Spanish pesetas to fund a German subsidiary, even though peseta interest rates were higher than D-mark rates — because it was betting on a peseta devaluation. Firms are reluctant to admit to speculating with the treasury because stockholders and regulators might be displeased.

Even were the hedging story a fuller explanation of derivatives markets than it seems to be, is hedging necessarily a good thing? Barry Schachter's (1992) review of options theory makes it clear that mainstream finance theorists do not speak with one voice on whether options make sense or not — whether, in their absurdly mathematical world, options promote equilibrium or perturb it, whether they're functional or "redundant." There are plenty of theories, none of them predominant or terribly convincing. Schachter is reduced to saying that "The huge volume of trade in options worldwide could be taken as supporting the conclusion that options make a difference." No doubt they do, but of what sort?[19]

It's possible that hedging leaves society as a whole worse off than it would be if unhedged. David Newberry (1992) offered this example. Compare two arrangements for growing rice, one safe, the other higher yielding and more profitable, but riskier (for example, a high-yield strain subject to disease in certain climates). Without futures markets, farmers would be less likely to grow the risky rice than they would if they could sell a portion of the crop forward to speculators. In the second world, supplies would be more volatile than in the first, and spot prices probably would be too. In this case, hedging promotes instability.

But even if markets did neutralize price exposure, prices are only part of the story. "[I]f prices are stabilized," wrote Newberry, "but quantities remain unstable, incomes may be less stable than if prices were free to move in response to the quantity changes." Both Newberry's and Schachter's inability to summon powerful arguments in support of the derivatives markets is striking, given their growth over the last 20 years.

Journalists, however, have no problem in composing apologias. Well along in the 1994 derivatives hysteria, true to its role as the organ of reasssurance, the *New York Times* (Hansell 1994) pointed up the virtues of derivatives, calling as lead witness William McDonough, president of the New York Fed. McDonough warned against "derivatives angst," which threatened the smooth functioning of the market, which threatened everything good: "The existence of derivatives," McDonough said, speaking in the midst of the weakest U.S. economic expansion since World War II with investment well below Golden Age levels, "increases the level of investment and makes possible greater economic growth."

As the *Times* put it, derivatives are lovely if they're in the right hands, dangerous otherwise. "You don't put an average pilot in an F-15 fighter without special training," Harvard finance professor Andre Perold told correspondent Saul Hansell. Hansell picked up on Perold's martial metaphor, noting that "once companies learn how to use this advanced financial weaponry for defensive purposes, it's natural and often profitable for them to take on some extra risk." Just who is the enemy here? Is there any risk of collateral damage? Instead of interrogating its own metaphors, however, the *Times* instead solicited the opinion of Walter Shipley, chair of Chemical Bank, which the paper acknowledged to be "a large derivatives dealer," who declared that "all of the regulators...have fundamentally affirmed that most of the market functions responsibly."

"Responsible" users look to derivatives to shield them against volatility, particularly in interest rate and currency markets — a private, market-based attempt to solve the social problem of profound economic uncertainty. MNCs do business in scores of currencies, and have debts in quite a few too. Volatile currency and debt markets make good financial projections impossible, but if firms hedge properly with derivatives, they can theoretically insulate themselves against such risks.[20]

The irony of these individualized approaches to risk management is that they seem to increase systemic risk even as they lower individual risk, at least for the smarter or luckier or more practiced users. People who think they're hedged can turn out not to be when markets go wild; all the assumptions on which they've based their positions fall to pieces. Normal price relationships — between long and short interest rates, or between two currencies that normally trade in near-unison — fall apart; vast imbalances between supply and demand can result in wide spreads between bid and asked prices; and liquidity may disappear (a market can suddenly become all sellers, no buyers). Prices gap and career in ways that computers can't model. But since many custom derivatives do not trade on the open market, there's no fair way to price them; a great deal of guessing is at work. (Derivatives portfolios are often priced to model — they're carried on their owners' books at the price the computer deems rational, rather than any price arrived at through open trading.)

When things go wrong, as they did in 1994, seemingly prudent hedges can generate losses, and selective hedges even bigger ones. The 1994 losses resulted in a marked slowdown of OTC derivatives growth in that year; whether this is a pause for breath or a real leveling off is an open question. Historically, new futures contracts have typically started slowly, then grown rapidly, and then leveled off; it may be that the OTC derivatives world is now rounding the top of this classic S-curve.

While derivatives goose up systemic risk, expose central banks to huge potential losses, and provide often illusory benefits to users at great profit to their makers, they seem innocent of the charge of increasing volatility. There's no significant difference between pre- and post-1980 stock market volatility; Treasury bill volatility was lower after 1980 than before.[21] Volatility was lower in stocks from 1990 to early 1995 than in any five-year period since the late 1940s; interest rate volatility was higher, but still only half the 1950s average. Currencies, of course, are a major exception, but they were once fixed by decree and then freed, so their derivatives boom is clearly a reaction to fundamentals, not a cause of increased volatility.

currencies

Trading in currencies is the largest and probably the oldest market of all. It used to be that the buying and selling of foreign exchange (a/k/a forex or FX) was an intermediate process, a step between, say, liquidating a U.S. Treasury bond and buying shares of Matsushita in its place, or between a multinational corporation's taking its profits in German marks and shipping them back to headquarters in London. Now, however, hedge funds, pension funds, and other institutional investors have increasingly been treating foreign exchange as an asset class in itself, separate from any underlying stock or bond (Bank for International Settlements 1993, p. 7). That means that trading in money itself, rather than monetary claims on underlying real assets, is now one of the most fashionable strategies available to big-time plungers.

Trade in foreign currencies is ancient — and not only in coins and bills, but in financial exotica. As Marcello de Cecco (1992a) noted, Aristotelian,[22] Christian, and Islamic restrictions on usury prompted clever forex transactions, so priced and structured as to allow the furtive bearing of interest. That means that from the outset, FX markets were only partly about the cross-border trade in real goods; financial considerations have long been central.

With the breakup of the Roman empire, currencies proliferated, as did opportunities to profit from their exchange and transformation. Italians were well placed to profit from the new trade — Italy being the center of the former empire, and also the home of the church doctors, who were adept at devising schemes for evading usury prohibitions. As the church ban began to lose its bite, and as the center of European economic activity moved north and west, Italian dominance of FX waned; first Belgian and Dutch dealers inherited the business, only to lose dominance to London, where it remains, though of course there's still plenty to go around.

In myth, the old days were ones of monetary stability, with gold acting as the universal equivalent for all national monetary forms. In fact, the temptation of states to manipulate their currencies — to declare their coins' purchasing power to be greater than the intrinsic value of their metal — is ancient and nearly irresistible, and the more insulated a country is from FX markets, the less resistible it seems to be. The triumph of the international gold standard was the result of the Enlightenment and the consolidation of British industrial and financial power; the political economists of the 18th and early 19th centuries provided the theory, and the development of capitalist finance provided the impetus from practice.

With Sir Isaac Newton as Master of the Mint, Britain set the value of the pound sterling at 123.274 grains of gold at the beginning of the 18th century. That standard was suspended in 1797, because of the financing needs of the Napoleonic Wars. When peace came, creditors' calls for restoration of the gold standard were resisted by industrialists and landowners. In 1818, the government faced major funding difficulties, and was forced to return to the old formula. The ensuing deflation savaged home demand, forcing British industrialists to search abroad for export markets.

The classical gold standard was nowhere near as stable nor as universal as it's usually painted by metal fetishists. Wild booms alternated with equally wild busts. And while the Bank of England stood at the center of the world gold market, silver prevailed elsewhere, especially in France, which provided Britain with a reservoir of liquidity in tight times.

And then there was America, which was constantly disrupting things throughout gold's heyday. The often imprudent, anarchic American credit system helped finance the country's extraordinary growth, but the system's indiscipline led to manias and panics in near-equal measure.[23] The Bank of England was often forced to act as a lender of last resort to the U.S., which had no central bank, and often little sense of fiscal management (de Cecco 1992b). Had America been forced by some pre-modern IMF to act according to modern orthodox principles, the U.S. and perhaps even the world would be a poorer place — at least in monetary terms.

The U.S. went off gold during the Civil War — war, it seems, is the greatest enemy of financial orthodoxy — and didn't return until 1879, with most other countries following suit. That began the period of the high classical gold standard, which lasted only until 1914, when it was destroyed by the outbreak of war — a much shorter reign than the propaganda of modern goldbugs suggests. There were attempts to put it back together between the two world wars, but countries set their currencies' values (relative to gold) unilaterally, with no sense of how the values fitted together. That system collapsed in the 1930s, and there was no stable global monetary order until after World War II, when the Bretton Woods fixed exchange rate system was established. Unlike the classic gold standard, in which all countries expressed their national currency in terms of gold, the Bretton Woods system used the dollar as the central value, and the dollar in turn was fixed to gold. Countries could hold dollar reserves in their central bank for the settlement of international trade and finance on the knowledge that they could cash those dollars in for a fixed amount of gold. The dollar, as was said, was as good as gold.

The designers of the Bretton Woods system feared floating rate systems were unstable, undermining trade through uncertainty and market over-reactions. Keynes wanted a much more elastic system than the U.S. pay-masters would permit; ironically, though, the emergence of the dollar as the central reserve currency meant that world reserves were essentially a matter of U.S. monetary policy, and the U.S. did not stint on supplying these. From soon after the war was over until today, the U.S. has acted as the final source of world demand. There was the Marshall Plan, global military expansion, investment abroad by newly globalizing U.S. multina-tionals, and always more and more imports — all of which scattered dol-lars around the world. That cascade of greenbacks, plus rising domestic inflation, meant that the dollar was no longer worth as much as it was supposed to be — that is, the gold price was artificially low — and that cashing in dollars for gold at posted prices was a marvellous deal. (No one took more pleasure in pointing this out than Charles de Gaulle.) Strains began appearing in the system in the late 1960s; the outflow of gold from the U.S. to London was so great during the week of the Tet Offensive in Vietnam (March 1968) that the floor of the Bank of England's weighing room collapsed (O'Callaghan 1993, p. 19). The German mark broke free and appreciated in 1969, and repeated the breakout in 1971. The French cashed in dollars for gold, and there were rumors that Britain was next. So in August 1971, Nixon closed the Treasury's gold window, ending the sale of cheap gold. After some attempts at patching the system together, currrencies began floating, one by one, in 1973. Now the value of a dollar or a D-mark is set by trading on this vast market.

While governments are not free to set the value of their national currencies, they aren't as powerless as casual opinion has it. Policies to manage the major currencies have been fairly successful since the major powers agreed to the gradual devaluation of the dollar in 1985 (the so-called Plaza agreement, named after the New York hotel where they met). Nor is central bank intervention necessarily the fruitless and expensive thing it's thought to be. From the last quarter of 1986 to the first of 1996, the U.S. government made over $10 billion on exchange market interventions, mainly to support a falling dollar (by buying lots of dollars).[24] The profits, divided about equally between the Treasury and the Fed, were added to the Treasury's Exchange Stabilization Fund — $28 billion in D-marks, yen, and Mexican pesos — and the Fed's holdings of $21 billion in FX reserves, denominated in the same currencies (Fisher 1996).[25]

Central banks can't change the underlying fundamentals that drive currency values — like productivity, inflation rates, and political stability — but they can influence the speed and gentleness of adjustment. But it's worth saying a few words about those fundamentals. As loopy as currency trading can get from day to day, it's no surprise that economic crises often take on the form of a foreign exchange melodrama. Despite all the hype about a borderless global economy, the world is still organized around national economies and national currencies; the foreign exchange market is where national price systems are joined to the world market. Problems in the relation between those countries and the outside world often express themselves as currency crises. Two recent examples of this are the European monetary crisis of 1992 and the Mexican peso crisis of 1994. In both cases, one could blame the turmoil on speculators, and one would be partly right — but also in both cases, the political momentum for economic integration had gotten way ahead of the fundamentals. Weaker economies like Italy's and Britain's were being thrust into direct competition with Germany's, just as Mexico was being thrown into competition with the U.S. The relative productivity of the weaker partners in both cases wasn't up to the valuations implied by the exchange rates prevailing before the outbreak of the crisis. Something had to give, and it did, with seismic force.

But day-to-day trading in money itself typically proceeds with little regard for such real-world considerations. That trading in money takes many forms. The longest-established are the spot and forward markets, dominated by the world's major commercial banks. A spot contract allows a customer to buy a specified amount of foreign exchange — a million U.S. dollars' worth of German marks, for example — for immediate delivery at prevailing market rates. (In practice, "immediate" usually means two business days.) The full amount involved actually changes hands. Conceptually, forward contracts are simple enough — they're a kind of delayed spot deal, with buyers today fixing a price today for a deal to be consummated in a month or three. In practice, such straightforward forward deals have been eclipsed by swaps, in which the two parties agree to exchange two currencies at a certain rate on one date, and then to reverse the transaction, usually at a different exchange rate, some specified time in the future. The "price" of a forward contract — the difference between the forward and spot prices — is determined largely by the difference in interest rates in the two currencies, with an adjustment for the markets' expectations of where the currencies are going in the near future. There are also futures and options contracts traded on the major currencies, and, of course, exotic custom derivatives are available as well.

A survey by the Bank for International Settlements (1996) reported that on an average day in the rather placid month of April 1995, $1.2 trillion in currencies changed hands, up from $880 billion in 1992, an increase of only 45% — insignificant compared to the doubling between 1986 and 1989.[26] To put that $1.2 trillion in perspective, it means that the currency markets turned over an amount equal to annual U.S. GDP in about a week, and world product in about a month. Turnover has certainly risen since 1992; the daily volume on the Clearing House Interbank Payment System (CHIPS), the network connecting all the major banks doing business involving U.S. dollars, rose about $200 billion in the three years after the survey (Grant 1995, 1998) — a big number, for sure, but one that implies a slower growth rate than that of the 1980s or early 1990s.

Britain (mainly London) was the biggest FX market, accounting for 30% of turnover; the U.S. (mainly New York) was next, with 16%; and Japan (mainly Tokyo) third, with 10%. So the big three centers accounted for 56% of world currency trading; surprisingly, Germany accounted for only 5% of the total, less than far smaller economies like Singapore, Switzerland, and Hong Kong. London's dominance of the game is revealed by two striking facts: more U.S. dollars are traded in London than in New York, and more D-marks than in Frankfurt.

According to the BIS survey, 44% of the turnover was in the spot market, 9% in the forward markets (which are dominated by real-world customers, doing actual trading of goods and services), and 48% in the swap markets. (In addition, a modest $15 billion a day in FX futures and options were traded on organized exchanges.) Around 64% of total daily turnover was between foreign exchange dealers themselves, and another 20% with other financial institutions. Only 16% involved real-world "customers."

Around 83% of all trades in the 1995 survey involved the U.S. dollar. While this is down from 90% three years earlier, it's evidence that the dollar is still the dominant world currency by far; even something as decentered as the FX market needs a fixed referent. Part of this dominance, however, is the result of "vehicle trading" — the practice of using the dollar as an intermediary currency. Instead of someone who wants to buy lire for D-marks waiting to find someone eager to sell D-marks for lire, the trader exchanges D-marks for dollars, and then dollars for lire. The dollar is also the world's main reserve currency — according to the IMF, 59% of world foreign exchange reserves were held in dollars in 1996, up from 1990's low of 50%. As the European Union moves towards its single currency, the euro is likely to account for a larger share of world reserves, making it a rival to the dollar as the world reserve and vehicle currency. Loss of the dollar's central role would decrease demand for the greenback, and would probably nudge up U.S. interest rates, and maybe even spell the end of the U.S.'s imperial privilege of borrowing in its own currency.

Though some sentimentalists still cling to the barbarous relic, the gold market is a fairly small one. Still, it remains a kind of money, worthy of discussion here rather than with more routine commodities like crude oil and pig parts. Trading takes the usual array of forms, from the spot and forward exchange of physical bullion — done mainly with the exchange of titles and warehouse certificates, rather than actual physical movement — to futures and options on futures. In 1989, total trading on world futures and options exchanges alone was the equivalent of 21 times the world supply of new gold, and about 38% of the total above-ground supply. That trading, plus trading in other markets, far outstrips the total of all the gold ever mined (about 80% of which is thought to be accounted for; people rarely lose or waste gold). Despite this vigorous trading, the world gold stock is not that impressive. At $400 an ounce, the total world supply of gold is worth about $1.5 trillion — about a quarter as much as all U.S. stocks are worth, less than half the value of all U.S. Treasury debt, and also less than half the U.S. M2 money supply.[27]

But not all the world's gold is available for trading. The leading holders are central banks, with 27% of the total world stock; they liquidate their holdings periodically, but are not major traders. Other official holders like the IMF account for another 6% of the world supply, meaning a third of all the world's gold is in the hands of state institutions, even though goldbugs celebrate their metal for its freedom from the state. Jewelry accounts for nearly a third (31%), and industrial use, another 12%. That leaves less than a quarter (24%) of the world's gold stock — under $400 billion, or not much more than the U.S. currency supply — in what are called "private stocks," those that are likely to be traded. London's annual bullion turn-over alone accounts for all this easily tradeable supply, and derivatives account for another 160%. Every grain of gold is spoken for many times, but as long as everyone doesn't demand physical delivery at once, the market will behave.

Despite the small physical foundation on which the gold market is built, the metal still has a psychological grip on financial players, who view its rise as a portent of inflation or political problems, and view its fall as a sign of deflation and placidity. Calls for a return to a gold standard regu-larly emanate from the right wing of Wall Street — supply-siders like Jude Wanniski and Larry Kudlow adore gold, and even Fed chair Alan Greenspan professes to be fond of paying close attention to it when setting monetary policy. Greenspan, a one-time Ayn Rand acolyte, wrote an essay (Greenspan 1966) for her *Objectivist* newsletter proclaiming gold the ulti-mate weapon of the haves against inflation, a way for the "owners of wealth" to "protect" themselves against all statist schemes to "confiscate the wealth of the productive members of society to support a wide variety of welfare schemes."[28]

Gold remains, in Keynes' (*CW* VI, p. 259) phrase, an important "part of the apparatus of conservatism," and in more senses than one. Attend a conference of goldbugs and you are likely to be surrounded by the most fervent denizens of the far right, who love not only the austerity that gold symbolizes, but also the fact that it's a non-state form of money. In a tre-mendous reversal of 19th century populist ideology, which was feverishly anti-gold, many of today's right populists are very pro-gold, as the only antidote to the parasitical rule of Washington and Wall Street. A cultural bonus to right-wing goldbugs was the large presence of South Africa in the industry and of South Africans at their conferences; many, though certainly not all, aurophiles were admirers of apartheid. Ironically, many leftish South Africans now root for monetary disorder in the North, which would result in heavy demand for gold, allowing the country to play the role of a "prosperous undertaker at a funeral." Though South African mines are getting pretty tapped out, the six largest South African firms controlled over a quarter of world gold production in 1993, with the huge Anglo-American combine alone responsible for over 18%. Canada, with 8%, and the U.S., with 7%, were a distant second and third (Tegen 1994).

Gold's actual performance is a source of constant frustration to goldbugs. The metal's main charm is that it retains its purchasing power over time; should inflation soar or the banking system implode, gold will not vanish like a paper claim. But its drawbacks are plentiful, and there are good reasons why all societies have gravitated to state-sponsored money. Gold pays no interest, is bulky, requires assay, and must be stored. It is heavy and physical in a world that tends towards ever more immateriality. Something that normally does no better than shadow the general price level is no fun, though goldbugs are always imagining some disaster — hyperinflation, the collapse of the state, climatic catastrophe — that will bring their beloved metal back to life.

For metallists, there were no better days than the 1970s. Gold first began trading freely in 1968, and it immediately broke away from the classic $35 an ounce price, set in 1934, when the Roosevelt administration banned private ownership of monetary gold. The price rose slowly, breaking gently above $40 as the decade turned. Once the U.S. abandoned convertibility, however, gold started a ripping bull market. Reaching a first peak just under $200 in oil-shocked 1974, the price settled back with the recession, and turned up with the world economy in 1976 in a spec-

tacular rise that ended at $850 an ounce in January 1980. From there, when the Volcker clampdown took hold, gold sank almost unrelievedly to below $300 in 1985. After 1985, it spent ten years going nowhere — which should be no surprise over the long term, given the metal's reputation as a sterile repository of value. Despite all the gyrations in between, the average gold price of $294 in early 1998 was 31% below 1934's $409 (in constant 1998 dollars). Seen in a long-term perspective, the 1970s merely corrected the steady erosion of the metal's purchasing power during the four previous decades when the price was fixed by law. From here on out, gold should rise with the average price level — making allowance, of course, for the occasional war, revolution, hyperinflation, or financial panic, should such a thing ever happen again.

innovation in general

This review is likely to be obsolete all too soon; the finest minds of Wall Street and similar precincts around the world are constantly inventing new instruments. At the risk of anthropomorphizing a social convention, money capital longs for exotic forms. One reason for this is that the highest-profit instruments are usually the newest; big gains go to the inventor of a new gimmick, but these fade as the product is imitated by everyone else on the Street. But that can't be the only reason; clearly there's a demand, not always fully thought through, for whizbang new tools to "manage risk," have a fling, or indulge some other lust for moneymaking.

John D. Finnerty, who compiled the Whitmanic catalogue of financial innovations since the 1960s reproduced on page 51, listed 10 stimuli to such creative enterprise. They include risk reduction or the shifting of risk towards one party or the other, reduction of agency costs (lender supervision of management) and issuance costs, tax angles, compliance with or evasion of regulation, changes in the level and volatility of interest and exchange rates, "academic and other research that result in advances in financial theories," accounting gimmickry, and technological advances.

This little survey of financial innovation would be incomplete without notice paid to the ease with which nearly anything can be absorbed into the circuit of money. On shutting down his family's 172-year-old London art dealership, Charles Leggatt observed, "When I started in art, what mattered was being able to spot a good picture. What counts now is to have a first-class financial brain. What I came into was the art trade; what I am leaving is a financial service" (ARTnewsletter 1992).

Art is but one example of capital's ability to capitalize nearly anything. The World Bank is a master at this practice; it capitalizes disaster itself. A headline in the April 13, 1995, issue of its weekly PR sheet, *World Bank News,* bragged, "Bank Prepares Emergency Help for Massive Russian Oil

Spill." Something had to be done to contain a huge spill that would be unleashed come the spring thaw, and the World Bank was ready. While many Americans think this means the World Bank gave away their tax dollars, in fact the Bank was turning Russian economic catastrophe into $99 million in claims held by the Bank and its creditors, to be serviced by Russian exports. For the World Bank, this is all in a day's work. It routinely "funds" greenhouse gas reduction programs — through loans, of course — in countries where it financed the gas-spewing power plants. It provides "Women in Development" loans in countries where gender relations, for good or ill, had been turned upside down by Bank-led liberalization. It provides new loans for the restructuring of old loans. For a public institution, the World Bank is quite innovative — and profitable. In 1995, it made $1.35 billion for itself, and $6.84 billion for its bondholders; it had $15.5 billion in retained assets on its balance sheet, accumulated from debts serviced by the world's poor (World Bank 1996).

But back to the more familiar terrain of workaday financial instruments. Most of the nearly 100 instruments shown nearby are merely hybrid products assembled from several basic building blocks — conversion of fixed to floating interest rates or vice versa; maturity transformation (turning long-term obligations into shorter-term ones, or the reverse) instruments crafted to move in the direction opposite some other price (inverse floaters, which pay less as interest rates rise and more as they fall); the creation of hermaphrodite securities (bond–stock warrant, bond–gold, bond–another country's currency, bond–stock future); tax, accounting, and regulatory footwork; the splitting of income streams ("stripped" bonds, ones divided into interest and principal sub-bonds, and then perhaps divided again between high- and low-risk); the swapping of income streams (interest rate swaps); the pooling of funds or of obligations into larger wholes to diversify against individual risks (mutual funds, securitization); schemes for increasing leverage (options, futures, payment-in-kind securities) or controlling volatility (options, futures, swaps). From these elements, however, infinitely strange creatures can be made.

Or, "Rather than developing new generic instruments," "financial innovation since the mid-1980s has tended to take the form of novel combinations of existing products to support complex and highly sophisticated investment strategies.... At the same time, a growing range of 'custom-tailored' investment products has been developed to maximise possibilities for matching actual portfolio structures to theoretically-based invesment models" (Bank for International Settlements 1993, p. 86). The more reality

financial innovations

adjustable rate convertible notes • adjustable rate preferred stock • adjustable/variable rate mortgages • All-Saver certificates • Americus trust • annuity notes • auction rate capital notes • auction rate notes/debentures • auction rate preferred stock • bull and bear CDs • capped floating rate notes • collateralized commercial paper • collateralized mortgage obligations/real estate mortgage investment conduits • collateralized preferred stock • commercial real estate-backed bonds • commodity-linked bonds • convertible adjustable preferred stock • convertible exchangeable preferred stock • convertible mortgages/reduction option loans • convertible reset debentures • currency swaps • deep discount/zero coupon bonds • deferred interest debentures • direct public sale of securities • dividend reinvestment plan • dollar BILS • dual currency bonds • employee stock ownership plan (ESOP) • Eurocurrency bonds • Euronotes/Euro-commercial paper • exchangeable auction rate preferred stock • exchangeable remarketed preferred stock • exchangeable variable rate notes • exchange-traded options • extendible notes • financial futures • floating rate/adjustable rate notes • floating rate extendible notes • floating rate, rating sensitive notes • floating rate tax-exempt notes • foreign-currency-denominated bonds • foreign currency futures and options • forward rate agreements • gold loans • high-yield (junk) bonds • increasing rate notes • indexed currency option notes/principal exchange linked securities • indexed floating rate preferred stock • indexed sinking fund debentures • interest rate caps/collars/floors • interest rate futures • interest rate reset notes • interest rate swaps • letter of credit/surety bond support • mandatory convertible/equity contract notes • master limited partnership • medium-term notes • money market notes • mortgage-backed bonds • mortgage pass-through securities • negotiable CDs • noncallable long-term bonds • options on futures contracts • paired common stock • participating bonds • pay-in-kind debentures • perpetual bonds • poison put bonds • puttable/adjustable tender bonds • puttable common stock • puttable convertible bonds • puttable-extendible notes • real estate-backed bonds • real yield securities • receivable-backed securities • remarketed preferred stock • remarketed reset notes • serial zero-coupon bonds • shelf registration process • single-point adjustable rate stock • Standard & Poor's indexed notes • state rate auction preferred stock • step-up put bonds • stock index futures and options • stripped mortgage-backed securities • stripped municipal securities • stripped U.S. Treasury securities • synthetic convertible debt • tuition futures • unbundled stock units • universal commercial paper • variable coupon/rate renewable notes • variable cumulative preferred stock • variable duration notes • warrants to purchase bonds • yield curve/maximum rate notes • zero-coupon convertible debt

source: Finnerty (1992)

can be made to correspond to the pure beauty of financial theory, the better life will be.

It's fashionable among liberal intellectuals to treat "financial engineering" as an invention of the Reaganbush years. But financial engineering was a favorite term of André Meyer, the supremo of Lazard Frères from the 1950s to the 1970s, who was the professional godfather of the liberal intellectuals' favorite investment banker, Felix Rohatyn. By that term, Meyer meant the creation of "a structure that somehow enabled him to wring all he could out of the deal with a minimum amount of risk." Rohatyn traced Meyer's skill at creating this artful risk–reward structure to his skill at negotiation. "André could peel people like bananas," said Rohatyn (Reich 1983, p. 19).

But financial innovations are more than mere bankers' fancy; hard issues of power and risk are settled through them. Floating rate instruments shift the risk of rising interest rates from lender to borrower. Adjustable rate notes protect bondholders against imprudent or capital-risking actions by management, like taking on gobs of new debt. Looser regulations on issuance like shelf registration, which allows corporations to file general prospectuses to be kept on file, rather than prepare custom prospectuses for a specific stock or bond issue, allow firms to hawk their paper when the market looks friendly.

Joseph Schumpeter (1939, vol. 2, p. 613), writing during a decade when financial innovation was deeply out of fashion, observed that "it is one of the most characteristic features of the financial side of capitalist evolution so to 'mobilize' all, even the longest, maturities as to make any commitment to a promise of future balances amenable to being in turn financed by any sort of funds and especially by funds available for short time, even overnight, only. This is not mere technique. This is part of the core of the capitalist process."

Mobilize, mobilize — this is Moses and the prophets!

notes

1. There is a curious reticence about money, not only in economics, but more throughout American culture — curious because both the discipline and the culture are built on an obsession with money. Along these lines is R.C. Lewontin's (1995) observation that the only two questions in the famous 1994 survey of Sex in America that were asked in private, written form rather than explored in face-to-face interviews were those on masturbation and household income. American culture is almost as obsessed with sex as it is with money, but the obsessions are fraught with ambivalence and denial.

2. In its own propaganda, the New York Stock Exchange (1994, p. 6) is vague — and one

guesses deliberately so — on this matter. Its annual *Fact Book* says only that the NYSE "contributes to the capital-raising and capital-allocating process that is the strength and hallmark of the U.S. economy." The NYSE "encourages savings and investment," "helps individuals save for their future," and "encourages the creation and development of new ideas, new products and new services that build successful enterprises and create jobs." (On a floor tour, the exchange's press officer used almost exactly the same words.) Just how it does all that is left to the reader's imagination; the NYSE's centrality to all these happy processes is, of course, obvious.

3. Ironically, the first chair of the U.S. Securities and Exchange Commission was Joe Kennedy, who made a fortune from two classic 1920s pursuits, bootlegging and stock manipulation. Presumably this qualified him to root out other rascals.

4. The Mexican debacle of 1994–1995 slowed the boom a bit, but hardly killed it.

5. One needn't control 100% of a firm's shares to exercise a controlling interest. Anyone holding 50% of the outstanding shares plus one can dictate policy, and in practice, 10% can be enough to do the trick, especially if the other 90% of the shares are widely dispersed among numerous and disorganized shareholders.

6. The smart money/dumb money distinction is very popular among Wall Street professionals and wannabes — typically people who assume themselves to be among the smart — though academic students of finance dismiss it as mythology. In general, smart money consists of specialists and other exchange members and celebrity money managers; dumb money, of small-time speculators among the public. Ironically, that means that analysts and traders in brokerage houses use the behavior of their own customers as a contrary indicator. It's hard to place the mass of big-time money managers on the smart–dumb spectrum. The charitable reason for such agnosticism is that they essentially *are* the market, since they dominate daily trading. The uncharitable reason is that despite their alleged sophistication and wealth of financial and analytical resources, they turn in a mediocre performance. The smart/dumb classification scheme also fits in with the paranoid we/they mindset of many traders, who are convinced that "they" manipulate the market, though who "they" are is not clear. A hint of who they are can be found in the remark of an options trader who once defined a bear market to me as the time "when money returns to its rightful owners, like, you know, the Rockefellers."

7. Figures for the yen's share of foreign trade are for 1987; reserves, 1990; both cited in Goldstein et al. 1992b, p. 8. For more on the yen, see McKenzie and Stutchbury 1992.

8. The Federal National Mortgage Association, the Federal Home Loan Bank, and the Student Loan Marketing Association, respectively. More about them in Chapter 2.

9. Specifically, these are repurchase and reverse repurchase agreements. A repurchase agreement (repo) is the sale of an asset done with the pledge to buy it back at a specific time and price. Essentially it's a loan with the underlying asset — typically U.S. Treasury paper — as collateral. A reverse repo is the opposite side of this transaction.

10. According to Fed regulations, banks must keep a specified percentage of deposits either as vault cash or on deposit with the central bank. The requirement is a constraint on the share of deposits that banks can lend out. Banks with reserves in excess of those required by the Fed — usually small banks with more deposits than lending outlets — lend money to those short of reserves, generally the larger banks, who often have more would-be borrowers than they can satisfy, from manufacturing companies eager to build inventory to financial operators and real estate developers.

11. In practice, the gap is usually narrower, because municipal debt is not as safe as U.S. Treasury bonds. In 1995, the best muni bonds, rated Aaa by Moody's, paid an average of 5.80%, while long-term Treasuries paid 6.93%.

12. But only in part, because the derivatives were a fancy-dress version of a classic strategy, borrowing lots of money to make bad investments. You don't need instruments

jointly concocted by MBAs and theoretical physicists to lose at that game.

13. Anyone who thinks an option on a future is too abstract to exist is obviously not schooled in the higher financial consciousness.

14. An old Wall Street rhyme says of short-selling: "He who sells what isn't his'n/Buys it back or goes to prison."

15. What follows describes futures markets, but options markets are very similar.

16. Long before stock options were traded on exchanges, stock warrants were traded on the NYSE and other exchanges. Warrants are essentially long-term options to buy a stock, with maturities typically measured in years rather than months; they're frequently attached to new bond issues to make them more attractive.

17. Note that public sector institutions were the pioneers of swap techniques.

18. Briese's figures are based on September 28, 1993, filings with the U.S. Commodity Futures Trading Commission, reported in *Commitments of Traders*.

19. A study of 675 mutual funds showed no "statistically or economically significant" differences in returns between funds that used derivatives and those that didn't (Koski and Pontiff 1996).

20. One of Chase Manhattan's top risk managers was a designer on the Chernobyl team. The ex-designer, a mathematician and physicist named Victor Makarov, kept an eye on some of Chase's positions in 36 currencies, bonds, loans, stocks, and derivatives; his history, he says, made him especially risk-averse (Lipin 1994).

21. Volatility is measured by the standard deviation of yearly percentage changes; 1980 is as good a dividing time as any between the New Era and the Old. Interest derivatives began trading in 1977; stock derivatives in 1981; 1980 also marked the first bite of Volcker's sadomonetarism, was about the midpoint of financial deregulation, and was the eve of the Reagan transformation.

22. "Aristotle thought that only living beings could bear fruit. Money, not a living being, was by its nature barren, and any attempt to make it bear fruit (*tokos*, in Greek, the same word used for interest), was a crime against nature" (de Cecco 1992a).

23. Nearly half of the late 19th century in the U.S. was spent in periods of recession or depression; since World War II, only about a fifth of the time has been.

24. The Fed does not make it easy to get this information. Calls to the press office inquiring about profits and losses from FX interventions are met with the declaration that the Fed isn't in that business to make money, and no further help is offered. My research assistant, Josh Mason, was able to put together figures going back to 1986 at the New York Fed library, but the staff made it very hard to get earlier information.

25. Dollar policy is the only area where the Fed takes instructions from the elected government, specifically the Secretary of the Treasury. On domestic monetary policy the Fed is largely its own boss. The ESF was tapped by the Clinton administration for the 1995 Mexican bailout, when it was prevented by Congress from using conventional sources of funding.

26. These figures are adjusted to eliminate all forms of double-counting (i.e., in which the same trade might be reported by both sides and counted twice). Gross reported turnover, before this adjustment, was nearly $1.4 trillion.

27. U.S. figures are end-1994. Governments typically value gold reserves at well below market rates; the Fed values U.S. gold at $42.22 an ounce.

28. Greenspan no longer speaks with that clarity, though his preference for near-zero inflation speaks for him. In his essay for Rand, Greenspan denounced government borrowing in what for him are heated terms, but now in his role as Fed chief he is banker to the Treasury and responsible for maintaining the orderliness of the market for the Treasury's bonds. In another irony for the antistatist Greenspan — who, by the way, has never repudiated Rand and who attended her funeral — also presided over the

great state bailout of the U.S. financial system that ran from roughly 1989–93. Other Greenspan contributions to the Randian collection in which his 1966 essay is reprinted include an attack on antitrust and consumer protection laws.

2 Players

Despite years of deregulation, mergers, internationalization, and other transformations, U.S. finance still bears traces of New Deal strictures and an ancient hatred of monopolistic big city finance. To 1933's Glass–Steagall Act we owe the distinction between investment and commercial banking. Commercial banks were forbidden to play in the stock market and similarly racy arenas; they were to use their depositors' money mainly to make business loans. Glass–Steagall also affirmed long-standing restrictions on bank branching, regulations that sprang from American suspicions of a centralizing money trust. Banking emerged from the Depression a tightly regulated industry laden with government guarantees, and the rest of the system was sedate and fairly well-defined.

Things are no longer sedate nor well-defined. Institutional borders have faded, bank interest rates are no longer fixed by law, and interstate bank branching restrictions are gone. But the U.S. financial system still remains highly fragmented. The New York Stock Exchange has over 500 member firms; as of 1995, the nation was blessed with 10,450 banks, 2,152 thrifts, 7,361 mutual funds, and over 12,500 credit unions; in 1990, corporate America had 51,440,000 individual and hundreds of thousands of institutional shareholders.[1] Calling this hodge-podge a financial system requires a certain taste for abstraction — though of course it all comes together around money.

the matrix of claims

Maybe the best way to get a sense of how the hodge-podge does fit together is to use the Federal Reserve's flow of funds (FoF) accounts as a skeleton and connective tissue. The FoF are not as well known as the national income and product accounts (NIPA), which measure gross domestic product and its components, but they're a rich source of information on how the various pieces of the financial system connect with each other and with the real world.

In the inelegant words of their keepers, "[t]he flow of funds system of national accounts is designed to bring the many financial activities of the U.S. economy into explicit statistical relationship with one another and into direct relation to data on the nonfinancial activities that generate income and production…[and] to identify both the influences of the nonfinancial economy on financial markets and the reciprocal influences of development in financial markets on demand for goods and services, sources and amounts of saving and investment, and the structure of income" (Federal Reserve Board 1980, p. 2). Individuals, firms, and governments all save, borrow, and buy; the FoF accounts bring these activities together within a single set of covers. The national income accounts have nothing to say about the proliferation of financial claims or the size of the capital stock; these are the province of the FoF accounts.[2]

At the heart of the FoF system is a matrix that divides the economy into 34 major sectors. These 34 can be boiled down into five basic sectors: households, nonfinancial businesses, governments, and financial institutions, for the domestic economy, along with "rest of world," a catch-all sector that includes every player outside the U.S., private or public, individual or corporate. Each of these entities saves, borrows, and accumulates physical capital with its own and borrowed funds. All these flows must balance in the end; A cannot borrow unless B has saved (or, in this dizzy world, which is always getting ahead of itself, A cannot borrow unless the lender can find some of B's money to pass along) — nor can B save profitably if there is no A available to invest the money. All the instruments invented by modern financial alchemists haven't altered these essential facts, even though they can bend them pretty far out of shape.

Besides sectoral data, the FoF also reports "transactions" data — the form the transmission of money takes. Though over 50 kinds are listed in the flow of funds manual (Federal Reserve Board 1993, p. 19), these too can be boiled down into several major categories: insurance and pension fund reserves; interbank dealings; deposits (in banks and thrifts, mainly); stocks and mutual funds; credit market instruments (like bonds, mortgages, consumer credit, commercial paper, bank loans); and "other" (loans by brokers to customers to cover security purchases; trade credits, like those between GM and its parts suppliers or between garment makers and department stores).

There are two ways of looking at FoF data, flows and stocks. Flows represent a sector's contributions and withdrawals from the capital markets (saving and borrowing, the creation of new assets and new liabilities) over the course of a quarter or a year. Stocks are the total value of assets and liabilities outstanding (essentially the sum of prior years' flows, less losses to obsolescence, repayment of principal, or financial tragedies like bankruptcy). The size of one's bank account at the end of a year is the stock value; the year's deposits and withdrawals are flows. If the stock at the end of this year is larger than a year earlier, then the year's net flows were positive.

Each sector has a basic income flow — wages for households, taxes for governments, sales for businesses, investment income for all. This income is then spent, with part of the money going to cover current expenses (like food and rent for households, or raw materials and salaries for businesses) and part to long-term "investments." These investments may either be in tangible assets (cars and houses for households, or computers and office buildings for businesses) or financial ones (stocks, bonds, bank deposits). In the FoF world, borrowing is considered a negative financial investment, so the net financial investment for each sector consists of what it saves less what it borrows.

Conceptually, all these accounts must balance; neither people nor businesses can spend more than they take in through income and borrowing. In practice, the accounts never quite balance, because it's nearly impossible to account for every transaction — something the FoF accountants take care of by throwing in "discrepancy" terms. These are usually quite tiny, and can be safely ignored. Conceptually and practically, the FoF accounts are an extraordinary achievement in the vastly underrated field of social statistics.

who owes what to whom

Decades of financial innovation aside, most financial market activity still involves some variation on borrowing and lending, and this section focuses mainly on these traditional areas.

A chart nearby shows that most sectors have been busily tapping the credit markets. While the U.S. government spent the first half of the post-World War II years paying down its war debt, households were exploring consumer and mortgage credit, nonfinancial firms were gradually ratcheting up their leverage, and financial firms went rather wild.[3] All this borrowing

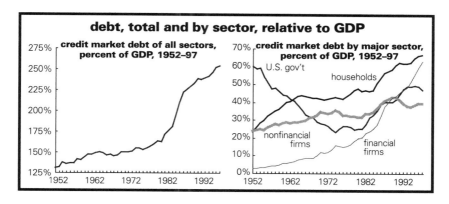

debt, total and by sector, relative to GDP

by the main economic sectors pushed up the total debt/GDP ratio, gradually from the 1950s through the late 1970s, with an acceleration beginning around 1982 — the year the Reagan boom really got underway, along with the bull market in stocks. Though the pace of new credit-making slowed a bit in the early 1990s, it wasn't thrown into reverse overall; note that the only major sector to rethink its relation with debt was nonfinancial business — though it looks like the U.S. government will follow suit in the late 1990s, should the budget actually remain in balance after 1998. This continued upward rise in the aggregate debt line contradicts the clichéd picture of the 1990s as a sober corrective to the wicked indulgences of the 1980s.

In official mythology, the credit markets exist to collect the savings of households in order to lend to businesses that need other people's money in order to make productive investments that allow them, and the whole economy, to grow. In some deep sense, this may be true; debts are claims on future growth in incomes, and under capitalism, the principal engine of growth is investment by nonfinancial corporations. But while such deep truths are not irrelevant, reality is a lot messier. Nonfinancial business accounted for just 22% of outstanding credit market debt in 1997, well under the 26% share owed by households, and just a bit above the 19% share owed by the U.S. government. These debts are not claims on future profits, but on future wages and taxes. Unlike business debts, there are no real income-producing capital assets offsetting these obligations.

It must be acknowledged that it's a bit misleading to focus on debts without taking note of assets. On debts alone, households, for example, are deep in the red — but households also have assets like durable goods, houses, mutual funds, and stock in unincorporated businesses. Businesses

who owes, who's owed
credit market debt, end-1997

	US$ billion	percent
owed by		
total	$21,118.9	100.0%
domestic nonfinancial	15,194.1	71.9
US government	3,804.9	18.0
nonfederal	11,389.3	53.9
household	5,571.5	26.4
business	4,532.9	21.5
noncorporate	1,250.1	5.9
corporate	3,282.8	15.5
state & local government	1,128.7	5.3
other	156.2	0.7
foreign	558.8	2.6
financial	5,366.0	25.4
GSEs/federal mortgage pool	2,821.7	13.4
banks	309.7	1.5
thrifts	160.3	0.8
finance companies	554.5	2.6
ABS issuers	998.4	4.7
other	521.5	2.5
held by		
total	$21,118.9	100.0%
domestic nonfinancial	2,955.1	14.0
US government	201.4	1.0
domestic nonfederal nonfinancial	2,753.7	13.0
household	1,826.9	8.7
business	335.3	1.6
noncorporate	39.1	0.2
corporate	296.3	1.4
state & local government	591.5	2.8
rest of world	2,270.0	10.7
financial	15,893.8	75.3
GSEs/federal mortgage pool	2,734.4	12.9
Federal Reserve	431.4	2.0
banks	4,031.9	19.1
thrifts	925.5	4.4
credit unions	304.2	1.4
insurance companies	2,289.8	10.8
pension funds	1,409.2	6.7
finance companies	566.7	2.7
mutual funds	894.8	4.2
ABS issuers	859.5	4.1
other	1,446.4	6.8

GSEs: government-sponsored enterprises. ABS: asset-backed securities issuers. Source: flow of funds accounts.

have substantial physical assets as well. There's no level of debt that's magically fatal; debts only become insupportable when the incomes or assets underlying them aren't sufficient to cover interest and principal.

For every borrower, there must be a lender. A chart of who holds these debts would lack the visual drama of the borrowers' charts. It would mainly show a rise in the financial sector's holdings that tracks the overall rise in debt — not surprising, really, since the manufacture of debt is one of the financial sector's main roles in life. Socially, though, financial institutions are merely intermediaries; the ultimate creditors and debtors are human beings — or households, as demographers call them. This is why the distribution of household assets discussed below matters — that is the truest picture of who owes, and who is owed, after all the institutional mystifications are stripped away.

That, of course, is domestically speaking. In order to consume more than it produces, and invest more than it saves, the U.S. has gone deeply into hock abroad; another way of looking at this is that the U.S. economy hasn't generated enough of a financial surplus to satisfy all its borrowers, so it's turned to countries that have, like Japan. In 1952, the U.S. held

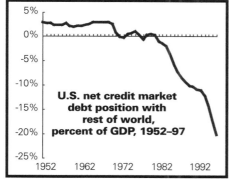

U.S. net credit market debt position with rest of world, percent of GDP, 1952–97

claims on foreigners equal to 4.2% of GDP; in 1997, that number had risen a bit, to 6.7%. But foreign claims on American borrowers exploded, from 1.4% of GDP in 1952 to 26.8% in 1997. As the graph shows, on credit market debts alone (leaving out direct investment and stock positions), the U.S. went from a net creditor position of 2.8% of GDP to a net debtor figure of 20.2%. The U.S. had been a net creditor internationally since Britain fell into the red after World War I. In both mainstream and Marxist theory, international political power — call it imperialism if you like — is inseparable from financial power, and an erosion in international position like that seen by the U.S. could be tantamount to the toppling of a hegemon — typically a period of great international disorder. So far, U.S. military, political, and cultural power has largely failed to follow the credit line into the abyss, but ghouls and pessimists await the dropping of the other shoe.

Let's look at each of the major sectors — who they are, how much they lend and borrow, and why.

households

In the national income accounts, households are the ultimate claimants in the financial system; the category "net interest," which appears throughout the accounts, refers to the amount that businesses hand over to households after all cross-payments are netted out. On one hand, this makes intuitive sense; though they are undoubtedly social actors, corporations are ultimately legal fictions, institutions that serve the pooled interests of individuals. In the flow of funds system, though, there is no final resting place; households are equal citizens in the republic of finance, along with the 33 other major sectors.

Households get about two-thirds of their income from wages, salaries, and fringe benefits, with the balance about equally divided between investment income (interest and dividends) and transfer payments (like pensions, alimony, and welfare).[4] From this income, taxes are paid and the necessities and indulgences of life are bought. If anything else is left over, it can be saved.

According to the FoF, households saved and invested $1.13 trillion in 1997, with around 95% of that total going to physical investment in housing and durable goods like cars and appliances, and the balance going into financial assets. But that net financial investment figure, remember, consists of the excess of saving over new borrowing; in 1997, households took on $404 billion in new debt at the same time they added $491 billion to their stock of savings. Since the net figure is positive, households can be thought of as net providers of funds to the financial markets: they put in more than they take out.[5]

Behind those bottom-line figures, however, lurk some odd conventions. To take one important example, unlike the national income accounts, the FoF treats purchases of consumer durables as investments rather than current consumption. According to the Fed's flow of funds handbook (Federal Reserve Board 1993), there are three major reasons for this: (1) like capital goods, consumer durables are long-lasting; (2) consumer durables "provide services that otherwise would be provided by businesses through their purchases of equipment," and (3) durables purchases are usually financed by debt, and the logic of FoF accounting requires some asset to offset this debt.

Of the three, only the longevity argument is remotely convincing; cars and computers last for years, even though the NIPAs treat them as being used up in the quarter they were bought. But the other arguments seem to be motivated by ideology and convenience more than anything else. Though they may make life easier or happier, consumer durables, unlike real capital assets, do not produce a stream of cash in return. Consumer debts, especially debts unsecured by assets like houses or cars, are merely a wage earner's promise to pay; they capitalize labor income, often at very high rates of interest. Business liabilities capitalize future profits (in the case of the stock market) or payments made out of future profits (in the case of debt); they capitalize capital income.

As odd as this may seem, the national income accounts treat owner-occupied housing even more surreally. Housing purchases are defined as investments, but since by U.S. definitions only businesses can invest, interest payments on residential mortgages are listed in the business rather than the household accounts. Owner-occupiers are treated as landlords who pay themselves rent, and deduct upkeep, mortgage, and property tax payments as "business" expenses. The net return on housing investments is imputed to households as the consumption of housing services. Official statisticians argue that they are trying to separate the consumption and investment aspects of housing; though people do speculate in primary residences, hoping to make a killing on a well-timed purchase or sale, most of these gains are rolled into the acquisition of a new house.

FoF accountants, free of the prejudice that only businesses invest, continue to treat housing purchases as investment, but shift most activity to the household sector. One practical advantage of this is to expose the sharp increase in mortgage debt relative to the underlying value of the housing. In 1945, home mortgages outstanding were 14% of the value of all owner-occupied housing; this rose steadily to 34% in 1965, fell gently into the high 20s in the late 1970s and early 1980s, and then rose with hardly a pause to a record 43% in 1997. Almost certainly, this long rise helped bring about the steady inflation in housing prices — though rising house prices are, in mainstream discourse, taken as a sign of a healthy market; in the words of the late FNN credit market analyst Ed Hart, "housing inflation is the American national religion." It also meant that mortgage creditors were taking an ever-increasing share of personal income.

This rising trend of mortgage debt was aided by the invention of the home equity loan, which allowed people to borrow against the value of their house to finance college tuition, vacation expenses, or whatever.

But unless people are willing to sell their houses, or turn them over to the bank, that equity is even more purely fictitious than a stock option, especially if house prices are stagnant or declining. If the owner–occupier loses his or her job, the inadequacy of the home as capital asset comes quickly clear: it demands cash without producing any in return. You can't pay the mortgage banker with imputed rent. Or as the Fed puts it, the increase in mortgage debt has been "unrelated to new capital formation" (Federal Reserve Board 1980, p. 31), a formulation that if carried to the extreme suggests inflation, insolvency, or some unpleasant combination of both as its ultimate resolution. Carried short of that apocalyptic resolution, it suggests strains on personal housing budgets for all but the most affluent.

Another officially defined asset of the household sector that looks less impressive on closer scrutiny is private pension funds. FoF accountants treat these as being held in trust for households, which is conceptually accurate but politically misleading: like children, future beneficiaries have little or no say in how their trust funds are managed. And only a minority — about 40% and falling — of workers are in pension plans. According to Ed Wolff's (1996) examination of Fed's Survey of Consumer Finances (SCF), the bottom 90% of the population held just 38% of pension assets in 1992.

debts sink to the bottom, wealth rises to the top

For all their virtues, the FoF accounts do erase all distinctions among the members of a sector. This is always a danger with aggregate data, but it's especially dangerous with households. While it is true, for example, that households are net providers of funds to to other sectors, not all households keep their ledgers in black ink.[6] According to the 1992 SCF (Kennickell and Starr-McCluer 1994), 30% of families with incomes under $10,000 had no financial assets at all, as did 12% of those in the $10–25,000 range; overall, almost one in 10 American families had nothing in the bank, figuratively speaking. The median assets of all families having assets was $13,100 — compared to a median of $17,600 in debts, for the three-quarters of all households carrying debts.[7]

Back in the 1980s, you used to read about the rising debt burden on households; for some reason, you don't read about it much in the 1990s anymore, even though the burden has continued to grow. You do still read about the concentration of wealth. The two phenomena are rarely seen as linked. But because of the decline in real hourly wages, and the stagnation in household incomes, the middle and lower classes have borrowed more to stay in place; they've borrowed from the very rich who have gotten richer. The rich need a place to earn interest on their surplus funds, and the rest of the population makes a juicy lending target.

Just how this works out can be seen in data from the 1983 survey; unfortunately, the Fed didn't publish the 1995 survey data in sufficient detail. In 1983, leaving aside the primary residence and mortgage debt on it, over half of all families were net debtors, and fewer than 10% accounted for 85% of the household sector's net lending (Avery et al. 1984). As William Greider (1987, p. 39) put it, the few lend to the many.

At the end of 1997, U.S. households spent $1 trillion, or 17% of their after-tax incomes, on debt service — just a smidgen below 1989's record of 17.4% (unpublished Federal Reserve staff estimates). This represents a

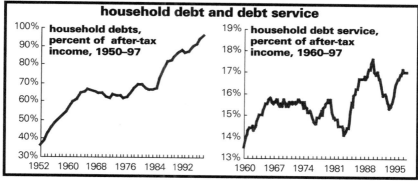

massive upward redistribution of income. The share would have been higher had not interest rates declined sharply over the period. But this borrowing has been a tremendous stimulus to consumer demand; between 1950 and 1997, the growth in consumer credit (excluding mortgages) financed 23% of the growth in consumption; between 1991 and 1997, the figure was 29%, the highest of any post-World War II expansion.[8]

Why do people borrow? Robert Pollin (1990) concluded from a study of the SCF that the bottom 40% of the income distribution borrowed to compensate for stagnant or falling incomes (what Pollin called "necessitous" or "compensatory" borrowing), while the upper 20% borrowed mainly to invest (or speculate, if you prefer). Pollin's findings are echoed in British experience: a survey of that country's households concluded that "[C]redit fulfils two different roles in household budgets. Poorer families, on the whole, use credit to ease financial difficulties; those who are better-off take on credit commitments to finance a consumer life-style. Both would use it to improve their lot: one to reduce their poverty; the other to increase their prosperity" (Berthoud and Kempson 1992, p. 64).[9]

Economically, then, consumer credit can be thought of as a way to sustain mass consumption in the face of stagnant or falling wages. But there's an additional social and political bonus, from the point of view of the creditor class: it reduces pressure for higher wages by allowing people to buy goods they couldn't otherwise afford. It helps to nourish both the appearance and reality of a middle-class standard of living in a time of polarization. And debt can be a great conservatizing force; with a large monthly mortgage and/or MasterCard bill, strikes and other forms of troublemaking look less appealing than they would otherwise.

Though the household sector as a whole has a steeply positive net worth, the liabilities are found disproportionally at the lower end, and assets at the high end of the distribution. Subtract liabilities from assets, and you find net worth to be concentrated far more densely than income. In 1995, the richest 1% of households claimed 11% of total income — but had 31% of all assets, 35% of all net worth, and 43% of net worth if you disregard the principal residence, which is the lion's share of most middle-class wealth. *The richest 1/2% had a larger share of total nonresidential net worth than the bottom 90% of the population (34% vs. 22%); the richest 10% accounted for 78% of nonresidential net worth.*[10]

Revisions to older estimates show that despite the decade's reputation, there was no great concentration of wealth in the 1980s; the real concentration has happened in the 1990s, with the share of the top 1% rising by nearly five percentage points. That gain came mostly at the expense of the next 9%; the share of the bottom 90% continued its long erosion. Wealth is now the most concentrated it's been since the 1920s. According to Edward Wolff (1995, pp. 28, 62–63), this trend is probably the result of several things, among them the increasing "dispersion" of wages and salaries — economists prefer this morally neutral term to the more value-laden "inequality" — which has depressed saving among the middle class and boosted it among the rich, and also the relative stagnation of house prices (the main repository of middle-class wealth) along with the phenomenal rise in stock and bond prices from the early 1980s into the late 1990s.

Ownership of the most valuable financial assets — real claims, like stocks and bonds — is densely packed in the upper crust. In 1995, the richest 1% of households — about 2 million adults — owned 42% of the stock owned by individuals, and 56% of the bonds (Kennickell and Woodburn 1997); the top 10% together own nearly 90% of both.[11] Since households own about half of all corporate stock, that posh 1% owns a quarter of the productive capital and future profits of corporate America;

distribution of wealth, debts, and income, 1995

	bottom 90%	top 10%	top 10%, percentile breakdown		
			90–98.9	99–99.4	99.5–100
PERCENT OF TOTALS					
family income	68.9%	31.1	19.6	3.4	8.1
assets	**37.9**	**62.1**	**31.0**	**6.9**	**24.2**
principal residence	66.4	33.6	25.7	2.7	5.2
other real estate	20.2	79.7	43.9	8.8	27.1
stocks	15.6	84.4	42.2	10.7	31.5
bonds	9.7	90.2	34.5	9.2	46.5
trusts	13.1	86.8	42.6	10.4	33.8
life insurance	55.0	45.0	27.8	6.1	11.0
checking accounts	57.7	42.3	26.0	4.6	11.6
thrift accounts	43.1	56.9	40.9	8.2	7.8
other accounts	37.9	62.1	35.2	7.0	19.8
business	7.7	92.2	20.8	11.5	59.9
autos	77.6	22.4	17.8	1.9	2.6
other	29.3	70.6	39.2	4.8	26.6
liabilities	**70.9**	**29.1**	**19.3**	**3.0**	**6.7**
principal residence	78.4	21.6	17.2	1.8	2.6
other real estate	25.2	74.7	41.0	10.2	23.5
other	80.6	19.4	9.6	1.5	8.3
net worth	**31.5**	**68.4**	**33.2**	**7.6**	**27.5**
nonresidential	22.5	77.5	34.2	9.1	34.2
DOLLAR VALUES					
income	$33,273	134,933	94,690	293,565	700,677
net worth	72,654	1,418,022	765,622	3,163,956	11,415,294
nonresidential	39,252	1,217,375	596,974	2,844,934	10,757,046

source: Kennickell and Woodburn 1997

the top 10%, nearly half. These stockholders are overwhelmingly white; fewer than 6% of black and Hispanic households owned any stock in 1991 (U.S. Bureau of the Census 1995, p. 513).

Those numbers are based on sorting households by their net worth; if you sort households by their stock ownership, the concentration is even more intense. In 1992 (the most recent year available), the top 0.5% of stockowners held 58.6% of all publicly traded stock; the next 0.5%, 11.7%; the next 4%, 24.2%; add those together and you discover that *the top 5% owns 94.5% of all stock held by individuals* (Poterba and Samwick 1995).

Despite the omnipresence of stock news in the papers and on TV, especially "public" TV, the active investor population, presumably the target of all these pitches, is tiny. In 1983, only 19% of households owned any stock at all, and of those almost half owned just one; 4% owned two to four, and only 4% owned five or more. The share who traded stock was even smaller: only 6% bought or sold a share of stock that year, and only 2% made five or more trades (Avery and Elliehausen 1986). While more recent SCF data have not been published, the New York Stock Exchange's 1990 shareholder survey (New York Stock Exchange 1990) showed a modest uptick in the percentage of the population owning shares, to 21%, with two-thirds of them men. This increase looks like a bit of an anticlimax, considering the grand bull market of the 1980s. Trading picked up somewhat more, with 12% making at least one stock purchase or sale, and 4% making five or more trades. Despite the expansion of these numbers, the stockholding and trading share of the population is quite small — but the amount of wealth they control is not: almost $1.5 trillion in stocks and bonds alone in 1989.[12]

the transmission of privilege

Edward Wolff's analysis of the Fed's 1962, 1983, and 1989 Surveys of Consumer Finances showed that 70–75% of the growth in wealth over the long term is from the appreciation of assets, and only 20–25% from new savings — and the wealthy are about the only people who have appreciable amounts of spare money to save (Wolff 1992, cited in Mishel and Bernstein 1994, p. 246). Elsewhere, Wolff (1996) reports that between 1983 and 1992, 57% of the increase in financial wealth went to the richest 1%, 39% to the next 19%, and just 4% to the bottom 80%.

Things were a bit less lopsided between the 1962 and 1983 surveys; the upper middle class (the 90th to 99th percentiles) did notably better and the bottom 80% even gained wealth rather than losing it. Even so, wealth concentrated between 1962 and 1983. It seems to be in the very nature of wealth to concentrate, much as interest compounds over time.

Despite myths of affirmative action and upward mobility, the tendency of wealth to concentrate, for advantage to breed advantage, makes it hard on people who start with nothing. Quite surprisingly, economists don't really have a very solid idea of what share of personal wealth comes from savings during individuals' lifetimes, and what share is inherited. This is in sharp contrast to the reams of studies on the "intergenerational transmission of welfare dependency." Estate taxes, a possible source of information, are widely evaded; also, surveys of the wealthy are rare, and any answers they elicit would have to be taken with a grain of salt. Economists have used a variety of techniques to simulate inheritance. Daphne Greenwood and Edward Wolff (1992), for example, using age group data from various years of the Survey of Consumer Finances found that younger families had higher net worths, and older families, lower, than their saving behavior would suggest; attributing the difference to intergenerational transfers either during life or at death, they estimated that 50–70% of the wealth of households under age 50 was inherited. Laurence Kotlikoff and Lawrence Summers (1981), using a variety of simulation techniques, estimated that as much as 80% of personal wealth came either from direct inheritance or the income on inherited wealth. Franco Modigliani (1988), one of the inventors of the life cycle hypothesis (LCH) of savings — that people save in their early years to finance retirement, implying that their wealth approaches zero as they stumble towards the grave — came up with results that were a mirror image of Kotlikoff and Summers: only 20% of personal wealth, by his estimate, was the result of inheritance. The major reason for his low estimate was that he counted income on inherited wealth as lifetime savings rather than as an inheritance, rather a conceptual stretch, but one essential to preserve the LCH, something he understandably feels a personal attachment to.

During the 1980s, about half the fortunes in the *Forbes* 400 were the result of inheritance, by the magazine's classification; this inexplicably fell to under a quarter in the early 1990s. But the magazine was probably defining things too strictly. A study of the 1995 and 1996 editions by the Boston-based group United for a Fair Economy (1996) showed that 43% were born with enough wealth to make it onto the elite list; another 7% had inherited $50 million or more — not enough to make it onto the list, but nothing to sneeze at; 6% had inherited at least $1 million or a family business; and 14% were born into the upper middle class. Just 30% of the 400 plutocrats were "self-made" — but they controlled only 25% of the list's total wealth, making them the elite's poor relations.

Putting all the evidence together, a cautious guess is that about half of all personal wealth can be traced to inheritance (Gale and Scholz 1994), though one is perfectly justified at believing three-quarters.

"Nonwhite" Americans — the SCF offers no finer distinction than that — suffer badly in a wealth comparison with whites.[13] In 1992, nonwhites' median income was 58% of whites', but their median net worth was only 20% of whites'; looking at only financial assets, nonwhite wealth was a mere 1% of white levels. (Wolff 1996). The racial wealth gap is vast even for households at the same income level. In 1989, the poorest whites, those with incomes under $10,000, had four times the net worth of nonwhites in the same income class; whites with incomes over $50,000 were twice as wealthy as nonwhites in the same class. Nonwhite single-mother households had only one-fifth the wealth of white ones. Obviously this leaves nonwhite households much more vulnerable to economic crises (sickness, job loss) and much less capable of taking advantage of opportunities (moves, schooling, entrepreneurship) than white ones.

In mainstream speech, "saving" rarely travels without a moralizing subtext, one that apologizes for vast inequalities by arguing that the poor are profligate, live in the eternal present, and are unable to control their impulses, while the rich are the virtuous opposite of all these things. Or as Texas Senator Phil Gramm puts it in his homey way, society consists of those who pull the wagon (his rich Dallas and Houston constituents) and those who ride in it (the shiftless poor). The middle classes, obviously, fall somewhere between vice and virtue. From this black-is-white premise, it follows that the rich should be lightly taxed, and the poor, soaked; this is the rationale behind consumption taxes, like sales taxes and VATs, which spare the saver and punish the consumer.

But according to SCF data, only 57% of households — 61% of "white non-Hispanics" and 44% of "Nonwhites or Hispanics" (Kennickell and Starr-McCluer 1994) — saved in 1989. Most people reported saving for "liquidity" purposes, like illness and unemployment; next came retirement and education. In America, private savings substitute for a welfare state, to the great disadvantage of the nonwealthy.

Another look at savings comes from the Bureau of Labor Statistics Consumer Expenditure Survey (CES). These findings must be regarded as very rough approximations of actual experience. While some people in the lowest income bracket are just temporarily down on their luck, and are able to draw on savings or family help, most people cannot consume more than twice their income for very long. The table's report that they do is probably wrong. Poor people work off the books, and hide it from Census enumerators. Rich people are almost certainly undersampled, and those who are surveyed heavily understate their income. The U.S. has a low savings rate, but it's not 0.7% of income. Incomes are probably understated at the bottom and the top, meaning that low-end "dissaving" is smaller and high-end saving, higher than they appear.

Still, the overall patterns are undoubtedly correct, though of course boilerplate caveats about exceptions to every rule apply. On average, poor people consume all their income and then some; middle-income people come out more or less flat; and only the well-off save significant amounts. Young people usually start out borrowing heavily, accumulate savings into

consumption and savings, 1991

	income				
	before tax	after tax	expenditures	saving	assets
dollars					
total	$33,901	$30,729	$30,487	$ 242	
poorest fifth	5,981	5,648	13,464	-7,816	
second fifth	14,821	14,308	18,986	-4,678	
middle fifth	26,073	23,973	26,144	-2,171	
fourth fifth	40,868	37,237	36,151	1,086	
richest fifth	81,594	72,332	57,597	14,735	
under 25	14,319	13,521	16,745	-3,224	
25–34	34,032	30,863	29,280	1,583	$ 2,500
35–44	41,871	37,583	36,446	1,137	11,200
45–54	48,413	43,828	38,137	5,691	14,500
55–64	38,285	34,401	31,945	2,456	20,000
65+	20,004	18,515	19,692	-1,177	
65–74	22,723	21,339	22,564	-1,225	18,200
75+	16,247	14,612	15,782	-1,170	21,000
percent of pretax income					
total		90.6%	89.9%	0.7%	
poorest fifth		94.4	225.1	-130.7	
second fifth		96.5	128.1	-31.6	
middle fifth		91.9	100.3	-8.3	
fourth fifth		91.1	88.5	2.7	
richest fifth		88.6	70.6	18.1	
under 25		94.4	116.9	-22.5	
25–34		90.7	86.0	4.7	7.3%
35–44		89.8	87.0	2.7	26.7
45–54		90.5	78.8	11.8	30.0
55–64		89.9	83.4	6.4	52.2
65+		92.6	98.4	-5.9	
65–74		93.9	99.3	-5.4	80.1
75+		89.9	97.1	-7.2	129.3

Figures are from the BLS's Consumer Expenditure Survey. Age refers to reference person, the person mentioned by the respondent when asked who owns or rents the home. Saving is after-tax income less expenditures.

middle age, and spend them in retirement. But Census data shows that there is "no evidence that net worth decreased among the oldest age groups within any income group," at least in 1991 (U.S. Bureau of the Census 1994b, pp. x-xi); in fact, there's some evidence that older households continue to save (Menchik and David 1983). The American dream, if you believe estate schemer Barry Kaye's TV ads, is to die rich and tax-free.

nonfinancial business

Like households, businesses have incomes, which they devote to current expenses and to investments. If they need extra, they can borrow, like households, or sell stock to outside investors. The need to borrow and sell stock is said to be a "discipline" on corporate behavior: poor managers will find it difficult and/or expensive to borrow money or sell stock, while sharp managers will find eager investors camping on their doorsteps. These alternatives will presumably reward good managers and discipline bad ones, forcing the hapless or incompetent to improve performance or find themselves shut out of the financial markets.

While these influences do operate on some level, the significance of external financing is greatly exaggerated, as the table on page 75 shows.[14] Either the U.S. financial markets function very badly, and good investments are not made because external finance is wanting, or nonfinancial businesses don't want to make the investments. Capital expenditures — capex, in Wall Street jargon — rose as a share of GDP during the Golden Age and even into the troubled 1970s, peaking late that decade and early the next, and then drifting downward through the Reagan boom and Bush slump. Things perked up in the Clinton era, but not by much.

Almost all of this investment — about 92% of the total between 1952 and 1997 — was paid for by the firms' own cash. Or to turn that notion upside down, the financing gap — the difference between the nonfinancial corporate sector's capital expenditures (like buildings, machinery, and inventory) and its own internal funds (profits plus depreciation allowances), which has to be funded by outside borrowing or stock sales — has averaged around 8% of capex. Even at the financing gap's widest chasm, the early 1970s, corporations still managed to fund almost 70% of their gross investment with internal funds. During the 1980s and 1990s, it's been common to hear of large industrial corporations with several billion dollars in cash and no idea of what to do with the money.

And the stock market contributes virtually nothing to the financing of outside investment. Between 1901 and 1996, net flotations of new stock amounted to just 4% of nonfinancial corporations' capex. That average is inflated by the experience of the early years of the century, when corporations were going public in large number; new stock offerings were equal to 11% of real investment from 1901 through 1929. Given the wave of takeovers and buybacks in recent years, far more stock has been retired than issued; net new stock offerings were –11% of capex between 1980 and 1997, making the stock market, surreally, a negative source of funds.

But if you exclude that period, and look only at 1946–1979, stocks financed just 5% of real invesment. This is true of most other First World countries; in the Third World, the figures are more like those of the early 20th century in the U.S., but again, that's because firms are going public for the first time, not because existing ones are raising funds through fresh stock offerings (international and pre-1952 U.S. data are from Mullin 1993; U.S. figures since 1952 are from the flow of funds accounts).

That huge negative number for stock-financed investment after 1980 is part of a larger phenomenon of swelling rentier claims. Nonfinancial firms have been distributing ever more of their profits to outside investors, who typically contribute no capital to real firms, but simply buy their bonds or stocks from previous holders. Start with the basic distribution, dividends. From the early 1950s through the mid-1970s, firms paid out 44% of their after-tax profits in dividends. That sank a bit in the late 1970s, and then rose sharply; from 1990–1997, nonfinancial corporations paid 60% of their after-tax profits out as dividends. Presumably they saw no alluring opportunities for investing the cash in their own firms, at least at a profit rate that would satisfy shareholders. Wall Street wants cash today, not promises about tomorrow. But dividends are not all. Firms are also paying lots of interest to their creditors. What might be called the rentier share of the corporate surplus — dividends plus interest as a percentage of pretax profits and interest — has risen sharply, from 20–30% in the 1950s to 60% in the 1990s.[15] Far from turning to Wall Street for outside finance, nonfinancial firms have been stuffing Wall Street's pockets with money.

But corporate America borrowed heavily in the 1980s; debt levels zoomed upward (see chart, p. 74), though they've come down quite a bit since, thanks to bankruptcies, debt reschedulings, and healthy profits. Why all the borrowing, if not to finance investment? To fund stock buybacks and takeovers.

rentier share of corporate surplus, 1945–97

interest + dividends / pretax profits + interest

Outside "investors" are laying claim to a far larger share of the corporate money machine than 20 or 30 years ago. This shows interest plus dividends as a percentage of the pretax profits and interest of nonfinancial corporations. Interest is added back into the denominator because it is deducted before profits are computed; dividends, on the other hand, are paid out of profits. *Source: national income accounts.*

Firms have bought back immense quantities of their own stock — $864 billion between 1984 and 1997 (Securities Data Corp., unpublished data). That amount is larger than total mutual fund buying over the period, and twice as large as state and local government pension fund buying over the period — the two largest stock-buying sectors. In the 1980s, firms bought back their stocks with borrowed funds (Remolona 1990); in the 1990s, they've used their happily rising profits rather than debt, but they've continued to buy their own stock with both hands. They also borrowed because having lots of debt was seen as a possible defense against takeover — not only would its burden be something an acquiring company would have to deal with, but if the borrowed money were used to support the share price, stockholders would be happy, and predators far less likely to be on the prowl.

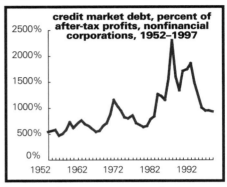

They also borrowed to do mergers and acquisitions (M&A). Between 1980 and 1997, U.S. nonfinancial firms spent $3 trillion buying each other, 38% of what they spent on capital expenditures over the period. Like buybacks, they have continued to do this throughout the 1990s, but again without borrowing, just with bountiful profits (and inflated stock).[16] With M&A fees, according to Securities Data Corp., running from 1–2% of the value of a deal, bankers and lawyers raked in some $20–40 billion from combinations alone over the period.

If you put all the cash-like payments together — dividends, interest, M&A, and buybacks — then between 1985 and 1997, nonfinancial firms transferred to rentiers an amount about 5% greater than their capital expenditures. These funds were then plowed into the stock market, where they've contributed to its wondrous rise.

A final point: just because the nonfinancial sector, on average, financed investment internally, doesn't mean all firms did. Smaller and newer firms almost certainly would invest more if outside finance were available, but this unmet desire doesn't show up in a FoF cell. Cash-rich corporations pull down the averages, too. Both these extremes suggest that the capital markets aren't channeling social capital too well.

At a finer level of detail, U.S. Census Data, analyzed by Fazzari et al.

nonfinancial corporations: financing investment						
	capex	internal	financing gap		dividends,	M&A,	stock
	% of	funds, %	% of	% of	% posttax	% of	buybacks,
	GDP	of capex	capex	GDP	profits	capex	% of capex
1952–54	9.1%	93.9	6.1	0.5	43.8		
1955–59	8.9	94.5	5.5	0.5	43.4		
1960–64	7.8	100.5	-0.5	0.0	47.2		
1965–69	8.3	87.1	12.9	1.1	44.4		
1970–74	6.4	76.6	23.4	2.0	44.5		
1975–79	7.5	86.7	13.3	1.2	32.5		
1980–84	5.2	85.6	14.4	1.3	53.5	20.1	
1985–89	4.3	98.1	1.9	0.2	71.5	47.5	8.3
1990–94	4.5	99.7	0.3	0.0	77.8	30.8	8.5
1995–97	6.2	94.5	5.5	0.4	61.4	67.1	18.2
average	6.8	91.5	8.5	0.7	52.0	35.0	9.5

"Capex" is capital expenditures, both on fixed assets and inventories. *Source: flow of funds accounts, except buybacks and M&A, from Securities Data Corp.*

(1988) show that from 1970 throuh 1984 (a period of relatively high reliance on external funds overall), manufacturing corporations financed an average of 71.1% of investment with retained earnings, with much less variation by firm size than one might imagine. Retained earnings — those not distributed as dividends or taxes — for firms with less than $10 million in assets covered 75.9% of funding needs; firms in the $50–100 million category, 78.7%; firms in the over $1 billion category, 67.9% — a variation of less than 11% around the average. These figures exclude depreciation allowances, the other major source of internal funds, which would be roughly equal to retained earnings — meaning that firms of all sizes fund most of their investments without having to resort to markets or banks.

Two things that do vary greatly by size are the portion of profits a firm keeps rather than paying out as dividends to shareholders (the retention ratio) and the importance of banks as a source of finance. Retention ratios ranged from 79% for the smallest firms to 52% for the largest. Firms with assets under $100 million relied on banks for around 70% of their long-term debt (though remember that all forms of external sources accounted for well under a third of all funding); those with assets from $250 million to $1 billion, 41%; and those with over $1 billion in assets, 15%. Bank finance is generally more expensive than bond interest rates, and bankers are generally more inquisitive, even interventionist, than bondholders, who generally keep their distance in non-critical times. And much of the non-bank finance raised by small firms is in the form of private placements done directly with institutional investors, usually with restrictions on borrower behavior (working capital requirements, minimum equity levels, limits on dividend payouts and capital spending) stricter than public bond covenants. That's not to say that strict conditions are unwarranted; banks take risks by lending to smaller, less-established firms, and may even do the world at large a favor by reining in the enthusiasms of entrepreneurs, who can tend towards a Panglossian view of life.

Sales of new stock are insignificant for smaller firms, confirming the big-picture figures presented above from a worm's-eye view. Fazzari et al. cite research by Philip Vasan showing that manufacturing corporations with under $100 million in assets raised only 2% of their total finance from new share issues between 1960 and 1980. It is very expensive for small firms to prepare the legal and financial documents for a public stock offering, and, outside of bubbly times, it can be difficult to sell obscure names to investors. Smallish entrepreneurs may chafe at the snoopiness of outside investors, the press, and Wall Street analysts — unpleasantries that have to be added to the costs of going public.

Of course, small firms do occasionally get finance from stock sales at moments that may be crucial in their evolution, meaning that these aggregate numbers may understate the importance of the securities markets in bringing together entrepreneurs and rentiers. Even if it were possible to adjust for the timeliness of a cash injection, it's hard to imagine any multiplier that would turn Vasan's 2% into something significant.

In sum, big corporations, the ones with easy access to the public (non-bank) capital markets, have more money than they know what to do with; small ones, who invest most of what they earn, don't find a generous reception in the capital markets.

financial institutions

In theory, the financial sector exists to gather a society's savings and direct them towards their worthiest, which means most profitable, investment pursuits. Whether it accomplishes this or not, finance is very handsomely rewarded for its efforts. There are several ways of making this point.

In 1991, finance, insurance, and real estate, collectively nicknamed "FIRE," surpassed manufacturing's contribution to GDP, and widened their lead in subsequent years; as recently as 1985, FIRE was 15% smaller. In 1996, manufacturing accounted for $1.3 trillion of output, and finance for $1.4 trillion. That year, investment was $1.1 trillion — meaning FIRE "produced" 30% more than the savings it theoretically channeled into investment.

The nearby chart shows the take of what mainstream economists call the two major factors of production, capital (whose reward is profit) and labor (whose reward is wages and salaries) for the FIRE sector, calculated as a percentage of gross private domestic investment (GPDI).[17] After all, if FIRE's social task is to allocate investment, this is probably the most relevant measure of how cheaply or expensively it does its work. Real estate is included along with finance and insurance because residential investment (housebuilding) accounts for over a quarter of total investment, and nonresidential structures another quarter.

The most striking feature of the chart is the extraordinary ascent since the early 1980s, from just under 20% in 1981 to peak at 47% in 1991, then falling back gently to 40% in 1996. This spectacular explosion, which occurred because of a simultaneous stagnation in investment (and a decline in its share of GDP) along with a sharp growth in FIRE income, threatens to overwhelm the message of the rest of the chart: even in bygone years, financiers, developers, brokers, realtors, and the rest of the gang pocketed rewards equal to 20–25% of gross investment — rather a large take for a supposed neutral intermediary. The 1990–94 average of 43% is a grand reward indeed.

Had the chart begun in 1929, when the national income accounts begin, the graph would be much harder to read, but its story would be no less compelling. In 1929, FIRE's rewards were 28.4% of gross investment, a bit above the 24.1% average for the 1950–79 period. But the figure exploded in the 1930s, as investment collapsed but the profits of finance didn't, hitting 228% in 1932 — meaning that the allocators earned over twice as much as the investment funds they were allocating! It was not until the recovery of invest-

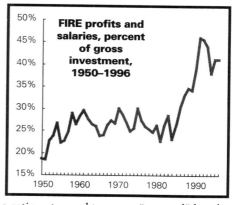

ment at the end of the war that the ratio returned to more "normal" levels.

With the growth of consumer credit since the 1920s, it might be argued that consumer durable goods, like cars and appliances, should be added to the denominator of the calculation, since these, too, are financed (though, of course, they produce no monetary return to their owners — unless they're taking in their neighbors' laundry). While this adjustment produces slightly less eye-popping figures, the trend remains the same: FIRE's income as a percent of GPDI plus expenditures on durable consumer goods rose from the 1950–79 average of 17% to a peak of 28% in 1991, before retreating to a more modest 26% in 1996.

In 1992, FIRE corporations filed 17% of all corporate tax returns, reporting 16% of total revenues, but 37% of profits (U.S. Bureau of the Census 1994, p. 539). FIRE's profit share has risen steadily, from 14% of the corporate total in 1980, to 25% in 1985, and upwards to 1992's figure. Manufacturing's share was almost a mirror image, falling from 53% of profits in 1980 to 36% in 1992.

Rewards to individual FIRE workers are usually quite generous. As part of the national income accounts, the Bureau of Economic Analysis reports average wage and salary figures for 85 different occupational categories. At the very top are routinely the elite moneyspinners of the field, "security and commodity brokers," who earned on average $108,760 in 1996. (No doubt the brokers would have done a lot better if their secretaries and clerks weren't depressing the industry average.) That disparity is the widest since the accounts began in 1929, breaking the previous record, set in 1993. In the memorable year of the Great Crash, brokers earned a bit over twice as much as the average worker; they picked up a bit on average in the 1930s, and then began losing ground from the end of the war until the late 1960s; in 1970, employees of brokers earned just 58% more than the average worker. The brokerage premium has climbed, almost without interruption, ever since. FIRE workers as a whole do somewhat less well than brokerage employees. Average earnings for all FIRE workers were 39% above the national average in 1996 — up sharply from the 1960s and 1970s, when they bounced around the national mean.

These high numbers are a bit deceptive. Hourly pay for nonsupervisory workers in all of FIRE was just 9% above the private sector average in December 1997, and earnings at depository institutions (like banks and thrifts), 16% below. Tellers and check processors don't lunch anywhere near as grandly as investment bankers.

Though they are exceedingly well-paid, there aren't that many people employed at brokerage houses — just 616,000 in January 1998, or 0.5% of total employment, though this is a considerable increase from 1950's 0.1% share. Brokers are overwhelmingly white men — two-thirds of the total, according to 1990 census data. Under 2% of all brokers were black women; 25% were white women. Women occupy only about 5–10% of the top jobs at the high-end investment banks (Passell 1996b). Less elite financial jobs show greater diversity: almost 90% of all bank tellers were women, and 8% were black women — more than the 7% who were white men.

This demographic mix comports quite predictably with the salary rankings reported in the previous paragraph. All in all, FIRE employment grew from 4.3% of the total in 1950 to 6.0% in 1996 — significant growth, but nowhere near as significant as the growth in FIRE's monetary haul.

In one of the interesting analytical articles based on the 1983 Survey of Consumer Finances — part of an analytical exercise that the Fed hasn't replicated with later surveys — it was reported that 31% of families with incomes over $200,000 a year were "headed" by someone in banking, insurance, or real estate, even though they represented only 2% of the population (Avery and Elliehausen 1986); FIRE's representation among the well-heeled was the most of any sector.[18]

FIRE has created a strange economy in its headquarters city, New York. In the words of New York Fed apologist Rae Rosen (1993, p. 23), "on a per capita basis, each job in the FIRE sector generates *2.4 times as much output as all other sectors.* The wages and salaries that are paid in the FIRE sector reflect this degree of productivity." Rosen's reasoning is dizzily circular. How do you measure the "output" of FIRE? By its revenues, which are a function of its costs. What are its costs? The salaries and profits of FIRE. What Rosen's numbers mean is that FIRE creates a city with a small elite and a mass of excluded. This is what makes New York different from many other cities, which have only the excluded without the elite. It's also what makes Manhattan the most income-unequal county in the U.S. after one in Hawaii that used to be the site of a leper colony, according to Queens College professor Andrew Beveridge (personal communication).

Lest we close this section with the implication that Wall Streeters are without redeeming social value, here's a kind word for them from the New York call-girl-turned-writer Tracy Quan (personal communication):

> Wall Street guys generally like working girls and were among my sweetest clients when I was active. On the whole, they are nicer to do business with than doctors (who are often quite vain, neurotic and selfish) — and they are often more giving than lawyers (who pride themselves on their negotiating skills). Wall Streeters tend to be very indulgent — once they leave the office or the pit, and enter the bedroom.... Also, they basically see themselves as hookers see themselves, which colors their humor.[19]

IRE: insurance and real estate

So far in this section I've centered my attention on finance, the F in FIRE. The rest of this book will sustain that bias, but a few words about IRE are in order. Real estate is based on milking wealth from land and tenants, with the help of government subsidies (in the form of tax breaks and infrastructure development) whenever possible. Its connection with construction and infrastructure puts it a mite closer to the physical world than pure finance, but to many financial investors, buildings are just streams of revenues — rents — that can be capitalized just like a bond or a stock.[20] As an industry, real estate accounts for only about 13% of the total FIRE dollar payroll, but 20% of employment, meaning real estate workers are the poor relations of finance.

There's also little here about insurance as an industry in itself, though insurance companies are major players in the major markets, and they control huge lumps of capital — $3.4 trillion in assets at the end of 1997. The industry is largely exempt from federal regulation — the states handle it — but it carries plenty of weight in Washington, as the failure of Clinton's health insurance scheme showed. Insurance companies are heavily represented on the boards of major nonfinancial firms; everyone wants to remain on good terms with these rich sources of capital. Corporations often tap insurance companies through "private placements" — custom loans that aren't publicly traded.

In general, insurance is the private socialization of risk.[21] People buy insurance to protect themselves against devastating things that happen rarely. Risks are pooled across a large population, and the losses are paid from the common pool. If the pool is large enough, the risks are fairly predictable, meaning that insurers can invest most of their premium income in the financial markets, especially in bonds. Most of the time it is highly profitable, as long as they can keep price wars under control and keep their payments to policyholders to a minimum, though thanks to dexterous accounting, the industry can make profits look like losses.

Price wars are confined mainly to the property–casualty subspecialty, where there seems to be a pricing cycle. Firms under-price insurance in order to take in cash from premiums, which is then invested. They hope investment profits will exceed payout on claims, but if the pricing is too low, they end up under water, and they're cured of the temptation to under-price for a while. Property–casualty insurers keep their reserves in much shorter-term paper than do life insurers; disasters and accidents can happen at any time, but people tend to die on a predictable schedule. Riots and natural disasters, made worse by global climatic tremors, have recently hammered property insurers, however, and disturbed their old risk models. One could think of this as social and environmental crisis taking a financial form — an example of James O'Connor's (1988) second contradiction of capitalism — but like the classic contradiction, it hasn't proven systemically fatal yet.

Insurance companies have lost some market share in the provision of credit, falling from around 16% total credit market debt in the early 1950s to around 11% in 1997. Still, they are vast buyers of paper assets; life insurance companies owned almost a third of all corporate bonds outstanding in 1997. They were major funders of corporate buyouts and takeovers during the middle and late 1980s, though on review, a buyout specialist for a brand-name insurance company told me his firm could have done better investing in Treasury bills, so lousy was the return on his deals.

As financial popstar Andrew Tobias (1982) once argued, the insurance industry thrives on its reputation for dullness, which keeps prying eyes away from examining its wealth. So-called mutual life insurance companies, which are owned by their policyholders, are especially fat and obscure, because few small policyholders have the means or will to check out what "their" firm is up to with "their" money. Executives of such firms are among the most cosseted of a cosseted class, though financial deregulation is beginning to bite at the industry.

banks, commercial and investment

And now to the players that attract the most attention — commercial and investment banks and other star institutions that are synonymous with Wall Street. A striking feature of the general credit scene is that old-style banking has taken a backseat to "the markets." This is a matter of both numbers and style. From the 1950s through the mid-1970s, banks held an average of 28% of total credit market debt; at the end of 1997, their share had fallen to 19%. Thrifts have lost even more market share than the banks. They held 18% of credit market debt in 1977, a near-doubling from 1952, but that share eroded throughout the 1980s and early 1990s, falling to under 5% in 1997. What banks and thrifts lost was gained in part by pension funds, who have more than doubled their share over the last 40 years, and mutual funds, who had 0.2% of all credit market debt in 1952, and 7.6% in 1997.

These asset figures are misleading, since banks still have a hand in most financial transactions — it's hard to sell a stock or trade a currency without one — and also since the flow of funds figures exclude banks' "off-balance-sheet" activities — unsupervised, under-reported adventures in leverage in derivatives markets and anywhere else their inventive minds might take them. At the end of 1993, the 20 largest banks had off-balance-sheet exposures equal to 39% of assets and 573% of their "core capital" (retained profits plus the proceeds of past stock sales), meaning that if all hell broke loose many would be legally insolvent. Additionally, many banks have extensive proprietary trading accounts (for their own accounts rather than clients'), in which they turn over foreign exchange, government bonds, and other fictitious claims; the 20 largest banks had trading accounts equal to 45% of assets and 749% of core capital (computed from Sheshunoff data reported in Schlesinger 1995). Many of these activities are not only off balance sheets, they're off the mainland as well, in London or the Cayman Islands.[22] But the central banks would not allow all hell to break loose, meaning that a public safety net has been placed under a market no one really understands or can even accurately measure.[23]

Fear-mongering aside, whatever the virtues of off-balance-sheet financing and proprietary trading, it has little in common with J.P. Morgan's "character" banking — making a loan based on a judgment of personal character rather than a balance sheet — or classic credit scrutiny. Often, banks are quick to syndicate loans — farm bits of a deal out to other banks — or to securitize them (to package a bunch of similar loans and sell them as bonds on the open market). And the biggest commercial banks are rapidly becoming securities firms, so their founding uniqueness — making commercial loans while being prohibited from underwriting new securities — no longer exists. Money-center banks — the giants based in New York, Chicago, and California — derive large portions of their profits from trading operations; merely paying your depositors less than you charge your borrowers seems a very retro approach to the business.[24] Big banks no longer nurture long-term ties with big corporations; the big corporations can borrow for themselves in the commercial paper market, and the bankers bid on the rest of the corporate business like traders juggling stock. Banking is now largely an affair of transactions, not relationships.

Now we get to the rich heart of what people mean by "Wall Street." Commercial banks, though undoubtedly major presences in the financial world — and which are becoming more like investment banks every day — are still looked down on by investment bankers as dull and incompetent. The peak of the Wall Street hierarchy, measured by both prestige and money — and money, of course, is what really matters — are the "bulge bracket" underwriting and trading monsters like Morgan Stanley and Goldman Sachs. They bring forth new securities issues to their customers, and trade them for their own and their customers' accounts.

The sociology of modern Wall Street is worth a book in itself. It's notable how few high-flyers from the 1980s mania made it into the ruling class. Henry Kravis, the major figure of the leveraged buyout mania, did make it to the chair of New York City's public TV station and the board of the Metropolitan Museum, the latter an inner sanctum of the Establishment — but Kravis' father was rich and well-connected on Wall Street, even if he was from Oklahoma (Bartlett 1991). Many 1980s hotshots have disappeared from the headlines; one, Kirk Kerkorian, made a pass at Chrysler in the spring of 1995, but wasn't taken seriously, because there was no longer any Drexel Burnham Lambert around to float junk bonds in his name. Boone Pickens' firm, Mesa Petroleum, is in terrible shape, and his shareholders booted him out. Alumni of the financing arm of the upstarts, the now-dead Drexel, are scattered around Wall Street, but they're no longer financing a New Class's claims to power.

In the old days, investment banking was much more about connections — who roomed with whom at Andover could determine both partnerships and client relationships. During the 1950s and 1960s, investment bankers raised money for and offered counsel to the managers of the American Century, and fixed fees and gentlemanliness kept competition from getting out of control. Andover connections still matter, of course, though not as much, but the rest is utterly transformed. Fees and commissions aren't fixed, and neither are customer relationships.

Wall Street does business with both financial institutions and the general public, with the general public ranging from billionaires down to "odd lotters" (literally people who trade stocks in units smaller than a round lot of 100 shares, but more colloquially the naïfs who lose money because they're in over their head). Some firms, like Merrill Lynch, deal with the general public, from odd lotters upwards to rich individuals and institutions, while some, like Morgan Stanley, deal with only institutions and the very rich. Since fixed commissions were abolished in 1975, an industry of discount brokers has sprouted, dealing mainly with the general public. They offer little or no research from professional analysts, and their brokers don't give investment advice. At the bottom of the heap are bucket shops, boiler rooms, and hawkers of cheap penny stocks. These operations range from the negligently optimistic to the outright criminal, and show a special fondness for locating in places like Long Island, Florida, and Vancouver.

This survey excludes the lowlifes who take in $200–300 billion a year by preying on the poor and desperate — brokers who demand 20% on a second mortgage, pawn shops who charge 240% on loans, finance companies who charge 300%, check-cashing services that charge 2,000% for quick "payday" loans, layaway artists and rent-to-own schemers (Hudson 1996). While they're undoubtedly part of the financial industry, I'll ignore them; the point of this book is to tar the folks with the good reputations, if only to preempt the "bad apple" defense.

funds of several sorts

Individuals who deal with brokers can trade stocks, bonds, options, and other exotic instruments, but many also turn to mutual funds and other managed investment vehicles to do the research and trading work for them. Mutual funds have grown steadily since Wall Street recovered its reputation after the Depression — 11% a year on average through the 1960s and 1970s, and about twice that ever since. The 1990s have been notable not only for the continued rush of dollars into mutual funds as people despaired of low interest rates — with many of them plunging into bond and foreign stock markets completely unaware of the risks involved, though with dreams of 20–30% returns in perpetuity — but also the sheer proliferation of entities. As of February 1998, there were 6,867 U.S. mutual funds (far more stocks than are listed on the New York Stock Exchange), more than double 1990's number, a birthrate of almost two funds per business day. From 1991 to 1997, $992 billion flowed into mutual funds, well over half of new savings over the period, and even exceeding the fresh supply of savings in several quarters. It is one of the most remarkable financial developments of modern times — assuming it lasts, and that it's not a bubble of sublime proportions, like the Japanese financial markets were in 1989.[25]

Mutual funds collect money from public investors, use a bit of it to hire managers who select securities and trade them. (A "bit" from the big picture perspective, perhaps, but considering the small staff it takes to manage big bucks, a thin slice of a massive pile means the managers and directors are paid very very well.) Styles vary; some funds are aggressive, some conservative; some invest only in bonds, or stocks, or certain kinds of bonds (municipal, Treasury) or stocks (medical companies, new or small companies), or certain regions (Mexico, Asia). There is a huge industry about them, too — TV shows, software, websites, newsletters. Mutual funds have become the favorite indoor sport of the upper half.

"Hedge funds" might be thought of as high-end mutual funds.[26] Though there's no strict definition of what they are, in general a hedge fund is the pooled capital of usually 100 or fewer partners (rich individuals or institutions), led by a single manager or a small team. They're barely regulated, if at all; many are registered in offshore havens, even though they're often managed from places like New York and London; and can do pretty much whatever they like with their money, from U.S. bonds to Turkish stocks to silver futures to Moscow real estate. Since there's no strict definition, and since they need file no reports — even the partners aren't always informed of their investments — one can only guess at their size. As of 1994, best estimates were that there were 800 to 900 hedge funds with total capital of $75–100 billion; a small fund would be one with $75 million under management, and a large one, as much as $10 billion. Since hedge funds borrow aggressively, they can take positions anywhere from 5 to 20 times their paid-in capital, meaning that they can control anywhere from $375 billion to $2 trillion in securities (Goldstein et al. 1994, pp. 6–9). Not only are these big numbers, even by the standards of today's capital markets, but they move very quickly in and out of investments. They were responsible for much of the turbulence in the European Monetary System in 1992, and for the U.S. bond market debacle of 1994 (the worst year in the modern history of that market), and for the Mexican crisis of that year as well. While many hedge fund stars lost big money in 1994, their performance in the years leading up to that plague year was impressive: an average yearly return of almost 20% between 1987 and 1993, compared with "only" 13% for mutual funds and the U.S. stock market (measured by the S&P 500), and with much greater consistency as well. Such superior returns compound miraculously over time; $1 million placed with the average hedge fund in 1986 would have grown to $3.5 million at the end of 1993, compared with a mere $2.4 million in the average stock or mutual fund (Republic New York Securities data, presented in Goldstein et al., p. 8).

Despite these returns for the lucky few, hedge funds are not without dangers for the rest of us. Since they borrow so heavily from banks, a really disastrous year for the speculators could do serious damage to the broad financial system — meaning that central bankers and regulators may face the choice of a bailout or systemic collapse. There is also the worry that they increase the volatility of the markets, though it may also be that their willingness to tread where others fear may help put a floor under weak markets. Another worry is that hedge fund operators could manipulate markets, either through calculated buying and selling designed to mislead the general public — slowly bidding up the price of some asset, say, and then unloading a large position on gullible buyers, or using calculated leaks to the press to create a mania or panic profitable to the well-positioned. The authorities play down the dangers of manipulation, but that's what authorities are paid to do.

A highly romanticized corner of finance is the venture capital industry, which supplies funds to small, new firms, prominently though not exclusively in high-tech. Typically, money is pooled by institutions and rich individuals into partnerships under the management of a small expert team. The failure rate is high, but the successes can make it all worthwhile; everyone wants to hit the next Compaq. Rates of return run between 0% in bad years (like 1984 and 1990) to 60% in good ones (like 1980 and 1995), averaging around 20% since 1980 (Venture Economics data, reported in Mehta 1996). Many initial public offerings (IPOs) are designed to cash out the original investors; though some venture capitalists keep their money and even a management presence at companies once they go public, the idea is not to nurture a large portfolio of mature operating companies, but to provide finance and guidance at the embryonic stage.

As important as that sounds, the venture capital industry is surprisingly small. In 1995, venture pools totaled $34 billion, down a bit from 1990's $36 billion, and dwarfed by the stock market's $8.4 trillion capitalization. Inflows of $4.4 billion exceeded new commitments of $3.9 billion — well under 1% of that year's nonresidential investment — suggesting that the venture industry isn't going wanting for funds (*Venture Capital Journal,* various issues). This looks like further proof that the outside financing of real investment, Wall Street's advertised social role, is actually a rather tiny part of what the racket is all about.

the thrift disaster

No book on modern finance would be complete without a look at one of the greatest monetary disasters of all time, the savings & loan (S&L) debacle of the 1980s. While hotshot S&Ls were among the most enthusiastic makers of the great boom, they collapsed at a cost of $200 billion to the U.S. government, to be paid for well into the next century. S&Ls, also known as thrifts, are disappearing; they've pretty much lost their rationale for being.

S&Ls have their roots in 19th century mutual savings banks, cooperative institutions that pooled the savings of workers to finance home mortgage loans.[27] Patterned after European credit cooperatives, thrifts offered credit to customers whose custom was refused by snobbish commercial banks. Since a mutual's depositors are also its borrowers and shareholders, 19th century thrifts offered protection from the predations of the "monied classes" — usurious interest rates, speculative bubbles, and bank failures (O'Hara 1992). Some more conventional stockholder-owned thrifts popped up, but a spate of failures in the 1890s led several states, notably New York, to require that all thrifts be structured as mutuals. As late as 1974, only 11 states permitted stockholder-owned S&Ls.

Nearly 2,000 S&Ls failed in the Depression, and a third of deposits were wiped out, though cooperative associations survived illiquidity and technical insolvency by restricting withdrawals. Two New Deal institutions transformed the industry, the Federal Savings and Loan Insurance Corp. (FSLIC) and the Federal Home Loan Bank Board (FHLBB). The first provided deposit insurance, and the second was a central bank, to oversee the industry and provide credit to troubled institutions. Thrifts' investments were limited largely to mortgage loans at fixed rates. No other industrial country offered fixed-rate loans, since they put all the financial risk of higher interest rates onto the lender; with floating-rate or adjustable loans, the borrower bears all the risk (Lomax 1991; U.S. Congressional Budget Office 1993). Thrifts were insulated from competition by limits on commercial bank deposits

Thrifts prospered during the housing boom that followed World War II. Deposits and mortgage loans soared, though capital ratios sank as profits lagged growth. Growing competition from banks for both deposits and mortgage loans in the 1960s and money market funds for deposits in the 1970s drew customers away from thrifts. Worse, the inflation and high interest rates of the later 1970s exposed the S&Ls' tragic flaw, borrowing short to lend long: depositors tempted by higher rates in the unregulated world were free to withdraw on a whim, but their funds had been committed by thrift managers to 30-year mortgages. As rates rose, the value of outstanding mortgages sank (like bonds, loan values move in the opposite direction of interest rates). Balance sheets and income statements turned deep shades of red.

Deregulation was the answer. If thrifts couldn't make money the old-fashioned way, they would be liberated from the ancient strictures and allowed to enter the playpen of high finance. The Depository Intermediary Deregulation and Monetary Control Act of 1980 — passed by a Democratic Congress and signed by a Democratic president, refuting popular associations of the disaster with "Reaganism" — removed all interest rate ceilings, and the Garn–St. Germain Act of 1983 let thrifts get out of housing and into whatever they liked. The laws and regulations governing thrifts had long been written by industry lobbyists, and their regulators were in thrall to the S&Ls as well, but this cozy relationship became particularly dangerous as they were free to go wild. That wildness, as everyone knows by now, included showering money on superfluous shopping centers in the middle of nowhere, windmill farms, prostitutes, speculative housing, speculative office buildings, cocaine, junk bonds, art for the CEO's house, the Nicaraguan contras, and yacht parties on the Potomac. Hot for funds to get into these pursuits, and subsequently hotter for funds to cover losses, thrifts pushed up interest rates to attract deposits from Wall Street. It used to be said that nobody got rich in the thrift industry and nobody went bust; during the freeplay of the 1980s, people did both.

Conservatives love to point to the web of perverse incentives that spawned the affair. Deposit insurance removed all incentive for depositors to scrutinize the thrift's portfolio (a situation bankers and their friends call "moral hazard"). The mutual structure reinforced this, since individual depositor–shareholders have neither time nor interest nor expertise to scrutinize management. Abolish deposit insurance, said the right radicals, or rein it in, said the centrists. Of course, without deposit insurance, the entire financial system would probably have collapsed in a climactic run sometime between 1987 and 1990. If you're going to insure deposits, you'd better supervise bankers pretty closely; the price of the S&L bailout would have funded the presence of 10 full-time bank examiners in every thrift in the country for close to 200 years.

Financial radicals should pay attention to the lesson about dispersed cooperative ownership: there's little incentive for smallish depositors, or the owners of any large cooperative, to pay attention to the management of the enterprise they legally own. Unless there's some institutionalized oversight, a serious and representative supervisory board, managers can easily commandeer the institution for their own interest. But unfortunately for those who want to damn cooperative ownership entirely, shareholders in non-mutual thrifts did little better. One of the crucial junk bond buyers in Michael Milken's network was a public thrift, Columbia Savings. Shareholders can be as dispersed and inattentive as small depositors.

Economists have their own understanding. Thrift pundit Robert Litan (1992) rejected popular explanations of the crisis, which center on "venality, greed and incompetence," out of professional discomfort. Instead, Litan preferred the terrain of conventional economics — inflation, interest rate volatility, moral hazard, real estate slump, and the rest — and, like a loyal economist, was eager to get deregulation off the hook.

Of course inflation and the rest are to blame. But it would be impoverishing to stop there. Litan's fellow economists assured us that financial deregulation was supposed to release untold energies by liberating the self-adjusting mechanisms of the capital markets. Instead, it released imprudence, incompetence, and fraud throughout the entire system. As a *Wall Street Journal* piece on the thrift disaster noted, the list of malefactors is "so long that some observers conclude there is something profoundly wrong with the country's political and financial systems, which appear easily undone by feckless and reckless behavior. In fact, they say, the behavior of this legion calls into question the performance of this nation's professional class itself" (McCoy et al. 1990). The "calls into question" is a little euphemizing, and the "some observers conclude" a classic journalist's dodge for offering the forbidden controversial opinion, but the *Journal's* analysis is a fine corrective to Litan's. Unfortunately, the paper did not go into the sorry performance of the media, the *Journal* included, during the 1980s, as the thrifts and everything else were spinning out of control.

Every institution that was supposed to watch the S&Ls botched the task. Topping the roster of failures are the regulators, federal and state, in the grip of the early-Reagan-era euphoria, who failed to supervise the institutions — often run by dim provincials — that they had just set free to enter businesses they'd never been in before. Congress had long been in the industry's pocket. Even a president's son, Neil Bush, helped drive an S&L into the ground, Denver's Silverado (Wilmsen 1991). The administration, with the complicity of an uncurious press, successfully kept Silverado out of the 1992 campaign, no doubt helped by equal Democratic political and financial collusion in the disaster.

But it's wrong to blame only the government, despite the American habit of doing so. Virtually every high-end profession around was involved (a point made well by Martin Mayer [1990]). Auditors repeatedly certified fictitious financial statements, lawyers argued on behalf of con artists and incompetents, investment banks bilked naïve S&L managers, and consultants testified as character witnesses for felons. One of these character witnesses was Alan Greenspan, then an undistinguished economist from whom "you could order the opinion you needed" (Mayer 1990). Greenspan praised thrift-killer Charles Keating's "seasoned and expert" management team for rescuing a "badly burdened" thrift through "sound and profitable" investments. Every word of this was untrue. Greenspan's reputation, however, survived intact (just as it did his earlier demented jottings for Ayn Rand's *Objectivist* newsletter).

In its infinite generosity, Washington came to the rescue. Of course it had no choice; no modern government would dare let a financial crisis turn into a general collapse. Yet the situation is rich with irony. In the early 1990s, Greenspan would craft the Federal Reserve's bailout of the 1980s mania. And the braindead caretaker administration of George Bush crafted the greatest socialization of private loss in history, the S&L bailout. And, remarkably, almost nobody has suffered serious criminal penalties or political disgrace for this rampant abuse of trust. Huge quantities of public money — some $200 billion, though definitive accountings are hard to come by — were spent with little discussion or analysis, and the affair is now largely forgotten. The chance to use the industry's partial liquidation as an opportunity to develop new public and cooperative financial institutions was blown. Within a couple of years of the crisis' passing, no one paid it any mind any longer. It's as if it never happened.

government, especially the Fed

The S&L crisis exhibits several roles of government in finance: to look the other way during a riot on the upside, and then pay for the rescue when it's done. But of course that's not the only role of government on Wall Street. Governments are heavy players in the financial markets — not merely as debtors, though certainly the public bond markets are quite important. But government is more than a debtor; it is a heavy spender and regulator. In the decentralized U.S. financial system, both state and federal governments supervise and regulate finance; there is virtually no federal regulation of insurance, which is mainly a state-by-state affair.

At the federal level, many agencies regulate finance. The issuance and trading of securities is mainly the province of the Securities and Exchange Commission (SEC); firms wishing to sell stocks or bonds to the public must register them with the SEC, disclosing a reasonably large amount of information about the securities and the firm peddling them. Public firms must also file their annual and quarterly reports with the SEC; such reports, along with more technical annexes known as proxies and 10-Ks, include lots of info about officers' and directors' pay, business relationship between the firm and its boardmembers, as well as financial statements.[28] The SEC also supervises trading on organized stock exchanges and, to a lesser extent, keeps an eye on over-the-counter trading. The SEC, and its disclosure requirements, were the creation of the New Deal, an attempt to prevent a recurrence of the lunacies of the 1920s — market manipulations, the issuance of fraudulent securities, and the like. Though plenty of hype and con artists still pervade the securities markets, brokers routinely clip their customers in pricing trades, and insiders profit from knowledge of what their customers and the general public are up to, the markets are pretty clean — aside, that is, from their systemic parasitism. While firms don't always tell the truth, and do their best to put the most positive spin on their reports, U.S. corporate disclosure requirements are strict by world standards; it's amazing how many junk bonds that went bad during the 1980s contained explicit warnings in their prospectuses of just how risky they really were. Information and understanding are apparently very different things.

To avoid getting bogged down in Washingtonia, I'll add only a few more words about regulators. Commodities and futures market are regulated by the much newer Commodities Futures Trading Commission (CFTC). The commercial banking system is regulated by the the Comptroller of the Currency (part of the Treasury Department), the Federal Deposit Insurance Corp. (which also insures deposits), and the Federal Reserve system. State banking departments are also important, especially the New York State authorities, since the biggest commercial banks are headquartered there. As with the U.S. financial system — the whole society, it's tempting to say — the regulators are very fragmented.

Quasi-federal agencies are also important financial intermediaries. For example, the Federal National Mortgage Association (Fannie Mae) and the Federal Home Loan Mortgage Corp. (Freddie Mac), are monsters in the mortgage market; they led its transformation from a sleepy, localized business into a hot, liquid national and even global one. In the old days, thrifts and banks made mortgage loans and kept them on their books, often for the full 30 years of their duration. Now, they're more likely to sell the loans to Fannie Mae or its much smaller cousin Freddie Mac, who take the loans and package them into bonds for sale to institutional investors and rich individuals (a process known as securitization); they were behind $1 trillion in oustanding securities in 1996 (Calmes 1996). Fannie Mae, once a public entity created during the New Deal, and Freddie Mac, a 1970 creation, have both been partly privatized — though everyone on Wall Street correctly believes that they are implicitly guaranteed against failure by the U.S. government, even though their stock trades on the NYSE as if they were private firms.

That implied guarantee allows them to borrow cheaply, leverage up their balance sheets, and buy loans on more favorable terms than their truly private competitors. These competitors, as well as the fiscally prudent, argue that the corporations' implicit guarantees are a form of corporate welfare, for which the government should be paid, and that their over-leveraging exposes the government to the risk of a bailout more expensive than the S&L extravaganza. To protect their privileged status, Fannie and Freddie deploy the usual weapons with unusual skill. In 1996, for example, Fannie Mae saw its ex-chair move on to direct Clinton's budget office, and lent a volunteer PR expert to the cash-starved Dole campaign (while he continued to draw his Fannie Mae paycheck). Its lobbyists include former Senators, Representatives, and White House officials of both parties, and it throws around campaign contributions with great verve. It makes friends in academia with the lure of fat consulting contracts (a seductive trick also practiced by the Fed and the World Bank). The U.S. Congressional Budget Office (1996) estimated that only two-thirds of the benefits of lower interest rates from the implied federal guarantee are passed through to borrowers; the rest is skimmed by managers and stockholders.[29] Fannie Mae earned $2.1 billion in profits in 1995, and its shareholders have done quite well. Who says government doesn't have the knack for business?

the Fed

The most important government agency in the realm of money is undoubtedly the Federal Reserve. If something as decentered as a financial system has a center, it's the central bank, and since the dollar remains the world's central currency, the Fed is the most important of all central banks. All eyes are on it, and the tone of both financial and real business is heavily dependent on its stance. When a central bank is in an expansive mood, finance bubbles; when it's tight, things sag.

The Federal Reserve is a study in how money and the monied constitute themselves politically. Ironically, though it's now an anathema to populists of the left and right, its creation perversely fulfilled one of the demands of 19th century populists: for an "elastic" currency — one administered by the government that could provide emergency credit when a financial implosion seemed imminent — as an alternative to the inflexibility of the gold standard. Instead of becoming the flexible, indulgent institution the populists dreamed of, the Fed quickly evolved into Wall Street's very own fourth branch of government (Greider 1987, chapter 8).

There were a couple of attempts in the early and mid-19th century to create an American central bank, but they were allowed to die because of

Jeffersonian–Jacksonian objections to concentrated financial power. That left the anarchic, volatile U.S. financial system without any kind of lender of last resort, but in booms all kinds of funny money passed.[30]

Canonically, it was the panic of 1907 that led to the Fed's creation. In the frequent panics of the late 19th century, a cabal of New York bankers would typically band together to organize lifeboat operations in emergencies; in the panic of 1895, J.P. Morgan and his cronies bailed out the U.S. Treasury itself with an emergency loan of gold. The panic of 1907, however, proved too much for these private arrangements; that time, the Treasury had to be called in to bail out the cabal. After that brush with disaster, Wall Street and its friends in Washington came around to thinking that the U.S. could go no longer without a central bank (Greider 1987, chapter 9; Carosso 1987, pp. 535–549).

Gabriel Kolko (1963) traced the loss of the Wall Street circle's power to several things — the aging of personalities like Morgan and Stillman (the Rockefeller representative); the growth of the economy and financial markets, and the evolution of financial centers outside New York; and the shift of industry towards internal finance, which lessened Wall Street's influence. The loss of raw financial power, however, was compensated for by the creation of the Fed, an institution that has been dominated by Wall Street since its birth in 1913. To Kolko, the Fed was an example of an interest group using the state to reverse its fading market fortunes. This line resonates in populist discourse today.

That canonical story, however, doesn't comport with the convincing evidence massed by James Livingston (1986). To Livingston, the struggle for a U.S. central bank had a much longer history, and one central to the creation of the modern corporate–Wall Street ruling class beginning in the 1890s. Livingston showed that the campaign for a more rational system of money and credit was not a movement of Wall Street vs. industry or regional finance, but a broad movement of elite bankers and the managers of the new corporations as well as academics and business journalists. The emergence of the Fed was the culmination of attempts to define a standard of value that began in the 1890s with the emergence of the modern professionally managed corporation owned not by its managers but by dispersed public shareholders.

Though the U.S. had become a national market deeply involved in global trade and finance in the decades following the Civil War, in the early 1890s it was still dominated by small producers and banks. As any Marxian or Keynesian crisis theorist can tell you, the separation of purchase and sale is one of the great flashpoints of capitalism; an expected sale that goes unmade can drive a capitalist under, and unravel a chain of financial commitments. Multiply that by a thousand or two and you have great potential for mischief. This is one reason the last third of the 19th century was characterized by violent booms and busts, in nearly equal measure, since almost half the period was one of panic and depression. In panics, the thousands of decentralized banks would hoard reserves, thus starving the system for liquidity precisely at the moment it was most badly needed. But the up cycles were also extraordinary, powered by loose credit and kinky currencies (like privately issued banknotes). There was no central standard of value, unlike the way we think of assets of all kinds, from cash to inverse floaters, as denominated in the same fundamental unit, the dollar. "Progressive" corporate thought, which had mastered the rhetoric of modernization, wanted a central bank that would control inflationary finance on the upswing — which in the mind of larger interests, meant keeping small operators from "overinvesting" and laying the groundwork for a deflationary panic — and extend crucial support in a crunch.

Trusts were one attempt by leading industrialists and bankers to manage the system's instabilities, but those were prohibited by the Sherman Act of 1890. The corporation, argued Livingston, was a response to the outlawing of trusts. By internalizing lots of the the competitive system's gaps — by bringing more transactions within the same institutional walls — corporations greatly stabilized the economy.

With the emergence of the modern firm at the turn of the century came a broader rethink of the business system. Writing in 1905, Charles Conant, a celebrity banker–intellectual, explicitly cited Marx (and anticipated Keynes) in emphasizing that the presence of money as a store of value, the possibility of keeping wealth in financial form rather than spending it promptly on commodities, always introduces the possibility of crisis. In other words, the possibility asserted by Marx but denied by classical economics, the possibility of an excess of capital lacking a profitable investment outlet, and an excess of goods that couldn't be sold profitably on the open market, had proved all too real in practice. A system for regulating credit was essential — one that while operating through the state would be taken out of politics; the regulation of money and credit would be turned over to "experts," that is, creditors, industrialists, and technocrats who thought like them.

The struggle around the definition of money, Livingston showed, marked the emergence of corporate and Wall Street bigwigs as a true ruling class:

energized, confident, highly conscious of its mission — capable of promoting its case to a broader public using PR and friendly expertise, and to Congress with deft lobbying. Universities became rich sources of expertise for the new class, and they endowed institutes and foundations to act as a marketing and distribution mechanism for the new ideas.

The fight for sound money was also consciously expansive, even imperial; the economic theory of the day held that chronic oversupplies of capital and goods could be alleviated by conquering foreign markets. Industrialists with global ambitions wanted their bankers to be international, and wanted the dollar to be firm against the British pound rather than a junk currency. They wanted their paper accepted in London money markets in dollars, not pounds, and that required a central bank.

The panic of 1907, rather than being the catalyst it's sometimes presented as, was taken as the "evidence that validated conclusions [the corporate–financial establishment] had already reached" (Livingston 1986, p. 172). The elite had been agitating for sterner money for a decade. The PR campaign heated up, as did the political campaign; in 1908, Congress formed a monetary commission led by the blue-chip Senator Nelson Aldrich, and the next year, the *Wall Street Journal* ran a 14-part editorial on its front page (written by Conant) arguing the case for a central bank. This institution would regulate "the ebb and flow of capital," and stabilize the economy. Among the elite there was a great loss of faith in the self-regulating powers of the free market; a central bank was just the sort of expert and dispassionate intervention required to brake its frequent tendency towards derailment.

This history helps explain the absence of a finance–industry split, minor family quarrels excepted, over central bank policy in the U.S. and elsewhere. There was remarkable regional and sectoral agreement on the need to rationalize the banking system, both for reasons of stabilizing the economy and to promote overseas commercial and imperial interests. This history also helps explain populist thinking in the U.S. today, with a similar analysis often shared by left and right, greens and libertarians. Their opposition to central banks, centralizing corporations, and global entanglements in favor of a decentered, small-scale system reflects the historical processes by which these modern institutions formed each other. They typically forget the volatile, panic-ridden history of the late 19th century in their dreams of simpler times.

From its founding, the Fed has consisted of twelve district banks scattered around the country — a concession to the decentralized traditions of American finance and politics — and a central governing board in Washington. The district Federal Reserve banks are technically owned by the private banks in their regions, which choose six of each district bank's nine directors. Of the New York district's nine serving in 1996, three were bankers (from the Bank of New York, and smallish banks on Long Island and in Buffalo); two were CEOs of giant companies (AT&T and Pfizer). The balance: conservative New York City teachers' union leader, Sandra Feldman;[31] private investor John Whitehead, formerly of Goldman, Sachs and the Carter cabinet; investment banker Pete Peterson of The Blackstone Group, formerly of the Nixon administration, and sworn enemy of Social Security; and the head of a giant pension fund, Thomas Jones of TIAA–CREF. Recent alumni include the CEO of a large insurance company, a small business-owner, and the head of an elite foundation. Of all these, only two were outside the Big Business/Big Finance orbit — three if you're generous, and want to count the foundation executive, but foundations have big financial holdings, and are politically and socially intimate with the corporate class. So while the Federal Reserve System is technically an agency of the federal government, an important part of the system is directly owned and controlled by private interests.

Despite the original decentralizing intent of the district structure, power quickly gravitated toward two centers — Washington, where the Fed is headquartered, and New York, the site of the most important of the regional banks because of its location just blocks from Wall Street. Day-to-day monetary policy is carried out, based on broad instructions from Washington, at the New York Fed's trading desk. The system's executive body is a Board of Governors, consisting of seven members nominated by the President and confirmed by the Senate, who serve for a term of fourteen years. That long term is supposed to insulate the governors from political pressures; in reality, it insulates them almost completely from anything like democratic accountability. From the seven board members, the President nominates, subject to Senate confirmation, a chair and a vice chair, who serve four-year terms. The board has in practice been pretty well dominated by the chair; after leaving the vice chairship in 1996, Alan Blinder complained publicly about his difficulty in even getting information out of the staff economists. From the chair down to the vice presidents and directors of the district banks, the Fed's senior staff is overwhelmingly male, white and privileged (Mfume 1993).

Unlike ordinary government agencies, the Fed is entirely self-financing; it need never go to Congress, hat in hand. Almost all its income comes from its portfolio of nearly $400 billion in U.S. Treasury securities. It's not difficult to build up a huge piggy bank when you can buy bonds with money you create out of thin air, as the Fed does. In fact, at the end of every year, the Fed returns a profit of some $20 billion to the Treasury — after deducting what it considers to be "reasonable" expenses. Salaries are far more generous and working conditions far more comfortable, than in more mundane branches of government — and there's not much that mere civilians can do to challenge its definition of reasonableness.

Monetary policy is set by a Federal Open Market Committee (FOMC), which consists of the seven governors plus five of the district bank presidents, who serve in rotation —five of the twelve votes are cast by the heads of institutions owned by commercial banks, a strange feature in a nominally democratic government. Imagine the outcry if almost half the seats on the National Labor Relations Board were reserved for unionists.

The FOMC meets in secret every five to eight weeks to set the tone of monetary policy — restrictive, accommodative or neutral, in Fed jargon. Until very recently, the committee didn't announce policy decisions until six to eight weeks after they'd been made. In a departure from almost eighty years of history, the sequence of tightenings started in February 1994 were announced immediately, a frank attempt to steal some of the populist reformers' thunder. Until early 1995, those reformers were led by Texas Representative Henry Gonzalez, who spent his few years as chair of the House Banking Committee deliciously torturing the Fed in every way possible. The threat of subpoenas from Gonzalez caused a sudden bout of recovered memory syndrome at the Fed; for 17 years, it had denied that it even took detailed minutes at FOMC meetings; in fact, it had been taping and transcribing them all along. The Republican takeover of Congress in 1994, however, ended Gonzalez' reign of terror.

Still, despite this whiff of *glasnost*, the Fed remains an intensely secretive institution. This opaqueness has spawned an entire Fed-watching industry, a trade reminiscent of Kremlinology, in which every institutional twitch is scrutinized for clues to policy changes. Fed watchers "earn" salaries well into the six figures for such work; greater openness at the Fed would reduce their importance, if not put them out of business, a rare form of unemployment that would be entirely welcome. The Fed also manipulates the media ably; reporters, eager for a leak from a central bank insider, will print anything whispered in their ears, whether or not it's true — leaks sometimes designed to mislead or enlighten the markets, and other times the product of some internal struggle.

Even though FOMC members would no doubt invent all sorts of clever euphemisms to express the dangers of excessively low unemployment, televising the FOMC's proceedings on C-SPAN would still provide an enlightening glimpse into the mentality of power.

Wall Street ideology

Since this section is about the state, some words about Wall Street's politics. As do most plutocrats, financiers take their own, usually crude, thoughts quite seriously, and are also rich enough to pay lots of other people to think for them. Their opinions range from establishment liberal (especially on social issues) to ravingly right wing; the rightwingers, all fans of *laissez-faire,* can be subdivided into those whose libertarianism extends to social tolerance, and those who are fulminant bigots. (Not all the bigots are on the right. According to someone who used to work for one of Wall Street's more prominent "liberal" Democrats, he was quite the racist in private.) Probably 95% of Wall Street — and that includes similar outposts in Chicago and California — would agree with the mantra, "markets good, government bad" — even those who trade government bonds for a living. Despite their reputation for sophistication, most Wall Streeters hold to a raw, selfish view of the world.

Finance, both U.S. and international, is heavily represented on the boards of Washington thinktanks, from hotbeds of centrism like the Brookings Institution to right-wing outposts like Cato and Heritage. Buyout artist Ted Forstman, a man barely capable of articulating even his own primitive libertarian philosophy when not supported by a script, is a major supporter of the right-wing *American Spectator.* Financiers are quite heavy political givers. FIRE's political action committees (PACs) "invested far more...dollars in the '94 campaign than any other group of business interests," with the securities industry tilting heavily towards the Democrats, even in that Republican year (Goldstein 1995). While it may be seen as a sign of enlightenment that Wall Street contains more Democrats than do most other business sectors, in fact finance is a heavily conservatizing influence on the supposed party of the people. More recently, hedge fund hotshots emerged as major supporters of the 1994 Newt Gingrich Republican counterrevolution. And again in 1996, reports the Center for Responsive Politics, the FIRE sector was the heaviest political giver of all.

Even though their worldview often seems formed by nothing deeper than the endless play of headlines that scroll by on their computer screens, Wall Street analysts and economists are favored sources for reporters to turn to when they need a quote. For a somewhat more scholarly take, reporters call experts at the thinktanks Wall Street supports. And so does money express itself ideologically.

information: "reflexively fellative"

No survey of the cast of characters would be complete without a look at the various financial media. Pundits and economists are fond of pointing out that the markets are about "information," a chic and spongy word that often serves as an unexamined euphemism for money and power, and not just in finance.[32] But just because pundits and economists say something repeatedly doesn't mean that it isn't at least partly true. There are, however, many different kinds of information.

Most precious of all is inside information, which comes in many forms. The most famous kind is news about some dramatic business development, like an unexpected drop in profits, or a takeover attempt, or an imminent indictment. Obviously, whoever knows this before the public can make big money when the news hits the Street. But that's not the only kind of inside info that can be turned into ready money. News that a brokers' research department is about to recommend Intel, or that a client is about to place an order for a million shares of IBM, can be valuable to the firm's trading desk, which can take a position ahead of the event and profit from the ensuing price thrust as the news spreads. The trading desk is supposed to be insulated from the rest of the firm through a so-called "Chinese wall," but these walls aren't always poreless. As a veteran financial journalist told me in the midst of all the insider scandals of the late 1980s, people have been coming to Wall Street for generations to make money off inside info; Boesky & Co. just got too piggy for their own good. Or as a celebrity trader once put it, "Whoever doesn't know something everyone else doesn't know is a fucking chump."

Wall Street is awash in less sexy forms of information, too, ranging from gossip that traders pass along to each other on the phone, to serious-seeming financial and economic analysis published by brokerage firms and research boutiques, to the daily news that appears in the papers and on the wires. The financial wire services — Reuters, Dow Jones, Bloomberg — have computer terminals scattered all over the financial world, pouring live news into the eyes of easily distracted players, and offering a range of market prices, historical information, and analysis as well.

One shouldn't overestimate the quality of a lot of that news product.

While the news pages of the *Wall Street Journal* contain some of the best daily journalism in America, the market news in that and other major papers is often quite superficial, an uncritical repackaging of the blather coming out of the big brokerage houses. The research produced by those brokers is typically little more than an adjunct to the sales effort. Analysts rarely say anything unkind about companies they cover; firms don't want to alienate potential investment banking clients, and the analysts don't want to alienate their sources in management, for fear they'll stop taking their phone calls.[33] As a result, you almost never see a "sell" recommendation; the nastiest thing most analysts will say about a stock is to call it a "hold" rather than a "buy."

The most famous example of the pressures at work was when Marvin Roffman, a gambling analyst then in the employ of Janney Montgomery Scott, dared tell the *Wall Street Journal* in 1990 that Donald Trump's frightening Taj Mahal casino in Atlantic City was a debt-heavy house of cards that "won't make it." Trump threatened to sue Janney, and the firm quickly fired Roffman (who turned out, as of 1996, to be wrong, alas).

That's an extreme case. The more normal pressures were described by John Keefe, formerly a banking analyst with Drexel Burnham Lambert who now runs his own research shop in New York. According to Keefe, since the services brokers offer to clients are pretty undifferentiated, it's hard for a firm, beyond a basic level of competence, to stand out at executing buy and sell orders. So, the research a firm offers clients is what's supposed to distinguish it from its rivals.

But, "in fact," Keefe notes, analysts "spend most of their time 'selling' their ideas to their clients, and very little of their time researching." When he was at Drexel, Keefe said he was expected to pay two or three personal visits a year to major clients, and one a year to lesser clients. Aside from the personal sit-downs, analysts are expected to make a least 100 phone calls a month to clients, with some of the "more obsessive (and successful)" ones making as many as 300 calls a month — or 15 a work day. Obviously, there isn't much time left over after the clients are serviced to do serious corporate and industry research.

One thing analysts rarely do is second-guess the numbers that firms report to their shareholders, which are certified by outside auditors, typically a brand-name global accounting firm. Accountancy may have a reputation for dullness, but it can be the scene of great creativity. Accountants are notoriously eager to say kind things about the companies they audit; after all, the subject of the audit pays the fees. Notorious bankrupts of the

1980s, from Drexel Burnham Lambert to BCCI to several hundred S&Ls, were repeatedly given clean bills of health by prominent accounting firms — the very outside auditors who are supposed to provide an external check on a firm's numerical self-representation. More pedestrian companies are transformed through creative arithmetic and legal interpretations into dazzling growers.

Sluttish accountancy is a long-standing practice. During the 1960s, John Brooks (1973, pp. 160–162) reported, accountants painted a glowing picture in numbers that merger promoters wanted. Investors, many of them naïfs, eagerly bought paper that only a few years later would turn out to be near worthless. "By following conservative practices and their consciences, accountants could have prevented this jiggery-pokery; they did not." You could say exactly the same thing about the financial disasters of the last 15 years. Had Wall Street analysts, who are presumably competent to do so, given the accountants' numbers a serious second look, much recent jiggery-pokery might have been detected.[34]

Even economic analysis must serve the sales effort. One economist who'd been making accurately bullish forecasts about U.S. economic growth in 1993 and 1994, when the rest of Wall Street was unanimous in projecting sluggishness, was called in by his superiors and told to rethink his forecasts. (Strong economic growth is usually bad for bonds, and the firm had lots of bonds to sell.) The economist did as told, and marked down his forecasts. Wall Street's favorite economist, Ed Hyman, winner of the *Institutional Investor* poll for a dozen years running, was one of those (wrongly) predicting sluggishness in 1993 and 1994; by coincidence, his firm not only sells bonds, but he also manages a large bond portfolio.

As Keefe said, if the markets are the casino that Keynes famously said they were, then the analysts are like lounge singers. After all, the casinos all offer the same games and the same odds; the only difference among them is the entertainment and decor. While there are "many analysts who take their work quite seriously," Keefe concluded, "many times the competition among them degenerates into a contest to see who can get the most attention with the most daring forecast." Other times, however, less flamboyant analysts simply tune their forecasts to the consensus, so as not to stand out, and thereby avoid potential embarrassment. In either case, flamboyant or shrinking, the forecast is driven by the consensus rather than the facts of the case.

These analysts and economists provide the raw material for financial reporters. Here's a view of how that trade is plied, from a long-time practitioner, John Liscio, a former *Barron's* columnist who now publishes his own high-priced newsletter:

> Financial writers are nothing more than glorified recording secretaries. Unlike their colleagues in other fields like theatre, cinema, food, sports, politics, and fashion, financial writers and even columnists refuse to think for themselves. Because they cherish access to highly-placed sources, they serve as nothing more than conduits for the received wisdom, which is almost always wrong…. Whatever the moron economists and analysts tell the financial press gets smeared across the page. There's no filter.
>
> Imagine how ridiculous it would be if a sports writer, assigned to a perennial also-ran, persisted in printing the absurdly optimistic rantings of the managers, owner, and aging pitching staff, and little or nothing else. Or if a food critic's review of a restaurant was built around the opinion of the master chef and maître d'. Asking a Wall Street hack his opinion on the economy is like asking a producer how he feels about a play he just mounted, or a runway model what she thinks about the new line. Yet that's exactly how the financial press plays it: reflexively fellative.

Historically, the financial press has served a deeply ideological role. As Wayne Parsons (1990) showed, the dissemination of price and product information was crucial to the development of national markets in Britain and America from the 17th through the 19th century. Like today, some of that information was good, but some of it was little more than shilling for the touts of the day; the South Sea Bubble, for example, probably never would have inflated without the help of the London press.

But more than prices were circulated — so were ideas. *The Economist,* under editor Walter Bagehot, was crucial to the spread of the free-trade and *laissez-faire* religion through the British elite. As Bagehot said, *The Economist,* the magazine that mysteriously calls itself a newspaper, was a great "belief producer" for the new bourgeoisie. As Parsons (1990, p. 41) put it, "the historical importance of the financial press does not lie so much in its contribution to the development of a literary form as in its role in defining a capitalist language and culture: free markets, individualism, profit and speculation. Not only did the publication of information facilitate the growth of the internationalization of markets, it also assisted in no small way in the promotion of capitalist culture" (Parsons 1990, pp. 27, 41).

That culture had a very narrow conception of economic news; it was that "which impacted on the state of the market and City opinion. The economic condition of the people…was not something which…greatly preoccupied the attention of financial journalists and newspaper editors" (Parsons 1990, p. 31).

Parsons was speaking of the 19th century, but much the same can be said today, with cable TV channels running the stock ticker all day, the *Financial Times* and *Wall Street Journal* publishing editions on each other's home turf, and *The Economist* telling yuppies and senior bureaucrats around the world what to think, with a heavy dose of British attitude that insecure Americans find intoxicating. Economic news is largely confined to the "business" section, with all the biases that implies; needless to say, no daily paper has a "labor" section.

Further, Parsons argues, the transformation of economics into a largely obscure branch of mathematics and the retreat of economists into the academy have left a great vacuum in the dissemination of economic ideas, a vacuum that has been filled by the business press. The conversion of *The Economist* from a Keynesian sheet to an anti-Keynesian one during the 1970s was of great importance in the repudiation of the postwar Keynesian consensus.

Supply-side economics, a ludicrous but enriching doctrine that became national policy in the U.S. in the early Reagan years, was developed in large part on the editorial page of the *Wall Street Journal* by Jude Wanniski and Robert Bartley. Wanniski left the paper to become an economic consultant (famous for his fervid screeds promoting a return to the gold standard), but Bartley and his minions still push the early Reagan years as an economic model for all time, with ever-increasing disregard for fact, reason, and opposing views. Many *Journal* reporters are embarrassed by Bartleyism, but the chair of Dow Jones, Peter Kann, and his wife, Karen Elliott House, a fire-breathing vice president of the company, adore it. Kann is said to have denounced James Stewart, the paper's page one editor in the late 1980s, for being "too liberal." The "liberal" Stewart went on to win the Pulitzer prize for his book on Drexel and the insider scandals of the 1980s (Stewart 1991), and from there went on to become a big cheese at *Smart Money*, a joint venture between Dow Jones and Hearst. At *Smart Money*, a slick and empty personal finance magazine, Stewart overcame his ignorance of the stock market and wrote stories naming the ten stocks you *have* to own — names supplied by a money manager, James Cramer, who just happened to own many of the stocks he recommended to Stewart.

One might think that the scads of independent newsletters, with subscription prices ranging from several hundred to thousands of dollars a year, might be a better source of investment analysis, but they rarely are.

The long-term performance of popular newsletters is little different from a guess, but even the high-end ones are not too impressive either.

The consulting service Johnson Smick, which charges up to $100,000 for subscriptions to its tout sheets, is a case in point. The Johnson is Manuel Johnson, former vice chair of the Federal Reserve. When Johnson was at the central bank, the firm, then Smick Medley, showed an uncanny ability to forecast Fed policy changes; when Johnson left the Fed, the firm became Johnson Smick Medley — and their prescience about Fed policy seemed to lose some of its edge. In 1994, the firm reported to its clients that the Whitewater scandal was about to take a spectacular turn that would be very damaging to President Clinton; the stock and bond markets swooned on the report, which turned out to be completely untrue (Kurtz 1994; Fromson 1994). So why would people pay $100,000 a year for such bad journalism? Because it moves the markets when it spreads beyond the circle of subscribers; if you hear it first, you can make money on it, whether it's true or not. This is admittedly an extreme example, and a newsletter that repeatedly was very wrong would stop moving markets, but while a service is hot — and sometimes for long after — people will pay big to feel the first warmth.

Lower-grade tout sheets often disguise their poor performance by manipulating history. According to Liscio, who reads tons of the stuff, one of the most ambitious rewriters is James Dale Davidson, who mixes right-wing politics with financial advice in his *Strategic Investing* newsletter. Bad picks — and there's no shortage of those — simply disappear from the recommended portfolio from one issue to the next. Passionately anti-Clinton, Davidson has recommended shorting stocks of Arkansas-based companies simply because of some imagined connection to the president. At the time of his death, former CIA director William Colby was writing for a Davidson *SI* spinoff, promoting tales of Clintonian criminality; the conspiracy wires heated up after Colby met his end in the Chesapeake.

styles of play

This isn't a manual of investment technique, though it would probably sell a lot more copies if it were. But a few words on how people sling around their cash wouldn't be excessive pandering to commerce. People who trade financial assets can be divided into several categories. One common distinction is between traders and investors, that is, between people who take a position with an eye to getting out of it in a time measured in units somewhere between seconds and weeks, as opposed to those who intend to hold it for months or even, on occasion, years.

Another distinction is between fundamental and technical traders. Though details vary by market, people who trade on fundamentals look at the realities underlying price movements — broad economic developments, government policies, demography, corporate strategies. A fundamental analyst in the stock market, for example, might examine a company's finances in depth, or talk to managers, customers, and rivals. Technical traders couldn't care less about such ephemera — all they care about is the movement of security prices, which they trace to underlying supply and demand patterns in the markets themselves.

To a technical stock trader, it doesn't matter whether a firm makes potato chips or memory chips. Some technical analysts do fairly rigorous statistical work, tracking changes in trading volume or price momentum, looking for possible clues of imminent trend reversal. Others, little better than haruspices, try to divine patterns in price graphs that supposedly portend dramatic upward or downward moves. Such "chartists" speak enthusiastically of pennants, rising wedges, head and shoulders, saucer bottoms. There is little evidence that chart-reading works at all; the patterns seen are probably little different from the butterflies and genitalia that one sees in a Rorschach test. The economist Burton Malkiel, author of the popular investment text *A Random Walk Down Wall Street,* had his students construct mythical stock price charts by flipping coins. When Malkiel showed these to practicing chartists, they discovered their favorite patterns lurking in the random squiggles (Malkiel 1990, pp. 135–136).

Most market participants use some combination of technical and fundamental analysis, but that doesn't mean their performance is terribly successful. According to Norm Zadeh, who rates the performance of money managers, only about 1–2% of all money-slingers have a consistent and substantial record of good performance. Most do a little less well than the market averages, which isn't surprising, since they *are* the market, and because fees and commissions shave a bit off their returns. Truly outstanding performances — the 1,239% returns you see trumpeted in ads — are almost always flukes.

What's the secret of consistent winners, the household names (at least in affluent households)? According to Zadeh, it often involves market manipulation, bribery to get inside information, and clever use of the press; "they view investing as war," and in war, all is fair. Investors with deep pockets can move markets simply by moving lots of money around; strong movements in one direction or another will attract attention from the broader public, moving prices in a favorable direction. Star investors — names are omitted to avoid lawsuits — will often let it drop that they think the yen is overvalued, or that they've just bought gold; when the masses act on this information, the position, whatever its initial wisdom, becomes a winner. No unknowing chumps here.

capital unbound

So far, this review has concentrated on the U.S. While this simplifies things, it's hardly a fair representation of how we invest today. Capital and commodities traverse the globe with remarkable freedom. Though casual observers treat this borderless world as a recent invention, it's more than a little reminiscent of life before World War I. That idyllic world was nicely evoked by John Maynard Keynes (1988, pp. 11–12), no doubt one of these once-charmed Londoners he wrote about:

> The inhabitant of London could order by telephone, sipping his morning tea in bed, the various products of the whole earth, in such quantity as he might see fit, and reasonably expect their early delivery upon his doorstep; he could at the same moment and by the same means adventure his wealth in the natural resources and new enterprises of any quarter of the world, and share, without exertion or even trouble, in their prospective fruits and advantages; or he could decide to couple the security of his fortunes with the good faith of the townspeople of any substantial municipality in any continent that fancy or information might recommend. He could secure forthwith, if he wished it, cheap and comfortable means of transit to any country or climate without passport or other formality, could despatch his servant to the neighboring office of a bank for such supply of the precious metals as might seem convenient, and could then proceed abroad to foreign quarters, without knowledge of their religion, language, or customs, bearing coined wealth upon his person, and would consider himself greatly aggrieved and much surpised at the least interference. But, most important of all, he regarded this state of affairs as normal, certain, and permanent, except in the direction of improvement, and any deviation from it as aberrant, scandalous, and avoidable. The projects and politics of militarism and imperialism, of racial and cultural rivalries, of monopolies, restrictions, and exclusion, which were to play the serpent to this paradise, were litle more than the amusements of his daily newspaper, and appeared to exercise al-

most no influence at all on the ordinary course of social and economic life, the internationalization of which was nearly complete in practice.

This attitude of entitlement and permanence equally characterizes capital's sense of itself today. Aside from the occasional trade skirmish, often whipped up by politicians eager to excite domestic audiences, further global economic integration, of which free capital flows are the avant garde, is thought to be inevitable. We'll see if it is.

The world Keynes described first came apart during World War I, though the global overprivileged did their best to put it back together again in the 1920s. While European economies hardly thrived in the 1920s — British unemployment was above 10% for almost the entire decade, and Germany spent the Roaring Twenties in crisis — it still seemed as if parts of the prewar order had been restored, and the U.S. spent most of the decade in a boom that marked the beginning of modern consumer capitalism. Capital began flowing across borders again, and bold debts were contracted. But the old order finally fell apart for good with the 1929 crash.

How badly that world came unstuck in the Depression can be seen in the experience of "sovereign default" — countries that went bust. Of 58 countries that issued international bonds in the 1920s, 25 defaulted between 1929 and 1935. In dollar terms, 70% of all foreign debt issued in the U.S. between 1926 and 1929 (excluding Canada) went bad — compared with a default rate of "only" 30% on corporate debt issued in the late 1920s. Most of the sovereign defaulters, by the way, had good ratings from Moody's (Cantor and Packer 1995).

But now those defaults are a distant memory, and today's capital markets look seamless. Statistics confirm the decreasing importance of borders for the financial markets.[35] In the 1970s, the correlation coefficient between interest rates on 10-year U.S. government bonds and German bonds of similar maturity was 0.191, but from 1990 to 1994, it was 0.934; Japan and the U.S., 0.182 and 0.965, respectively; and the U.S. and the U.K., 0.590 and 0.949 (Bank of England data, reported in Goldstein et al. 1994, p. 5).[36] While it would be an exaggeration to say that there's now a single global credit market, we're definitely moving in that direction.

Though all this seems as natural as the sunrise, this incarnation of globalism isn't all that old. Most countries imposed extensive capital controls well into the 1970s. Even now, the IMF Articles of Agreement (Article VI, Section 3) allow members to "exercise such controls as are necessary to regulate international capital movements," as long as they don't unduly interfere with routine payments that go with trade. Though official opinion of the 1950s urged a liberal regime, balance of payments imbalances in the 1960s led to a tightening of controls, with the U.S. trying to restrict capital outflows and several surplus countries trying to limit inflows.

As Philip Turner (1991), an economist with the Bank for International Settlements, noted, capital flows have tended to exaggerate imbalances in trade. Cross-border movements of private capital were "driven to an important extent by expectations of exchange rate realignments," themselves driven largely by current-account considerations. Deficit countries, then, typically faced outflows, as capital tried to beat a coming devaluation; surplus countries faced inflows, as investors hoped to benefit from the likely revaluation. With the advent of floating exchange rates in 1973, these tendencies were only reinforced.

Margaret Thatcher's prompt removal of exchange controls upon her ascension in 1979 set the tone for the 1980s. Ten years later, none of the major and few of the minor rich industrial countries significantly restricted the right of their citizens to hold foreign property.

As Turner noted, things were very different the last time capital roamed the globe so freely. One difference is evoked by Keynes' memoir — "coined wealth." Contrary to the myths proffered by modern goldbugs, current-account imbalances (and the consequent capital flows) of the pre-1914 gold standard — with sterling serving as a good-as-gold substitute — were both large and persistent. From 1880 to 1914, Britain's current account surplus was 4½% of GNP, which yielded a net foreign investment position of 130–140% of GNP in 1914. Returns on foreign invest-

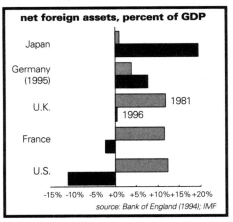

net foreign assets, percent of GDP

source: Bank of England (1994); IMF

ment were 5%, twice the return available from U.K. government bonds. By contrast, Japan's surplus of 19% of GDP looks modest (see chart) compared to Britain at its peak, and 5% returns are regarded as minimal today.

Since almost all these flows were denominated in gold, there was no currency risk — unless some country was bold enough to take the wicked step of renouncing gold. Of course, the flip side of currency risk — the opportunity to speculate in currencies themselves (more than in the underlying assets denominated in those currencies), which became one of the prime movers behind global capital flows in the 1980s — was reduced. What inspired capital to move about then was interest rate differentials.

Aside from gold, Turner noted two other features of the pre-1914 period, a limited range of vehicles and the prominence of long-term investments in real assets. Because of the stability of the gold–sterling system, there was no need for today's hedging instruments like options, swaps, and futures — and it's hard to imagine a deep market in such alchemy in a computerless age. There were stocks, bonds, direct investments — many of these euphemisms for imperial claims — and not much else.

More stunning to the modern observer is how much of border-crossing capital took the form of productive investment, either through the direct European ownership of railroads in the colonies or through holdings of railroad bonds. This had, as Turner (1991, pp. 13–20) pointed out, two economically fortunate sequelae (leaving aside the social questions of colonial "development"). First, real assets were created, assets that could service their debts. And second, the inflow typically found its way back to capital exporting countries in the form of demand for capital equipment.

Unlike the 19th century, the free capital flows in the 1980s largely bypassed the so-called Third World, standing the logic of conventional economics on its head. One would think that potential profit rates would be higher in what are optimistically called "developing countries," but aside from a handful of favored newly industrializing countries (NICs), capital largely shunned the Southern Hemisphere until the "emerging markets" boom of the early 1990s. (Even then, flows were concentrated in a handful of countries — and still, flows among First World countries predominated.) Governments and quasi-public institutions like the World Bank provided two-thirds of the finance to the poor countries during the 1980s. But, as Turner (1991, p. 25) pointed out, "the classical function of international capital markets" — allocating funds to areas of the highest return — "has become even less evident in recent capital flows even among industrial nations." He continued:

> In the 1950s, the United States (high capital/labour ratio) exported capital to Europe (lower capital/labor ratio), a process that contributed to faster growth in Europe than in the United States and a narrowing of wage differentials. Within Europe, Switzerland (high capital/labour ratio) was the largest per capita exporter of capital. Viewed in this light, it appears somewhat anomalous that the United States has been the largest importer

of capital for much of the 1980s; there is little evidence that the US rate of return on real assets was higher in the 1980s than that in other countries.[37]

Turner surmises that this inflow was largely a function of the depth of U.S. capital markets. Well-developed markets, it seems, can pervert the allocation of capital as well as lubricate it. The increasing sophistication of the capital markets is a reaction to the post-Bretton Woods instability of the global system. Turner concludes that "the *financial diversification and intermediation* function of international capital markets has come to eclipse the classical allocation of capital function." Joan Robinson was right when she said that the financial markets are mainly "convenience for rentiers."

Things changed somewhat around 1990, however, as Turner's paper was published. The decline in U.S. interest rates eased the stress on Latin American borrowers as much as it did in the U.S., but those lower rates left investors hungry for yield. They overcame their memories of the debt crisis and began plowing money into the Third World. Official development finance grew just 28% between 1989 and 1994 — but private finance swelled by 313%, led by stock market investment, which exploded by 1029%. Much of this flowed into privatized firms, particularly in Latin America. Old 1970s and 1980s debts were converted into equity in these de-statified firms, giving foreign investors and domestic political cronies big stakes, often at generous prices, in monopoly or near-monopoly businesses. Private debt flows, mainly bonds rather than bank loans, grew 337%, and direct investment — taking a position in existing real enterprise or the establishment of a new one — rose 203%. As a result, the official share of long-term finance fell from over half in 1989 to a third in 1994.

Mexico was the poster country of the emerging markets bubble. The wave of privatization, deregulation, and capital market opening led to a rush of capital — $68 billion in portfolio capital between 1991 and the first half of 1994, compared to a net outflow of $3.6 billion from 1988 through 1990. Mexican financial markets, a fraction of the size of the U.S. market, boomed. The real Mexican economy, however, was performing poorly, turning in tepid growth rates and low real investment levels, while average Mexicans suffered only the mildest of recoveries from the ravages of the 1980s. When the bubble burst, the real economy fell apart under the pressure of the austerity program designed to calm the financial markets, and living standards collapsed once again (Henwood 1995).

The Third World's share of total global direct investment rose from under 15% in 1990 to nearly 40% in 1993 (World Bank 1994, volume 1, chapter 1). That increase in direct investment in the Third World followed on a remarkable increase in cross-border holdings among the First World countries during the 1980s, which doubled or tripled from the levels of the 1970s (Turner 1991, p. 32). According to the UN Centre on Transnational Corporations (UNCTC 1991), unlike the 1970s and early 1980s, when direct investment grew roughly in line with trade, in the late 1980s, cross-border direct investment grew at two to three times the pace of trade.

But direct investment flows to the Third World were concentrated in only a handful of countries, mainly in East Asia and Latin America; the Middle East, Africa, and South Asia were barely in the picture. In fact, that's true of all private capital flows in general — portfolio (stock and bond) as well as direct. Just five countries — China, Mexico, Argentina, Thailand, and Korea — accounted for half the private capital flow total between 1989 and 1993; add another eight (Brazil, Portugal, Malaysia, Turkey, Greece, India, Indonesia, and Chile), and you're over 80%. Private markets are not known for spreading the wealth.

As a series of annual *World Investment Reports* published by the United Nations has argued, these investment flows are driven by the production strategies of multinational corporations (MNCs).[38] Though foreign investment is old, the truly global corporation is a relatively recent development. For centuries, direct investment was mainly the mechanism by which the First World corporations relieved Third World countries of their oil, tin, and rubber. Starting in the 1960s, however, with a big push by U.S. consumer products firms into Europe, the modern MNC began to take shape. As the 1960s and 1970s progressed, U.S. multinationals continued to expand overseas, choosing to serve foreign markets with local operations rather than exporting from the U.S. European MNCs soon followed suit, and during the 1980s — especially as the yen rose in value after 1985, making Japanese exports more expensive on world markets — Japanese firms hopped on the globalization bandwagon.

The UNCTC (1991) calls the three great geographical sources of direct investment — the U.S., Western Europe, and Japan — the Triad. And despite the recent upsurge in direct investment in the Third World, as their study says, "in terms of both foreign direct investment and in terms of trade, interactions *within* the Triad have outpaced interactions in the rest of the world, and between the Triad and the rest of the world, indicating a faster rate of integration among the Triad than between the Triad and the rest of the world." Since the three poles of this trilateral world collectively account for two-thirds of global product, it's not surprising that MNCs are gravitating to where the market action is. As global competition continues to intensify, eliminating the weak and increasing the stakes for the survivors, it won't be surprising to see even further concentration of capital and markets as the decade wears on.

At the same time, however, the UNCTC spied "a pattern whereby host countries *located in the same geographical region* [emphasis in original] are clustered around a single Triad member." Though the Centre wouldn't phrase it this way, each member of the Triad has gathered under itself a relative handful of poor countries to act as sweatshop, plantation, and mine: the U.S. has Latin America, particularly Mexico; the European Union has Eastern and Southern Europe and Africa; and Japan, Southeast Asia. In a few cases, two Triad members share a country — Taiwan and Singapore are split between Japan and the U.S.; Argentina, between the U.S. and the EU; Malaysia, between the EC and Japan; and India is shared by all three. According to the UNCTC, the number of countries dominated by U.S. capital declined somewhat during the 1980s, especially in Asia, and those dominated by Japan and the EU increased.

Only about 25 countries fit into this clustering about the Triad, leaving around 100 mainly small and poor countries on the margins. Though being a member of one of these clusters is no guarantee of prosperity, being left out is probably an even worse fate.

So far, I've talked a lot about direct investment, and rather promiscuously so for a book more concerned with the financial sector than the real. There's a good reason for this. Stephen Hymer (1979) argued that the integration of national financial markets into a single global system — a process that was only beginning when he wrote this in 1972 — developed in symbiosis with the growth of the MNC. "The multinational corporation's need for short-term loans and investment arising from the continuous inflow and outflow of money from all nations, never quite in balance, has encouraged international banking and has helped integrate short-term money markets; its long-term financial requirements...have broadened the demand for international bond and equity capital" (Hymer 1979, p. 82). Production must be financed, and if all goes well, it throws off profits in money form, and globalized production is no exception, meaning that MNCs inevitably create financial flows alongside their productive activities.[39] While the global markets that surround them may seem monstrously bloated next to their real-world base, much the same can be said of the U.S. national financial system, which has been growing far beyond its tangible base for decades.

Just as national capital markets join together fragmented surplus and deficit units who may be miles apart, this global market joins creditors and debtors around the world. And just as shareholder-owned, professionally managed, nation-sized firms emerged from family-owned and - run local units of the 19th century, the MNC emerged from the national corporation. Shareholders and creditors would, Hymer rightly imagined, develop an interest in the global function of the system, not their national piece of it, just as they had developed an interest in their national system more than any specific corporate piece of it.

Two pungent quotes give the flavor of this global solidarity. A senior executive of Colgate–Palmolive told the *New York Times* in 1991: "The United States does not have an automatic call on our resources. There is no mindset that puts this country first" (quoted in Reich 1991, p. 141). Not only Americans are so free of patriotic sentiment. "To be in business," said Frank Stronach, chair of Magna International, a Canadian auto-parts maker that has shifted its production to Mexico, "your first mandate is to make money, and money has no heart, soul, conscience, homeland" (quoted in Bilello 1992). This is very far from the constraints on capital flows imagined by David Ricardo (1911/1987, chapter 7), the founding father of modern free trade theory:

> Experience, however, shows that the fancied or real insecurity of capital, when not under the immediate control of its owner, together with the natural disinclination which every man has to quit the country of his birth and connections, and intrust himself, with all his habits fixed, to a strange government and new laws, check the emigration of capital. These feelings, which I should be sorry to see weakened, induce most men of property to be satisfied with a low rate of profits in their own country, rather than seek a more advantageous employment for their wealth in foreign nations.[40]

Ricardo's sentimental patriotism is a long way from the heartless, landless sentiments of Stronach and the Colgate exec. It remains to be seen whether this borderless world is more permanent than the one described by Keynes, or whether war, depression, and/or political rebellion will smash the idyll once again.

Recalling Keynes, though, should caution against the common habit of treating the globalized present as something utterly new. The share of exports in Britain's GDP was only a bit higher in 1992 than it was in 1913, and the U.S. of 1996 is no match for either. By that same measure, Mexico was more internationalized in 1913 than it was in 1992 (Maddison 1995). Capitalism has from its birth been a deeply international, and internationalizing, system. In many ways, the globalization characteristic of the late 20th century resembles the world of 100 years ago, with goods and capital crossing borders with a freedom unknown since the old world broke apart in 1914. I leave it to soothsayers to answer the question of whether another 1914 — or 1929 — is in our future.

notes

1. How big is institutional finance? In 1991, 1,291,000 tax returns were filed by individual proprietorships claiming either finance, insurance, or real estate (FIRE) as their main line of business, 804,000 partnerships, and 618,000 corporations (U.S. Bureau of the Census 1995, table 847, p. 543).
2. The NIPAs also have little to say about U.S. relations with the outside world; these are covered in the balance of payments (BoP) accounts, which, like the NIPAs, are compiled by the Commerce Department's Bureau of Economic Analysis. The UN's System of National Accounts covers all these bases — NIPAs, BoP, and FoF — in a unified way, but the U.S. is only slowly moving towards compliance with the SNA standard.
3. Not shown is state and local government debt, which had a short burst in the 1950s, fell back in the early 1980s, and then rose some in the late 1980s; 1995's figure of 14.9% of GDP is little different from 1962's 14.0%.
4. This ignores self-employment income, part of which is a return to labor and part to capital; it accounts for well under a tenth of personal income.
5. 1994 figures are used because the 1995 balance sheet figures were delayed by the benchmark revisions of the national income accounts. Financial accounts were published for 1995, but data on tangible assets and capital stocks were unavailable as this book was prepared for publication.
6. Note that in terms of credit market lending alone, households are net borrowers — but households have many other kinds of assets, from houses to mutual funds, that don't show up as credit market assets. As a whole, the household sector has a highly positive net worth.
7. The SCF is the most detailed and accurate survey of the financial state of the population that exists, certainly for the U.S. and quite probably the world, but because of funding shortages, it is done only every three years. Despite its detail and breadth — the interview on which it's based is an hour long, involving reviews of actual financial records and not just sums done from memory, and it catches far more rich people in its net than routine Census surveys — it isn't perfect. According to work by Edward Wolff (1994), the SCF numbers don't really match the FoF. People report their houses and privately owned businesses to be worth almost a third more than the accountants estimate them to be worth, which isn't surprising, because the FoF figure is an estimate based on historical investment figures, and people report current market prices (inflated, no doubt, by an optimism premium). They understate their security holdings by half. People also report lower debts to SCF surveyors than the FoF's sums, meaning that SCF net worth is substantially higher than FoF net worth estimates.
8. These figures are computed by dividing the annual dollar change in consumer credit by the annual change in personal consumption expenditures.
9. People who get deeply into debt are "significantly more likely" to have reported a

sharp drop in income, as are those who ultimately file for bankruptcy — most probably because of job loss or medical emergency (Sullivan et al 1989, pp. 95–102, 185–187). Credit seems again to be a private substitute for a civilized public welfare state.

10. One way of measuring the (in)equality of income or wealth distribution is with the Gini index, which ranges from 0 (perfect equality) to 1 (perfect inequality, i.e., one person has all the money). Gini indexes on wealth are astonishing. In 1989, the Census Bureau's household income Gini was .431; on the SCF, it was .505; for wealth, it was .793 overall, and .966 excluding houses and cars (Weicher 1995).

11. The Fed has lately been doing its best to bury these numbers. Detailed reports on the 1983 Survey of Consumer Finances were published in its main journal, the *Federal Reserve Bulletin;* only a very general report was published on the 1989 survey, and the wealth distribution data was circulated only in the form of an unpublished working paper, buried under 36 pages of technique. The Fed also sat on the wealth data for month, delaying the release of the computer tapes until after the 1992 presidential campaign election — for ostensibly technical reasons, but the official explanation must be met with some skepticism. When the Democrats won, the forces interested in doing the wealth arithmetic lost some of their zeal. The 1992 survey received similarly cursory treatment.

12. Who knows how underreporting affects this? It may be that despite the SCF's best efforts, rich people are still falling through the net, or it may mean that nonrich people are underreporting their holdings. The best one can do is say, if it's good enough for the Fed, it's good enough for me.

13. The SCF's catchall "nonwhite" is as misleading as it is callous. It includes Asians and Hispanics, who are notably better off than blacks, and since their numbers are increasing faster than African Americans, they're boosting the nonwhite average.

14. Other paths of influence — direct ones like takeover threats and shareholder rebellions, or indirect ones like stock prices and interest rates — are more important than the regulation of market access, and will be taken up later.

15. The rationale for the formula is given in the graph's caption.

16. When stock prices are high, one firm can take over another without spending cash, but just by offering shares of its own stock as payment.

17. For different reasons, Post-Keynesian and Marxist economies object to making capital into a factor of production on a par with labor, but those objections, as accurate as they are, don't really bear on the point being made here.

18. Later surveys lumped FIRE workers into "infrastructure, wholesale trade, and FIRE," mixing bus drivers in with bond traders.

19. Elsewhere, a source familiar with the New York gay S&M world said that most of the Wall Streeters he's met have been bottoms. As one explained to him, "The more power I have, the greater my need to be humiliated."

20. A building is thought to be worth x times its rent roll, with the x varying with interest rates, the present state of the real estate market, investors' general optimism or pessimism about the future, and various tax considerations. That x is the inverse of the building's yield. If interest rates are 5%, then a real estate investor might want annual rental income to equal 10%, since real estate is riskier than a sound government or corporate bond — so the building would be priced at ten times the rent roll. But real estate is a game usually played with borrowed money, so the interest rate on that borrowed money would have to be subtracted from the rent to get the building's net yield. If the building appreciates over time, so much the better; rent can cover the mortgage, with the price appreciation almost all gravy.

21. Insurance companies often manage pension fund assets, but in doing so they're acting more as portfolio managers than insurers in the narrow sense.

22. London may look onshore, but it's largely unregulated. "Offshore" is really more a state of mind than a place, anyway; the ultimate beneficiaries of offshore transactions are usually very rich citizens of very rich countries.

23. In April 1995, the Bank for International Settlements (BIS), the Basel-based central bankers club, proposed allowing banks to use their own internal computer models for judging the riskiness of their exposure to derivatives and off-balance-sheet items, subject to the approval of national regulators. The BIS, normally a fairly conservative institution, is here showing great faith in both the models' accuracy and the banks' honesty (Basel Committee on Banking Supervision 1995).

24. In the 1950s and 1960s, it was said that a good deal of banking followed the 3-6-3 rule: borrow money from your depositors at 3%, lend it to another set of customers at 6%, and be at the golf course by 3.

25. I have become very shy about predicting the future. But it *looks* like a bubble of sublime proportions.

26. The name "hedge fund" originally came from the fact that unlike most institutional investors, they were free to sell short and play with options, supposedly to protect ("hedge") their positions. Hedging is regarded as a conservative thing to do, but hedge funds are anything but conservative.

27. These were not entirely spontaneous formations: they were guided by upper-class reformers and philanthropists encouraging the moral development of the lower orders (Kristov and Olmstead 1992). It seems that saving and borrowing are always intimate companions of virtue, especially if they make the rich richer and the poor quiescent.

28. For the moment — barring privatization — SEC filings are available on the World Wide Web, at www.sec.gov. They are a rich source of information about corporate America, if you can hack through the jargon.

29. Snipped from the CBO study, the *Wall Street Journal* reported, was math showing that the $2 billion that goes annually to Fannie's and Freddie's managers and shareholders "could provide a 10% down payment on homes for 250,000 low-income families."

30. Most European countries had central banks, some of them going back hundreds of years. The world's first was Sweden's Riksbank, founded in 1668; the Bank of England, the world's second, was founded (as a private banker to the government) in 1694.

31. That union leader, Sandra Feldman, refused to appear at a labor-backed "tax the rich" rally in New York City in 1993, because, her spokesperson told me, she wouldn't share a platform with "avowed Communists."

32. As, for example, with patent protection for drugs and microchips, where "information" is really about the preservation of monopoly power and profits.

33. An article in the *Public Relations Journal* (Shell 1990) said that "investor relations" staffers — corporate PR specialists whose audience is Wall Street — shouldn't "stonewall"; instead they should "provide 'more' information." The use of quotes around "more" — they're in the original — suggests that the provision of more information should never be confused with telling the truth.

34. One check on this confederacy of optimists are professional shorts — people who look for companies with inflated reputations and stock prices, dig out the info, short the stock, and then leak the bad news to reporters eager for a hot tip. If the news takes, then the stock will suffer damage. Sometimes it doesn't matter whether the bad news is true; if the short can take a position and undertake a successful disinformation campaign, he or she can profitably cover the short.

35. For the "real" sector, however, borders still matter, and the "global assembly line" is a bit of an exaggeration.

36. The correlation coefficient is a measure of how tightly two sets of numbers are related to each other, ranging from -1 (a perfect mirror image) through 0 (no relation at all) to

+1 (perfect lockstep). A correlation coefficient under 0.2 marks a fairly cacophanous relation, but figures over 0.9 signify great intimacy.

37. In fact, many foreign investments made in the U.S. during the 1980s have had apparently dismal rates of return. The dollar's decline has savaged financial invesments, and real investments haven't done much better. According to official U.S. figures for 1993 (U.S. Department of Commerce, Bureau of Economic Analysis 1994), foreigners earned a return of 1.4% (income divided by the total value of assets) on their direct investments in the U.S., while U.S. firms earned 10.3% on their invest-ments abroad. Japan ran in the red — a return of –2.4%. These figures are admittedly only very rough approximations; it's very hard to value the capital stock properly, and companies scheme and cheat to reduce reported profits. But these numbers fit well with anecdotal evidence that Japanese investors took a bath on their invest-ments in the U.S. during the 1980s.

38. The agency that publishes the *World Investment Reports* was once known as the UN Centre on Transnational Corporations (UNCTC). Though this was once a mildly sub-versive institution during the 1970s, when calls from the South for a new international economic order were popular — meaning a more equitable distribution of global wealth and power — the UNCTC grew tame along with everyone else by the 1980s. Still, the Reagan and Bush administrations regarded the Centre as a nest of Bolsheviks, and pressured the UN into reducing its status to the point where it is now a sub-speck within UNCTAD, the UN Conference on Trade and Development. For the sake of con-sistency, I'm calling it the UNCTC anyway, even though the Centre no longer exists.

39. Again, it must be emphasized that the globalization of production shouldn't be exag-gerated. Most multinational firms make products in the country or region of their final sale; the amount of shipment of parts and semifinished goods around the world is nowhere near as great as is sometimes thought (Whichard and Lowe 1995).

40. Ironically, though born in London, Ricardo was of Dutch origin, and he was educated in Holland.

3 **Ensemble**

Though it often seems like Wall Street inhabits a world entirely of its own imaginative making, it is connected to the real world, in often indirect and mysterious ways. So too the individual markets; though they often seem to dance to their own music, what happens in one can affect another, or sets of markets may simultaneously react to the same news. Having outlined the pieces, let's now try to fit them together.

Mother Credit

If there is a mother of all financial markets it is the one for credit.[1] Changes in the terms on which some people let other people use their money move both the financial markets and the real economy. When credit is easily gotten, and when interest rates are low and/or falling, the financial markets typically sizzle; when credit is scarce, and rates are high and/or rising, financial markets do badly.

Why is this? Several reasons, the simple ones first. The focus here is on stocks, which are typically the focus of speculators' most ardent attentions, but the reasoning can be applied with only slight modifications to other assets, like real estate, art, and even baseball cards.

- *Cost of playing with other people's money.* Speculators — and in this instance the word is used in a morally neutral sense to mean anyone who buys a financial asset in the hope of selling it at a higher price in the near or distant future — typically operate on borrowed money. Any increase in the cost of funds increases their costs of doing business, with obvious effects on both their enthusiasm and buying power. Someone who borrows money at 5% needs to make well over 5% to justify the great risks of holding stocks or futures — say, just for the sake of argument, 10% or more. Should rates rise to 7%, the margin of safety at a hoped-for 10% return would be reduced, meaning that a return of 12% would be required. And returns of 12% are much rarer than 10%, rare as those are. Consequently, speculative enthusiasm dampens, and prices of speculative assets typically sag, when interest rates rise.

- *Effects on sentiment.* When interest rates rise or fall a nontrivial amount, it's usually with the consent or even the intention of the central bank. When central banks lower rates, they're trying to stimulate the real and financial economies; when they raise rates, they're trying to slow them down. Sane speculators never bet against central banks, the center of the entire financial universe: they create money, regulate credit, and often decide whether troubled private banks will live or die. While not almighty, central banks often get what they want, so they affect speculators' sense of the future very powerfully. (Major central banks, that is; the Fed and the Bundesbank are mighty, but the Bank of Mexico is weak and the Bank of Zaïre little more than a joke.) Since financial asset prices are built largely of expectations about the future, stimuli or depressants to those expectations bear very directly on their prices. Optimism boosts prices, and pessimism depresses them.

- *Relative attractiveness of alternative investments.* When interest rates are low or falling, people despair of the earnings on their Treasury bills, bank deposits, or money market funds; they search for juicier profits, and plunge into stocks or long-term bonds, which typically pay higher interest rates than short-term instruments. But when rates are rising, the relative attractiveness of short-term investments rises. If you can earn 7% on a CD, it may not be worth taking the extra risk of holding stocks; but at 2% interest rates, stocks seem much less intimidating — irresistible even.

- *Valuation.* This is a bit more complicated: it depends on the future value of money, one of the elementary concepts of financial analysis. What is the value of $10,000 in 10 years? It's the amount you'd have to set aside today, at current interest rates, to have that $10,000 in 10 years. If you were guaranteed to earn a 5% interest rate every year for the next 10, you'd hit $10,000 if you made a bank deposit of $6,139, or bought a bond of that value. That $6,139 would grow to $6,446 in a year (the original amount plus 5% interest, $6,768 in the second year...and so on, until year 10, when the $10,000 target would be hit. In financial jargon, the present value (PV) of $10,000 at 5% over 10 years is $6,139. But what would happen if interest rates were to rise to, say, 10%? You'd need to set aside a lot less, because each year's interest earnings would be twice as high — and since you'd be earning interest on interest, that effect is greatly magnified. At 10%, the PV of $10,000 in 10 years is $3,855, a lot less than the PV at 5%. This is illustrated graphically nearby.

How does this affect asset prices? The value of a stock, fundamentally speaking — leaving aside all influences of optimistic or pessimistic psychology — is a function of the profits that its issuer will earn over time, or the dividends it will pay to shareholders out of those prof-

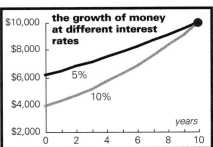

its.[2] In a normal world, those profits or dividends can be assumed to grow with the economy every year. Some years, of course, will be better than others, but over time, it's not unreasonable to assume that the joys of ownership will grow by 5–10% a year. Take, for example, a corporation that earns $10 in profits for every share of stock outstanding. Assume further that that amount will grow by 7.5% every year for the next 20. What is its stock worth? In theory, its price should be some function of the PV of that future stream of profits, discounted at prevailing interest rates. In this example, the stock that "earns" $10 today, growing 7.5% a year to $39.51 at the end of 20 years, will throw off $433.05 in profits over the 20-year period. At 5% interest rates, the PV of that stream is $240.39; at 10%, $147.43. So even if the future prospects of a corporation remain unchanged, a rise or fall in interest rates greatly changes the arithmetic used to value stocks. And if the change in rates changes one's estimates of future growth prospects — if, say, higher interest rates lead the prospective stockholder to mark down estimates of future profit growth, because of a less friendly economic environment — then these simple arithmetic changes are magnified.

- *Economic conditions.* Stock prices rise when investors anticipate an increase in profits and fall when they anticipate a decrease, and profits move with the business cycle, rising in expansions and falling in contractions. I'll have more to say about this in a bit, but on the matter of immediate relevance, higher rates often portend a slump and lower rates a recovery. Consequently, movements in interest rates color investors' estimation of the future course of profits.

With assets other than stocks, the economic environment counts less directly. In a recession, speculators assume that other players will be or at least feel less flush, making the prospects for unloading an asset — whether it be a Rothko or 1,000 shares of Microsoft — at a higher price less friendly. Words of caution are in order here too; no one knows for sure when a recession will hit, so speculators may bet that there will always be some "greater fool" to take a rare baseball card off their hands, or that things are different this time and higher rates won't bring about a recession.

These are some of the reasons why interest rates have such a profound impact on the prices of stocks and other speculative financial assets. Since many of the same techniques used to value stocks are applied to real-world assets as well — like an ongoing business that may be up for sale, or the willingness of a firm to undertake a new project or expand an existing one — rates are a powerful influence on real activity as well. And I haven't even mentioned the effects that changes in interest rates have on the finances of both debtors and creditors.

finance and the economy

Changes in interest rates do affect the finances of households and business: rising interest rates will divert funds away from real spending and towards debt service, while falling rates can deliver a windfall. One shouldn't make too much of this; in a strong expansion, rising employment, incomes, and profits will probably outweigh a modest increase in interest rates, and in a deep slump, low rates can be only a weak antidote to the general economic despair. To take two notorious historical examples, microscopic T-bill rates of 0.28% in 1934 were not enough to end the Depression, and it took a sustained bout of 15–20% short-term rates in 1980 and 1981 to shut down the U.S. economy under the Volcker repression. But in both cases, those were extraordinary times.

Instead, let's look at the behavior of the major markets in more normal times. Shown nearby are idealized — idealized by averaging, not by imagination — representations of the behavior of the stocks and interest rates around business cycle peaks and troughs. Interest rates fall sharply as a recession matures; because the average post-World War II recession has lasted about nine months, you can say that short-term rates begin drop-

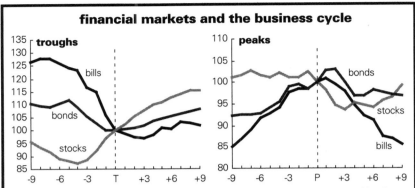

financial markets and the business cycle

These charts show the behavior of interest rates and stock prices around business cycle peaks and troughs, based on the average of nine U.S. business cycles between 1948 and 1995, with either the peak or trough month indexed to 100. "Bills" are three-month U.S. Treasury bills; "bonds" are long-term U.S. Treasury bonds (maturity greater than 10 years); and "stocks" are the Standard & Poor's 500 average, all as reported by the Federal Reserve.

ping only a few months into a slump, with long rates acting a bit more stickily. After a few months of declining rates — usually encouraged by the Federal Reserve — the stock market begins reponding to one of its favorite stimuli, lower rates. At business cycle peaks, the process is thrown into reverse gear, with interest rates steadily rising and the stock market flattening and finally sinking. Note that short-term rates move far more dramatically in both directions than long-term rates; the yield curve normally flattens or even goes negative as the economy approaches recession, then turns steeply positive as the slowdown ends. In fact, the yield curve "significantly outperforms other financial and macroeconomic indicators in predicting recessions two to six quarters ahead" (Estrella and Mishkin 1996) — and not only in the U.S., but in most of the rich industrial countries (Bernard and Gerlach 1996). It outdoes the stock market and composite leading indicators at this distance, with stocks and the composites having a forward vision of only about a single quarter.[3]

The bond market's fear of economic strength, and its love of weakness, used to be something of a Wall Street secret, at least until around 1993, when it became a more open secret. Though it often shocks people when they first hear about it, the reasoning isn't that hard to follow. Creditors hate inflation, since it erodes the value of their stock-in-trade, money itself. If the economy grows too fast and unemployment gets too low, then inflation will almost inevitably rise. The real value of their bonds will deteriorate with the pickup in prices, and the interest rate agreed to in the days when inflation was lower will seem much less satisfying when the consumer price index is heading northwards.

There are several reasons for this. At the highest level of abstraction, growth beyond the economy's presumed capacity limits will strain human and physical resources, resulting in an "overheating." If left unchecked, this will turn into a runaway boom, to be followed by a stunning collapse. More concretely, if markets get too tight, then shortages and bottlenecks will develop, resulting in price rises and order backlogs rather than healthy growth. What is true of markets for goods and services is also true for markets in human labor: if the pool of skilled workers runs dry, then wages will rise, as employers bid for the scarce resource and workers feel their power and turn more demanding. Consequently, when the economy looks too strong, Wall Street demands that the Fed tighten in order to slow the economy down to a crawl — and to push the unemployment rate significantly higher.

Many liberals and populists dismiss such reasoning as paranoid. Though the history of actual economies shows that there's no simple relationship between growth and inflation, financiers are near-unanimous in their belief that a strong economy means rising prices, and is something to be feared. And painful as it is to admit it, the financiers have a point — within the limitations of the conventional worldview. While there may be no neat mathematical trigger point when strength translates into inflation, tight markets — whether measured by the percentage of total factory capacity that's in use, or the percentage of the workforce unemployed by the (inadequate and misleading) official measure, or the ratio of actual GDP to its long-term trend growth rate — tend to lead to a higher inflation rate. The reverse is also true, which is why the long and deep recession of the early 1980s — much longer and deeper than policymakers had tolerated in the 1970s — "broke the back" of inflation, as the cliché runs. It also broke more than a few workers, but to Wall Street, that was mere collateral damage in a holy war for price stability.

Liberals and populists often search for potential allies among industrialists, reasoning that even if financial interests suffer in a boom, firms that trade in real, rather than fictitious, products would thrive when growth is strong. In general, industrialists are less than sympathetic to these arguments. Employers in any industry like slack in the labor market; it makes for a pliant workforce, one unlikely to make demands or resist speedups. If a sizeable portion of industry objected fundamentally to central bank policy — not only in the U.S., but in the rest of the rich world — then central banks wouldn't operate the way they do.[4] While rentiers might like a slightly higher unemployment rate than industrialists, the differences aren't big enough to inspire a big political fight.

Bond markets may hate economic strength, but what about stocks? Street-level wisdom — Main Street, not Wall Street — usually holds that a boom is good for stocks, but this isn't the case. Most of the gains in a bull market are made in the late recession–early recovery period. Stocks generally behave badly just as the real economy is at its strongest. Since the early 1950s, reported investment advisor James Stack in the August 19, 1994, issue of his *InvesTech* newsletter, annual stock returns have averaged +20.1% when capacity utilization was below 82%, and +6.0% when it was above; +16.9% when the Columbia University Center for International Business Cycle Research's leading index of inflation was below 0%, and +8.3% when it was above; and +17.7% when the annual change in spot raw materials prices was below 0%, and -0.7% when it was above. Other work by Stack, inspired by Martin Zweig and reported in the April 28, 1995, issue of *InvestTech,* showed that conventional thinking, which sees the best time to buy stocks as when corporate profits are soaring and the worst time when they are collapsing, is exactly wrong. Between 1938 and 1994, Stack reported, excitedly, "the most profitable period to be invested *(with almost a 20% annualized return)* was when the S&P 500's four-quarter earnings were *tumbling* at over a -25% annual rate!" Next best was during a profit decline of -10% to -25%, and so on, up to the worst period, when profits were growing at over a 20% annual rate, when returns were barely positive. Stocks thrive on a cool economy, and wither in a hot one.

That apparent contradiction may be resolved by timing: the stock market, following interest rates, tends to lead the real economy, as work by Ahmad A. Kader (1985) shows — though Kader aptly points out that the market's leading role should not be confused with causation, since both stocks and the real economy often respond similarly to the same stimuli (notably, lower interest rates are typically manna to both worlds). Kader reported that from 1963 to 1983, stock market changes were most highly correlated with GNP growth two quarters later.

But that correlation is far from perfect. The market gave false signals in 1966 and 1976, dropping sharply with no subsequent recession. Kader concludes that though the correlation is high, it is still "not as strong as one might expect," and should only be used "with caution" as a leading economic indicator. The 1987 market crash had no economic effects — but undoubtedly because of prompt, aggressive salvage operations launched by the world's central banks; without those, the collapse would probably have spread, 1929-style. The market must be seen as a somewhat unreliable narrator; it gets lost in its own stories as it tries to divine the near future. And about the distant future, it thinks hardly at all.

Stepping into the wider world beyond the U.S. and beyond the merely cyclical makes the picture even blurrier. John Mullin, an economist with the Federal Reserve Bank of New York, marshalled a sample of 13 countries, six of them industrialized and seven of them "developing" (Mullin 1993). Over the 15-year period from 1976 to 1991, Mullin's data show that long-term stock market performance can best be explained by dividend growth — but even this is not the tightest of relations, since only 31% of the variation in stock prices can be "explained" by variations in dividend growth.[5] On second glance, this statistical relation is even less satisfying than it may seem; the equation delivered up by the regression suggests that with an annual rate of 0% dividend growth, the average stock market among the Mullin 13 would nonetheless go up by 16.6% a year. Stock market investors are inveterate optimists. A less emotional explanation might be that in a world where the rich tend to get richer, and park a lot of their ever-expanding wealth in stocks, the market can rise despite a general economic torpor.

For the Mullin 13, the relationship between economic growth and stock market performance is as good as random. Whether you use real GDP figures in national currency, as reported in *International Financial Statistics,* or U.S. dollar GDP per capita figures, as reported in the World Bank's *World Tables,* the relationship between stock performance and economic growth is essentially patternless.[6]

Back to the U.S. economy, and more rigorous statistical work than either Stack's, Kader's, or mine. Nai-Fu Chen (1991), following up on some earlier research (Chen, Roll, and Ross 1986), finds that stock returns can be predicted by several indicators, notably the yield curve (the steeper the curve, the better stocks and the economy will do over the next several quarters); dividend yields (high relative to stock prices when the market is poised to do well, and low when the market is likely to be weak); and industrial production growth (which moves inversely to the market — that is, the market does well when the economy doesn't and vice versa).

These relations are mostly loose and noisy. It is interesting, though, that Chen's data shows that the real economy can also be thought of as predicting the stock market (with real weakness portending financial strength), turning the conventional notion of the stock market as the leader

and the real world as the follower on its head. When things move in opposite directions, it's admittedly hard to say which is the cause and which
is the effect.

allocation

A good deal of Wall Street time is devoted to asset allocation — figuring
out where to put money. Analysts are deployed, both on the buy (customer) and sell (broker) sides, to scrutinize the health of the national economies, industrial sectors, and classes of assets. Though lots of institutional
investors are restricted in what they can buy — managers of high-tech
mutual funds can't buy auto stocks, and insurance companies don't buy
penny stocks — even the most tightly specified have to figure out just
what to buy, sell, and hold. The less restricted have an array of choices to
make: financial assets vs. real commodities, domestic vs. foreign assets, if
foreign then Latin American vs. African, stocks vs. bonds, various kinds of
stocks (by industrial sector, by size of underlying company, by various
financial measures like price/earnings ratios) or bonds (government vs.
corporate, high-quality corporate vs. low-, long-term vs. short-), and so
on. Over the very long term stocks greatly outperform any other asset
class, but most people don't care about the long term; they want to be in
today's hot sector, the day after tomorrow be damned.

While stocks do outperform over the very long term, it's not really clear
why; their performance can't be explained by most conventional financial
models (Mehra and Prescott 1985; Siegel 1992). This is known as the *equity premium puzzle* in the trade. Many ingenious attempts have been
made to solve the puzzle — like "nonaddictive habit formation"
(Shrikhande 1996), whatever that means — but none have done so defini-
tively. When measured against long-term economic growth — and Siegel's
work covers the U.S. from 1802 through 1990, about as long-term as an
anlysis can get — stock returns seem too high and bond returns too low.
Of course, the underlying models may be nonsense, but if orthodox economics can't explain the stock market, one of the central institutions of
modern capitalism, what *can* the discipline explain?

But no one on Wall Street cares about such fundamental questions.
Instead, the game is to play the cycle and the microcycle. Wall Street apologists might point to attempts to ride emerging long-term trends — biotech,
the Internet — with both great risk and promise, but the Street is often
wrong about these things; they're far more passions of the moment than

they are serious, detached prognostications. Talk of structural transformations is often just part of the sales rhetoric, a way to hawk a fresh asset
class or defend a favored old one. Few people pay as much attention to
the business cycle as Wall Streeters — understandable, given the chart
patterns around cyclical turning points. But understanding the cycle isn't
enough; it's also tempting to catch deviations from the cycle — "growth
recesssions," "soft landings," and the like. Great effort goes into predicting important numbers; meaningless factoids like "in four of the last five
Aprils, employment came in under the consensus" circulate, assertions
that are often wrong, but are nonetheless believed and solemnly repeated.
But if enough people believe them, and the market moves in accordance
with belief, what does it matter? Truth is what makes you money.

a trading week

Let's take a look at a week's trading in the financial markets to see how
they play against each other and the real world. I chose, part by chance
and part by design, the first week of May 1994. It was an interesting week
because several significant economic reports were due, notably the report on employment for April. In this instance, Wall Street was actually
interested in an important thing, since the state of the labor markets is,
aside from being the most humanly important of all the products of the
federal data mills, the best contemporaneous indicator of the general state
of the economy.

What follows was written in "real time" — which explains, and I hope
excuses, the use of the historical present — to capture the sentiments, as
ephemeral as they are, that moved the markets, and to avoid retrospective
wisdom. Traders, analysts, and some academics frequently argue that the
markets often dance to their own beat, and newsy explanations of their
choreography are simply after-the-fact rationalizations. Undoubtedly there's
some truth to that, but for the moment this diary is offered in an agnostic
spirit. This is what happened, and how Wall Street represented itself to
itself and the outside world.[7]

the week

For some time now, analysts have been preoccupied with trying to divine
the strength and durability of the economic recovery that began formally
in March 1991, but which qualified as probably the weakest and most
tentative post-recession upswing in modern U.S. history.

Wall Street has come to love this sluggishness — weak enough to keep inflation at bay, but just strong enough to stifle political pressures for fiscal stimulus, and with job growth tepid enough to keep labor appropriately disciplined. Yet this spate of fair weather now seemed a pleasant but fading memory. The real economy began picking up steam in late 1993, to the alarm of the financial markets, and the monthly count of new jobs was averaging around 200,000. If that pace of employment growth continued, the unemployment rate of 6.5%, stubbornly high for the third year of an economic expansion, might decline. Though the job figures for January and February were depressed by unusually nasty winter weather, there was a sharp rebound in March. Should April also show a brisk pace, then all hell could break loose in the markets on Friday.

The language used to describe this economic strengthening would seem surreal to one untrained in the subtle wisdom of Wall Street. Phrases like "dark clouds" and "threat overhanging the market" have been thrown around for the last six months or so to describe a situation that might seem like good news to the outside world. Wall Street has become convinced that GDP growth over 2.5–3.0% and unemployment rates below 6.5% are now "unsustainably strong," and must be reined in by tighter Federal Reserve policies.

After nearly four years of falling interest rates, the Fed began reversing the trend in early 1994. As of this week, the central bank had tightened policy in three notches, starting on February 4, and was expected to continue to do so over the next several months. With that tightening came the first signs of serious troubles in the U.S. financial markets — and the world's — since Iraq's hostile takeover of Kuwait in 1990. Markets thrive on lower interest rates and swoon on higher ones. Bond prices have fallen about 20% from their 1993 peaks, and stock prices about 10%. Everyone's favorite "emerging market," Mexico, has also sold off sharply, becoming a "submerging market," and the whole "miracle" — or "bubble," if you prefer — seems on the verge of coming unstuck. The recent declines were fairly widespread; a Salomon Brothers report released early in the week showed that of all the world's major bond markets, only Japan's showed gains in price (and declines in yield) during April.

These early cracks were showing in financial markets that were among the most overvalued in history. Though the U.S. stock market, and most other world markets, experienced a massive crash in 1987, and a mini-crash in 1989, they hadn't experienced a sustained bear market like the one of the mid-1970s in 20 years. But despite those cracks, the general mood was one of confidence; while the markets might stumble, most players were convinced that the unpleasantness would be no more than transitory. As the brokerage house Wheat First said in a commentary reported on CNBC, the markets were experiencing no more than "an infrequent period of extraneous volatility."

Monday, May 2, 1994. At 10 AM, the National Association of Purchasing Management (NAPM) released its April survey of the executives who buy things for large corporations. Instead of falling slightly, it rose slightly. The NAPM index has become one of Wall Street's current faves, since it's supposed to be a good guide to the state of the manufacturing economy, and one that comes out more quickly than official government numbers. Whether this is actually the case has never been proved, but the markets believe it to be, so no one can ignore the event. Bond prices fell on the news that the economy was doing better than the consensus allowed.

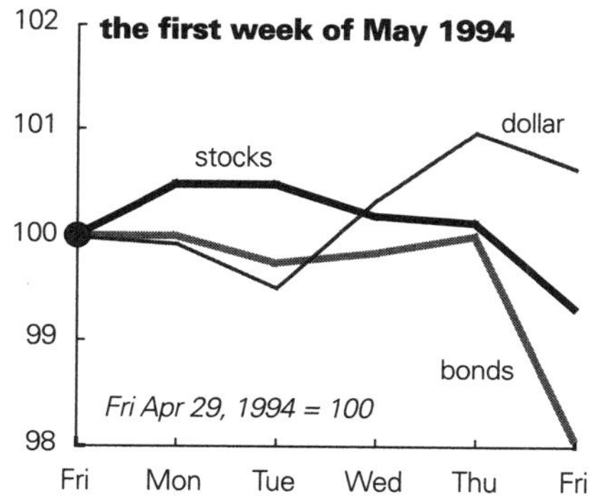

the first week of May 1994
102
101
100
99
98
dollar
stocks
bonds
Fri Apr 29, 1994 = 100
Fri
Mon
Tue
Wed
Thu
Fri

All values are at market closes. Stocks are the S&P 500; bonds, the near futures contract in U.S. Treasury bonds; and the dollar, the Fed's index of 10 currencies against the U.S. dollar. All are indexed so that the closing value on April 29, 1994, equals 100. Monday is May 2, 1994.

Stocks shrugged off the weak bond market, and rose, though not with an overpowering strength. The market was led higher by news that the Swiss drug company Roche would buy the California-based drugmaker Syntex for $5.3 billion, creating the world's fourth-largest drug company. Syntex, once a high-flying stock, had crashed recently because many of its most important patents had been expiring, and it had nothing in its R&D pipeline to match the old hits. Other drug stocks rose in sympathy with Syntex's; since health reform and cost-containment pressures had been pressing the consolidation of the industry, it didn't seem outlandish to bet on the possibility of other mergers. And even if they didn't happen, well, it was today's story. Who knows what tomorrow's will be?

Tuesday. At 8:30 AM, the Commerce Department reported that its index of leading economic indicators (LEI), so-called not because of their prominence but because of their tendency to lead changes in the real economy by 6 to 9 months, rose 0.7% in March, and the reading for February was revised from down 0.1% to unchanged.[8] Both were a hair above expectations. The message is that the economy survived the winter and is bouncing back strongly in the spring. Since this message is now quite familiar, and since the numbers came in more or less in line with expectations, and since most of the components of the index are known in advance of the formal announcement, the markets shrugged off the news, and some began speculating about next month's number.

The U.S. dollar was weak on the foreign exchange markets, continuing a multiweek slide that defies short-term economic logic. European interest rates have been tending lower, thanks to the grudging easing by the German Bundesbank, and U.S. rates tending higher, developments that should argue for a higher dollar (developments that should attract capital to the U.S., thereby pushing up the currency). The only immediate rationale was political — the Clinton administration would like to see a higher value for the yen to press Japan into making trade concessions. But that doesn't explain why the dollar should fall against European currencies. A longer-term explanation — that the U.S. is a debtor country whose export industries are addicted to the stimulus of a cheap currency — is attractive, but the timing is a bit hard to explain.

Though the Fed and other central banks came to the dollar's defense late last week, it could be that currency speculators found the interventions half-hearted, and they might be testing the authorities' resolve. If central banks defend a sickly currency with only half measures, then these defenses can be little more than a gift to traders.[9] In this example, the central banks bought dollars with marks and yen to prop up the U.S. unit's value. But from the traders' point of view, the central bankers were just buying a depreciating asset with appreciating ones without having any lasting effect on the market's trend. A casino operator who played by these rules would quickly be out of business.

Bond prices were depressed by the weak dollar, because, should intervention fail, the Fed will be forced to hike interest rates even more than they want to otherwise, and more than the markets had been expecting.

Stocks, despite the weakness in bonds, staggered indecisively, with broader indexes down modestly and the blue-chip Dow up, led higher by Eastman Kodak, which announced that it would spin off its Sterling drug division. Stock jockeys endorsed the move as evidence that Kodak would now be free to focus on its core businesses; only a few years ago, the acquisition of Sterling was cheered as a diversification away from its stodgy old film business, widely thought to be a technology in decline in these days of electronic imaging. In other merger news, the software firms Broderbund and Electronic Arts called off their marriage, saying that the market's negative judgment, expressed in declining share prices since the announcement, made the union look unwise. Thus do market gyrations affect the real world.

Wednesday. The New York morning brought news of heavy central bank intervention to prop up the sagging U.S. dollar, which reached seven-month lows in yesterday's trading. In a statement to the press, Treasury Secretary Lloyd Bentsen, who is in charge of the dollar — currency market intervention is the only instance where the Fed is legally required to defer to executive branch wishes — said that the administration "sees no advantage to an undervalued currency," and that the intervention was designed to counter "recent moves in exchange markets [that] have gone beyond what is justified by economic fundamentals." By day's end, the central banks of 17 countries bought $3–5 billion to prop up the currency's value — the most massive currency operations in a decade — with the Fed alone intervening 17 times. But in a market where trading averages around $1 trillion a day, it's unlikely that intervention alone will reverse the trend; should the greenback resume its slide after the smoke clears, then the Fed might be forced to raise interest rates if it really wants to defend the dollar's value. The U.S. bond market's weakness in the face of the intervention led to market gossip that a Fed tightening — specifically, an increase in the discount rate — was imminent.

Foreign exchange traders suspect that the Clinton adminstration would be happy to see the dollar fall some more, suspicions that were reinforced by Labor Secretary Robert Reich's remark that the dollar's swoon wasn't inflationary, because "currency valuations are relatively short-term phenomena." The Labor Department quickly issued a "clarification" of Reich's remark, saying that it was not intended as a comment on exchange rate policy. As the week progressed, adminstration officials refused to utter a word about the dollar, robotically saying that only Bentsen was authorized to make such statements. Even after the intervention, suspicions lingered that Clinton & Co. would be happy to see the dollar decline some more — just not too quickly, and as long as it didn't threaten the stability of U.S. financial markets.

At noon, the Fed released its "beige book" — or "tan book," depending on your preferences — a compilation of reports about economic conditions around the country issued every six weeks in advance of the policy-setting Federal Open Market Committee's (FOMC) meeting. (The name comes from the fact that the copy presented to FOMC members has a beige cover; market participants see mainly wire service accounts of the volume, and the version mailed to mere civilians has only a white paper cover and very low production values.) The report is based on work at the twelve regional Federal Reserve Banks, each of which has a formidable intelligence network in its district, based on interviews with executives, bankers, real estate developers, tax collectors, and other inhabitants of what financial players call the "real sector."

For years, beige books have been reporting tepid economic conditions, with regional or sectoral pockets of strength amidst a fairly tentative recovery. This issue, however, reported "solid" growth everywhere but California, and even the first signs of a pickup there. Several important sectors — autos, steel, and building materials — were said to be "near capacity." In Fedcode, this means that bottlenecks and price rises are probably not far behind, conditions which must be addressed through another tightening. Since the economy's growth was described as "solid," this must be taken as evidence that the Fed thinks the tightening can be done without much damage. That the at-capacity sectors are very interest-rate sensitive — the strength of the auto and housing markets correlates strongly with the expense or cheapness of auto and mortgage loans — no doubt reinforces Fed resolve to tighten, if not now, than at the May FOMC meeting.

In the stock market, drug and other health care stocks remained hot, thanks to the spillover from the Syntex and Sterling news, and to continued buzz that industry consolidation was inevitable.

Thursday. Markets were fairly quiet today, as the dust settled in the forex markets, and stock and bond players awaited tomorrow's employment report. At 8:30, the BLS reported a drop in the number of workers applying for unemployment insurance last week; this was taken as a sign that tomorrow's employment report would be on the strong side. For some reason, Wall Street takes this so-called initial claims series as a picture of the present employment picture; in reality, it's a better predictor of the near future, which is why it's one of the components of the official leading indicators index.

Entertainment was provided by Democrats on the housing subcommittee of the Senate Banking Committee, which offered a forum for homebuilders to complain about the Fed's growing stinginess. An industry lobbyist estimated that higher rates have already trimmed construction payrolls by 80,000 jobs, and another 100,000 were at risk were the rises not to be reversed. Senator Paul Sarbanes, the subcommitee chair, said he was "puzzled" and "deeply concerned" by the Fed's tightening, which is fairly hard to believe, since Sarbanes isn't stupid by Senatorial standards and the Fed's behavior is perfectly consistent with what it and Wall Street see as its mission — keeping the economy slack enough to prevent inflationary pressures from developing. Congressional posturing, some of it sincere, is little more than steam-venting, since no respectable legislator would ever seriously challenge the primacy of money capital; in fact, politicians are often happy to have the Fed take the heat for them.

Stocks, bonds, and other major asset markets closed nearly unchanged, as they often do ahead of important news; only the bravest make big bets 16 hours before an announcement that may prove their guesses very wrong. The only exception was the Dow Jones Utility Average, which sagged, suggesting underlying weakness in confidence and an upward bias to interest rates lurking behind the apparent calm.

Friday. According to a survey taken a week ago by MMS International, a research boutique, the market's average expectations are that the U.S. economy added 175,000 jobs in April, or more precisely, that the Bureau of Labor Statistics will report that as the estimate of the month's job growth. While the BLS's monthly survey of employers is "the largest monthly sampling operation in the field of social statistics," as the Bureau's boilerplate in every issue of *Employment and Earnings* reads, it is still only an estimate, and is subject to numerous revisions, as are most economic numbers. Still, what really matters for the markets is the number that prints on the news ticker an eyeblink after the report is released; serious analysts may scrutinize the release for clues to the truth behind the headlines, but if you're slinging paper around, what matters more than anything else is whether a number comes in meaningfully above or below the consensus.

For the working class, April turned out to be a better month than Wall Street imagined: employment grew by 267,000, and the previous two months' estimates were revised up fairly sharply. (Connoisseurs sometimes view revisions as a clue to an underlying trend; upward revisions suggest a strong underlying trend, and one that official numbers may be underestimating; downward revisions suggest the reverse. Not that there's any serious evidence this is the case, though.) Bond prices instantly fell over a full point, a moderately dramatic move, ignoring news elsewhere in the statistical release showing that average hourly earnings grew only three cents, to $11.06 — an annual rate of just over 3%, in line with inflation. For U.S. workers, who've experienced 20 years of declining real hourly wages, even this strong employment growth has been unable to deliver any wage improvement. To Wall Street eyes, however, that's good news: "wage inflation" is under control for now. There's nothing the bond ghouls hate more than real wage increases for anyone but themselves.

Despite that wage sluggishness, and the good behavior of the general price indexes, the consensus is that the Fed will tighten again before long. This supposition was confirmed by Fed governor Lawrence Lindsey, who said that monetary policy was "not quite in neutral." Neutral, in Fedspeak, is a euphemism for moderately tight; for months the central bank's line has been that its low interest rate policies, which had saved the financial system from the indiscretions of the 1980s, were excessively stimulative now that the financial system had healed, and that it was merely shifting policy back to "neutral" by pushing up rates.

Weekend. The lead headline in Sunday's *New York Times* declares "U.S. Shifts Stance In Effort To Slow Economic Growth," and its first sentence reads: "After a year and a half of seeking faster economic growth, the Clinton Administration has now reluctantly changed course, putting the stability of financial markets ahead of rapid economic expansion." Deeper into the story, the author Keith Bradsher notes that this shift "could be unpopular with liberal Democrats…[b]ut it is in keeping with Mr. Clinton's political goal of positioning himself as a Democrat who is not feared on Wall Street." Growth must be throttled back to no more than 2.5%, or maybe 3% tops — below levels that might make possible sharper reductions in unemployment, strengthen labor's bargaining position, and maybe even reverse, however temporarily, the 20-year decline in real wages.

This story may be a plant, an attempt to calm the markets through leaking; Bradsher is a reporter who has had no trouble serving as a frictionless conduit for administration or Fed propaganda. But it does fit with events; challenging the Wall Street demand for slower growth would be political dynamite — just the kind of fight a not-feared-on-Wall-Street Democrat would shy away from. The bond-market vigilantes have won.

Postscript. This book is being prepared for publication two-and-a-half years after that diary was written. Growth continued to be strong for the rest of

1994, consistently surprising Wall Street, which was touting an imminent slowdown, and the Fed tightened several more times. 1994 turned out to be the bond market's worst year in modern history, and perhaps ever; higher U.S. interest rates helped throw Mexico into crisis. For a moment, it looked like a bear market and maybe even a recession was in order, but the Fed, apparently fearing that it had overdone the tightening, backed off a bit, pushing down fed funds from their spring 1995 peak. Growth slowed considerably — whether because of the Fed's tightening, tight fiscal policy, or the economy's immanent torpor — to the 2.0–2.5% range, below the targets mentioned in Bradsher's *Times* article, but still above recession levels. Despite the slow growth, the labor market tightened over the next two years, with unemployment falling by a percentage point. The dollar continued its decline into the summer of 1995, stabilized, and then regained about half its losses by mid-1996. The bond market retraced a bit more than half its decline, and the stock market, already grandly overvalued, rose 46% over the next two years. Though presumably Fed tightening would be in order someday, 1995 and 1996 were wonderful years to own stocks.

notes

1. The allusion is not only to Saddam Hussein, but to Karl Marx (1981, p. 596): "[I]nterest-bearing capital always being the mother of every insane form, so that debts, for example, can appear as commodities in the mind of the banker...."
2. Dividends are generally more stable than profits, but depend ultimately on them, so for the purposes of this exercise, they are pretty well interchangeable. Academics prefer looking at dividends, and Wall Streeters, profits.
3. This weak predictive value of the stock market was confirmed in a study of banks that failed or weakened in the 1980s. Katerina Simons and Stephen Cross (1991) found that stock prices "fail[ed] to anticipate bank downgrades by examiners." Stock traders learned when everyone else did that a bank was in trouble. Despite this record, Wall Street folk wisdom attributes almost mystical fortune-telling power to financial markets; some partisans even argue that agricultural futures markets are better at forecasting the weather than meteorologists.
4. There is the additional fact that many nonfinancial corporations have heavy financial interests; GE, an ideal type of the large U.S.-based industrial enterprise, derived 24% of its 1994 profits from financial services (S&P Online).
5. That is, in a linear regression of stock market return on dividend growth, the adjusted r^2 is .31, with p=.0282. Firms tend to smooth dividend payouts over the economic cycle (that is, dividends are less volatile than profits or economic growth), so some of this correlation may be spurious. Thanks to Mullin for sharing the data behind his article.
6. That is, a linear regression relating both to real stock returns, p=.737 and p=.5271, respectively.
7. For the sake of economy, detailed references are omitted. This diary was compiled

using the following sources: *New York Times, Financial Times, Wall Street Journal, Washington Post,* Reuters, Associated Press, Dow Jones, MMS International, CNBC (the cable TV financial news channel), as well as phone chats with market observers and participants.

8. This index, along with the lagging and coincident indicators, was privatized in 1996; the Commerce Department turned over its production and publication to the business-funded Conference Board. Since the indexes are compiled from previously reported data, almost all of it from the government, the Department deemed it a low-priority item in the face of stiff budget cuts. Still, the indexes and their components are useful, and until late 1995 were published in the "yellow pages" of the Department's flagship economic journal, *Survey of Current Business*. These pages were a residue of another casualty of budget constraint, the *Business Conditions Digest,* snuffed in 1990; the *BCD*'s yellow pages were folded into the *Survey*. (The *BCD* was origianlly known as the *Business Cycle Digest,* but in the optimistic days of the late 1960s, when it was thought the business cycle had been conquered by adept Keynesian management, the *Cycle* was changed to *Conditions*.) They join in death the *Survey*'s "blue pages," another compendium of useful indicators, snuffed in 1994. No doubt, the Conference Board will do a fine job in assembling and distributing the indicators. But they apparently feel no sense of public duty in pricing their new service, *Business Cycle Indicators;* a year will go for $95 and up. A subscription to the *Survey of Current Business,* however, was $41 in 1996, and the journal also contains huge amounts of original information.

9. Though intervention is far from the suicidal thing it's thought to be for the central banks, as we saw in Chapter 1. In this case, the U.S. dollar continued to sink, with the Fed's dollar index losing about 5% of its value through the end of 1994, and about that much again in 1995. Still, the central bank made $706 million in profits on foreign exchange intervention in all of 1994.

4   Market models

So far, this has largely been a Wall Street vulgate. What has the dismal science done with finance on a more rigorous level?

In (neo)classical economics, money is held to be neutral — a mere lubricant to trade, but not a force in itself. Ironically, though, theories from that tradition were part of the intellectual foundation as well as the marketing garb for the financial experiments of the 1980s.

The place of finance — lumping together money and credit in disregard of all distinctions between them[1] — in economics is quite odd. As Claudio Borio (1995, p. 3), an economist with the Bank for International Settlements, put it:

> It seems fair to say that central bankers, accustomed to tracing the effects of their actions through the financial system, have probably laid more emphasis on credit than academics, who are more used to thinking in terms of simple paradigms where credit may not even appear explicitly. Similarly, credit has traditionally been more prominent in policy discussions in several continental European countries than in some Anglo-Saxon ones, especially in the United States, partly because of a less pervasive monetarist tradition....

Borio is right that central bankers, and economists working for central banks, are often much more interesting than academics on the subject of how finance and the concrete relate to each other. His "simple paradigms" are the neat mathematical models that economists build to represent social reality, or at least to convey some theory about social reality, paradigms that often ignore money and finance completely, or treat it as an afterthought. (The irony of "monetarism" being partly responsible for this strange indifference to money and credit is one I'll return to.) Those American economists who haven't ignored finance have built their own paradigms, simple and complex, that return the favor by often treating the "real" sector as an afterthought.

A web of financial theories, spun from the 1950s onward, became the orthodoxy of business schools and editorial boards in the 1970s onward. These theories held that the markets are efficient and rational, that they optimize the allocation of social capital, and that the capital structure of firms (how much debt and how much equity are on the balance sheet) hardly matters. Finance became capital's master control panel; liberated from the fetters of regulation, it could spontaneously drain capital from declining sectors and flood more promising ones with cash — without introducing any mischief of its own. To argue this, economists and professors of finance built many lovely models.[2]

the technique of economics

Charles Plosser (1984) listed some of the basic assumptions on which modern financial theory is based:

> Most of the fundamental contributions to financial economics, including portfolio theory, the Modigliani–Miller Theorem, efficient markets, and virtually all of the asset-pricing models, have been developed under the assumption of a *perfect market* by which I mean (1) no transaction costs, (2) complete and costless information, and (3) competition.

As Plosser noted, "theorists, especially of the Keynesian variety, are quick to assume the existence of arbitrary constraints and/or market failures," such as "institutional and/or wage–price rigidities, nonmarket clearing, exogenously determined long-term contracts, and the money illusion, to which you may add your favorites." But, argued Plosser, we need pure models of market function so we may better understand the departures from purity. In economics, reality is often treated not as the starting point of analysis, but as a set of unfortunate constraints on or exceptions to the theoretical utopia of perfect markets.

If you read neoclassical — or what used to be called bourgeois — economics, the market performs its magic for free. Prices float gently to their natural level, goods and capital are led magnetically to their most fruitful roles, and material production and human happiness are thereby maximized. But markets are expensive to create and maintain, and even if the "adjustments" promoted by free-flowing markets were efficient, there's no guarantee the efficiency gains exceed the costs of the market. The con-

sumer sphere, for example, is powered by a massive regime of psycho-
metricians and image merchants. And finance, as was shown in Chapter
2, is very expensive. Information gathering is hardly costless; both consumers and industrialists spend plenty of time and money researching the
stuff they buy. Nor are all participants equally informed; what small shareholder could undertake the research a huge investment fund can, or eaves-
drop on the secrets that leak through Chinese walls?

A nonacademic confronting the academic economics literature is confronted with a largely terrible thing. Much of it consists of building elaborate models, and empirical work consists in fitting data to the model.[3]
Financial theory is one of the most mathematized branches of economics.

Economics was once known as political economy; class, power, institutions, and even a vision of how the world should be mattered at least as
much as numbers. Politics began to disappear in the 19th century, and
mathematics came to dominate in the mid-20th. Economics, at least in the
English-speaking world, has become more and more a matter of econometrics. As Peter Kennedy (1987, p. 1) noted in his excellent primer on
the subject, "strange as it may seem," there is no generally accepted definition of econometrics. Kennedy said his guide to econometrics was devoted to "the development of statistical techniques appropriate to the
empirical problems characterizing the science of economics." Kennedy
used the word "science" without any quotation marks.

As one of the field's major adepts, Gerard Debreu (1991) noted in his
1990 presidential address to the American Economic Association (AEA),
in 1940, one only needed basic college math to follow the trade; in 1990,
"graduate training in mathematics is necessary." To Debreu, the field has
been "helped by greater abstraction," though details on the nature of this
claimed improvement are sparse in his text. But Debreu does concede
one problem with this numerical turn — that it has promoted an insularity
in the profession, so that mathematical sophistication itself, regardless of
its referent, is rewarded, and so that its very incompehensibility to a general audience is part of the thrill. "Since its messages cannot be deciphered
by economists who do not have the proper key, their evaluation is entrusted to those who have access to the code." And so economics has
walled itself off from the other social sciences, intoxicated by fantasies of
its own rigor.

Economic numbers are dirty statistics — not because of deviousness or
incompetence on the part of the data gatherers, but by the very nature of
the animal. National income accounting is carried out to the nearest hun-

dred million dollars, but the figures are only estimates, imperfectly collected and imperfectly organized. GDP estimates can never be as accurate as blood counts. Run two or three time series, estimates all, through your statistical software and you may either compound errors or fall prey to spurious correlations. Investment is hard enough to measure (is software capital?), and depreciation is even harder, but these estimates in turn form the basis of measuring growth, profitability, and productivity. Income and production figures are often extrapolated from employment estimates, so any link discovered between can be less than revealing. Econometricians use ever more sophisticated techniques to try to outwit the deficiencies in their data, but all fall prey to Goodheart's Law, "namely that all econometric models break down when used for policy" (Kennedy 1987, p. 6).

Though the machinery has gotten considerably more complicated over the years, econometricians essentially compare two or more variables with each other to find some pattern among them — or to find it missing, if they're trying to disprove something. An analyst might devise a model in which changes in money growth, interest rates, private investment, and government spending were tested separately and together for their capacity to anticipate changes in GDP growth. In such a model, GDP would be the dependent, and the others the independent, variables. Kennedy (1987, p. 69) offered this advice on how to choose the variables for your model:

> The first and most important ingredient in such a search is economic theory. If economic theory cannot defend the use of a variable as an explanatory variable, it should not be included in the set of potential independent variables. Such theorizing should take place *before* any empirical testing of the appropriateness of potential independent variables; this guards against the adoption of an independent variable just because it happens to "explain" a significant portion of the variation in the dependent variable in the particular sample at hand.

This takes hypothesis testing — hypotheses presumably being derived from the informed observation of reality — into a purely ideal realm. Observation and experience are distrusted, and theory instead is the lodestar. Given the bias of most theorists and theories, then, this style of economics can generally be trusted to produce results proving unfettered markets to be the finest principle of social organization.

There's one sterling example of that dependable bias, the minimum wage, almost universally regarded by economists to be a job-killer. Their reasoning is pure Econ 101 — raise the price of something (and a wage is the price of labor), and you depress demand for it. Therefore, boosting the minimum wage *has* to result in an employment decline for low-end workers. But in surveys of employers taken just before and after changes in the minimum wage, David Card and Alan Krueger (1995) showed that this just isn't true. They paused for a few pages in the middle of their book, *Myth and Measurement,* to review some reasons why the academic literature has almost unanimously found the minimum wage guilty as charged. They surmised that earlier studies showing that higher wages reduced employment were the result of "publication bias" among journal editors. They also surmised, very diplomatically, that economists have been aware of this bias, and played those notorious scholarly games, "specification searching and data mining" — bending the numbers to obtain the desired result. They also noted that some of the early studies were based on seriously flawed data, but since the results were desirable from both the political and professional points of view, they went undiscovered for several years.

In its forecasting, math-happy economics exposes its limits to the world, proving Wassily Leontief (1971) too kind in his remark that "in no other field of empirical inquiry has so massive and sophisticated a statistical machinery been used with such indifferent results." Two examples of self-criticism come to mind. In a review of the forecasting accuracy of the IMF's *World Economic Outlook* and that of the Organization for Economic Cooperation and Development, Fund staff economist M.J. Artis (1988) found them roughly comparable, with a decent record if you go no further than one year out, but likely to miss turning points. In other words, if next year is pretty much like this year, the forecast will be accurate.

Economists from the U.S. Bureau of Labor Statistics (Fullerton 1992, Saunders 1992, Rosenthal 1992) reviewed the Bureau's own employment projections and found similar failings. The 1973 forecast for 1990 greatly underestimated the continuing surge of women into the workforce. Projections of the female labor force participation rate (LFPR) in 1990 made in 1978, 1980, 1983, and 1985 were a lot closer to the mark, but by 1978, women's LFPR had already risen sharply enough to be noticeable. In its macroeconomic projections, the 1978 and 1981 GNP forecasts for 1990 were too optimistic — the 1978 forecast by a margin of 11.5%, a not inconsiderable $386 billion. Though the error got smaller as time went on, there was a persistent tendency to overestimate the growth of labor productivity. Forecasts for the composition of GNP were even worse than the aggregate numbers: the consumption share projected for 1990 in 1978 was too high; that predicted in 1981 was too low; 1983 and 1985 projections were much closer to the market — but all missed the fall in spending on nondurable goods and the rise in spending on medical and financial services. The BLS also missed deindustrialization and the overbuilding of commercial real estate — trends that unhappily shaped the U.S. macroeconomy of the early 1990s. In the words of the Bureau's own summary of its review, "the projections improve the nearer to the target year they are made...; the downside is that they often fail to forsee major structural shifts in the U.S. economy" (Saunders 1992, p. 15). In other words, forecasts are least accurate when they are most needed — when the world is about to change. They are best at predicting the present and the near future, assuming the status quo isn't overturned.

The point of this little review is not just to embarrass official wisdom, though certainly that is always fun, but to undermine confidence in the entire enterprise of conventional mathematized economics. And few subfields are as math-dense as finance. A lot of neat theories grew up in the 1950s, 1960s, and 1970s, only to be challenged by some neater theories in the 1980s and 1990s, but the entire project of clever, influential, and largely empty theorizing about capital markets and the invisible hand has yet to be severely questioned. Even the extensive empirical work by a number of financial economists, often based on thousands, even millions, of data points, fails to provide any significant enlightenment, because it asks such self-contained, even puerile, questions.[4]

As Leontief argued — in the presidential address to the AEA given 20 years before Debreu's — that self-contained quality is a significant reason for the failings of econometric analysis.

> The same well-known sets of figures are used again and again in all possible combinations to pit different theoretical models against each other in formal statistical combat. For obvious reasons a decision is reached in most cases not by a knock-out, but by a few points. The orderly and systematic nature of the entire procedure generates a feeling of comfortable self-sufficiency.[5]

Real progress, he continued, would require crossing disciplinary boundaries — towards engineering (or, he might have added, industrial organization) to understand the process of production, or anthropology and demographics (or psychology) to understand consumption. But in the hermetic world of conventional analysis, prices are explained with regard to other prices, output with regard to other outputs, and so on — a circular, almost onanistic process of analysis. The interesting stuff — OPEC's rise in the 1970s, for example, and its fall in the 1980s — is typically relegated to the realm of "exogenous shocks." Some theories of the business cycle explain recessions as purely exogenous phenomena — an intellectual convenience, since it allows the theorist to avoid the labor of explaining booms and busts, and an ideological one as well, since it exonerates market processes themselves as the source of instability.

Studying economics also seems to make you a nastier person. Psychological studies have shown that economics graduate students are more likely to "free ride" — shirk contributions to an experimental "public goods" account in the pursuit of higher private returns — than the general public. Economists also are less generous than other academics in charitable giving. Undergraduate economics majors are more likely to defect in the classic prisoner's dilemma game than are other majors.[6] And on other tests, students grow less honest — expressing less of a tendency, for example, to return found money — after studying economics, but not after studying a control subject like astronomy (Frank, Gilovich, and Regan 1993).

This is no surprise, really. Mainstream economics is built entirely on a notion of self-interested individuals, rational self-maximizers who can order their wants and spend accordingly. There's little room for sentiment, uncertainty, selflessness, and social institutions. Whether this is an accurate picture of the average human is open to question, but there's no question that capitalism as a system and economics as a discipline both reward people who conform to the model.[7]

After this overture, let's examine three of the most prominent theories that financial economists developed over the years — Tobin's q, the Modigliani–Miller theorem, and the efficient market hypothesis. The first is a theory of how finance influences the real world; the second, a vision of how finance is largely irrelevant to the real world; and the third, a deeply influential story about how markets are wondrous instruments of adjustment and allocation. Like all models, they tried to simplify the world in order to explain it. All are wrong.

A footnote: high finance theory is often associated with the political right (the University of Chicago being virtually synonymous with both). But Modigliani and especially Tobin are among the most "liberal" of the mainstream economists. Like American foreign policy, modeling markets is a bipartisan affair.

In fairness to Tobin, though, he is critical of the financial system. He famously mourned the proclivity of his Yale students to head towards Wall

Street, to waste human and financial resources on "financial activities remote from the production of goods and services...activities that generate
high private rewards disproportionate to their social productivity" (Tobin
1984). He stood out among his peers in a Twentieth Century Fund (1992,
p. 23) report on "market speculation and corporate governance" for recommending a securities transaction tax. So far right has the center moved
that this old-style Keynesian looks like a rebel.

Tobin's q

James Tobin and William Brainard followed up on a few sentences from
Keynes's *General Theory* to create a theory of how the financial markets
regulate investment. Keynes (1936/1964, p. 151) said:

> [The] daily revaluations of the Stock Exchange, though they are primarily
> made to facilitate transfers of old investments between one individual and
> another, inevitably assert a decisive influence on the rate of current invest-
> ment. For there is no sense in building up a new enterprise at a cost greater
> than that at which a similar existing asset can be purchased; whilst there is
> an inducement to spend on a new project what may seem an extravagant
> sum, if it can be floated off on the Stock Exchange at an immediate profit.

Being modern economists, Tobin and Brainard (1977) wanted to translate Keynes's prose into numbers, replacing his "common sense" with sci-
entific rigor. In their model, firms invest more if the market values them
highly, and hold back if they are assigned a lowly value. Keynes spoke
only of the stock market, but Tobin and Brainard added debt. Specifically,
they defined q as the market value of a firm's shares and long-term debt
divided by the value of its real capital. When q is above 1, firms should
invest, because the market will mark up their value by more than the investment. When it's below 1, firms will see their market value — mainly
their stock price, since debt prices fluctuate far less — rise by less than the
value of investment. Good managers should follow these signals.

Tobin, writing with and without Brainard, has claimed that changes in
q are an important way for a central bank to manipulate the real economy.
When interest rates are forced down by the Fed, stock and bond prices
usually rally; when tightness reins, security prices generally sink. Higher
markets will then induce real corporate investment. Similar reasoning has
been applied to households, with changes in the value of financial assets
stimulating or stifling the lust for houses, cars, and gadgets.

Most central bankers agree that changes in asset prices — not only stocks, but also bonds and real estate — have some influence on personal and business spending. But as the BIS economist J.T. Kneeshaw (1995, p. 3) conceded, the mechanisms are still "not well understood," despite a century of experience with modern central banking. The deregulation and financial innovation of the last 20 years have made things even murkier.

In the U.S., the Fed assumes that half the impact of monetary policy on the real economy occurs through effects on household balance sheets; increases or decreases in paper wealth, especially changes in stock prices, influence consumer spending. A policy-led decline in interest rates pushes up stock prices, and stockholding households spend more. Recently, however, that relationship seems to have broken down. Why this should be isn't clear; it could be that both the stock market and consumer spending were independently responding to lower interest rates, and that the conclusion that stocks were "causing" the spending changes are a classic example of confusing correlation with causation. Or it may be that the increasing institutionalization of the market has reduced the effect of stock prices on personal spending. Or it may have been that household balance sheets were in such terrible shape in the early 1990s that a bull market was of little help (Steindel 1992). But whatever the reason, this household application of q theory isn't quite as impressive as it once was.

But we've strayed a bit from Tobin's original formulation, which was about the financial influence on real corporate investment. Empirically speaking, the business relation broke down long before the household one did. But before we look at the record, a few words on how exactly to compute q. In their numerator, Tobin and Brainard used the market value of stocks plus the market value of long-term debt. While good estimates of the market value of equity are available for both individual firms and the entire corporate sector, almost on a minute-to-minute basis, the market value of debt can only be estimated, and rather roughly. Keynes's original observation mentioned only the stock market, and that market is the one that is constantly valuing and re-valuing corporate capital. The denominator is the value of the firm's capital stock at replacement cost, though other researchers have used net worth (assets minus liabilities) in its place. In practice, the details seem to make little difference, with different versions of q all moving pretty much in unison.[8] So for what follows, it hardly matters which version of q you use.

The data for Tobin and Brainard's 1977 paper covers 1960 to 1974, a period for which q seemed to explain investment pretty well. But as the

the q ratio and...

...capital expenditures as percent of GDP

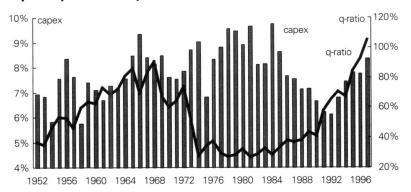

...three-year real price change in the S&P 500

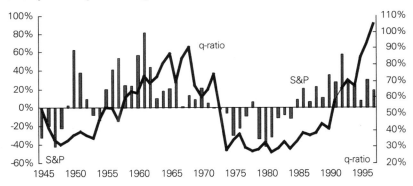

This version of the q ratio is the total market value of the stocks of non-financial corporations divided by the value of the tangible assets (fixed capital plus inventories), from the Federal Reserve's flow of funds accounts. Capital expenditures, also from the flow of funds accounts, include fixed investment plus inventory investment. The S&P 500 is the Standard and Poor's index of 500 stocks, deflated by the consumer price index. Charts cover different years because the quarterly figures on capital expenditures begin in 1952, while the balance sheet data begins in 1945. While it looks like investment is once again traveling along with the q-ratio, record q's have brought about only a cyclical expansion in investment, not record-smashing highs. Cash flow (facing page) still looks like the better explanation.

capital expenditures of nonfinancial firms and...

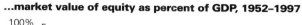

...market value of equity as percent of GDP, 1952–1997

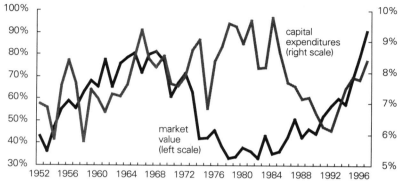

...internal funds, two-year change, 1954–1997

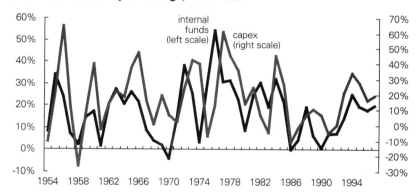

Internal funds consist of profits plus depreciation allowance, after taxes and dividends. Capital expenditures include fixed and inventory investment. Rates of change are nominal (uncorrected for inflation). All figures come from the flow of funds accounts, except for GDP, which is from the national income accounts. Note the tight correlation between internal funds and investment, and the loose, sometimes inverse, relation between market values and investment. These charts lend great visual support to the position that firms invest depending on their cash flow, and not stock market measures like q or share price changes. The alleged power of stock prices to explain investment may just be a result of their imperfect reflection of corporate cash flows.

chart on page 148 shows, things started going awry even before the paper was published. While q and investment seemed to move together for the first half of the chart, they part ways almost at the middle; q collapsed during the bearish stock markets of the 1970s, yet investment rose.[9] And as q rose with the bull market of the 1980s, investment failed to follow. In fact, since 1970, a high q has been associated with low investment, and a low q, with high investment — exactly the opposite of q theory.

The divergence of the 1970s is sometimes explained by the rise in oil prices, which rendered a lot of older capital equipment obsolete, forcing firms to invest in new energy-efficient technology. That points up a theoretical problem at the heart of q. The theory is about new investment, or investment at the margin, as economists say: a new investment will be undertaken only if it will be applauded by the stock market. But we can only know how the markets value existing assets; one can only guess at marginal q. If managers were investing because they had to, they were apparently doing so without the approval of the stock market. The marginal rationalization may work for a short period of time, but if the marginal q were substantially higher than average q, several years of sustained investment should have brought up the ratio's value, and it didn't. It wasn't until the bull market that began in the early 1980s that q began to take off.

Other analysts have argued that while q is a weak explanation of real investment, changes in stock prices do a better job (Barro 1990). But it may be that the stock market is simply a leading indicator of the business cycle, responding quickly to changes in interest rates and central bank policy, rather than being the independent cause of anything. Randall Morck, Andrei Shleifer, and Robert Vishny (1990) found that over the period 1960–1987, the stock market explained very little of the change in real investment once fundamentals like sales and profit growth were controlled for — relations that held for the stock market and economy taken as a whole, and for individual firms examined in detail.[10] Introducing external financing — new stock and debt issues — added a bit of explanatory power to their equations, but not much, with new debt doing a better job than equity. Morck & Co. theorize that this may be because firms borrow to sustain investment spending in lean profit years. Their results are confirmed by Blanchard et al. (1993); fundamentals like profits do a far better job of explaining changes in real investment than stock market developments.

While it does a terrible job explaining investment, q seems to predict the stock market and explain mergers. This isn't surprising; q is another way of doing what Wall Street analysts call the market-to-book ratio — the market value of a firm's stock compared with its net worth. Firms selling below their book value are thought to be bargains, while firms selling well over book — "well over" being an admittedly spongy concept — are overpriced. The second of the q charts shows that high q ratios have portended years of poor performance, and low q values, years of bubbliness. This confirms the notion of so-called "value investors" like Ben Graham and Warren Buffett that it pays to buy stocks when they're "cheap," and shun or sell them when they're not.

It's also almost certain that the takeover and restructuring boom of the 1980s was inspired by the low q of the 1970s. From the late 1970s through the mid-1980s, it made financial sense to borrow money, buy stock in undervalued firms, and squeeze them harder. This demand for stock, though, drove prices higher, and by the end of the 1980s, leveraged buyers were taking on overvalued assets, which is as good an explanation as any for why the boom collapsed.

Modigliani–Miller: almost nothing matters

Perhaps one of the loveliest financial models was one of the earliest, the Modigliani–Miller theorem, known as MM among connoisseurs. MM said that it didn't really matter how a firm financed itself, with debt or equity, it was all the same in the end. Before the theorists got hold of the matter, it was received wisdom that managers are happiest to rely on internal funds, since, unlike outside investors or lenders, your own money asks no embarrassing questions and makes no unpleasant demands. Next favorite is debt, though within reason. Loan payments are unforgiving in hard times, and borrowing should be done with care. Missing a single interest payment can trigger cross-default clauses in loan and bond contracts (an injury to one is an injury to all — solidarity is still in fashion among the creditor class), meaning the firm can be thrown into involuntary bankruptcy. But as long as you can earn a safely higher rate of return on new investments than you pay your creditors on new loans, borrowing can raise profits, and with it the stock price, the criterion of corporate performance. Unlike other countries, lenders usually have little say in the running of a healthy firm in the U.S.; you get outside money with minimal outside supervision.

Last on the list is selling new stock to public investors. While dividends are not a fixed payment — though markets do pummel a firm's stock when it skips a dividend — selling new stock means a new set of intrusive absentee owners. It also means that existing stockholders see their claims diminished ("diluted," in the jargon) by the new shareholders.

Along with this pecking-order theory was the supposition that there was an "ideal" level of debt, that ideal being measured by the financial structure that maximizes the stock market value of a public corporation. If a firm had an investment opportunity that offered profits greater than the interest it would pay on borrowed money, it would make sense to go into debt to make the investment. But there are only so many opportunities to earn profits well above the rate of interest; a firm can only expand existing operations so far before it saturates its market, and managers straying far from their usual business often screw up badly. Lenders are likely to get nervous when they see firms piling on debt, and will charge ever higher rates of interest until they shut off the credit flow. At some point, the profit rate on new investments will fall below the interest rate on new loans. At that point, new borrowing would depress profits, and with it the firm's stock price. So if you graphed the debt level on the vertical axis and the stock price on the horizontal, the resulting line would be an upside-down U — as debt increased, the stock price would rise until the ideal debt level had been reached, and then turn down again as the firm looked increasingly risky. At least that was the Old Wisdom.

A 1958 article by Franco Modgliani and Merton Miller rejected this orthodoxy, asserting, scandalously, that the "*market value of any firm is independent of its capital structure*" and "*the average cost of capital to any firm is completely independent of its capital structure*" (Modigliani and Miller 1958; italics in original).[11] Even for an unleveraged firm, debt is no cheaper than equity, and managers cannot increase the market value of their firm by moving towards some ideal point of leverage.

Their argument was highly abstract and formal, but boiled down to the idea that investors could undo the supposed gains from leverage by selling the stocks of firms that increase their indebtedness (since risk increases with leverage), thereby depressing the share price — or, conversely, investors can create their own leverage by buying bonds directly, preempting the strategies of corporate managers. As Modigliani and Miller put it, "the gains from being able to tap cheap, borrowed funds are more than offset for the stockholders by the market's discounting of the stock for the added leverage assumed." Or as Miller once put it in an interview, you can't make yourself richer by moving money from one pocket to the other.

Modigliani was actually initially skeptical about their theory, but Miller, "a passionate believer in the power of free markets to forge optimal and predictable outcomes, stood his ground. 'I *believed* it! I felt from the very beginning that this is right.'" (Bernstein 1992, p. 174). Marxists have often been accused of practicing religion rather than science, but Miller's remark shows that market partisans also thrive on busloads of faith.

Though MM argued more by equation than example, they did present some empirical evidence showing little relation between corporations' cost of capital and their financial structure. Their scatter diagrams plotting the cost of capital versus leverage ratios for 43 electric utilities and 42 oil companies showed no significant pattern.

MM concluded their paper with a list of their model's shortcomings, among them its static quality; its assumption of perfect competition, meaning instantaneous and rational price adjustment to new information; and ease of access to the capital markets. In reality, time frustrates the best plans; perfect competition exists nowhere, even in the capital markets where it comes closest to realization; and only giant corporations enjoy cheap, frictionless access to the financial markets. Model-builders proceed with the faith that such shortcomings (that is, essential features of actually existing capitalism) only complicate their work without rendering it pointless.

Modigliani and Miller, good bourgeois subjects, looked most closely at individual firms, not bothering to consider what happens when individual capitals are aggregated. The possibility that a debt contraction could choke an economy, just as debt expansion can stimulate it, or signal one in trouble, or both are all conveniently overlooked by the assumptions. So too the possibility that a highly indebted economy is more vulnerable to shock than a mildly indebted one, or that firms with high interest expenses do less R&D than those with low ones. Nor did Modigliani and Miller consider the different institutional arrangements and social patterns behind the words "debt" and "equity" — the dispersed patterns of U.S. financial markets, say, compared to the tighter worlds of Germany and Japan.

Five years later, Modigliani and Miller (1963) revised themselves, confessing that they had ignored the tax benefits of going into hock. Since U.S. corporations can deduct interest payments, but not stock dividends, from their taxable income, an increase in leverage is certain to reduce a firm's tax rate. MM counseled that this does not mean that corporations should borrow themselves silly; lenders get stricter as a firm's indebtedness rises, and managers would never want to run up all their credit lines and leave no reserve for bad times.

The MM thesis, even with its tax modifications, became so widely accepted in the academic literature that interest in the relation between finance and the real world faded to near-invisibility. In the words of a paper that would challenge this orthodoxy 30 years later, MM's triumph "dominated the investment literature until recently...largely because of [its] theoretical appeal" (Cantor 1990). It also made the life of model-building economists much easier; as Mark Gertler (1988) put it, "Apart from its formal elegance, the MM theorem was attractive because it provided researchers with a rigorous justification for abstracting from the complications induced by financial considerations." For one thing, you needed fewer variables in your equations if you did, and for another, it fit in nicely with the orthodox preference for individualism: you could focus only on the firm or the household as your unit of analysis, and ignore broader social institutions like the structure of financial markets (or even the state). Neoclassical theories of investment, for example, were developed without any regard to finance. Under the influence of Milton Friedman, economists paid attention only to money but not credit — that is, the medium of exchange used to grease immediate purchases and sales, but not the longer-term obligations used to finance investment and consumption.

But MM's influence went well beyond the academy, as leverage artists, their bankers, and their apologists chanted a debt-doesn't-matter mantra throughout the 1980s mania. Forgetting the message in the 1958 paper about how debt can't really make you better off, another MM, Michael Milken, used the theory to convince people that debt doesn't hurt either, and thanks to tax deductibility, it really can make you better off. Here's how *Business Week* (Farrell and Nathans 1989) characterized the popular influence of the MM theory, just after a wave of high-profile leveraged buyouts went bad in the summer of 1989:

> The rationale for such financings...dates back to seminal work in the late 1950s by two eminent economists, Merton H. Miller and Franco Modigliani. In essence, the economists reasoned that a company's earning power, not its financial makeup, is what determines its market value. So high leverage makes sense, since the tax code lets companies deduct the interest they pay.... Depite their bold logic — remember, debt was anathema back then — it was more than two decades before their ideas took hold, and that was largely through Mike Milken's canny nurturing of the market for less-than-investment-grade [i.e., junk] bonds.

Similar arguments, without the skepticism inspired by the sequence of leverage disasters in the summer of 1989, were common in the business press throughout the 1980s. For example, writing just before the Summer of Defaults, *Euromoney* (Thackray 1989) argued that the $200–400 billion in recent corporate restructurings were not enough — that work had only just begun, and that a quasi-Trotskyist doctrine of permanent restructuring was well advised by "the rise of modern corporate finance theory." Work that had originally said that capital structure didn't matter had spawned an industry, or at least an apology for that industry, based on the perpetual transformation of those structures.

how finance matters

Such observations drawn from mere journalism might be dismissed as hopelessly anecdotal by academics, but the notion that finance matters began bubbling up to prominence in the late 1970s. Ironically, one of the papers often cited by the finance revisionists, Gurley and Shaw (1955), was quickly eclipsed by the MM theorem, barely to resurface for more than 20 years. But Gurley and Shaw's arguments are still important. They claimed that one of the important differences between developed and undeveloped economies is the depth of the financial system; in a youthful economy, banks may play a primary role as a repository for savings and a source of credit, but in a more advanced economy, a far broader array of institutional forms connect savers and borrowers. So, in the simpler economy, the Friedmanite focus on money, defined as currency, checking accounts, and short-term savings deposits, is sensible, because it captures most of the financial aspects of exchange, but in a complex one, financial innovation leaves simpler forms of money way behind. According to Gurley and Shaw, what really mattered most in a complex economy was "financial capacity," a measure of borrowers' ability to absorb debt. Thus financial structure mattered a great deal to real economic activity; an economy populated by firms and households burdened by debt was one that was near a breaking point, but one populated by units light on debt had plenty of room to grow. A few economists continued this tradition during the 1960s and early 1970s, but the MM orthodoxy prevailed — and was a staple of the business school curriculum that shaped a generation of managers and financiers.

Economics is rarely given a chance to be tested by experimentation on real societies, but finance theory underwent an exhaustive real-world test during the 1980s and early 1990s. After that experience, it's hard to argue that financial structure doesn't matter. For example, a study by Richard Cantor (1990) of the behavior of 586 companies over the 17-year period from 1971 to 1986 showed that highly indebted firms showed greater volatility in investment and employment than those with low debt levels. That is, in good times, high-debt firms were likely to expand quickly, but in bad times, they tended to cut back just as quickly — a generalization that certainly fit the U.S. economy in the 1980s and early 1990s.

Cantor speculated that high leverage may encourage "a risk-averse attitude on the part of management," so that a drop in sales (of the sort one sees in a normal recession) "may lead firms to postpone investment and strenuously avoid inventory buildup, even if they are experiencing offsetting improvements in interest or other expenses." The need to remain current in servicing one's debts may take precedence over all else in the managerial mind.

Cantor was influenced by the work of Steven M. Fazzari, R. Glenn Hubbard, and Bruce C. Petersen (1988), who found rich links between financial structure and investment practices. Most investment models, Fazzari et al. argued, are based on a "representative firm" that responds to the cues of the securities markets. If the representative firm lacks the funds for an investment that passes orthodox financial muster, that should be no obstacle; external funds are a perfect substitute for internal funds. "[W]ith perfect capital markets, a firm's investment decisions are independent of its financial condition." After MM, classic notions that firms have a hierarchy of preferences in raising funds — internal funds, debt, and stock, in descending order of appeal — were out of fashion.

Much turns on how you define a representative firm. While large, established corporations may enjoy easy access to other people's money, small, youngish ones don't. To measure the importance of this distinction, Fazzari and his colleagues looked at 422 manufacturing firms in the Value Line database that were alive for the entire period from 1969 to 1984, sorting them into three groups depending on what portion of their profits they paid out in dividends.

Fazzari and colleagues reasoned that if financial constraints were unimportant, investment would be largely independent of a firm's cash flow: firms facing lean times could maintain their investment program simply by raising outside money. They used dividend payout ratios (percentage of profits paid out in dividends) as a proxy for financial constraint. Firms paying out less than 10% — 49 of the sample 422 firms — were placed in class 1; those paying more than 10% but less than 20%, class 2; and those paying more than 20%, class 3. As the table shows, sales growth and investment rates decline as you mount the class ladder, as does the correlation between cash flow (mainly profits plus depreciation allowances) and investment. Since cash flow is volatile, investment among the constrained firms is also more volatile than among unconstrained firms (as their respective standard deviation figures show).

At least three conclusions emerge. First, firms that could most profitably use external finance seem to have the least access to it, while those firms with the least promising investment prospects are suffused with sur-

financial constraints and investment			
	FIRM CLASSIFICATION		
	1	2	3
number of firms	49	39	334
retention ratio [%]	94	83	58
annual sales growth [%]	13.7	8.7	4.6
investment/capital ratio [%]			
average	26	18	12
standard deviation	17	9	6
cash flow/investment			
correlation	.92	.82	.20

For explanations of classes, see text. Source: Fazzari et al. 1988.

plus cash. Second, smaller, cash-constrained firms are extremely vulnerable to changes in the economic environment; changes in interest rates and sales growth will quickly translate into rapid changes in investment.[12] An anti-inflation regime of tight money will leave large, mature firms mostly unscathed, while squeezing those with the best prospects. And third, theorizing aside, financial structure does matter, and it matters a lot.

Examples drawn from recent experience are nothing compared to those drawn from the 1930s. Ben S. Bernanke (1983) argued that the Great Depression's length and severity were aggravated by the increased costs of credit intermediation, which is an economist's way of saying that the banking system stopped working as it's supposed to — efficiently matching savers and borrowers.

In severely abnormal times, Bernanke argued, this process of intermediation is disrupted, as savers shun the banking system and bankers hoard what little funds are entrusted to them. Though we saw some of these abnormal behaviors during the late 1980s and early 1990s, the recent events were nothing when compared with the 1930s. From 1929 to 1933, almost

10,000 banks failed; between failures and mergers, the number of banks was reduced by nearly half over those four years. At the same time, individual and business borrowers were going bust in unprecedented number. Of 22 major cities surveyed in 1934, default rates on residential properties ranged from a low of 21% in Richmond to 62% in Cleveland, with the majority clustering around 40%. A year earlier, 45% of all U.S. farmers were delinquent on mortgages. As of March 1934, 37 of the 310 cities with populations over 30,000 were in default, as were three states.

Among businesses, however, the picture was uneven. Aggregate corporate profits before taxes were negative in 1931 and 1932, the only years the business sector as a whole has been in the red since the national income accounts began in 1929. But these losses were borne mainly by small and mid-sized businesses; firms with assets over $50 million remained profitable throughout the period, while those with assets under $50,000 suffered losses equal to 33% of their capitalization in 1932 alone.[13]

In these circumstances, it's not hard to see why the process of credit intermediation froze nearly solid. Customers with spare cash — an increasingly rare species in the early 1930s — avoided depositing it in banks. Simultaneously, frightened bankers called in loans — those, of course, that weren't already in default — and refused to make new ones, preferring instead to stash their money in U.S. Treasury bills. Though big corporations remained largely unscathed, the shutdown of bank credit hurt small businesses, farmers, and households. No doubt the cascade of defaults, insolvencies, and bank failures fed on itself, since credit was denied even to borrowers who could have put it to good use.

Though the banking crisis came to an end in March 1933 with Roosevelt's bank holiday — the very month officially recognized as the trough of the 1929–33 contraction — small businesses still found it difficult to borrow money at least through 1935, and possibly 1938, according to a number of surveys cited by Bernanke. The home mortgage market was similarly frozen; what lending took place was the result of New Deal credit programs.

Frederic S. Mishkin (1978) argued, in a paper now seen as a milepost in the revival of interest in finance, that financial mechanisms at the household level were also important in propagating the Depression — not as causes, really, but as part of the transmission mechanism of the economic implosion. During the 1920s, almost certainly encouraged by the stock market boom, households had taken on enormous liabilities, which suddenly became quite "embarrassing," in the charming old formulation, when the prices of stocks and real estate began their collapse in late 1929. Worse, the general deflation — consumer prices fell by almost 25% between 1929 and 1933 — sharply increased the real debt burden. From 1929 to 1935, real household net worth fell almost 12% (according to Mishkin's estimates), a function of simultaneously declining asset values and rising liabilities. The situation improved in the mid-1930s, but the recession and stock market decline of 1937–38 brought a rerun, in less dramatic form, of the 1929–33 horrorshow. Mishkin speculated that these balance sheet pressures (and the psychological pressures they gave rise to) caused solvent consumers to defer major purchases. Financial crisis, in other words, translated into a decline in demand for housing and durable goods, purchases that typically require both borrowed funds and faith that there will be sufficient income in the future to service the loans.

In a classic paper, Irving Fisher (1933) argued that financial involvement made all the difference between routine downturns (not yet called recessions) and big-time collapses like 1873 and 1929. Typically, such a collapse followed upon a credit-powered boom, which left businesses excessively debt-burdened, unable to cope with an economic slowdown. The process, which he labeled a debt deflation, was fairly simple, and makes great intuitive sense, but it was an argument largely forgotten by mainstream economics in the years after World War II. A mild slowdown, caused perhaps by some shock to confidence, leaves debtors unable to meet their obligations out of current cash flows. To satisfy their creditors, they liquidate assets, which depresses the prices of real goods. The general deflation in prices makes their current production unprofitable, since cost structures were predicated on older, higher sales prices, at the same time it increases the real value of their debt burden. So firms cut back on production, employment falls and demand falls with it, profits turn into losses, the debt burdens further increase, net worths sink into negative territory — and so on into perdition. Fisher argued that there was nothing on the horizon to stop the process from continuing in 1933 — until Roosevelt took office and declared a bank holiday on March 4. This state intervention broke the destructive pattern; otherwise, claimed Fisher, the collapse would have taken out whole new realms of the economy, leading inevitably to the bankruptcy of the U.S. government.[14] The implication, then, is that such deflations are impossible today, because governments will intervene at a far earlier stage (Minsky 1982b).

The theoretical message of the Depression experience is that finance matters a great deal to both businesses and households, and is anything but neutral. The impact seems to come less from valuation (shown by the irrelevance of q to investment spending and the weak relations between asset prices and consumer spending) than from the bite of interest payments on current incomes and the availability of credit (that is, the ability to roll over old debts and get fresh loans). Finance is a powerful stimulus on the way up, and can be a powerful depressant on the way down.

These analyses of the financial mechanisms behind the Great Depression are illuminating for recent history as well, particularly the recession of the early 1990s, which confused no less an observer than Fed chair Alan Greenspan. "No models can explain the types of patterns we are having," Greenspan said on an October 1992 visit to Japan. "This is really a quite extraordinarily difficult type of environment" (Sterngold 1992). In his theorizing, Greenspan was a conventional economist schooled in the neutrality-of-money faith — but as a practical central banker, he knew that the Fed had to drive interest rates down or the economy would have sunk into depression. He did just that, and it didn't.

A telephone-book-sized compendium of studies by New York Fed economists (Federal Reserve Bank of New York 1994) confirms the thesis that the fevered boom of the 1980s was fueled by an exceptionally heavy use of credit — federal, business, and household — and that the 1989–92 slump (a broader period of sluggishness than the official recession of July 1990 to March 1991) was caused by a breakdown in the credit machinery. While it's difficult to specify precisely the components of that breakdown — how much could be ascribed to a loss of Gurley and Shaw's financial capacity, as debt-burdened borrowers found themselves unwilling or unable to borrow more; how much to the collapse of the S&Ls and the junk bond market, and the resulting shrinkage in the supply of new credit; and how much to the reluctance of surviving lenders to lend to risky clients — it's almost certain that all these elements contributed something to the slump. The loss of bank credit to small business seems, from the New York Fed's work, to be of crucial importance. Extrapolating from their work, it's also virtually certain that the initially weak recovery from the 1991 recession low was in large part a result of the crippling of the credit machinery. Even the extraordinary fiscal stringency of recent years can be seen in this light, as the U.S. government's own financial capacity was severely strained, and deficit reduction kept the brake on real economic activity from the 1990 budget deal onwards (the mirror image of the intensely stimulative Reagan deficits of the 1980s).[15]

When the early 1990s recession officially began in July 1990, it was not unreasonable to expect the first debt deflation in 60 years. Total debts of nonfinancial corporations (NFCs) were almost 15 times pretax profits, compared with under 11 times in 1929. Interest payments claimed 39% of pretax profits, compared with 14% in 1929.[16]

Here again, Bernanke and colleagues (Bernanke and Campbell 1988; Bernanke, Campbell, and Whited 1990 — BCW) have done illuminating work. BCW discovered that the increase in corporate debt averages was not across-the-board, but was instead concentrated among a small number of firms. But the debt leaders had driven themselves into a hideous bind. The median firm in the BCW sample of about 1,200 publicly traded firms devoted 22% of its cash flow to interest payments in 1988, up from 13% in 1969, but no increase from 1980's 22%. At the 90th percentile, however, firms devoted 186% of their cash flow to interest in 1988, up from 34% in 1969, and 56% in 1980. The calculation is impossible at the 95th percentile, since those firms lost money — a situation that had persisted since 1982; in 1969, these firms were profitable, and paid 44% of cash flow in interest. Though BCW did not say, it is safe to assume that firms at the 70th and 80th percentile were barely earning their interest payments.

Using financial data like profits, stock prices, and interest rates running through 1986, Bernanke and Campbell (1988) simulated recessions as severe as those of 1973–75 and 1980–82; they projected that 10% of U.S. corporations could face bankruptcy in a comparable downturn. Updating their work in 1990, incorporating data from the debt-mad years 1987 and 1988, BCW estimated that 20–25% would face insolvency in a deep recession. The authors emphasized that these were measures of financial stress, not literal predictions. Needless to say, if anything like 10% of U.S. firms had gone under, the crisis would almost certainly have cascaded into a severe depression.

We had a recession, but no depression. While thousands of firms — 60,746 in 1990, 87,266 in 1991, and some 90,000 in 1992 — went bust, each year's failures represented fewer than 1% of all U.S. businesses. Liabilities of firms that failed in 1991 totaled $108.8 billion, a lot of money, but less than 2% of business debts.

The charts help explain why things never got worse. They show the course of some important financial variables over three recessions, 1973–75, 1980–82, and 1990–92. To be sure, the timing of the three slumps isn't perfectly matched; their official lifespans are November 1973–March 1975, January 1980–July 1980 and again from July 1981–November 1982 (two back-to-back downdrafts that felt like one long one), and July 1990–March 1991 (though real recovery didn't begin until 1992). But all three show peaks in the first year, and two of them show troughs in the third, so this is close enough.

Scrutiny of the graphs shows: in the 1990–92 swoon, interest rates fell, but in the others they rose; profits were flat, unlike 1980–82, when they fell 40%; and stock prices rose 20%, instead of falling, as they did in the

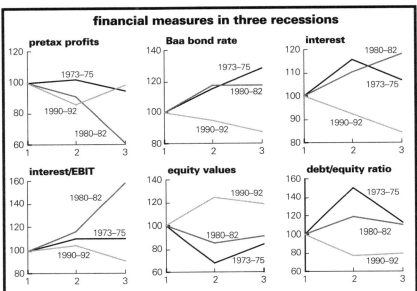

financial measures in three recessions

Charts show the course of several important financial measures affecting nonfinancial corporations during three recessionary periods, 1973–75, 1980–82, and 1990–92. For each indicator, the value of the first year (1973, 1980, 1990) is set to 100, and values for the second and third years of each period are expressed as an index number relative to the first. The absolute levels for each period vary; the point of this exercise is to examine changes, not absolutes. In order, charts show interest rate for Baa-rated corporate bonds (firms rated Baa lie between blue-chip and junk status); net interest paid by nonfinancial corporations (NFCs); pretax profits of NFCs; the ratio of those interest payments to earnings [profits] before interest and taxes (EBIT); equity [stock] values of NFCs; and the ratio of those equity values to the debts of NFCs. Assets and liabilities from the flow of funds accounts; interest and profits, from the NIPAs.

two prior recessions. Consequently, the average business was able to meet its interest bill, and the value of its equity stayed above the value of its debt, keeping it solvent. Had the 1990–91 recession been more like the earlier two, average debt/equity ratios would have been 100% (meaning that heavily indebted firms would have been under deep water) instead of 60%, and interest would have taken a bigger bite of profits — in the range of 42–55%, close to the levels of 1933–34 (though still below those of 1931 and 1932). Bond rates would have been 12–13%, not 9%. BCW haven't updated their work, but it's likely that firms at their 95th percentile went to the wall but those at the 85th got by, or something like that.

Both borrowers and lenders got debt-shy in the early 1990s. After retiring a net of $641 billion in stock between 1984 and 1990, mainly through leveraged buyouts, share repurchases, and takeovers (hostile and otherwise), U.S. nonfinancial corporations finally used the stock market for its alleged purpose from 1991 to 1993, raising a total of $67 billion total in net new equity. Rather than financing new investment, those stock issues mainly went to pay off old debts. Debt issuance slowed from $1.3 trillion from 1984 through 1990, an average of $185 billion a year, to $77 billion from 1991–93, or $26 billion a year, an 86% fall in the annual pace of debt creation. The low level of net borrowing for 1991–93 disguises a heavy gross issuance; firms were busily exchanging new, lower-interest-rate debt, for old, high-rate debt, and short-term debt for long (Remolona et al. 1992–93, pp. 15–19). By 1994, firms' balance sheets were significantly repaired, and the debt service burden was considerably lightened.[17]

It wasn't luck that gave us this turn of events, but government policy — the bank and S&L bailouts and sustained indulgence by the Fed. The welfare state may have been shredded for the poor, but not for big finance, which can screw up grandly and still count on an expensive rescue.

efficient markets

Does it matter to a larger public whether the stock market is "efficient" or not? Here's one view of why it does, from some conventional economists:

> To reject the Efficient Market Hypothesis for the whole stock market…implies broadly that production decisions based on stock prices will lead to inefficient capital allocations. More generally, if the application of rational expectations theory to the virtually "ideal" conditions provided by the stock market fails, then what confidence can economists have in its application to other areas of economics…? (Marsh and Merton 1986, quoted in Fortune 1991).

The answer to the confidence question, as we'll see, is not much.

the view from 1970

Perhaps the easiest way to consider the vast literature on market efficiency is to focus on two reviews of the state of the art written by Eugene Fama of the University of Chicago, the first in 1970, when the theory was in high flower, and the second in 1991, when it had taken serious hits. Fama opened his canonical 1970 review of the efficient market theory[18] as follows:

> The primary role of the capital market is allocation of ownership of the economy's capital stock. In general terms, the ideal is a market in which prices provide accurate signals for resource allocation: that is, a market in which firms can make production–investment decisions, and investors can choose among the securities that represent ownership of firms' activities under the assumption that security prices at any time "fully reflect" all available information. A market in which prices always "fully reflect" available information is called "efficient."[19]

The words in quotation marks carry heavy baggage. Fama acknowledged that "fully reflect" is a pretty mushy phrase, so vague as to be statistically untestable. Stock prices must always represent investors' best opinions of the prospects of their underlying firms; if this is the case, then the allocation of capital they symbolize must be optimal. To a purely financial theorist, efficient prices are ones that reflect all available information. To an economist, an efficient allocation is one that produces the maximum output for a given set of inputs — a rare case of economics echoing colloquial usage. Unfortunately the two meanings are easily confused, leading to much intellectual and political mischief.

Fama distinguished among three varieties of the EMH: the weak, semistrong, and strong forms. The weak form asserts that the past course of security prices says nothing about their future meanderings. The semistrong form asserts that security prices adjust almost instantaneously to significant news (profits announcements, dividend changes, etc.). And the strong form asserts that there is no such thing as a hidden cadre of "smart money" investors who enjoy privileged access to information that isn't reflected in public market prices.

EM theory turns in part on what the definition of the "right" price of a stock or other financial asset should be, since in an efficient world, the market price should be more or less identical to the right one. How, then, should a stock be priced?[20] The preferred model that grew up alongside the EMH holds that the key to pricing any asset is its riskiness. That has a common-sense appeal, but the professors of finance have a special view of risk. In the Sharpe–Lintner–Black model (SLB, named after William Sharpe, John Lintner, and Fisher Black), also known as the capital asset pricing model (CAPM, pronounced cap-em), risk is defined as the volatility of an asset's expected returns — its variance around a norm — expressed in comparison to some benchmark, usually a "riskless" investment like Treasury bills. Risk, then, is not the possibility of loss in the colloquial sense, but the likelihood of deviation from an expected return.

A security's characteristic risk is called its beta (or β, depending on your typographical preferences). The higher the beta, the higher the "expected" return. In the CAPM, a riskless investment like a bank deposit or a Treasury bill sets the baseline return; the further up the risk scale you move, the higher the expected return. Stocks in general are riskier than T-bills, so stocks in general should offer higher compensatory rewards; the stock of a high-tech firm is likelier to be far more volatile than a soapmakers's, so the high-tech stock should offer the better return. In the classic formula, then, the return on an individual stock equals the riskless interest rate plus a premium for its relative volaility.

Were these risk and return relationships graphed, they would yield an upward-sloping line, known as the security market line (SML), because the return demanded rises with risk. In an efficient market, asset prices should fall on the line. Should one fall above it — indicating a return higher than warranted by risk — or below it, then the market is inefficient.

Needless to say, the real world is far messier than the theory, and Fama himself would challenge it in a 1992 paper (discussed below). But over the long term, the relationship between risk and reward does more or less hold, even if not with mathematical perfection; while year-to-year returns may vary wildly, over decades, stocks are far more profitable than riskless investments — though why this is has not been convincingly explained.

Most theory speaks of *expected* returns, which are little more than guesses based on history. In the early days of EM theory, this was largely ignored, since expectations were assumed to be rational, but the devils hiding in this assumption will be revealed later on. Fama acknowledged, in his typically fair-minded way, that this notion of expected returns is a mathematical concept that should not be imbued "with any special importance." Instead, it is a methodological necessity, "the unavoidable price one must pay to give the theory of efficient markets empirical content." No one can see an expected return; one can only extrapolate from past experience. In more popular, more ideological versions of efficient market theory, expectations are imbued with an almost mystical importance: the collective wisdom of "the market" is treated as if it were omniscient.

Notions of market efficiency have their roots in a long-standing observation that it's damn hard to beat the market, and that prices seem to move in random ways. Louis Bachelier argued in a 1900 study (that was ignored for 60 years) that over the long term, speculators should consistently earn no extraordinary profits; market prices, in other words, are a "fair game." Another precursor of EM theory was Alfred Cowles, who showed in two studies (Cowles 1933; 1944) that a variety of forecasts by pundits and investment professionals yielded results that were at best no better than the overall market, and often quite worse.

In the more modern form, market efficiency partisans hold that the courses of prices constitute something like a "random walk," meaning that they cannot be predicted, since their day-to-day variations — oscillations around some fundamental value, as determined by expected future return — do not follow a pattern significantly different from what chance would specify. Almost no one has access to special information denied most market participants. The practical implication is that punters can't beat the market by moving in and out of the stock market as a whole or from one set of stocks to another in accordance with their evaluations of the market's prospects; the best thing they can do is buy a broad variety of stocks and hold them patiently through good times and bad.

As Fama noted, these notions of efficiency all assume: (1) there are no transaction costs in trading securities; (2) information is disseminated equally among all market participants; and (3) all participants hold similar interpretations of that information. Efficient prices are those formed by the frictionless buying and selling of equally endowed participants.

Of course, none of these conditions are true. Commissions and taxes make buying and selling relatively expensive; institutional investors employ a bevy of pricey analysts and subscribe to hundreds of equally pricey news and analytical services, while smaller fry depend on instinct or rumor; and interpretations diverge. As they say on Wall Street, people buy a stock because they think it's going to go up, but they usually buy it from someone who thinks it's likely to go down. If everyone held identical opinions, there would be no trading. These real-world conditions should not be fatal to the EM enterprise, Fama argued; reality is close enough to theory to justify the theoretical pursuit.

Even the occasional anomalies that were uncovered in the 1960s — mainly those showing serial correlations (that is, some persistence in price changes from one period to the next, or in plain English, trends) in stock prices over the very short term, meaning a single day or just several hours — were too small to be traded profitably; even professionals who trade at minuscule commissions could not take advantage of these trendlets. Other evidence cited by Fama showed that large price changes are likely to be followed by large price changes, though there was no pattern to the signs of the successor changes; a large upward change one day would probably be followed by a large change the next day, but the change on the second day was as likely to be down as up. Needless to say, such a discovery is not of much help to speculators.

Tests of the semi-strong form of the EMH during the 1960s consisted of observations of stock prices just before and after important announcements like stock splits, dividend changes, and the like. These provide statistical confirmation of the Wall Street axiom to buy the rumor and sell the news: most of the change in price around such announcements occurs before their public release, suggesting that a significant fraction of investors are remarkably prescient, remarkably skilled at analyzing public information, or remarkably well-informed.

Even in 1970, the strong form of the EMH was empirically the weakest of the three versions. One 1966 study cited by Fama showed that stock exchange specialists generally traded profitably over 80% of the time, a sharp blow to the idea that smart money investors do not exist. This fits with popular belief that being a specialist is virtually a license to print money (though specialists, of course, deny this). Other studies during the 1960s showed that corporate insiders — senior managers and boardmembers of publicly held firms — were also able to buy and sell with better-than-average timing. This observation concerns only legal insider trading, which must be reported to the SEC and which is not supposed to be based on access to specific juicy bits of information. It would be illegal for a CEO to sell her stock a week in advance of a nasty announcement that will take Wall Street by surprise — a disastrous loss, perhaps, or an unfavorable regulatory development. But should she sell on the basis of an informed judgment that the firm faced a rocky year or two, that would not only be entirely legal, but also quite well-advised.

Even if they do have access to privileged information on which they can profitably trade, specialists and corporate insiders are nonetheless a small class of investors. Studies of professional money managers, supposedly the most sophisticated investors outside denizens of boardrooms and the stock exchange floor, show them consistently unable to beat the market. Of course, as professionals have come to dominate trading, replacing individual investors, pros have *become* the market, and cannot reasonably be expected to beat themselves. Still, if most professional money managers can do no better than market averages, why do they deserve those high salaries?

In sum, the weak form of market efficiency looked quite firmly established in 1970, despite a few minor anomalies. So too the semi-strong form. Even the strong form, which Fama said should be "best viewed as a benchmark against which deviations from market efficiency...can be judged," looked respectable, despite the specialist and insider exceptions.

It is quite a leap to say that because it is unpredictable, the stock market is efficient, and another broad leap to argue that such efficiency means that the stock market's influence over the allocation of real capital is efficient in the economic sense. But in 1970, Fama's analysis seemed to be irrefutable on its own terms.

the view from 1991

Twenty-one years later, Fama (1991) returned to survey the state of efficient market theory, and found it under challenge from several quarters.

Fama began by defining efficiency as the "simple statement that security prices fully reflect all available information." What is that information? The sum of investor expectations about the future. But are these stable or rational, and where do they come from anyway? In testing for market efficiency, Fama pointed out, "we can only test whether information is properly reflected in prices in the context of a pricing model that defines the meaning of 'properly.'" Tests of the EMH, then, are simultaneously tests of how accurately investors divine the future and how accurately stock prices represent that consensus — meaning that the EMH had a "joint hypothesis" problem, in the jargon of the trade.

If prices reflect bad information efficiently, is that a good thing? Investors overvalued U.S. corporations in the early 1970s, and undervalued them later in the decade; prices correctly reflected this consensus, but in both cases the consensus was "wrong" in retrospect. Fama brought up the point only to drop it, but it does seem to have rather serious implications for the wisdom and reliability of stock market pricing and investment decisions influenced by its signals.

Terminology, Fama noted, had changed over the two decades since his last review. The weak, semi-strong, and strong forms of the EMH had earned more descriptive names: tests for return predictability, event studies, and tests for private information. Following Fama, let's look at the state of the art in the early 1990s.

Return predictability. Work in the 1980s, using different — a skeptic on econometrics hesitates to use the phrase "more powerful" — statistical techniques, repeatedly found more patterns in prices than classic random walk theory allowed, especially if you examine portfolios consisting of a number of stocks. In other words, individual shares may follow more-or-less random patterns, but the market as a whole moves in trends (or, in statistical language, returns are autocorrelated), especially over the long term. "[R]ecent research," Fama concluded, "is able to show confidently that daily and weekly returns are predictable from past returns."

Even more challenging to EMH orthodoxy is research that goes beyond price history. A number of studies during the 1970s and 1980s showed that stocks with low price/earnings ratios and/or high dividend yields — "cheap" stocks, in slang — would likely outperform stocks that were expensive by these measures, a sophisticated confirmation of old Wall Street wisdom. Other research, including Fama's own (Fama and French 1989), showed that stocks are a good buy when the long-term interest rates are well above short-term ones, and when the gap between interest rates on risky and safe corporate bonds is wide, and a bad buy when the opposite conditions prevail, though the relationship is far from perfect. The first set of circumstances is usually associated with recession and/or financial anxiety, and the second set with good times — another way of saying that stocks anticipate turns in the business cycle, though not without giving quite a few false signals. Again, this looks like a fancy confirmation of Street wisdom.

Fama also reported some bad news for the Sharpe–Lintner–Black/CAPM pricing model. The early 1970s, Fama recalled, were a euphoric time for financial theorists; the SLB theory for a moment seemed to have "solved" the problem of pricing securities. "We should have known better," Fama wrote. "The SLB model is just a model and so surely false." For a model building profession, this is an odd discovery, but Fama went on to defend SLB and model-building in general by saying it was useful to discover the ways in which it is proved false, which might be true if the model builders had approached the world with humility rather than euphoria.

Though it is still reverently taught to business school students, there are simply too many anomalies to sustain the pure SLB beta model, most importantly the size effect. "Small" stocks, as measured by market capitalization (price times the number of shares outstanding) show excessively high returns relative to their betas, and "big" stocks, excessively low returns. Also, the relation between beta and return (with more volatile stocks showing higher returns), which was first posited in the 1960s and 1970s, breaks down when applied to more recent price history. Either the first "discovery" was anomalous, or it ceased to work as the investing public became aware of the technique.

A 1992 paper by Fama and Kenneth French that reported very damaging evidence for the beta model — that firm size and the ratio of market value to book value are better predictors of return than relative volatility — excited the ideologists at *The Economist* (1992c) to a defense. "Should analysts stop using the CAPM? Probably not," the magazine declared in its best *ex cathedra* tone. And why not? Because while Fama and French "have produced intriguing results, they lack a theory to explain them." That is true enough; Fama and French were uncertain whether they'd uncovered something rational or not rational. (It's quite amazing to see the 1970 partisan of market efficiency even entertain the notion of irrationality 22 years later.) But as *The Economist* put it, the choice for practitioners and theorists is whether to believe evidence without theory, or "stick with a theory that, despite the data, is built on impeccable logic." The magazine's preference, clearly enough, was for theory over evidence.

A small flood of studies appeared in the years after the Fama–French paper, subjecting the CAPM to fresh scrutiny, some defending it against the heretics, and others supporting the heresy (for example, Kothari et al. 1995, and Cohen and Polk 1996). A review of recent work (Jagannathan and McGrattan 1995) makes it clear that evaluations of the model are highly dependent on the nature of the evidence used.[21] Different time periods, or different sets of stocks, or different measures of return (monthly or annual) produce wildly different results. The message seems to be that, yes, the more volatile an asset, the higher its likely return over the very long term, but the relation escapes precise quanitification of the sort most conventional economists crave. Since CAPM is not only used to analyze financial markets, but is also used by corporate managers to decide on real investments, the model's fate is of more than technical interest.

Though CAPM still has its adherents, one of the more influential alternative approaches to stock valuation is arbitrage pricing theory (APT) (Ross 1976). In APT, the price of an asset depends on the prices of a number of related assets, though the number of other assets and their nature isn't specified by the theory. An APT model of the stock market (Chen, Roll, and Ross 1986), for example, found that the best predictors of future return are the growth rate of industrial production (with future returns high when industrial production has been weak, and vice versa) and the spread between interest rates on low-grade corporate bonds and long-term government bonds (with future returns high when the spread is wide). This looks remarkably like Wall Street common sense; common sense can often be stupid, but not always.

The problem, though, with so-called multifactor models like APT is that analysts can play with the data, adding and subtracting influences, until they find a combination that works. This danger is always present in mathematical economics; Fama's review is full of warnings about the dangers of data farming and model dredging. In economics, one rarely knows for sure, despite all the pretense of science. And, as always, one uses historical relations to predict future prices — which is admittedly all one can use, but it's still a long way from physics.

Event studies. These studies are relatively easy to do, and can offer more definitive results than most. Stock prices will either react or not react to an announcement; the reaction will either persist or decay. So it's no wonder that the finance literature is filled with event studies.

There's little doubt now that stocks do respond quickly to new information, with occasional exceptions. Two interesting recent discoveries, however, dethrone some classic theoretical notions. The first is that unexpected changes in dividends tend to push stock prices in the same direction — up when the dividend is boosted, down when it's cut. This violates MM theory, which holds that dividend policy should be irrelevant to the stock price. There may be several reasons for this. One possibility is that investors are more emotional than theoreticians allow for, and their reaction to dividend changes is a triumph of gut reaction over rational analysis. Another possibility is that corporate managers use dividends to signal major changes in the long-term prospects for the firm (or that investors perceive them as such). A dividend cut is a way of saying the corporation is in deep trouble; a boost, especially a large, unexpected one, a way of saying the future is brighter than anyone had realized.

The second interesting discovery is that a new issue of stock tends to be bad news for future prices. The classic assumption was that a stock issue is a sign of a firm's confidence in its future; additionally, the infusion of fresh capital should be good nourishment for future profits. But this seems not to be the case. The most reasonable explanation is that managers issue stock when they think it's overvalued — another sharp blow at the notion of efficiency. More on both these topics a little later.

(Out)performance. Here, 20 years of studies generally confirm classic EM theory: it's devilishly difficult to beat the market. The exceptions discussed

above, stock exchange specialists and corporate insiders, still prevail. Even though information on (legal) insider trading is fairly widely available, the market apparently does not make adequate use of it — though it's hard to imagine this anomaly persisting forever. Professional security analysts and money managers are largely unable to do better than the market, with one notable exception, the stock rankings published by the *Value Line Investment Survey*.

Unfortunately, even the Value Line information, while theoretically interesting, is of little practical importance. Stock prices adjust speedily to Value Line upgradings, meaning that all but the nimblest or best-connected investors are denied the opportunity to profit from the information; by the time most subscribers get the news, it's already in the price.

Some readers may have noticed a contradiction here. On the one hand, Fama conceded that returns are "predictable," at least in the statistical sense, but on the other, it's still near-impossible to beat the market. This apparent contradiction is easily resolved. The kinds of predictability statisticians talk about are very difficult to translate into practical trading advice. Things that seem "predictable" in retrospect aren't easy to see in real time. Mortal traders, who have to worry about commissions, taxes, and other worldly complications, can't easily translate an anomaly announced in the *Journal of Finance* into a profitable trading system. And as soon as news of the anomaly circulates, a traders would pounce on the opportunity; once discovered, anomalies can be self-unfulfilling prophecies.

An exception, though, are longer-term anomalies, particularly those around valuation. Buying undervalued stocks, and avoiding overvalued ones, might be a way to beat the market over the long term. Here, the difficulty isn't so much technical as psychological: it means going against the consensus, and suffering the scorn of your colleagues. It also means measuring performance over years, even decades, rather than months and quarters — impossible for professional portfolio managers, who are under constant short-term review, and difficult even for amateurs, who might be embarrassed to describe their strange preferences at cocktail parties.

disinformation, noise, fads, and bubbles

Efficient market theory depends on the universal, costless dissemination of accurate information about economic and corporate prospects. The uncritical stance of most Wall Street analysts and much of the financial press reviewed in Chapter 2 makes this a bit hard to take just on the grounds of daily evidence. But even if analysts were universally honest and wise, there would still be serious communications problems between managers and stockholders. For example, according to Jeremy Stein (1989), something like a prisoners' dilemma prevails in relations between managers and the stock market. Even if participants are aware of an upward bias to earnings estimates, and even if they correct for it, managers still have an incentive to try to fool the market. If you tell the truth, your accurate estimates will be marked down by a skeptical market. So, it's entirely rational for managers to boost profits in the short term, either through accounting gimmickry or by making only investments with quick paybacks.

If the markets see high costs as bad, and low costs as good, then firms may shun expensive investments because they will be taken as signs of managerial incompetence. Throughout the late 1980s and early 1990s, the stock market rewarded firms announcing write-offs and mass firings — a bulimic strategy of management — since the cost-cutting was seen as contributing rather quickly to profits. Firms and economies can't get richer by starving themselves, but stock market investors can get richer when the companies they own go hungry — at least in the short term. As for the long term, well, that's someone else's problem the week after next.

Managers facing a market that is famous for its preference for quick profits today rather than patient long-term growth have little choice but to do its bidding. Otherwise, their stock will be marked down, and the firm will be ripe for takeover. Stein cited surveys showing that "U.S. executives ranked share price increases as their second most important objectives out of nine choices, ahead of such alternatives as improved product portfolio,[22] market share, or company image. In contrast, Japanese executives ranked share price increases as the least important of the nine objectives." This is no mere cultural difference, but a reflection of the contrasting systems under which the two nations' managers operate.

Stein's analysis is related to a branch of economics that sprouted during the 1980s from seeds planted in the 1970s — the study of information asymmetry. Since a party to a transaction can never know if the other is telling the truth, each has to be at least a little suspicious of the other. But protective actions resulting from such suspicions may leave both parties worse off than they would have been had both parties been honest and trusting. What, for example, does a low price mean? It may mean a real bargain — but it may also be a hint of damaged goods. (To take an extreme example, an offer of half-price sushi might drive away more customers than it attracts.) A price can convey more than is visible on first glance. This greatly complicates the mainstream notion of prices as a signaling mechanism for balancing supply and demand; there may be lots of noise mixed in with the signals.

As they say on Wall Street, when something looks too good to be true, it probably is. Or as one of the major figures in the development of information asymmetry theory, Joseph Stiglitz, put it, "If it's such a good idea, why are you telling me, instead of investing your own money?" (quoted in Kane 1993). This is a remarkably blunt statement for Stiglitz, whose normal mode is the symbols of pure mathematized theory.

Interest in "information asymmetry" is usually traced to George Akerlof's 1969 paper on the "lemons" problem — not the fruit, but bum autos. Would-be buyers of used cars have no way of knowing whether the vehicle they're contemplating is any good. So the price must reflect the *possibility* that it is a lemon, meaning that the sellers of good cars get an unfairly low price — while the sellers of bad ones still get an unfairly high one. If the lemon discount is deep enough, it may keep the sellers of good cars out of the market, because they can't get the price they think they deserve. But since textbook markets aren't supposed to work this way, this has to be counted as a serious flaw, because so many participants, actual or potential, are dissatisfied with the relation between price and product.

Stilgitz and Andrew Weiss (1981) applied this principle to the credit markets, arguing, almost entirely in math, that at a given interest rate, lenders will earn lower returns by lending to bad borrowers (because of defaults) than to good borrowers. If lenders try to jack up the interest rate to compensate for this risk, they may chase away good borrowers, who are unwilling to pay a higher rate, while perversely not chasing away incompetent, criminal, or malignantly optimistic borrowers. Such a market doesn't clear; there will always be unsatisfied players at a given rate of interest. Stiglitz and his collaborators (Greenwald and Stiglitz 1984; 1987; Stiglitz 1988) argue that informational problems explain credit rationing, which in turn can explain both the business cycle and unemployment.[23]

Though economists treat the lemons problem as if it were a recent discovery, it's really as old as the classics. Adam Smith (1976, Book II, Chapter 4), in recommending a legal ceiling on the rate of interest, observed:

> If the legal rate of interest in Great Britain, for example, was fixed so high
> as eight or ten percent, the greater part of the money which was to be lent
> would be lent to prodigals and projectors, who alone would be willing to
> give this high interest. Sober people, who will give for the use of money no

more than a part of what they are likely to make by the use of it, would not venture into the competition. A great part of the capital of the country would thus be kept out of the hands which were most likely to make a profitable and advantageous use of it, and thrown into those which were most likely to waste and destroy it.[24]

This provides an interesting gloss on the junk bond era. Or, as David Ricardo (1911/1987, Chapter 21), put it:

> To the question, "who would lend money to farmers, manufacturers, and merchants, at 5 per cent. per annum, when another borrower, having little credit would give 7 or 8?" I reply, that every prudent or reasonable man would. Because the rate of interest is 7 or 8 per cent. there where the lender runs extraordinary risk is this any reason that it should be equally high in those places where they are secured from such risks?

Michael Perelman, who teaches economics at California State University–Chico, said that when he told Stiglitz about these classic prefigurations of his argument, Stiglitz, regarded as one of the prime theorists of his field, reacted with surprise. To become a famous economist, you need not be familiar with the founding documents of your discipline.[25] Besides, Smith and Ricardo used words, words that anyone can understand. It's much more serious to use math, which only a handful of people can decode; even professional economists report Stiglitz' work hard going.

The stock market is also afflicted with informational problems (Myers and Majluf 1984; Greenwald, Stiglitz, and Weiss 1984). Outside investors must decide whether a firm selling fresh equity is legitimately trying to raise money for a worthy pursuit, or just trying to leave outsiders holding the bag. Assuming managers know their firm's prospects better than outsiders, a firm with "overvalued" stock is more likely to issue shares than one with a low value relative to what managers think of its possibilities, a very perverse set of incentives. If the markets realize this, then it will be very difficult to get any deals done. At the extreme, say Greenwald, Stiglitz, and Weiss, "the 'effective' cost of issuing equity may be so high as to be prohibitive, because any firm that issues equity obtains a 'bad' label." Obviously, firms *do* issue equity from time to time, but rarely, and mainly in euphoric bull markets, when suspicions are dulled (though such psychology is uncaptured in the models of Stiglitz & Co.).

In fact, euphoric self-deception seems to be what makes new equity offerings possible. Several recent studies show convincingly that new stock offerings — whether by firms issuing stock for the first time (initial public offerings — IPOs) or by already-public firms issuing fresh helpings of paper (seasoned equity offerings — SEOs) — greatly underperform the general market for years (Loughran and Ritter 1995; Cheng 1996).[26]

One prominent exception to poor IPO performance is that personally enjoyed by favored clients of the brokerages who underwrite the offerings. During a hot IPO market, prices typically rise in the early hours and days of trading, often quite dramatically, yielding quick and fat profits to those getting first dibs. For especially hot offerings, it can be hard to get a piece of the action — unless, of course, you have a friendly investment banker who reserves a fat tranche for you. Best known are the sweet deals earned by important politicans of both major parties — like former House Speaker Tom Foley and Senate Banking Committee chair Alfonse D'Amato (Glassman 1994; Kuntz and Simpson 1996). Even politicians with sterling reputations play the game; a former *Wall Street Journal* reporter told me he had confirmed information that a prestigious Senator beloved of the pundit class had played the game — but the journalist refused to publish the info because he was fond of the Senator.

Many rationales have been offered for poor post-offering performance, including managers' taking advantage of an "overpriced" stock — confirming the asymmetry theorists' speculation — and managerial manipulation of reported profits. Morck, Shleifer, and Vishny (1990) show that IPOs are far more likely when valuations are high than when average or low — formal proof of something that observers of Wall Street know in their bones. Teoh, Welch, and Wong (1995) show that accounting games played in advance of a stock offering should be visible at the time of the offering. If analysts were doing their jobs, these manipulations should have been noticed; but most analysts are in the pay of firms in the business of selling securities. Creative bookkeeping is a proven marketing tool.[27]

These problems may be mitigated through the development of long-term relationships between firms and their outside financiers. This is one of the advantages of bank, as opposed to bond or stock market, finance; bankers get to know their customers if they're together for a long time. But with the markets, the relationship is often the financial equivalent of a one-night stand; ecstasy is always possible, but so too is mortal disease.

Countries like Japan and Germany that are usually classified as bank-centered — because banks provide more outside finance than markets, and because more firms have long-term relationships with their banks — show greater growth in and stability of investment over time than the market-centered ones, like the U.S. and Britain. The reason seems to be that British and U.S. firms are more dependent on their internal funds for financing investment, in contrast with firms in the other countries, where outside finance is available from a familiar banker. Further, studies comparing German and Japanese firms with tight bank ties to those without them also show that firms with bank ties exhibit greater stability in investment over the business cycle (Corbett and Jenkinson 1993; Elston 1994).

It became fashionable in the mid-1990s to celebrate the American stock-market model as vindicated by the weak performance of the Japanese and German economies during the Clinton years. While it's not clear whether that U.S. outperformance is a permanent thing or just a shorter-term cyclical affair, it can't be denied that the old Axis powers experienced extraordinary growth in investment and income during the first 45 years after World War II's end. It may be that as capitalist economies mature, and liquid balances swell, they may tend toward a more fluid style of finance and ownership.

irrational expectations

Information asymmetry theorists generally assume that market participants are the rational self-maximizers of mainstream theory; they can just never be certain of the knowledge and motives of their counterparts. As Robert Gordon said of the closely related New Keynesian school, "any attempt to build a model based on irrational behavior or submaximizing behavior is viewed as cheating" (quoted in Dymski 1994).

While it's safe to believe that financial players are self-maximizers, their rationality is another matter. Academic students of finance have increasingly recognized that lots of old-fashioned impressionistic notions about market volatility may be truer than rationalists could imagine. The notion that fads and bubbles and panics drive security prices far from their fundamental value — deviations that end not by returning to that fundamental value but typically by overshooting it to the other extreme — now enjoys a scholarly respectability that it didn't 15 or 20 years ago.

In an influential series of papers published during the 1980s, Robert Shiller developed a theory of financial market volatility powered by horde psychology. His 1981 paper, "Do stock prices move too much to be justified by subsequent changes in dividends?" (reprinted in Shiller 1991) took aim at the EMH's claim that stock prices are the rational discounted present value of rationally anticipated future dividends or profits. On the second page of his article, Shiller charted the value of stock prices against the "true" value a perfectly rational market should have been assigning stocks based on how dividends actually turned out (a highly defensible use of 20/20 hindsight) from 1871–1979.[28] The line representing dividends is remarkably stable, even through the Great Depression, but the line representing stock prices zigs and zags wildly, remaining at extremes of over- and under-valuation for years, even decades.

Another perspective on the market's labile temperament is the "volatility paradox," the enormous variations in volatility in stock prices (Shiller 1988; Schwert 1989). This volatility bears no statistical relation to the volatility of real-world phenomena like inflation, money growth, industrial production, interest rates, or business failures.[29] Moreover, despite the advent of computerized trading techniques such as portfolio insurance and index arbitrage during the 1980s, day-to-day volatility during that decade was little different from that of the 1970s, though both decades were more volatile than the 1950s and 1960s (Davis and White 1987).

Schwert's data report stock volatility to have been low during times of great economic distress, like wars or the extended depression of the late 19th century, suggesting that in times of real social stress, people have more important things to worry about than their portfolios. That speculation, however, is upended by the fact that volatility during the Great Depression of the 1930s was the most extreme in financial history, far outpacing the increase in real-world volatility. Schwert finds only "weak" evidence that real-world (industrial production) volatility presages future financial volatility, and "somewhat stronger" evidence that financial volatility presages the real-world kind, but much of the time, it seems, the stock market dances to its own tune.

Why? Shiller (1984) points to various social phenomena to explain these departures from rationality. Efficient market enthusiasts deny any role to mass psychology; if, as they believe, markets are unforecastable, there's no room for psychological explanations of price behavior. Shiller dismisses this as "one of the most remarkable errors in the history of economic thought." Investing is a social activity: both amateur and professional investors spend lots of time gossiping, researching, and comparing performance. Financial markets are not the sum of the rational expectations of reasoning investors, but the collective judgment of a mob.

There is good evidence from experimental psychology showing that real people don't act in accordance with the assumptions of most financial models (cited in de Bondt and Thaler 1985; Kahneman and Tversky 1979). Specifically, people tend to overweight new information, rather than averaging it into a historical context. De Bondt and Thaler were able to use this information to predict stock prices: a portfolio composed of a broad array of "losers" — stocks that had been mercilessly beaten down by the market — outperformed the averages over the subsequent three years. In other words, the initial losses were the result of overreactions that corrected themselves, but not without the passage of quite a bit of time.[30]

In a series of papers, Lawrence Summers and his colleagues (Cutler et al. 1989; Cutler et al. 1990; Cutler et al. 1991; Poterba and Summers 1986; Poterba and Summers 1988; Summers 1986; these are clearly recounted in Shleifer and Summers 1990) developed "the noise trader approach to finance." In the words of Shleifer and Summers:

> Our approach rests on two assumptions. First, some investors are not fully rational and their demand for risky assets is affected by their beliefs or sentiments that are not fully justified by fundamental news. Second, arbitrage — defined as trading by fully rational investors not subject to such sentiment — is risky and therefore limited. The two assumptions together imply that changes in investor sentiment are not fully countered by arbitrageurs and so affect security returns.

Arbitrage in this sense refers to the efficient marketeers' assumption that should prices get out of line with their warranted value, rational investors will move in quickly and buy underpriced assets or sell overpriced ones. Thus mispricing can only be transient, never sustained. This makes sense if you're dealing with two very similar assets; were gold is selling for $350 an ounce in New York and $355 in London, then speculators would immediately move in and buy New York and sell London. But what if the whole U.S. stock market seems overpriced to a rational arbitrageur? What can she buy and sell to drive prices back into line? What about the danger that overpriced stocks may get even more overpriced before returning to a more "rational" value? How does the arb know what the rational price really is? What if profits are about to take off, and the apparently irrational value isn't so wacky after all? And what about the fact that a short-seller has to cover the dividends on the stock sold short (to the stockholder the shares were borrowed from); this isn't costless either.

While markets may be populated by the rational souls assumed by theory, as anyone familiar with the trade knows, they're also populated with a few less than perfectly rational souls as well. The irrationals trade on "noise" as well as information — pseudo-information (Black 1986). Were noise traders all truly listening to sounds of their own devising, they might cancel each other out, but instead "judgment biases afflicting investors in processing information tend to be the same. Subjects in psychological experiments tend to make the same mistake; they do not make random mistakes" (Shleifer and Summers 1990). In such experiments, subjects tend to be overconfident, which makes them take on more risk than they should; they tend to extrapolate the past into the future, which leads them to chase (sometimes spurious) trends; and they give too much weight to new information, at the expense of what they already knew.[31]

Technical traders — people who spot patterns like breakouts and breakdowns on price charts — spread noise. They frequently buy stocks that appear to be in strong uptrends, or sell those that have "violated" some perceived level of support. While these "signals" are almost certainly meaningless in the long term, they can be self-fulfilling in the short term.

Noise traders and faddists are the culprits in a market pattern called "mean reversion." In the short term, their trading strategies push prices further than they might have gone in a fully rational world, whatever that is, but when the prices get too far away, the bubble bursts, and prices revert to some fundamental value. But noise operates on the corrective side too, meaning that prices overshoot their target, which sets up another reversion. The statistics offered by Cutler, Poterba, Summers, & Co. are, as Fama noted, a "power failure" — the patterns they spot, while significant in the statistical sense, are less than overwhelmingly so.

But his own work with his Chicago colleague Kenneth French (Fama and French 1988) does offer long-term support to the pattern of mean reversion, specifically a three- to five-year timespan. Surveying stock prices over the 60-year period from 1926 to 1985, Fama and French argued that mean reversion accounts for about 35% of the behavior of stock prices. Though the tendency is strongest among the stocks of smaller firms, it holds for large stocks, across 17 industry groups, and among even the relative handful of individual stocks that survived the entire 1926–85 period. Fama and French quite reasonably offered no practical advice to speculators on what this all means; describing a tendency that operates broadly over the course of years isn't much help to traders whose idea of the long term is the day after tomorrow.

It is, however, of considerable economic interest. The two Chicagoans argue that this behavior is not necessarily testimony in support of the irrationality of financial markets. External "shocks" can encourage departures from rational evaluations of future returns. This is a favorite ploy of free-market theoreticians: instability must be seen as external to the market system, not inherent in it. But it does violence to language to call such regular, predictable features of the market system "external shocks."

Shiller, Summers, and the rest are onto something of more than statistical interest. But they don't draw some of the more interesting conclusions their work suggests. Shiller, who has probably done more than any single economist to damage EM theory, devoted a whole book (Shiller 1993) to playing with the idea of establishing futures markets so that businesses and people could hedge themselves against "macro" risks like big moves in GDP or house prices. No one, not even the biggest firm, is exposed to direct risk from GDP growth, and the practical problems in trading futures on a number that is revised frequently — twice in the months after its initial release, again in annual revisions, and yet again in periodic benchmark revisions — don't enter Shiller's mind.[32]

Why might an economist so prominently associated with the notion of excess volatility promote the development of new futures markets? Oh, convention has the perfect answer for this — a variation on Bill Clinton's favorite maxim, that what's wrong with America can be cured by what's right with America. That is, markets are volatile because markets are "incomplete" — if there were markets in absolutely everything, if every risk of life could be hedged with a futures contract, from the possibility of snow tomorrow to that of leukemia at age 60, then excess volatility would disappear, and rationality and placidity would reign.

Summers' academic work seemed to have no influence in his performance as the chief economist at the World Bank and later as the Clinton Treasury Department's top international official.[33] He was at the Bank when stock markets were heavily promoted as instruments of Third World development. Nor has he had any apparent influence on Clinton's financial policies; probably no Democratic president has been so in thrall to Wall Street. And Joseph Stiglitz, as a member of the President's Council of Economic Advisors and chief economist of the World Bank, has had little to say about what his research means for the real world.[34]

the marketeers defend themselves

Many of the architects of financial theory continued to defend their progeny's real world effects in the 1980s. In a speech reprinted in the *Wall Street Journal,* Harry Markowitz (1991), one of the creators of modern portfolio theory and CAPM, predictably summoned Adam Smith to defend program trading, Salomon Brothers' mortgage-backed bond department, and junk bond finance: "My own view is that the invisible hand could work its magic through mere humans is an essential part of Adam Smith's insight. Not many thousands of years ago, men like this would have clubbed each other over hunting rights. A few hundreds of years ago they would have hacked each other with axes and swords. Now they yelled at trainees while they brought together the supply and demand of [sic] home mortgages on a world-wide scale."

Through mere humans? Smith, a man of his time, saw the invisible hand as attached to God's invisible arm; are we to believe that Milken & Co. were divine agents? Has modern finance really made war obsolete?

And what about this sublime matchmaking that Salomon Brothers was allegedly performing in the mortgage markets? Markowitz was reacting in part to the book *Liar's Poker*, Michael Lewis' story of his short, intense, and comical life as an investment banker at Salomon Brothers in the late 1980s, an environment rich in gluttony and crudeness. Markowitz apparently overlooked Lewis' descriptions of how Salomon's traders bought mortgages from failing savings and loans, repackaged them into bonds, and sold them back to the thrifts at enormous profit to themselves and huge losses to the S&Ls — and eventually, U.S. taxpayers.[35] Deregulated and doomed, they were eager to play games on Wall Street.

Here is Lewis' (1989a, p. 105) description of the miraculous Smithian pricing mechanism at work:

> Trader Tom DiNapoli fondly remembers a call from one thrift president. "He wanted to sell a hundred million dollars' worth of his thirty-year loans …and buy a hundred million dollars of some other loans with the cash from the sale. I told him I'd bid [buy] his loans at seventy-five [cents on the dollar] and offer him the others at eighty-five." The thrift president scratched his head at the numbers. He was selling loans nearly identical to those he was buying, but the difference in yield would leave him out of pocket an unheard-of ten million dollars. Or, to put it another way, the thrift was being asked to pay a transaction fee of ten million dollars to Salomon Brothers. "That doesn't sound like a very good trade to me," he said. DiNapoli was ready for that one. "It isn't, from an economic point of view," he said, "but look at it this way, if you *don't* do it, you're out of a job." A fellow trader talking to another thrift president on another line overheard DiNapoli and cracked up. It was the funniest thing he had heard all day. He could picture the man on the other end of the phone, just oozing desperation.

Elsewhere, Lewis recalled some of the language his colleagues had used to hoodwink thrift executives, phrases like "risk-controlled arbitrage" and "CMO equity." The first, Lewis said, was a fashionable mid-1980s "euphemism...for big-time gambling in the mortgage bond market," and the second, a 1987 invention, was "a particularly slippery mortgage investment. The CMO stands for collateralized mortgage obligation, but bond salesmen call it 'toxic waste.'"[36] The language of portfolio theorists had become an elegant disguise for hucksters.

Markowitz argued accurately that the days of DiNapoli's 10-point, $10 million bid–ask spreads could not last; imitators quickly poached on Salomon's turf, ending the days of their monopoly profits. But how well did this mortgage market work even after competition had shaved down the point spreads to more reasonable levels? The 1980s were the first decade since the Depression during which homeownership rates fell — partly a function of declining real wages, for sure, but also a result of continued inflation in the cost of housing. It was also a time when mass homelessness became a permanent feature of the national landscape. And it was also a time when the ratio of home mortgages to the value of their underlying owner-occupied properties went from 28% in 1980 to 43% in 1990.[37]

The ideologists of the *Wall Street Journal*'s editorial page could not resist appending their own commentary to Markowitz' lecture, or more accurately, to lift some reasoning from another Nobelist's prize lecture, that of Merton Miller (1991). Miller began his address by denying that he, along with Modigliani, was the "co-inventor of the leveraged buyout — the transaction that perhaps more than any other has come to symbolize the financial excesses of the 1980s." Miller argued, accurately, that LBOs — specifically those in which "younger, active managers of a firm borrowed the funds to buy the controlling shares from a firm's retired founder (or from his estate)" — were around long before the first MM paper. "The LBO's of the 1980s differed only in scale, in that they involved publicly-held rather than privately-held corporations and in that the takeovers were often hostile." He might have added that interest rates were a lot lower in 1958 than they were in 1985. Miller conceded these points only to dismiss them, since they are enormously different from the often sensible transactions consummated before, say, 1984.

Miller also argued, again accurately, that it is ironic that he and Modigliani are credited as the theorists of LBOs, "since the central message of our M&M Propositions was that the value of the firm was independent of its capital structure" (aside from the tax correction of 1963). Miller insisted again that the MM propositions are the "finance equivalents of conservation laws" since a firm's risk depends on the profits from its real assets, not its financial structure: "leveraging or deleveraging...serves merely to partition that risk among the firm's security holders." In fact, wrote Miller, the real "gains in value achieved in the LBO's of the 1980s lies, in fact, not in our newly-recognized field of finance at all," but in the tremendous efficiency gains engineered by "LBO entrepreneurs," a title even more inflated than Alan Greenspan's "unaffiliated corporate restructurers."[38] Those gains, as we'll see in a moment, are figments of Miller's busy imagination.

Miller has lately been renting himsef out as an expert witness at the undoubtedly high fees a Nobel laureate can command. His paid testimony, however, is hardly of prizewinning quality. The Nasdaq hired Miller and several Chicago comrades, who collectively trade under the name Lexecon Inc., to show that its strange pricing practices (discussed in Chapter 1) were not evidence of market-maker collusion, but a simple manifestation of the tendency of prices to cluster around magic numbers like quarters and halves rather than eighths (Lexecon Inc. 1995). Why the NYSE does not exhibit this strange clustering was not well-explained; Miller & Co. simply found other markets that exhibited similar clustering.[39] Of course, Lexecon could not have anticipated that Nasdaq clustering would decline once the phenomenon was publicized, and legal action loomed. Nor could it have imagined conversations like the one quoted in Chapter 1 of this book, climaxing in the lovely line, "I'm goosing it, cuz."

A year later, Merrill Lynch hired Miller and Lexecon in an attempt to defend itself against a lawsuit by Orange County, California, in which the county accused the broker of selling it some bad derivatives that drove it into bankruptcy. In their report, the hired guns (Lexecon Inc. 1996) argued that had the county not liquidated its portfolio, and toughed it out instead, it would have emerged whole. Lexecon didn't mention the fact that long-term interest rates fell nearly two points over the term of the study; had they risen, the county would have been even deeper under water. In a letter to the *Wall Street Journal,* a lawyer for Orange County (Bennett 1996) pointed out that the firm didn't bother to submit Miller's paper as evidence, because the firm was "rightly concerned that its hired professor could not withstand cross-examination if he were to appear in court."[40] Merrill's claims were dismissed by the bankruptcy court.

Back to the Nobelist, and his case for leverage. When Miller spoke of gains in value, he meant the huge interest flows and stock market gains of the period. From 1982, the beginning of the great bull market, until 1989, the end of the LBO era, the market value of nonfinancial corporations' stock rose $1.83 trillion (from $1.38 trillion to $3.21 trillion), and the value of corporate bonds oustanding rose $519.1 billion (from $407.0 billion to $926.1 billion). But while stocks rose 133%, and bonds, 128% (and, of course, most of the gain in bonds was the result of new issues, not capital gains on old ones), business sector productivity rose 12.6%, and the broadest productivity measure of all, real GDP per hour worked throughout the entire economy (including the government and nonprofit sectors), rose 6.3% — quite weak by historical standards.

That great LBO boom suggests more interesting analytical territory, away from flows and valuations and towards what might be called the politics of money — the ownership and control of corporations and the exercise of power over governments.

notes

1. A quick way of drawing the distinction is that finance refers to claims exercised over time, like debts, and that money is the instrument in which such claims are settled. This distinction gets wobbly as soon as you push on it; a Treasury bill is a debt, but most creditors would be happy to receive one to settle a claim. T-bills, then, are a form of near-money. More on this later.
2. And traders trade on these models. There's evidence that new markets gravitate toward prices dictated by models that are later discovered to be inappropriate to their markets (Cherian and Jarrow 1993; Thomas 1995). In the case of the Value Line stock index futures contract, traders systematically mispriced the index for its first four years of trading, 1982 to 1986; they didn't understand that standard pricing formulas didn't apply to an index determined by geometric rather than arithmetic averages. Pricing may have been "efficient," but it was wrong — wrong, that is, according to the "right" model.
3. Over the last decade or two, radical economists — who now often call themselves heterodox, a far less confrontational term — have gone from criticizing this hyper-mathematical turn in the discipline to trying to outdo their mainstream colleagues at the game. They seem to think that building a better model will persuade the mainstreamers of the errors of their ways.
4. Of course they were asking these questions on behalf of money managers, who need advice on how to handle the trillions of dollars they "run."
5. Besides comfortable self-sufficiency, one shouldn't discount the macho feel of having dominated chaos with a complex model.
6. In a prisoners' dilemma, two experimental subjects, metaphorically partners in crime, are given the choice of betraying each other or hanging tough for monetary reward. If one defects and the other doesn't, the skunk gets 3 units. If both defect, each gets 1. If both cooperate, each gets 2.
7. One doesn't want to get too carried away naturalizing temperament and values, but the model seems particularly to drive away women and nonwhites, at least in America, because of its chilly irreality. It may just be that sex and race are simply convenient markers for hierarchy —that economics is an ideology of privilege, and the already privileged, or those who wish to become apologists for the privileged, are drawn to its study.

8. Correlation coefficients for the various versions of q suggested in the text are all well over .92. The correlation for the simple equity q (market value of stock divided by tangible assets, as shown in the charts and used in the text) and the values for 1960–74 reported in Tobin and Brainard (1977) is .97.

9. It's interesting that investment rose during what are usually considered the bad years of the 1970s. It may be that the rise in oil prices devalued old, energy-inefficient equipment, forcing firms to invest more than they would have otherwise. Most analysts, left and right, regard high investment as a good thing, but not so owners and their theorists. The "excessive" investment of the 1970s was taken care of by the shareholder revolutions of the 1980s and 1990s, which in part was designed to shift corporate profits out of real investment and into Wall Street hands, mainly through interest and capital gains on takeovers.

10. Specifically, they regressed changes in investment on changes in cash flow, sales, and stock valuations, allowing the fundamentals to enter the regressions first, and then adding in the stock measures. At the firm level, fundamentals explained 21% of the variation in investment (i.e., the r2 was .208); adding in stock values improved the explanatory power to 25% (r2 = .246), meaning that the stock market added less than 4 percentage points to their equations' power — in other words, very little. The "incremental r2," in the jargon, was even lower for small firms and lower still for the market and economy as a whole.

11. Cost of capital is the phrase MM use; it equals profits divided by the market value of all outstanding securities, debt and equity. This is the cost of capital from the issuing firm's point of view; outside investors might think of it as the return on their invested capital.

12. Fazzari et al. point out that investment tax credits, by reducing the cost of new investment, are not of much help to constrained firms; they would be better off with lower *average* tax rates, which would increase their cash flow, most of which would likely be invested.

13. All figures in the previous two paragraphs are from Bernanke (1983), except total bank failures, which is from U.S. Bureau of the Census 1975, p. 1038, and aggregate corporate profits, from the national income accounts.

14. Fisher is perhaps most famous for his ill-timed observation, made only days before the 1929 crash, that "Stock prices have reached what looks like a permanently high plateau" (quoted in Galbraith 1988, p. 70). Perhaps, then, his view of the collapse having no end should be regarded skeptically. But his analysis of the debt deflation process seems entirely sound.

15. Even though the U.S. economy entered its fifth year of expansion in the spring of 1996, the GDP growth rate was the slowest of any business cycle upswing since the end of World War II.

16. Interest here is measured against EBIT — or earnings (profits) before interest and taxes; a firm with $100 in pretax profits, and $50 in interest payments, has an interest burden of 33% of EBIT [(50/(100+50)=33%].

17. All figures are from the flow of funds accounts.

18. Hereafter, EM refers to efficient markets, and the EMH to the efficient markets hypothesis.

19. Though Chicago is the Vatican of free-market theory, Fama himself is an admirably fair-minded scholar, not shy about publicly changing his mind. But the kind of company he kept is telling. Among those Fama acknowledges at the outset of this paper are Arthur Laffer, who became famous for the preposterous curve he allegedly drew on a cocktail napkin that "proved" that a government could increase its revenue by cutting tax rates, and Michael Jensen, who was one of the intellectual godfathers of the 1980s, discussed below.

20. Though most EM theory is based on the stock market, it can be applied to the analysis of other financial asset prices as well. "Stock," in a sentence like this, is a stand-in for the whole array of instruments.

21. The debate over CAPM seems to be not without political aspects. For example, the defense by Kothari et al. (1995) was funded by the Olin Foundation and circulated by the Bradley Policy Research Center of the William E. Simon School of Business at the University of Rochester; Bradley and Olin are right-wing foundations, and Simon, besides being a financier, is a right-wing political figure who is famous for promoting right-wing philanthropy. Asked by email to comment, S.P. Kothari found the idea of political influence "amusing" and Jay Shanken said his "first reaction [was] to laugh." Shanken added: "if I were the type who is politically influenced, I would probably lie in response to your question," raising specters of the "all Cretans are liars" braintwister.

22. Not "improved products," note; the language of the financial markets seems to have captured even this critic of its influence.

23. Troubled firms, for example, could offer "contingent equity-like wage offers" — i.e., *we'll pay you if we don't go belly up first* — to unemployed workers; "but since the firms most likely to offer these contracts (e.g., Eastern Airlines) are just the firms from whom workers do not want to accept them, such arrangements are difficult to make" (Greenwald and Stiglitz 1987). Neat idea; too bad it's impossible.

24. Leave it to the ancient to be concerned more about the social good than the modern, who worries mainly about the mathematics of market clearance and the risk to creditors.

25. Some even celebrate this forgetfulness. Techno-Marxoid John Roemer, author of a preposterous scheme for stock market socialism (Roemer 1994), says frequently in conversation that to progress, a discipline must forget its founders.

26. Cheng also found that the stocks of bond issuers do not underperform the market, suggesting among other things that turning outside for finance isn't the crucial issue, but that the form it takes — debt or equity — does matter.

27. The findings about stock offerings smack of planned deception on the part of seller and broker, and even self-deception on the part of the buyer; pure info asymmetry theorists don't really have room for enthusiasts or liars in their models.

28. To be precise, Shiller "detrended" stock prices and profits, that is, he looked only at their departure from their long-term growth trend line. Econometric techniques often require detrended data, and it makes intuitive sense to scrutinize the stock market's skill at separating the ordinary from the extraordinary — the short- to medium-term oscillations around a long-term trend.

29. Shiller delivered his 1988 paper at a conference dominated by memories of the October 1987 stock market crash, an event that should have doomed all notions of market efficiency for good. What rational event could have justified the overnight markdown of world equity values by $1 trillion? Shiller was buoyed by his own survey of money managers showing that no news event prompted the debacle; 90% claimed to have thought the market overvalued prior to the crash, but it took the sight of the Dow falling several hundred points to get them to sell.

30. This confirms the earlier observation that the psychologically difficult strategy of "value" investing makes good economic sense.

31. In surveys of portfolio managers and housebuyers, Shiller (1990) discovered that both groups, the former supposedly sophisticated and the latter not, subscribe to extremely simple theories of market dynamics. The findings boil down to this: people, sophisticated or not, tend to follow the crowd. A survey of London fund managers (Taylor 1988) showed that these presumed rational traders of EM theory did a pretty mediocre job of forecasting critical economic variables — not completely awful, but not conso-

nant with rational expectations theory.

32. Shiller is a partner in a firm, Case Shiller Weiss, that computes and distributes regional house prices for a fee.

33. When he was still an academic, Summers did not like it that his paper tentatively promoting a transactions tax on securities to discourage pointless trading was going to be quoted in an editorial in *The Nation;* the editorial used his numbers, but was stripped of his timorous endorsement (Nation 1989).

34. Though I was dying to ask him what the policy implications of his work were, Stiglitz's office failed to respond to several requests for an interview.

35. Hijinks like these are why Jonathan Gray, a securities analyst with Sanford C. Bernstein, estimates that as much as a third of Wall Street's revenues between 1983 and 1987 — the heart of the Roaring Eighties — came from the thrifts. Aside from the mortgage chicanery, Wall Street firms also deposited their clients' funds with hotshot thrifts, who would then turn around and buy the (often dubious) securities the firms were peddling (Mayer 1990, pp. 296–297). Of course, the U.S. Treasury ultimately picked up the tab for this exercise in market efficiency.

36. Lewis 1989b, p. 31.

37. Figures from Federal Reserve's flow of funds statistics.

38. Greenspan explained that these freelancers pounced when they perceived "suboptimal asset allocations" (Greenspan 1989, p. 268; Jaroslovsky 1989).

39. Lexecon's argument is also damaged by Michael Barclay's (1996) findings that Nasdaq stocks with wide bid–ask spreads that subsequently shifted to the NYSE showed significant declines in the spread on exchange listing.

40. Several calls to Bennett asking for an interview went unreturned.

5   Renegades

In a better world, talk of noise, fads, imperfect knowledge, and emotional overreaction would have traveled beyond the arena of financial economics to the realm where political judgments are made. But such a passage might be inconvenient to the current mood of capitalist triumphalism.

So it's unsurprising that mainstream economists have been reluctant to draw too many theoretical conclusions from these empirical discoveries. Had they done so, it might give a lift to the reputation of an economist now regarded as unfashionable, John Maynard Keynes. The more interesting, and radical, aspects of Keynes's writing were forgotten in the years just after World War II, when his analysis of capitalism's tendencies towards polarization and volatility was domesticated into a banal strategy of business cycle management. The few modern economists who have developed those strains of Keynesian thought are marginalized by the discipline — especially those who mix Keynes with Marx.

For Keynes, the financial markets aren't neutral and efficient allocators of capital or the friends of social development, but rather irrational, destabilizing, and paradoxically conservative institutions that do more to expand rentier wealth than they do to nourish a broad and secure prosperity. Since, in his view, investment in real assets is the driving force of capitalist economies, and since the level and allocation of real investment depends heavily on the state of the financial markets, material progress is hostage to the whimsical forces of finance.

facts on the ground

Perhaps the best place to start this off-road tour is by exploring a fundamental social fact that efficient market theorists and Modigliani–Miller partisans have tried to finesse: financial investment and real investment are distinct activities undertaken "by different sets of people influenced by different sets of motives, each not paying very much attention to the other" (Keynes, *CW* V, p. 250).[1]

Capitalism was not always such. During the early days of the industrial revolution, firms were run by individuals, families, or a small circle of partners who reinvested their profits in the business. But with persistent growth and increasing technological complexity, this simple structure became untenable. For example, New England mill owners of the early 19th century found that their profits, as fat as they were, weren't sufficient to cover the financing needs of a rapidly growing and changing industry. Equipment had to be bought and maintained, and workers, previously paid irregularly in goods, had to be paid regularly in money, or they would starve. (Subsistence agriculture was no longer an option for urban workers.) So mill owners incorporated their enterprises — selling ownership shares to outsiders — in order to tap the surplus wealth of rich Boston merchants. Yet even then, the ownership circle was rather small; controlling shares in a typical Massachusetts mill were typically held by three or four close associates and their families (Chandler 1977, pp. 58–60).

Such financing and ownership structures were too intimate to cope with the railroad. Early lines first turned to farmers, merchants, and manufacturers living along the proposed route and to European money markets. But by the late 1840s, railroad builders began turning to Wall Street; just a decade later, all the instruments of modern finance — bonds, stocks, and even options — were well-established in the U.S., thanks to the railroads' hunger for capital (Chandler 1977, pp. 91–92).

The bounds of space and personal acquaintance had been broken. With these innovations came a whole set of institutions: the large national corporation, wage labor, professional management and sophisticated financial markets, institutions that evolved together as the 19th century progressed. In fact, these are all sides of the same coin — an appropriate metaphor, since the link among them all is money.

With the separation of savings and investment — and with it the separation of ownership and control — came the possibility of imbalances between the two. Keynes made much of this potential for dissonance in his *Treatise on Money,* a sprawling, two-volume work that preceded his *General Theory* by six years. Though the later volume rendered a good bit of the *Treatise's* theorizing obsolete, and though the earlier volume is largely forgotten except by Keynes cultists, it does include lots of useful schemas for thinking about an economy.

Talk of savings being unequal to investment sounds heretical and bizarre to modern ears. As defined by national income accountants, the two must always be in balance. In every issue of the U.S. Department of Commerce's flagship statistical publication, the *Survey of Current Business,* there appears NIPA table 5.1, "Gross Saving and Investment." The figures for 1995 are reproduced, with a bit of editing, in the nearby table.

In English, this means that gross savings — defined as the sum of personal savings, corporate profits not distributed to shareholders in the form

gross saving and investment, 1995 [billions of dollars]	
gross saving	**$1,141.6**
gross private saving	1,062.5
personal saving	240.8
undistributed corporate profits	142.5
consumption of fixed capital	
corporate	454.0
noncorporate	225.2
government saving (surplus/deficit)	79.1
federal	-88.7
state and local	167.9
capital grants received by the U.S.	0.0
gross investment	**1,146.1**
gross private domestic investment	1,065.3
gross government investment	221.9
net foreign investment	-141.1
statistical discrepancy	4.5
source: Survey of Current Business, *May 1996, p. 18.*	

of dividends, depreciation allowances, and the government deficit — must equal gross investment, which comprises business investment in buildings, machinery, and inventories; personal investment in housing; and acquisitions of foreign assets by U.S. residents less acquisitions of U.S. assets by foreigners. In even simpler English, income that isn't spent on consumption must be invested (leaving aside, of course, that which is stuffed into mattresses or lost down manholes). If savings are defined simply as income that isn't spent on consumption, and total production consists only of consumption and investment goods (a simplification, but not a violent one), then savings *must* equal investment, since consumption expenditures must equal the total sales of consumption goods. Voilà, savings = investment; otherwise, where would the money go? Or as Keynes said, "Savings and investment are merely alternative names for the difference between income and consumption" (*CW* XIII, p. 552).

In practical terms, savings and investment are balanced through changes in inventories, $37 billion of which are included in the investment figures in the table. In good times, or in anticipation of good times, firms increase production beyond demand to build inventories; in bad times, sales fall more quickly than production (since firms are producing according to recent demand), leading to a buildup in inventory. The first is planned, the second, unplanned. In 1974, for example, the belly of the 1973–75 recession, inventory buildup was 9% of gross nonresidential investment. Inventories were reduced in 1975, a form of disinvestment, as managers throttled back production and investment plans in the wake of 1974's disappointments. Fixed investment was also cut back. But the recovery that took hold in the latter part of 1975 drove sales above expectations, resulting in a voluntary accumulation of inventories in the following year — up by an amount equal to 9% gross nonresidential investment, and 37% of net, in 1976. Fixed investment perked up as well.

Life is never as neat as all that. The national income and product accounts, as their name implies, consist of two halves, mirror images of each other.[2] In business accounting, the halves are often referred to as sources and uses of funds; more colloquially, we could call them income and outgo. Government accountants estimate the two sides of the ledger, totaling income (wages, profits, etc.) and expenditures (consumption, physical investments, etc.) separately. In theory, the two counts should match — while not every product that is made can be sold, every sale must have a corresponding purchase. But in practice, they don't quite even up; in a $7+ trillion economy, it's not surprising that the sums don't work out to the penny. That mismatch is shown as the statistical discrepancy, which was negligible in 1995, but can run into eleven figures. And since personal saving cannot be measured directly, but only estimated as the difference between total income and spending, all these numbers should be considered as no more than a well-educated guess.

But let's give the national income accountants the benefit of the doubt and assume these estimates to be roughly correct, and that savings must equal investment by their definition. Put this way, however, the equivalence of savings and investment is on a par with saying 2+2=4 — accurate, useful, but not very interesting. Keynes's analysis in the *Treatise,* where he makes the inequality of savings and investment an important motor of economic change, is of far greater interest.

In the *Treatise,* Keynes battled one orthodoxy, the quantity theory of money, with another orthodoxy, the relation between "natural" and market rates of interest. The quantity theory of money, the root of modern monetarism, starts with an economic truism and ends in a religion. Though there are several variants, the most famous version of the truism is:

$$MV=PT.$$

That is, in one period, typically a year, the amount of money in circulation (M) times its velocity of turnover (V, or the number of times these units of money are spent) equals the sum of the prices (P) times the number of transactions (T). In practice, some definition of the money supply is substituted for M, GDP substituted for PT, and since velocity can't be seen, it's assumed to be whatever number makes the equation balance.

Of course, the equation is always true after the fact. But it fails to explain why the variables take on the values they do. They usually bob about wildly, often with little relation to the others. In the U.S., there are four official definitions of money, ranging from a narrow one called M1, basically currency plus checking accounts, to a very broad one, called M4 or L (for liquidity) which includes Treasury bills and other short-term securities. Each marches to its own drumbeat. Velocity is a slippery concept; monetarists assume it to be constant, but it isn't — in fact, it's all over the place. Speed of turnover is one of the fundamental variables of capitalist economies, but quantity theory has little to say about it. In the monetarists' view, changes in M cause changes in prices and volume of production; cause runs only from left to right in the basic quantity equation and since V is assumed to be a constant, it's ignored. Though modern monetarists, from Milton Friedman to Alan Greenspan's Fed staff, have tried to give their doctrine a dynamic spin, it's a flat, static, and trivializing view of a multidimensional, dynamic, and complex system.

Keynes's *Treatise*

In a considerable advance on static monetarism, Keynes began his model-building by separating a community's income into two parts, that earned in the production of consumer goods, and that in the production of investment goods, and separating its expenditures also into two parts, that spent on consumption goods and that on savings. This both rejects the homogeneity of the monetarists' T, and moves away from static identities towards a dynamic system.

Consumption goods prices, Keynes posited, were determined jointly by what are now called unit labor costs — wages per unit of output, or money wages adjusted for productivity — and the difference between savings and investment. Or, more precisely, *changes* in prices are caused by *changes* in the other two terms. The other motor of the model is the relation between savings and investment; changes in the relations between these two also motivate changes in the broad economy.

Changes in unit labor costs are important to price determination, and this relation is at the heart of Keynesian and post-Keynesian theories of inflation.[3] Empirically, the correlation between consumer price inflation and unit labor costs in the U.S. is very tight. If wage growth exceeds productivity growth, producers' costs will rise, and they will raise prices in compensation if they can get away with it. If these producers can't pass along price increases, they obviously will be forced to take other actions, ranging from mechanization to union-busting and moves overseas, to preserve profit margins.

More relevant to our terrain is the second relation, the (im)balance between savings and investment, which can generate deficient or excessive demand for consumption goods. If investment exceeds savings, fresh demand for investment goods will raise wages among workers in the capital goods industries without there being any offsetting decrease in consumption demand elsewhere (since a decline in consumption would be the obverse of an increase in savings). The prices of consumption goods will rise, and the value of money will decline. Conversely, should savings increase faster than investment, the decline in consumption demand would not be offset by any increase in capital goods demand (which would, in turn, raise consumption demand); therefore, the price of consumption goods would decline, and their producers would suffer losses.

Prices are "upset by the fact that the division of the output between investment and goods for consumption is not necessarily the same as the division of the income between savings and expenditure on consumption." And entrepreneurs are deciding independently what quantities of consumption and investment goods to produce (*CW* V, p. 121–123).

Financial markets are dominated by two forces — savers' willingness to part with cash to buy "securities" (or the choice between "hoarding" and "investing") and the generosity of the banking system. If "the public" — a City and Wall Street euphemism for rich people and investment managers — is bearish, anxious about the future, it will hold cash rather than making long-term investments. Unless the banking system eases credit to offset that bearishness, new investment will be choked. Price levels over-all depend, then, on the savings rate, the cost of new investment, the bear-ishness of the public, and the volume of savings deposits — a formula that boils down to the excess of saving over the cost of investment, and the disparity between the bearishness of the public and the offsetting loose-ness of the banking system (or bullishness and tightness).

Investment and savings, then, often conflated in mainstream theory, are quite different things that nonetheless are expected to balance. Invest-ment, in Keynes's words, is "the positive act of starting or maintaining some process of production or of withholding liquid goods. It is mea-sured by the net addition to wealth whether in the form of fixed capital, working capital or liquid capital."[4] It is "the act of the entrepreneur." Sav-ing, however, "is the act of the individual consumer and consists in the negative act of refraining from spending the whole of his current income on consumption" (*CW*V, p. 155). The two actors, savers and investors, are brought together by the banking system and financial markets, under the leadership of the central bank.

The balance or imbalance between savings and investment, in the *Treatise* model, is determined by the interest rate (setting aside, for con-venience, the fact that in the real world there are many interest rates) or, more precisely, the oscillation of the market rate of interest around a "natu-ral" rate. The natural rate is defined, somewhat circularly, as the rate that would equalize savings and investment, thereby keeping the price of in-vestment goods steady (*CW*V, p. 139). If the market rate rises relative to the natural rate, savings will be encouraged and investment depressed; if it falls, investment will rise relative to savings. "Booms and slumps...are simply...an oscillation of the terms of credit about their equilibrium posi-tion" (*CW*V, p. 165).[5] This assumes, of course, that savings are stimulated and investment is depressed by higher interest rates; although there's some truth to these axioms, and even more intuitive appeal, actual reality dem-onstrates much looseness in the relations. But let's not quibble for now.

If credit markets were perfect, changes in interest rates could balance savings and investment perfectly, just as price is supposed to equilibrate supply and demand in all competitive markets. Markets are imperfect (or don't clear) if not every buyer or seller can be satisfied at the "proper" price. Credit markets are far from perfect, Keynes argued; there always exists an "unsatisfied fringe" of borrowers who can't find credit because banks turn them down (*CW*V, p. 190). Or, the banks might say, they can't find enough qualified borrowers to soak up all their lending potential (hard to imagine before 1990). In the 1930s and the early 1990s, low interest rates did not encourage credit expansion because lenders, and possibly borrowers, had been scared by the recent credit implosion. This important notion of credit rationing would be largely forgotten as fantasies of perfect markets infected the economics profession during the 1960s and 1970s, but it would later reappear in the politically cautious "information assymetry" literature. It shows that not only the price of credit — the interest rate — is economically important, but also the ease of its availability — its quantity — as well. In high market theory, flexible prices assure a balance between supply and demand; but in real life, there may be unslaked urges to lend or borrow regardless of price.

Though the mood of the "public" counts for something — bearishness will drive up long-term rates — changes in interest rates are "normally" led by a nation's central bank, when it decides to change "the level of money incomes" (CWV, p. 142). Credit availability, and with it the size of the "unsatisfied fringe," will probably move in tandem with central bank policy. Sustained periods during which the market rate is held below the natural rate will result in explosive credit demand, runaway investment, and a rising price level, that will continue as long as the central bank permits (CWV, pp. 176–177). Conversely, periods during which the market rate is held above the natural rate will be ones of low investment and falling prices. Public sentiment can also move market rates; a bearish mood will push up long-term interest rates.

The natural rate itself is not a constant thing; a change in market rates often sets off a change in the natural rate in the opposite direction. For example, if market rates fall, the natural rate will rise, as entrepreneurs come to expect rising prices in the future. Higher future prices hold the promise of higher future profits, which makes new investments more attractive. While this may provoke a "reaction" sometime in the future — higher investment demand will drive up the price of investment goods, thereby offsetting the possibility of higher profits — the short-term effect is undeniably stimulative (CWV, p. 189–190).

Changes in the natural rate may also come from the "real" side of an economy. Keynes followed Joseph Schumpeter in arguing that technical and organizational innovations adopted by a handful of especially spirited entrepreneurs, which competition forces the less pioneering to adopt, are at the heart of capitalist progress. But these innovators would be nothing more than frustrated dreamers if the banking system — or, more broadly, financiers — didn't accommodate them by allowing them to rent other people's money (*CW* VI, pp. 85–86). A wave of innovation will raise average profit rates (at least in the short run, before imitators crash the innovators' party), raising the natural rate of interest. If market rates lag, as they usually do, changes in the natural rate, investment will be stimulated in the wake of the pioneers.

Keynes's heresy

Writing in 1930, Keynes was most interested in the process of deflation and in countering the dangerous advice of conventional finance. Orthodoxy put the pound back on gold at a punishingly high rate in 1925, torturing British industry and pushing up unemployment in the name of sound money. Central banks, Keynes feared, were being too timid about bringing down interest rates. Against orthodoxy's austerity nostrums, Keynes celebrated booms in a manner that would do a Texas populist proud. Shakespeare, said Keynes, died rich, and his days were "the palmy days of profit — one of the greatest 'bull' movements ever known until modern days in the United States…. [B]y far the greater proportion of the world's greatest writers and artists have flourished in the atmosphere of buoyancy, exhilaration and the freedom from economic cares felt by the governing class, which is engendered by profit inflations" (*CW* VI, p. 137). The Shakespeares of the era of junk finance have yet to be discovered, unless Bret Easton Ellis qualifies.

Keynes's repeated violations of the canons of orthodox finance are refreshing in these neo-Calvinist days of plant closures, mass layoffs, fiscal austerity, and mightily tightfisted central banks. We need not worry, argued Keynes, if entrepreneurs blow their money on riotous living; the money will return to their class in the form of excess profits in consumption industries. Investment, in so buoyant a clime, would take care of itself. This charming passage, which is bound to make a sadomonetarist scream, is worth quoting at length:

> [T]he opinion, which I have sometimes heard expressed, that the real wealth of the community increases faster, in spite of appearances to the contrary, during a depression than during a boom, must be erroneous. For it is a high rate of investment which must necessarily by definition be associated with a high rate of increment of accumulated wealth. Thus I am more disposed to sympathise with Mr D.H. Robertson, who thinks that much of the material progress of the nineteenth century might have been impossible without the artificial stimulus to capital accumulation afforded by the successive

periods of boom, than with the puritans of finance — sometimes extreme individualists, who are able, perhaps, to placate in this way their suppressed reactions against the distastefulness of capitalism — who draw a gloomy satisfaction from the speculative and business losses, the low prices, and the high real wages, accompanied, however, by unemployment, which characterise the typical depression. Nor is it a sufficient justification of the latter state of affairs, that, necessity being the mother of invention, there are certain economies and technical improvements which the business world will only make under the stimulus of distress; for there are other improvements which will only mature in an atmosphere of optimism and abundance (*CW* V, p. 246).

Booms are not automatic, and thrift campaigns are dangerous. It's not guaranteed that the savings encouraged by a thrift campaign — assuming they materialize at all, since the record of various tax breaks extended in the U.S., like IRAs, to encourage savings is dismal — will end up financing productive investments; they may end up causing an increase in unwanted inventories instead, or an inflation of stock prices as money pours into the market rather than the real world. If there's no increase in real investment, the excessive "savings" are merely offset by losses among consumer goods producers. "There is no increase of wealth in any shape or form corresponding to the increase of saving — the saving has resulted in nothing whatever except a change and change-about between those who consume and between those who own titles to wealth." Loss-making entrepreneurs would have to make up their shortfalls through borrowing; instead of financing new investment, the new savings in this unfortunate case merely finance losses. (*CW* V, pp. 121, 154–157; VI, pp. 185–186). The analysis is relevant in these days when increasing savings is touted as a social goal without any regard for how the savings will find their way into investment, or the risks of what could happen should they not.

In the *Treatise*, Keynes rebuked the world's central banks for being too slow to lower interest rates in the 1920s and into the 1930s. Massive savings in the years after World War I were simply "spilled," financing entrepreneurs' losses in the deflation that accompanied the effort to revive the pre-war gold standard (*CW* VI, p. 185). Keynes also rebuked the U.S. Federal Reserve for shutting down the 1920s bull market with high interest rates. Writing in 1930, before it became clear that capitalism was in the early days of its worst crisis ever, he argued that the slump was caused mainly by the period of tight money during the late 1920s, "and only secondarily" by the stock market crash itself. High rates simultaneously discouraged investment and encouraged savings — a double whammy — and the crash only made matters worse on both counts. Anticipating the role psychology would play in the *General Theory,* he argued that a bull market makes people feel richer, more likely to spend and less likely to save, and a bear run has just the opposite effect. Central bankers shouldn't worry about the price of *existing* securities (which is what a stock market overwhelmingly is); instead, they should concern themselves with keeping *new* savings and investment in balance (*CW* V, 230; VI, 176). How this balancing act can be managed was never revealed; presumably the central bank will be able to zero in on the natural rate, which is something that can never be seen. And Keynes essentially ignored the dangers of a financial mania — waste and fraud on a tremendous scale. While his celebration of excess may seem refreshing in a period of austerity, it seems less excusable in one of a market boom accompanied by widespread poverty, not to mention looming ecological crisis.

classical comforts

Instability, or at least the possibility of it, is built into Keynes's fundamental equations. Unlike the simple identity of MV=PT, his system is rich with potential imbalances — between consumption and savings, between savings and investment, between the public mood and the intentions of the central bank. These imbalances are a bit reminiscent of Marxian models of overproduction, disproportionalities between capital and consumer goods industries, and deflationary seizure. Keynes, however, displayed confidence in the ability of central bankers to guide the system safely around these rocks in its path.

Despite the emphasis on disequilibrium, "at a deeper level the theory is still comfortingly classical" (Leijonhufvud 1992). Considerable powers of self-adjustment still inhere in the *Treatise*'s system. At some point, for example, bearish speculators are likely to tire of selling bonds and find that interest rates had risen enough to make them a tempting purchase once again. In another classical touch, prices do the adjusting, not output, which makes no allowance for the extended unemployment of capital and labor.

The natural rate of interest is also an orthodox idea, though Keynes allowed for the market rate to deviate considerably from it. It is a notion associated most closely with Knut Wicksell, who was hot in pursuit of a "neutral" monetary system — one that behaved the same way a hypothetical world without paper money would behave. To Wicksell, the danger was that the credit system would keep market interest rates below their natural level, fuelling loan demand, increasing the money supply, and fostering inflation. The importance of the natural rate lies in its relation to the prevailing rate of profit: if money can be borrowed at 5%, and invested in real assets (or bonds representing real assets) at 7%, then prospective borrowers will mob their banks, baying for credit. Keynes, on the other hand, was worried about deflation.

This connection between the natural interest rate and the rate of profit takes us back to an even more classical world than Wicksell's, where profits ultimately determine the interest rate, rather than balancing savings and investment. Ricardo quoted this observation by Adam Smith approvingly: "[T]he market rate of interest will lead us to form some notion of the rate of profits, and the history of the progress of interest afford us that of the progress of profits." Unfortunately, Ricardo commented, states have, "from mistaken notions of policy," often kept interest rates from rising to appropriate levels, compromising their use as a proxy for profit rates.

Ricardo did concede that the interest rate, "though ultimately and permanently governed by the rate of profit, is, however, subject to temporary variations from other causes." Arguing like the faithful quantity theorist he was, Ricardo argued that changes in the stock of money will affect the price level, and with it interest rates, as will temporary fluctuations in trade. If, for example, prices fall because of an abundance of supply, a diminished demand, or a fall in the quantity of money, manufacturers will accumulate unsold inventories. To meet necessary payments, industrialists will have to borrow to cover the losses, pushing up market interest rates. But these stresses always contain the seeds of their own resolution: either prices rebound, and manufacturers are restored to solvency, or they don't and they go bust and disappear. "[M]oney and interest regain their real value." Like Ricardo, the Keynes of the *Treatise* thought that price changes were the way to restore equilibrium, though Keynes imagined a large role for the central bank in assuring the adjustments were made.

In the years after the *Treatise* was published, Keynes rethought these classical notions. It became clear that changes in output had to play a much larger role. In a 1931 lecture, Keynes offered the observation that an economy may come to rest at a "spurious equilibrium," with a low level of production and employment (*CW* XIII, p. 356). This was a rejection of one of the central features of classical economics: supply can never exceed demand, and consequently the long-term unemployment of people and machines can't happen. Obviously it does, though many mainstream economists still insist that human idleness can only be voluntary in such a miraculous self-equilibrating system as capitalism.

monetarism: money all, money nothing

In 1932 and 1933, Keynes began developing what he called a monetary theory of production, a phrase he used as the title of a short 1933 essay. The classical economists of the 18th and 19th centuries wrote as if money didn't exist, or, more precisely, existed only "as a neutral link between transactions in real things and real assets and does not allow it to enter into motives or decisions." In such a world, the level of prices has no effect on production, consumption, or the willingness to lend or borrow. But, as Keynes pointed out, wages are "sticky," meaning they don't change as rapidly as commodity prices, and debt contracts are denominated in money terms, meaning that if prices fall, entrepreneurs will have trouble meeting their wage bills and servicing their debts. In classical doctrine, a fall in prices would be either neutral, since money prices don't matter for real exchange, or possibly stimulative, since the fall in prices might increase demand. Conveniently, Keynes noted, in a world of neutral money, "crises *do not occur*" (emphasis in original). For someone writing in 1933, at the trough of depression, this "assumed away the very matter under investigation" (*CW* XIII, pp. 408–411).

Right-wing icon Friedrich Hayek introduced the term "neutrality of money" into English, attributing it wrongly to Wicksell; it was actually a product of Dutch and German writers of the 1920s (Hayek 1932, pp. 27–28; Patinkin 1992). The doctrine, though not the term, goes back to the mid-18th century and David Hume ("it is of no manner of consequence … whether money be in greater or less quantity"); two famous statements of the theory, incorporated into the creeds of many economists, belong to John Stuart Mill ("there cannot, in short, be intrinsically a more insignificant thing, in the economy of society, than money") and Irving Fisher ("money is a veil").

Quoting both Mill and Fisher approvingly, Milton Friedman and Anna Jacobson Schwartz (1963, p. 696) nonetheless spied a hole in the veil, one torn by governments, typically by their central banks, which make terrible errors when they try to reverse the fundamentally unappealable judgments of The Market. Most of these errors are misguided attempts to stimulate the economy, as for example the inflation of the 1960s and 1970s, which Friedman and his spawn argue was caused by excessive generosity by the world's central banks. They do have a point; the excessive extension of credit beyond an economy's capacity to satisfy the resultant demand will give rise to inflation. But this argument ignores the reason governments used to try to stimulate economies — chronically high levels of unemployment. (It also ignores the endogeneity of money, of which more later.) Friedman and Schwartz also blamed capitalism's most dire crisis, the Great Depression, on the allegedly tightfisted policies of the Federal Reserve, an argument that has the pleasant ideological effect of acquitting the inner workings of the market system — such as the overproduction of commodities combined with the polarization of incomes that characterized the 1920s — of any involvement. Crises may occur, inflationary or deflationary, but they're the state's fault.

Friedman (1962) used to urge that central banks be required by law or "monetary constitution" to increase the quantity of money at a constant rate of 3–5% a year. Thirty years later, Friedman's faith seemed a bit shaken: "It is tempting to conclude from the close average relation between changes in the quantity of money and changes in money income that control over the quantity of money can be used as a precision instrument for offsetting the forces making for instability in money income. Unfortunately, the loose relation between money and income over short periods, the long and variable lag between changes in the quantity of money and other variables, and the often conflicting objectives of policy-makers preclude precise offsetting control" (Friedman 1992). Now he tells us.

Quantity theorists have almost unanimously made exceptions for money's non-neutrality in the short term: a jolt of fresh money could, by goosing up prices, boost confidence, profits, and production for a little while. But, it was further argued, the stimulus would only be transitory, as a new equilibrium was reached. Put another way, as Friedman (1968b) did in his classic screed "The Role of Monetary Policy," central banks can only peg nominal quantities, not real ones: "the real rate of interest, the rate of unemployment, the level of real national income, the real quantity of money" are all beyond its powers. "The price level is then a joint outcome of the monetary forces determining nominal income and the real forces determining real income" (Friedman 1970). In other words, prices and output, the monetary and the real, are separately, not mutually, determined. So while money might be influential in the short view, it was neutral in the long. Why the long term should be fundamentally different from the sum of many short terms is a bit mysterious. And why too the quantity theorists, passionate believers in monetary neutrality, always care with equal passion about inflation is equally mysterious. If money prices don't matter, then why does inflation? But if inflation — "always and everywhere a monetary phenomenon," in the Friedmanite mantra — *does* matter, then money can't really be neutral, can it?

Monetarism officially prevailed in the U.S. from 1979, on Paul Volcker's ascension to the chair of the Federal Reserve, to 1982, when it was abandoned for ostensibly technical reasons, but actually because the U.S. economy was falling apart, the financial system was making horrible sounds, and Mexico was on the verge of default (Greider 1987). In truth, Volcker's adoption of monetarism was a ruse for driving up interest rates to unprecedentedly high levels to create a deep recession, to break inflation, and with it, to crush the last traces of labor militancy.

The Thatcher government inflicted an even more savage monetarism on Britain over the same period. According to Friedman's advice to the Iron Lady, the late-1970s inflation could easily have been defeated with "only a modest reduction in output and employment" (quoted in Gilmour 1992, p. 50). The theoretical reason for this confidence was, of course, the alleged neutrality of money: tightness by the central bank should have no effect on real output, only on prices. In fact, Britain, like the U.S., went into a deep and long recession, and one that inflicted far more serious long-term damage on Britain's fundamentally weaker economy. UK industrial production didn't return to 1979 levels until 1985. The U.S. did much better, no doubt thanks to the massive fiscal stimulus provided by the Reagan

money growth and inflation		
	UK	U.S.
money		
1975–79	14.9%	6.8%
1980–84	11.3	7.6
change	*-3.6*	*+0.8*
inflation		
1975–79	15.7	8.0
1980–84	9.6	7.5
change	*-6.1*	*-0.5*

Money is what the IMF calls "money plus quasi-money," which consists principally of currency, checking deposits, and time and savings deposits. It corresponds to M2 in the U.S. definition. Inflation refers to consumer price inflation. Figures shown are arithmetic averages of yearly rates of change as reported in *International Financial Statistics Yearbook,* 1992 edition.

deficit; both employment and production recouped their recession losses by 1983. Had Friedman's grand claims been true, the U.S. and UK recessions should never have happened.

Maybe these were the short-term dislocations that Friedman thought acceptable. There can be no doubt, however, that monetarism in both countries, and throughout the world from the Chilean coup onward, has been an important part of a conscious policy to crush labor and redistribute income and power toward capital — which certainly can't be considered neutral in the long term.

Ironically, even the periods of recession and recovery disprove monetarist dogma, as the nearby table shows. Britain showed a sharper decline in inflation than the decline in money growth would argue for, and the U.S. saw a decline in inflation despite a increase in the pace of money growth.[6] We'll return to this later, when looking at theories of where money comes from — from on high, or from below.

money changes everything

Having proven money to be non-neutral, and monetarism to be silly, it's time to move back to Keynes. In the years between the *Treatise* and the *General Theory,* Keynes came to see that money invalidated Say's law, the classical doctrine that assumed that supply creates its own demand. Here's how Ricardo (1911/1987, pp. 192–193) put it in a famous passage:

> No man produces but with a view to consume or sell, and he never sells but with an intention to purchase some other commodity, which may be immediately useful to him, or which he may contribute to future production. By producing, then, he necessarily becomes either the consumer of his own goods, or the purchaser and consumer of the goods of some other person.

But in the real world, a "man" sells only to accumulate money, and he may be slow in exchanging that money for either consumer ("immediately useful") or capital goods ("contribut[ions] to future production"). In the classical world, where money has no autonomous influence, goods' and securities' prices move so that interest rates fall into line with the returns on other assets. Keynes, however, was preparing to argue that the rate of interest is "determined by forces partly appropriate to itself, and that prices move until the marginal efficiency of other assets falls into line with the rate of interest" (*CW* XIV, p. 103).

In classical theory, Keynes also argued, the factors of production were assumed as given; at issue only was their use and relative rewards. Knowledge was assumed to be sound, and

> facts and expectations were assumed to be given in a definite and calculable form; and risks, of which, though admitted, not much notice was taken, were supposed to be capable of an exact actuarial computation. The calculus of probability, though mention of it was kept in the background, was

supposed to be capable of reducing uncertainty to the same calculable status as that of certainty itself; just as in the Benthamite calculus of pains and
pleasures or of advantage and disadvantage, by which the Benthamite philosophy assumed men to be influenced in their general ethical behavior
(*CW* XIV, p. 112).

In the real world, however, uncertainty could not be statistically domesticated. When the future looks especially uncertain, investors will be shy of
commitments, holding a large chunk of their wealth in cash. Uncertainty
in a world of non-neutral money can cause all kinds of trouble.

Keynes departed from his predecessors in placing expectations at the
center of economic decision-making. Take, for example, his idea of "effective demand." In Keynes's definition, effective demand is "simply the
aggregate income (or proceeds) which the entrepreneurs expect to receive, inclusive of the income which they will hand on to the other factors
of production, from the amount of current employment which they decide to give" (*CW* VII, p. 55). As Victoria Chick has written, the term is
somewhat unfortunate. It is sometimes misconstrued to refer to the "demand one can back up by purchasing power," in contrast to notional demand, which is what one would demand could one sell all one's labor
power for wages. (Given the power of imagination, notional demand could
be considered nearly infinite.) Effective demand is the aggregate of entrepreneurs' expectations of their sales on which they base their production
decisions — but their production decisions (how many workers to hire,
how long to work them, how many units to produce, etc.) in turn in large
part determine demand, since incomes from production are what provide
the juice for demand (Chick 1983, pp. 64–65).

Similarly, entrepreneurs' investment decisions and rentiers' decisions
about the allocation of their savings between cash and long-lived assets
are also based largely on expectations. Normally, economic actors derive
their expectations for the future from convention and from recent history,
assuming "that the present is a much more serviceable guide to the future
than a candid examination of past experience would show it to have been
hitherto" (*CW* XIV, p. 114). This self-deception is a stabilizing force, since
economic life, anarchists' appealing dreams aside, would be unimaginable in a world that was constantly turning itself upside down. In turbulent times, however, savers and investors, producers and consumers, all
will come to expect the worst, assuming that present turbulence will continue indefinitely. When people fear for the future, they pull in their horns

and keep whatever assets they have in something secure; usually that means cash, or something like it, rather than stocks, bonds, or factories.

In Classicalworld, expectations are always rational, resources employed to their fullest, and "*inactive balances are zero*" (*CW* XXIX, pp. 215, 256–257; VII, p. 26; italics in original). In Keynesworld, expectations are not necessarily rational, resources can remain unemployed for a long time, and inactive balances (hoards, in plain English) can be much greater than zero. Or, as George Shackle put it in his elegant summary of Keynes's *General Theory:* "To buy the means…of producing goods is to gamble on the eventual sale of those goods. From time to time businessmen lose their nerve and refuse this gamble, preferring to keep their wealth in money rather than embark it in the products of employment" (quoted in Moore 1988b, p. 249). The classicals were wrong; an economy will not necessarily come to rest with the full employment of capital and labor.

To Keynes, the most crucial problem of a modern capitalist economy was evoking a sufficiently high level of investment to assure full employment, and it's here that uncertainty and the comforts of money work their devilment. Entrepreneurs will only invest if they expect the new investment to yield a greater income over its life than it will cost them to finance the asset; in Keynes's jargon, the marginal efficiency of capital (MEC) must be greater than the interest rate they pay their bankers.[7]

While this may not seem like an extraordinarily original idea at first, there are at least two points of interest in the formulation. First is the notion that money is central to investment decisions; Keynes had no truck with mainstream pieties about production serving consumer needs. "The firm…has no object in the world except to end up with more money than it started with" (*CW* XXIX, p. 89). Second is the notion that *expectations* are central to investment decisions; the expectations may be wrong or right, rational or irrational, but whatever the case, they matter enormously.

It's not only the expectations of industrial managers that matter to investment; the MEC must be measured against the interest rate, and "the rate of interest is a highly psychological phenomenon" (*CW* VII, p. 202). *The General Theory* banished all notions of the interest rate balancing savings and investment (or, put another way, balancing the supply of and demand for savings), cut it free of any intimate relation with profit rates, and discarded the concept of a natural rate of interest. If the natural rate is defined as the one that maintains the status quo, there can be many natural rates of interest, each associated with a different level of employment — "and, in general, we have no predominant interest in the *status quo*."[8]

If there is any rate of interest that deserves special status, Keynes argued, it's the one associated with full employment (*CW* VII, p. 243). One of the goals of economic analysis and policy should be to discover and attain that optimum rate.

Interest rates are a function of the generosity or tightness of the central bank and the demand for money, which Keynes called the state of liquidity preference. Liquidity preference depended on three things in *The General Theory* (*CW* VII, pp. 168–174) — the transactions motive, the need for cash to cover personal and business expenses; the precautionary motive, the desire for a cash cushion in the face of future uncertainty; and the speculative motive, cash kept like dry powder, for taking quick advantage of market mis-valuations (like buying a stock that has been hammered down). To those three, Keynes later added a fourth, a finance motive, entrepreneurs' short-term demand for cash in the early stages of an investment project, "the credit required in the interval between planning and execution" (*CW* XIV, pp. 216, 218). In bad times, like the 1930s, fear increased the degree of liquidity preference to crippling levels; everyone wanted the safety of cash, and no one dared go out on a limb.

once more, with feeling

In the exposition of liquidity preference in *General Theory*, Keynes emphasized the psychological state of financial actors — rentiers and City professionals. When expectations are bearish, it takes a very high interest rate to lure rentiers from the security of cash; when they're bullish, it doesn't take much.[9] Rather than being the reward for not-spending, the classic Protestant–moralizing theory of interest, interest represents the reward for "not-hoarding" — for taking a risk, for becoming less liquid. But there's more to the demand for money than the desirability of hoarding, as Keynes emphasized in a letter to D.H. Robertson. Liquidity preference is also determined by "the scale of planning and activity and the level of costs" (*CW* XIV, p. 224). The demand for money can increase either out of enthusiasm or anxiety, in a boom or a panic, which will push up interest rates, other factors (like central bank policy) remaining unchanged.

Sentiment is at the center of Keynes's theory of investment, and his most justifiably famous exploration of the financial passions is Chapter 12 of *The General Theory*, "The State of Long-Term Expectations," one of the most splendid analyses of speculative markets ever written. Keynes argued that asset prices are powered by wild swings of temperament, the volatile judgments of an ignorant herd, and these noisy signals guide real investment, to the detriment of prosperity. Markets are populated by dispersed investors with little knowledge of the real businesses they own or lend money to. "Day-to-day fluctuations" in the fortunes of enterprises "of an ephemeral and non-significant character, tend to have an altogether excessive, and even an absurd, influence on the market. American companies which manufacture ice tend to sell at a higher price in summer when their profits are seasonally high than in winter when no one wants ice" (*CW* VII, pp. 153–154). Ice sounds quaint, but the principle still holds true; the stock prices of retailers respond to advance indexes of weekly sales that have little relation to final, definitive sales figures. "[T]he energies and skill of the professional investor and speculator" are concerned not with serious long-term forecasts, "but with foreseeing changes in the conventional basis of valuation a short time ahead of the general public."

> Thus the professional investor is forced to concern himself with the anticipation of impending changes, in the news or in the atmosphere, of the kind by which experience shows that the mass psychology of the market is most influenced. This is the inevitable result of investment markets organized with a view to so-called "liquidity." Of the maxims of orthodox finance none, surely, is more anti-social than the fetish of liquidity…. It forgets that there is no such thing as liquidity of investment for the community as a whole. The social object of skilled investment should be to defeat the dark forces of time and ignorance which envelop our future. The actual, private object of the most skilled investment to-day is to "beat the gun," as the Americans so well express it, to outwit the crowd, and to pass the bad, or depreciating, half-crown to the other fellow (*CW* VII, p. 155).

This game — which Keynes likened to Snap, or Old Maid, or Musical Chairs — is one of "the third degree where we devote our intelligences to anticipating what average opinion expects the average opinion to be. And there are some, I believe, who practice the fourth, fifth and higher degrees." Or, as he put it in *The Treatise,* the point is to "ape unreason proleptically" (*CW* VI, p. 323). Nothing could be truer. Some evidence that he was right is that unlike many economists, Keynes was a brilliant speculator who made himself and his Cambridge college a fortune.[10]

These gyrations might seem silly, decadent, or wasteful, but their danger lies in their influence on real investment. "Speculators may do no harm as bubbles on a steady stream of enterprise. But the position is serious when enterprise becomes the bubble on a whirlpool of speculation. When the capital development of a country becomes the by-product of the activities of a casino, the job is likely to be ill-done" (*CW* VII, p. 159). Keynes had the America of the 1920s in mind when he wrote this, but he could have been writing about this country, and increasingly many others, over the last 15–20 years.

In a narrow sense he was wrong. Changes in stock prices really don't have that much influence on real investment; insofar as they have an economic logic at all, they merely reflect (and usually amplify) changes in interest rates and the availability of credit, which in turn influence real demand, and eventually real investment. We saw this in Chapter 4, with the dissection of *q* theory and the review of the work of Morck, Shleifer, and Vishny (1990) showing that investment responds to fundamental variables like sales and cash flow, both at the firm and aggregate levels, with stock returns adding little or no explanatory power to their models. Further, Morck and comrades conclude that "The notion that the stock market evaluates the *long-term* prospects of the economy, and so guides long-term investment, is not supported by the data."

Thank God for that. Keynes's instinctive description of the forces behind stock markets are accurate, but their influence on investment is nothing like what he made it seem. But there's intense interest among Wall Streeters and their pet academics for forcing managers to be more obsessed with pushing up their stock prices than they already are. As a long-term strategy, this seems frightfully wrong.

But just looking at the relationship between stock prices and investment is to specify the matter too narrowly. The stock market isn't just about prices, it's about the control of whole corporations, which are bought and sold, combined and liquidated, often on purely financial considerations through the mechanisms of the stock exchange. So the judgments of an ignorant, greedy, and excitable mob do have considerable real world effects. Even less measurable is the effect of the new shareholder assertiveness. The effect of both active M&A and rentier assertiveness is to affect corporate policies in qualitiative ways that mere investment figures can't measure. We'll return to these topics in the Chapter 6.

Keynes: a heretic of sorts

Liquidity preference draws attention away from the level of savings and towards the question of how they're allocated. Orthodoxy argued in Keynes's day, and continues to argue in ours, that higher savings rates are to be encouraged, so that new investment could be more cheaply financed.

The implication is that investment capital is short. Keynes argued instead that while investment can be "congested" through a shortage of cash — difficulty in amassing borrowed money under the finance motive — it never can be congested by a shortage of savings. He called this "the most fundamental of my conclusions within this field." For the society as a whole, long-term investment can fund itself. "Increased investment will always be accompanied by increased saving," wrote the optimistic Keynes, "but it can never be preceded by it. Dishoarding and credit expansion provides not an *alternative* to increased saving, but a necessary preparation for it. It is the parent, not the twin, of increased saving." Attempts to reduce pressure on cash by cutting back consumption — the prescription of orthodox thrift-promoters of the 1920s and the 1990s — will do so, but only by depressing income and ultimately investment. Moreover, "*spending* releases funds just as much as saving does, and … these funds when released can then be used indifferently for the production either of capital goods or of consumption goods" (*CW* XIV, pp. 216, 219, 222, 229, 232, 281, 282). Money must circulate, not congeal into a hoard.

Like the *Treatise,* the *General Theory*'s message is resolutely expansive: spending, not sparing, generates wealth. Moralists, whether Calvinist, neoclassical, or even Marxist, find this aspect of Keynes scandalous, a reaction he seemingly went out of his way to provoke. Much of Chapter 23 is devoted to a rehabilitation of historical kindred spirits, of whom official opinion disapproves: mercantilists, immoralists, underconsumptionists, promoters of usury laws — even that old monetary crank Silvio Gesell.

Among the immoralists is a book that a Middlesex grand jury of 1723 convicted of being a nuisance, Bernard Mandeville's *Fable of the Bees.* The poem and commentaries "set forth the appalling plight of a prosperous community in which all the citizens suddenly take it into their heads to abandon luxurious living, and the State to cut down on armaments, in the interests of Saving" (*CW* VII, pp. 359–362). The community sinks into deflation and despair. Mandeville's tale is "not without a theoretical basis," as Keynes points out. In the commentary, Mandeville argued that while an individual family can save itself rich, a nation cannot — an observation that Adam Smith probably had in mind when he wrote, contrary to the fabulist, "What is prudence in the conduct of every private family can scarce be folly in that of a great Kingdom." Mandeville's advice to the state was to practice the economics of joy, encouraging manufactures, arts, and agriculture to produce to their fullest, and to cultivate "the Fruits of the Earth and the Labour of the People, both of which joined together are a more certain, a more inexhaustible and more real Treasure than the Gold of Brazil or the Silver of Potosi."

To this Keynes added his own fillip:

> No wonder that such wicked sentiments called down the opprobrium of two centuries of moralists and economists who felt much more virtuous in possession of their austere doctrine that no sound remedy was discoverable except in the utmost of thrift and economy both by the individual and by the state. Petty's "entertainments, magnificent shews, triumphal arches, etc." give place to the penny-wisdom of Gladstonian finance and to a state system which "could not afford" hospitals, open spaces, noble buildings, even the preservation of its ancient monuments, far less the splendours of music and the drama, all of which were consigned to the private charity or magnanimity of improvident individuals.

By Keynes's telling, Mandevillean exuberance disappeared from respectable circles until Malthus who, like Keynes, opposed Smith's doctrine that capital is increased by parsimony. Malthus feared that mass poverty would cause a chronic insufficiency of demand, leaving capital and labor to languish unemployed. Against this tendency towards anemia, Malthus celebrated the economically stimulative effect of "unproductive consumption on the part of the landlords and capitalists" (*CW* VII, p. 363).

Here Keynes seems very much like a rebel within his own class. As Marx (1963, pp. 170–172) argued, Mandeville and Malthus were part of an offensive to counter Adam Smith's distinction between productive and unproductive labor. Capitalism, Marx argued, reproduced "everything against which it had fought in feudal or absolutist form" — a parasitical elite. Smith, speaking for the early capitalists, found this stratum an obstacle; they contributed nothing useful, consuming social wealth but producing nothing in return. This was not well-received among the better orders. In Marx's words, the "'higher grade' workers — such as state officials, military people, artists, doctors, priests, judges, lawyers, etc. — some of whom are not only not productive but in essence destructive...found it not at all pleasant to be relegated *economically* to the same class as clowns and menial servants and to appear merely as...parasites on the actual producers." This "compromise" between the capitalists and the burdensome elite found "the *do-nothings* and their *parasites*...a place in this best possible order of things." Malthus and Mandeville, Marx conceded, were to be preferred to later apologists, because they recognized the parasitism of the unproductive even as they found their overconsumption helpful.

Mandeville even held that "Evil" is what makes us social creatures, and is "the solid Basis, the *Life and Support of all Trades and Employments* without exception" (Marx 1963, pp. 375–376).

Though Keynes declared himself an eternal immoralist (*CW* X, p. 447), there's no celebration of evil in his work, and he was too humane to celebrate the stimulative powers of parasites. But he often flinched when confronting the issue of what money should be invested in. Though he acknowledged that it would be better to "build houses and the like," it would be better than nothing to have the Treasury "fill old bottles with banknotes," bury them, and tender for contracts for people to dig them up again (*CW* VII, p. 129). Of course he was being ironic, but irony is a way of disguising an embarrassing truth. Later in the *General Theory,* Keynes said that in an economy with an unemployment rate of 10%, there's no reason to suppose that the employed 90% are seriously misemployed; the tragedy has nothing to do with what's produced, and only to do with the insufficiency of production. Despite his unmasking of markets as not self-adjusting, Keynes stated his aim to be indicating the "nature of the environment which the free play of economic forces requires" if the "Manchester System" is to realize its full potential. Once the planning bureaucrats get everything right, the "classical theory comes into its own again" (*CW* VII, pp. 378–379). Post-Keynesians rightly wail about the banalizing abuse Keynes suffered at the hands of the bastard Keynesians, but the Master himself had already done a good job showing them where to start. And remember he celebrated Gesell as the avatar of an anti-Marxian socialism who promised the flourishing of competition rather than its abolition.

Yet this apologia comes just pages after passages proclaiming the need for the "somewhat comprehensive socialisation of investment," arguing that extreme inequality of wealth and income hurt economic performance rather than helping it, and proposing the "euthanasia of the rentier, of the functionless investor" (*CW* VII, pp. 375–378). What the socialization of investment meant was left rather vague in the *General Theory.* It did not mean "state socialism," Keynes assured; most likely, it meant the state would merely determine investment levels and their rewards. Keynes offered some more detail in a letter to Hawtrey. While it was "theoretically conceivable that communal saving might have to be loaned to private enterprise," the "Board of National Investment would in one way or another control by far the greater part of investment. Private enterprise (meaning industry) requires such a tiny fragment of total savings that it could probably look after itself. Building, transport and public utilities are almost the only outlets for new capital on a large scale." Public sector investment would make capital so plentiful that it would lose its scarcity value, interest rates would drop to zero, and the functionless investor would disappear. It all could be done gradually, with no revolution, "without a break in the general traditions of society" (*CW* XIV, p. 49).

Yet even this program, for all its evasions and contradictions, is revolutionary in the eyes of capital. Private investment is largely self-financing, as Keynes argued, but to ignore it is to ignore what shapes the evolution of much of our physical and social environment. Capital could be made plentiful in the physical sense, but a system of production organized for money profits — which Keynes acknowledged capitalism to be — will have none of it. Rentiers, while they may be socially functionless, are nonetheless the owners of the productive capital stock, and the creditors of its hired managers. They would never concede to their "euthanasia," since they have never thought their condition terminal, at least since the mid-1930s. Nor would employers ever consent to a regime of full employment; it would be the death of work discipline.

One gets the sense, reading Keynes, that the driving force behind capitalism is sentiment, the bullish or bearish state of expectations, and that social reality is important only insofar as it changes expectations through surprise, pleasant or unpleasant. This is consonant with Keynes's highly aestheticized view of the world, his rebellion against what he called

> the extraordinary contraption of the Benthamite School, by which all possible consequences of alternative courses of action were supposed to have attached to them, first a number expressing their comparative advantage, and secondly another number expressing the probability of their following from the course of action in question; so that multiplying together the numbers attached to all the possible consequences of a given action and adding the results, we could discover what to do. In this way a mythical system of probable knowledge was employed to reduce the future to the same calculable status as the present (*CW* XIV, p. 124).

Keynes has a point; this is what mythmakers of the efficient market school do, transform radical uncertainty into statistical risk. In this reaction, however, Keynes returns to the spirit of his undergraduate circle at Cambridge, where "nothing mattered except states of mind, our own and other people's of course, but chiefly our own" (*CW* X, p. 436).

This reaction against Bentham was so extreme that Keynes could attribute the techniques of rational calculation imposed by competitive capitalism to a philosopher, rather than to the unsentimental, impersonal mechanisms of the market, and at the same time describe Marxism, the harshest systematic critique that the capitalist market has ever inspired, as "the final *reductio ad absurdam* of Benthamism" (*CW* X, p. 446).[11]

Maynard and Karl

Ironically, Keynes's interest in a "monetary theory of production" came in part from his reading of an account of Marx's classic formula of capitalist production, M-C-M' (*CW* XXIX, pp. 81–83). By this, Marx meant that the capitalist throws M[oney] into production — engaging both labor and capital — to create a C[ommodity] for sale, which returns, if all goes well, a sum of M'[oney] larger than that laid out at first. Keynes was struck by the contrast between this and the orthodox idea that entrepreneurs produce products in exchange for products (or the more modern, apologetic idea that they produce to satisfy consumers). Under capitalism, the satisfaction of needs is a positive externality of the pursuit of profit, to use the modern language — and the planned creation of needs a less positive externality.

Keynes learned this from a second-hand source because he found the original as unreadable as the Koran: "dreary, out-of-date, academic controversializing" (*CW* XXVIII, p. 38) — though Rolf Behrens (1985) argued that Keynes read more Marx than he admitted or his colleagues knew. As an economist, Keynes ranked Marx below the monetary cranks — something that caused Schumpeter (1936) to exclaim: "I am no Marxian. Yet I sufficiently recognize the greatness of Marx to be offended at seeing him classed with Silvio Gesell and Major Douglas."[12]

Marxism as a political philosophy was a "delusion" (*CW* XVII, p. 268), an "obsolete" and "erroneous...creed which, preferring the mud to the fish, exalts the boorish proletariat above the bourgeois and the intelligentsia who, with whatever faults, are the quality in life and surely carry the seeds of all human advancement." The hated doctrine could do nothing to "alter...human nature," to make "Jews less avaricious or Russians less extravagant than they were before" (*CW* IX, pp. 258–259). Workers he found "boorish," though he generously conceded that they were "not as ugly as they might be" (quoted in Perelman 1989, p.7). Civilization is not the product of humans working together, but "a thin and precarious crust erected by the personality and the will of a very few, and only maintained by rules and conventions skilfully put across and guilefully preserved" (*CW* X, p. 447). "The *class* war," he concluded charmingly, "will find me on the side of the educated bourgeoisie" (*CW* IX, p. 297).

The use of "educated" is an interesting qualification; it reeks of the English aristocrat's contempt for those ordinary souls engaged in trade; despite the anti-finance bias of much of his economic writing, in his heart he seemed closer to the City–gentry nexus than his subsequent reputation might suggest. His arrogance, another marker of his class, could be breathtaking at times. Unlike Marx, who wanted to "organize the myriad Lilliputians and arm them with poisoned arrows," Keynes thought that folks like him could manage everything through their disinterested sophistication. Marxism, he claimed, "enormously overestimates the significance of the economic problem. If you leave that to me, I will look after it" (*CW* XXVIII, p. 34).

In fact, he thought the *General Theory* had solved "the" economic problem, in both theory and practice. With that single shot, he claimed, he'd killed both Ricardo *and* Marx. To Keynes, both belonged to the "self-adjusting school" of "classical economics" (quoted in Behrens 1985), failing as they did to grasp the doctrine of liquidity preference and the drag on investment exerted by high interest rates. Here Marx and Ricardo are joined in their sunniness. But elsewhere he joined them in gloom: "Marxism is a highly plausible influence from the Ricardian economics, that capitalistic individualism cannot possibly work in practice." In both cases, the equivalence is as strange as Foucault's (1973, p. 262) declaration that the struggle between Marxians and Ricardians was "no more than storms in a children's paddling pool," since they both shared a common dream of an end to History. But Foucault had the excuse of deeming economics a 19th century concern, an excuse unavailable to an economist like Keynes.[13]

Keynes could not have read Marx's (1973, p. 410) succinct criticism of Ricardo and his colleagues for having "conceived production as directly identical with the self-realization of capital — and hence were heedless of the barriers to consumption or of the existing barriers of circulation itself," because the *Grundrisse* wasn't published until three years after the *General Theory*. But it would strike someone who'd bothered to read *Capital* as pretty familiar stuff; after all, Ricardo isn't exactly known as an impassioned prophet of capitalism's demise in quite the same way Marx is.

But Keynes could have read (in German, according to Behrens, which he read well) this from the third volume of *Capital;* "Those economists like Ricardo, who take the capitalist mode of production as an absolute, feel here that this mode of production creates a barrier for itself and seek the source of this barrier not in production but rather in nature (in the theory of rent)" (Marx 1981, p. 350). Were the parasitical landlords smashed, accumulation could continue apace. Keynes, you could say, sought the barrier not in nature, but in the mind of the capitalist and in the excessively austere policy preferences of a sadomonetarist central bank.[14] Were the rentiers smashed, then accumulation could continue apace. In that sense, Keynes had more in common with Ricardo than he would have liked to admit.

Keynes and the contradictions

Five pages of the *General Theory* (*CW* VII, pp. 353–358) are devoted to the rehabilitation of Gesell, a writer almost universally regarded as a monetary crank. Keynes sees him as a kindred renegade, vilified by the orthodox but really onto something (though of course not onto everything, having missed the centrality of liquidity preference). Keynes celebrated Gesell as the inventor of "an anti-Marxian socialism, a reaction against *laissez-faire* built on theoretical foundations totally unlike those of Marx in being based on a repudiation instead of on an acceptance of the classical hypotheses, and on an unfettering of competition instead of its abolition." To Gesell, the payment of interest holds back the accumulation of capital. If interest could be forced to zero, then accumulation would accelerate and universal prosperity would be our reward.

But of course interest rates can't be forced to zero, nor can the rentier be euthanized, nor can financial innovation be snuffed, without transforming capitalism in ways far more radical than Keynes envisioned. Recall Schumpeter's (1939, vol. 2, p. 613) observation that financial innovation "is one of the most characteristic features of the financial side of capitalist evolution…. This is not mere technique. This is part of the core of the capitalist process." An attack on liquidity and innovation is an attack on the core of the capitalist process, which is why Keynes's suggestions have been so thoroughly repressed by mainstream economics— rarely even argued with, but simply ignored. Many Keynesians seem mystified by this apparent oversight, apparently believing that ideas become dominant simply on their merits.

In times of reaction, when Marxism is regarded as beyond the pale by many even on the left, Keynes has become a more acceptable model, especially in these days of financial ascendancy. Few economists of any time have had as much to say about the financial markets themselves, or their relation to the real world. As Adorno said of Freud, "like all great bourgeois thinkers, he left standing undissolved such contradictions [those of bourgeois society] and disdained the assertion of pretended harmony where the thing itself was contradictory. He revealed the antagonistic character of the social reality" (quoted in Zizek 1994, p. 14).[15] The more fervent bits — like the call for the "somewhat comprehensive socialization of investment" — offer the appeal of radicalism, but in a calm, elegant form, and in one that may unsettle, but not shock, the ruling order. Keynes was a very seductive writer. But as Michael Perelman (1989, p. 1) put it in his very useful book on Keynes, he often sounded "more radical than he was."

Take, for example, the concept of "uncertainty," which he made a lot of, and his more loyal modern followers treat as revealed truth. It is an accurate description of the conditions under which real human beings, not Greek letters in a neat academic model, make real decisions about investment and many other aspects of life as well. It is a powerful antidote to the certainties of Chicago School economists. But it can only explain so much. Post-Keynesians hold that it is the main explanation for the existence of money; if there were no uncertainty, people would be happy to settle transactions in IOUs (backed by promises), but in an untrustworthy world, money (backed by the state) is essential to the settlement of debts.[16] While this is not without truth, this banalizes money, robbing it of its force as the fundamental principle of social organization under capitalism.

But the real problems with Keynes lie ultimately in the naïveté and conservatism lurking behind his sophisticated and iconoclastic style. Having (re)discovered that "entrepreneurs" (a word he and post-Keynesians like Davidson prefer to the more loaded "capitalists") are in business to make money, and nothing else, he somehow concluded that rentiers will consent to their euthanasia. Compare this vain wish to a 150-year-old observation: "In England there takes place a steady accumulation of additional wealth, which has a tendency ultimately to assume the form of money" (quoted in Marx 1981, p. 543). A tendency indeed: money, whatever its economic role, is most definitely not neutral in its social role; the accumulation of money is the fondest desire of every good capitalist citizen. Keynes realized this with one half of his mind, and then with the other half thought you could tweak this fundamental tendency out of existence almost unnoticed. Having laid bare some real contradictions, he spuriously proposed to resolve them.

And further, having discovered in two ways, those of the *Treatise* and the *General Theory*, that capitalism does not tend of its own accord to full employment and stability, Keynes (1936, p. 379) then declared at the end of the *General Theory* that his goal was not to overturn the "Manchester system," but merely to liberate its full potential.

The complaint against the present system is not that these 9,000,000 men ought to be employed on different tasks, but that tasks should be available for the remaining 1,000,000 men. It is in determining the volume, not the direction, of actual investment that the existing system has broken down. Thus I agree with Gesell that the result of filling the gaps in the classical theory is not to dispose of the 'Manchester System,' but to indicate the nature of the environment which the free play of economic forces requires if it is to realize the full potentialities of production.

The problem of capitalism lies not in the exploitation of labor, the creation of poverty amidst plenty, the abuse of nature, the atomization of society, nor the trivialization of culture, but simply in its incompleteness — that one in ten are denied its full delights. But given full license, Keynes and his epigones could solve that problem. Too bad the capitalists haven't let them do it yet.

But they did, in a sense — not the sense in which Keynes meant it, and post-Keynesians still mean it, but in a sense illuminated by Antonio Negri (1988). Here's how Keynes (*CW* XIV, pp. 112–122) defined uncertainty in a 1937 essay that was a response to critics of the *General Theory*:

> By "uncertain" knowledge, let me explain, I do not mean merely to distinguish what is known for certain from what is only probable. The game of roulette is not subject, in this sense, to uncertainty; nor is the prospect of a victory bond being drawn.... Even the weather is only moderately uncertain. The sense in which I am using the term is that in which the prospect of a European war is uncertain, or the price of copper and the rate of interest twenty years hence, or the obsolescence of a new invention, or the position of private wealth-owners in the social system in 1970. About these matters there is no scientific basis on which o form any calculable probability whatever. We simply do not know.

The examples given, notably the last — "the position of private wealth-owners in the social system in 1970" — are of a weighty sort, the kinds of doubts that nag investors in the midst of crises like those of the 1930s. In the First World, we haven't seen its like in 60 years. Here's how Negri read Keynesian uncertainty and the role of the state:

> Investment risks must be eliminated, or reduced to the convention, and the state must take on the function of guaranteeing the basic convention of economics. The state has to defend the present from the future. And if the only way to do this is to project the future from within the present, to plan

the future according to present expectations, then the state must extend its intervention to take up the role of planner, and the economic thus becomes incorporated in the juridical.... [The state] will not guarantee the certainty of future events, but it will guarantee the certainty of the convention.... In effect, the life of the system no longer depends on the spirit of entrepreneurialism, but on liberation from the fear of the future.

The role of the state, then, is to stabilize expectations — to guarantee there won't be depressions, and to guarantee (insofar as anything can be guaranteed) the position of private wealth-owners in the system. In these senses, bastard Keynesianism did the trick — of, to paraphrase Claus Offe, regulating the system politically without materially politicizing it. The establishment took what it needed from Keynes and left the rest.

posties

Though I've mentioned post-Keynesian economics several times in this chapter, I've barely fleshed out the mentions. But two matters deserve closer attention — theories of monetary endogeneity, and the work of Hyman Minsky. Both are barely acknowledged, much less known, in the mainstream.

money emerges from within

In conventional economics, of both the monetarist and the eclectically mainstream varieties, the money supply (not always precisely defined) is determined from "outside" the system of private exchange by the central bank; these are exogenous theories of money. The Fed or any of its siblings around the world injects money into the system, and banks, households, and firms do their business accordingly. Adherents to endogenous theories of money argue instead that the money supply is a function of the demand for credit, which is itself a function of the level of economic activity. The banking system, along with the central bank, creates as much money as people need, though there are disagreements on just how elastic this process is.[17]

Robert Pollin (1991; 1993) usefully divided the two major schools of post-Keynesian endogenists into the accommodative and the structural. Accommodative endogeneity holds that the central bank has no choice but to validate private credit demand by providing whatever reserves the banking system needs to accommodate the loans that it has already made;

that means there is no effective constraint on credit. Leading proponents of this school include Nicholas Kaldor and Basil Moore. Structural endogeneity — the branch that appeals to both Pollin and me — holds that central bank attempts to constrain the growth of credit are frequently evaded through creative finance.

Moore (1988a, p. 139), the leading living accommodationist, takes a good idea way too far, as he did in this surreal passage:

> The process of monetary accommodation, the validation of money wage increases which the data reveal, is mistakenly viewed, by both monetarists and post-Keynesians alike, as the result of a process of *active* policy intervention by the central bank. The notion appears to be that the monetary authorities keep their eyes focused on the state of the economy in general, and on the level of unemployment in particular.

Instead, Moore argues, the central bank passively validates decisions made by private creditors.

In fact, the Fed scrutinizes the real economy closely. Take, for example, the minutes of the December 22, 1992 meeting of the Federal Open Market Committee (Federal Open Market Committee 1993, p. 323)

> The information reviewed at this meeting suggested that economic activity was rising appreciably in the fourth quarter. Consumer spending, in association with an apparent upturn in wage income and a surge in confidence, had improved considerably; sizable gains were being registered in the sales and starts of single-family homes; and business spending for capital equipment remained strong. There also had been solid advances in industrial output, and private payroll employment had turned up. Data on wages and prices had been slightly less favorable recently [that is, wages have been rising, always a danger — D.H.], and on balance they raised the possibility that the trend toward lower inflation might be slowing a little.

The minutes went on to report detailed observations regarding employment, the average workweek, industrial production, retail sales, business invesment, construction, and the trade picture. (To give a measure of how detailed: "sales of heavy trucks rose sharply, and business purchases likely accounted for some of the recent sizable increase in sales of light trucks; on the other hand, shipments of complete aircraft were weak.") All this discussion of the real economy preceded discussion of financial and monetary affairs, and far exceeded it in volume as well. The central bank runs a huge economic data generation and analysis apparatus, which confidently second-guesses official statistics, and, a Fed economist once told me, frequently prompts corrections that are buried in routine monthly revisions in Commerce and Labor Department data. Every twitch in the statistics is noted and mused over to death.

And those conclusions are based on public releases of the Fed's minutes. According to Drew University economist Edwin Dickens (personal communication), who's read the full transcripts — which are released only 20 years after the fact, and read by almost no one — policymakers are exceedingly obsessed with wage increases and the state of labor militancy. They're not only concerned with the state of the macroeconomy, conventionally defined, they're also concerned with the state of the class struggle, to use the old-fashioned language.

When things look too bubbly for the Fed's satisfaction, it tightens policy, by lowering its targets for money supply growth and raising its target for the fed funds rate. In doing so, it hopes to slow down the economy, but there's often many a slip between tightening and slowdown. The reason for this gap was explored nearly 40 years ago by Hyman Minsky (1957) in a classic paper modestly titled "Central Bank and Money Market Changes." Minsky pointed to two innovations of that relatively sleepy time, the federal funds market, which allows aggressive banks to transcend the limits of their own reserves by borrowing from surplus banks, and the growing presence of nonfinancial corporations, eager to make money on spare cash, as providers as well as users of credit. Both were responses to rising short-term interest rates, which, as Minsky wrote, pushed actors "to find new ways to finance operations and new substitutes for cash assets." Market innovations, Minsky stressed, would complicate the work of central bankers, since tight policy could be partly offset with new instruments. Innovations, as Minsky (1975, p. 76) later pointed out, allow capital asset prices to continue rising (and economies to continue expanding) against the dampening influence of rising interest rates.

Over time, with the proliferation of financial innovations, the "compounded changes will result in an inherently unstable money market so that a slight reversal of prosperity can trigger a financial crisis," wrote Minsky 40 years ago. This would require an extension of the central bank safety net to the entire financial matrix, not merely the commercial banks that were its legal charges. Fighting inflation might entail a terrible financial cost, and so the Fed would be forced to err on the side of indulgence whenever the credit system looked rocky.

Perhaps Minsky was a little early — the first financial crisis of the post-

1945 period was the credit crunch of 1966 — but he described the mechanism perfectly: first the rising inflation of the 1960s and 1970s, followed by the Volcker clampdown, which was lifted when it looked like Mexico's default would bring the world banking system down. But the Volcker clampdown required driving interest rates far higher, and for a longer period of time, than anyone would have expected, to shut the economy down, so creative are the innovators at evading central bank restraints. In the 1980s and 1990s, innovations proliferated, as interest rates remained high by historical standards (despite their declining trend). Capital was mobilized as it hadn't been in 60 years, as it became clear that while the poor could expect no indulgence from the new economic order, the rentier class, some notorious bad apples aside, could count on a blank check.

Of course, Minskian innovations can't evade the tightening hand of the central bank forever. Perhaps the most sensible view of the whole matter was that expressed by a central banker, Alan Holmes (1969, p. 73), then a senior vice president at the New York Fed, speaking at a time when the monetarist challenge was marginal but on the rise: "In the real world, banks extend credit, creating deposits in the process, and look for the reserves later. The question then becomes one of whether and how the Federal Reserve will accommodate the demand for reserves. In the very short run, the Federal Reserve has little or no choice about accommodating that demand; over time, its influence can obviously be felt." This is a refreshing antidote both to the mechanistic nostrums of the monetarists and to the vision of limitless elasticity of the extreme endogeneists like Moore. The Fed, like all central banks, is mighty, but it is not almighty.

Why does this matter beyond the world of scholarship? If the endogenous money theorists are right — and they are — then money and commerce are inseparable; neutrality is a fantasy. That has several implications. It locates tendencies towards financial instability and crisis at the heart of the system, rather than outside it, as Friedman and other state-blamers would have it. It makes conventional monetary policy more difficult to manage, since "money" becomes a very slippery thing. And it makes radical reforms more difficult than many populists would like, since policies aimed at finance aim at a moving target, and one not easily separable from production, or from ownership.

Marx (1973, p. 126; 1981, p. 674; see also de Brunhoff 1976, pp. 80, 98) anticipated modern Keynesian endogenists, arguing (against Ricardo and the classical quantity theorists) that the quantity of money in circulation is determined by economic activity, and not the other way around. Not the least of the reasons for this influence is that the extension of credit is such a short step from simple exchange for money; an IOU can be exchanged between any agreeable partners, and it's only a small matter to bring in a bank to formalize the transaction. This was true even under a gold standard; these spontaneous contracts make the line between money and credit a porous one, and that explains why the modern money supply is so flexible. Of course, in Marx's view, these extensions of credit become worthless in a crisis, as everyone scrambles for gold; this kind of crisis hasn't been seen in this century, as central banks have learned how to contain crisis and make short-term government paper seem as good as gold.

Minsky

Of all the modern theorists in the Keynesian tradition, one of the most interesting is Hyman Minsky, who devoted his career to exploring the relations between finance and the real world.[18] We've already looked at his contribution to theories of monetary endogeneity; the rest of his work deserves a few more pages.

Following the lead of Keynes's *Treatise,* with its separate industrial and financial spheres, Minsky developed a two-sphere theory of a modern capitalist economy, one of current output and one for capital assets, which jointly determine the level of economic activity. Expectations about the short term determine how much of existing capacity will be used; expectations about the long term determine decisions about whether to expand capacity. Decisions of the latter sort have consequences over time; managers who make bad investments, and especially those who borrow money to make them, will suffer losses. If such losses are sustained and widespread, the system faces the risk of deflationary collapse. This analysis is familiar to a reader of Keynes's *General Theory,* but it got lost when Keynes was domesticated for textbooks and politicians.

A serious problem with Minsky's analysis, at least when applied to the modern U.S. economy, is that rather little real investment is financed by borrowed money. So while borrowing and investment decisions have long-term consequences, they're not simply two sides of the same coin. In the U.S. and most other First World economies, investments are overwhelmingly financed internally, through profits. Corporate managers have shown great reluctance in recent years to commit themselves to long-term investment, for fear of being stuck with useless capacity in a recession; investment has increasingly been skewed to short-lived, quick-payoff equipment.

But during the 1980s, managers were not shy about borrowing; here another portion of Minsky's analysis is illuminating. In a taxonomy that can be applied to individual units, like firms or households, or whole economies, Minsky (1978; 1986, pp. 207–209) divided financial structures into three types, hedged, speculative, and Ponzi. A unit with a "hedged" structure is one that can comfortably service all its debts, interest and principal, out of current income; a "speculative" unit can meet its interest payments, but must raise new funds, either through the sale of assets or the extension of new loans, to pay off principal; and a "Ponzi" unit can't make its interest payments, much less pay off principal, without finding fresh cash.[19]

Economies traverse the hedge–speculative–Ponzi sequence, until a bad financial accident scares players into prudence, and the cycle starts over again. In recent American experience, the late 1920s were a time when the border was crossed from speculative to Ponzi, until the great crash and subsequent Depression brought the scheme to a disastrous end. That bout made nearly everyone very debt shy, and the largely excellent performance of the U.S. economy in the 30 years after World War II meant that firms and households had little need for outside finance. But, Minsky argued, that kind of Golden Age makes people more complacent, reducing their fear of indebtedness: "stability is destabilizing," a formulation sometimes called the Minsky paradox. For a while, this new imprudence fuels a boom, but with few signs of general financial strain; individual units, and the whole economy, cross from hedged to speculative financial structures, as debts are rolled over. The margin of error narrows. While hedged financial structures are vulnerable to real-world shocks — firms might face new competition, or households face a period of unemployment — they're largely immune to financial disturbances. But speculative units are not only more vulnerable to real-world shocks, they're vulnerable to financial market troubles as well, since they need new credits to pay off old principal. If interest rates spike upwards, or credit gets hard to come by, a speculative unit is in trouble.

While it would be hard to draw a fine historical line, it seems that the U.S. economy entered the speculative realm sometime in the 1970s, as financial crises became more prominent features of the business cycle (Wojnilower 1980; Wolfson 1986). But in every case, the Federal Reserve stepped in to prevent the financial crisis from becoming generalized; individual institutions might be allowed to go under, but the authorities would never allow this localized crisis to spread into a broad deflationary collapse. Further, Big Government and its deficit spending put a floor under the economy, preventing a true cascade of failure from developing. But "validating threatened financial usages," in Minsky's (1986, p. 251) phrase, only emboldens players for further adventures in leverage on the next up cycle. And so the indulgence of the 1970s laid the groundwork for the even more exuberant 1980s, when the U.S. economy unquestionably entered a Ponzi phase. Corporate takeovers were frequently done with the open admission that the debt could never be comfortably serviced, and that only with asset sales or divine intervention could bankruptcy be avoided. Households, too, engaged in similar practices, as balloon mortgages were arranged — that final balloon payment could only be made by taking out another mortgage as the first one matured.

What does Minsky's model say about recent history? While the slump of the early 1990s was clearly the result of a Ponzi structure going sour, the authorities moved to contain the crisis. Between 1989 and early 1994, the Fed drove down interest rates hard and kept them there. At the same time, the U.S. government bailed out the savings and loan industry through the Resolution Trust Corp., spending $200 billion in public funds. These moves kept the financial system from utter collapse, but unlike the 1930s, debts were not written off. Thanks to lower interest rates, debts were easier to service, but the stock of debt — principal — tells a different story. The best way to measure this is by comparing the level of debts outstanding with the incomes that support them. For nonfinancial corporations, total indebtedness in 1995 was nearly 11 times after-tax profits — an improvement from the over 22 times level of 1986, but still twice the levels of the 1950s and 1960s. For households, the figures show no such improvement: in 1995, consumer debts were equal to 91% of after-tax income, the highest level since the Fed started collecting such data in 1945, and well above 1980s levels, which were themselves well above 1970s levels.

To use Minsky's language, the business sector seems to have settled back from Ponzi to speculative, but households continue to explore fresh Ponzi territory, with no signs of temperance. One message of these numbers is that the U.S. economy remains very vulnerable to higher interest rates. "At high enough short term interest rates speculative units become Ponzi units" (Minsky 1978), and Ponzi units explode.

Minsky emphasized financial factors in causing instability, with the real mentioned almost as an afterthought. A more balanced interpretation would say that financial structures are central to the propagation of a general economic crisis. Any shock to a highly leveraged structure — a business, household, or national economy — makes it impossible to service debts that seemed tolerable when they were contracted. For a system-wide crisis, the shocks are generally of a broad sort — a normal business cycle recession, capital flight, or a political crisis. For forward-thinking connoisseurs of crisis, one could imagine some ecological crisis causing crop failures or disastrous climate changes, which cause a spike in prices and/or a collapse in output. Regardless of the cause, a hedged financial structure might be able to cope with such threats, but a Ponzi couldn't.

money, mind, and matter: a psychocultural digression

Money is a kind of poetry.
— Wallace Stevens

Who drinks on credit gets twice as drunk.
— Turkish proverb

One virtue of Keynes's attention to psychology and sentiment is that it urges us to think about economics in a way that most economists find squishy and unscientific. This narrowness of vision has harmed the dismal science immeasurably.

Credit is money of the mind, as James Grant (1992) put it in a book title, though of course every now and then mental money faces an unpleasant coming to terms with matter. Still, in these days of multibillion-dollar bailouts, it seems that mind can sustain fantastic valuations for far longer than ever seemed imaginable in the past.

We could date the modern credit culture's beginning to the severance of paper currencies from gold in the early 1970s. It waxed during the 1983–89 binge, waned during the 1989–92 slump, and waxed again starting in 1993. At its root, it's based on the assumption that a munificent river of liquidity will flow for all time. Someone will always be willing to take an overvalued asset off your hands tomorrow at a price comfortably higher than today's. Two famous axioms from apostles of credit illustrate this faith. In the late 1970s, Citibank chair Walter Wriston, a promoter of Third World lending, rebutted skeptics with the argument that "Countries don't go bankrupt" (quoted in Kuczynski 1988, p. 5). The 1980s' chief debtmonger, the junk bond supremo Michael Milken, used to argue in the days before his incarceration that capital isn't a scarce resource, capital is abundant — it's vision that's scarce (quoted in Bruck 1988, p. 272).

This credit culture is a long way from that described by a 19th century Scottish banker, G.M. Bell (quoted in Marx 1981, p. 679), who thought his colleagues to be finer moralists than clerics:

Banking establishments are moral and religious institutions. How often has the fear of being seen by the watchful and reproving eye of his banker deterred the young tradesman from joining the company of riotous and extravagant friends…? Has he not trembled to be supposed guilty of deceit or the slightest misstatement, lest it should give rise to suspicion, and his accommodation be in consequence restricted or discontinued [by his banker]?… And has not that friendly advice been of more value to him than that of priest?

'The cult of money," wrote Marx (1973, p. 232), "has its asceticism, its self-denial, its self-sacrifice — economy and frugality, contempt for the mundane, temporal, and fleeting pleasures…. Hence the connection between English Puritanism or also Dutch Protestantism, and money-making." In a phrase Keynes also used, it is *auri sacra fames* — the sacred hunger for gold.

This austerity strikes moderns, saturated with commodities, as quaint — though there's nothing passé about sadomonetarist adjustment programs. But there's another sense in which money and religion travel together — especially when money takes the form of a promise rather than a hard form of settlement, that is, when money becomes credit (from Latin, "I believe"). A credit agreement is a profession of faith by both parties: short of a swindle, both parties believe the debtor will be able to repay the loan with interest. It is a bet on the future. This theological subtlety is lost on the information asymmetry theorists, who, even as they concede the possibility of deception, don't allow departures from rational self-interest.

For most of history, credit's dreamier excesses were limited by gold, a metal at once seen as both "natural money" and pure enough to touch the body of Christ. Marx (1973, p. 727):

The monetary system [i.e., gold-based] is essentially Catholic, the credit system essentially Protestant…. [T]he monetary existence of commodities has a purely social existence. It is *faith* that brings salvation. Faith in money value as the immanent spirit of commodities, faith in the mode of production and its predestined disposition, faith in the individual agents of production as mere personifications of self-valorizing capital. But the credit system is no more emancipated from the monetary system as its basis than Protestantism is from the foundations of Catholicism.

Money conflates the sacred and profane; it's no accident that U.S. currency confesses that "In God We Trust."

This conflation of high and low, of matter and spirit, is enough to send a student of money to Freud. By classical psychoanalysis, money is gold, and gold is transformed shit, and exchange relations, sublimated rituals of the anus. Though this is by now a commonplace, readers found this a rather shocking thesis almost 90 years ago. Freud's (1908) essay on the anal character began by noting the coexistence of a trio of features in such cases: orderliness, obstinacy, and thrift. Freud speculated that this unholy trinity — hallmarks of the Victorian bourgeois — springs from an infantile interest in the anus and its products. Orderliness, said Freud, gives "the impression of a reaction-formation against an interest in what is unclean and disturbing and should not be part of the body." Obstinacy represents the baby's lingering reluctance to part with stool on command.

And the infantile roots of thrift are perhaps the most interesting of all. Freud noted the rich associations between money and dirt found in folklore and everyday language. In English, there are expressions like "stinking rich" and "filthy lucre." In legends, "the gold which the devil gives his paramours turns into excrement after his departure.... We also know about the superstition which connects the finding of treasure with defaecation, and everyone is familiar with the figure of the 'shitter of ducats' [a German idiom for a wealthy spendthrift; we have our goose with its golden eggs, more fertile than fecal, but emerging from a neighboring bodily region]. Indeed, even according to ancient Babylonian doctrine gold is 'the faeces of hell.'" Finally, Freud suggested that "it is possible that the contrast between the most precious substance known to men and the most worthless...has led to th[e] specific identification of gold with faeces."

Freud's early followers — notably Abraham, Ferenczi, and Jones — trod the anal path blazed by the master. The accumulation of money is a sublimated urge to retain feces for the very pleasure of it, and the production of commodities is the psychic derivative of the expulsion of feces. Money, in Ferenczi's (1976) marvelous phrase, is "nothing other than odourless, dehydrated filth that has been made to shine."[20]

The psychological equivalence of dirt and money is suggested by the low social status of bankers in premodern times. Using nonfecal reasoning, philosopher of money Georg Simmel (1978, p. 221) speculated that "the importance of money as a means, independent of all specific ends, results in the fact that money becomes the center of interest and the proper domain of individuals and classes who, because of their social position, are excluded from many kinds of personal and specific goals." Among Simmel's examples are the emancipated Roman and Athenian slaves who became bankers, as did Armenians in Turkey; Moors in Spain; and Huguenots, Quakers, and Jews across Europe. Reading Simmel 80 years later, one thinks how the social prestige of banking increased along with the development of credit, that is, with its evolving liberation from gold.

Norman O. Brown, not the most fashionable of writers, found Freudian orthodoxy wanting. He returned the sacred to the analysis of money and demeaned both equally. For Brown (1985, p. 297), money and the sacred were both sublimated products of a revulsion from the body. Such sublimation, whether aimed at god or mammon, is "the denial of life and the body.... The more the life of the body passes into things, the less life there is in the body, and at the same time the increasing accumulation of things represents an ever fuller articulation of the lost life of the body."

To Brown, the exchange relation is imbued with guilt, and the debtor–creditor relation with sadomasochism. In this, Brown followed Nietzsche, for whom all religions are "systems of cruelties" and for whom creditors enjoy "a warrant for and a title to cruelty" (Nietzsche 1967, Second Essay). (Modern usage confirms the link of debt with both sadomasochism and the sacred: "bonds" impose conditions known as "covenants" on debtors.) Creditors in the ancient world "could inflict every kind of indignity and torture upon the body of the debtor; for example, cut from it as much as seemed commensurate with the size of the debt." Creditors can take pleasure in "being allowed to vent [their] power on one who is powerless, the voluptuous pleasure '*de faire le mal pour le plaisir de la faire,*' the enjoyment of violation." Nietzsche might have enjoyed these pleasures.

For Brown, debt is a sickly tribute paid by the present to the past. (Of course, we postmoderns often see — consciously or not — credit as a way to steal from the future.) But for a partisan of the body, Brown was nonetheless guilty of the ancient psychoanalytic habit of dematerializing its needs. As the early analyst Paul Schilder (1976) — who rightly lamented the absence of a psychoanalysis of work — noted, "When one looks over large parts of the psychoanalytic literature one would not conceive the idea that one eats because one is hungry and wants food for sustaining one's life but one would rather suppose that eating is a sly way of satisfying oral libido.... Silberer once said...[that] according to psychoanalytic conceptions...the Danube...is merely a projection of urine and birthwater."

Similarly, Brown's gold is more a fetishized projection of intrapsychic drama than an alienated embodiment of social power. His moneyed subjects lack class, race, nationality, and sex. For Marx, gold was valuable because it embodied human labor and served as the universal exchange equivalent for all other commodities, whose value arises from the labor that made them. But the nature of market relations — anonymous, mathematical — hides the social nature of production and exchange behind a veil of money. As psychoanalysis lacks a theory of work, so does orthodox Marxism lack an understanding of the passions that sustain the disguise. With credit comes a set of passions entirely different from those of gold.

Money, Brown said, is but part of the "commitment to mathematize the world, intrinsic to modern science." But modern science has mathematized money. Aside from doomsayers, survivalists, and other goldbugs, the monetary functions of dehydrated filth are all but forgotten. Even paper money is getting scarce — only about 10% of the broadly defined money supply (M2). Most money now lives a ghostly electronic life.

With this dematerialization of money has come at least a partial banishment of the guilty sadomasochism of the anus. That banishment was seen at its fullest in the 1980s, when fantasy ruled the financial scene; in the early 1990s, the repressed made a partial return, but the mid-1990s saw a relapse of exuberance. But the psychological dethronement, however complete or incomplete, of anality and guilt has an interesting analogue in the cultural and social transformations that so trouble American reactionaries. Capitalism, having undermined the authoritarian–patriarchal family, now produces fewer guilt-ridden obsessives and more hungry narcissists than it did in the days when gold and daddy reigned as the harsh taskmasters from whom there was no appeal. Like the narcissist, today's consumer seems less interested in the accumulation of possessions than in the (novelty-rich, credit-financed) act of purchase itself.[21] Rather than the guilty obstinacy of the anus — or the Puritan character identified by Max Weber as the spirit of capitalism — one detects a more primitive, fickle, and eternally dissatisfied orality. In contrast with the dry, tight, fixed, "masculine" aura of gold, modern credit money seems protean, liquid, and "feminine."[22]

Unlike the classic neurotic, whose conflicts centered around anxiety and guilt over what were seen as dangerous or forbidden desires, the modern narcissist complains most about a sense of emptiness, of disconnectedness, of a free-floating rage and anxiety attached to nothing in particular. Under a superficially well-functioning veneer, the upscale narcissist, in Joel Kovel's (1980) words, "is unable to affirm a unity of project or purpose, a common goal, with other people in a way that goes beyond immediacy or instrumentality."

According to Kovel, the transformations of domestic life that have occurred since the capitalist industrial revolution first gave us the authoritarian–patriarchal–obsessive personality type, only to be succeeded by the modern, or postmodern, narcissistic type. The breakup of traditional social arrangements that came with the development of the capitalist labor market meant that the scale of social life expanded — transportation and communication making people far more mobile and informed about life beyond their locality — and shrank, as the nuclear family became the central focus of all non-work life. "Childhood" in the sense of a protected, privileged phase of life was invented sometime in the 19th century.

This child-centered, father-dominated life became increasingly penetrated, Kovel argued, by the state, the media, and the increasing power of the commodity form. The family, in Kovel's coinage, became de-sociated. People's lives became increasingly determined by institutions far beyond their immediate sphere of experience. Decisions about lives in New Jersey are often made by executives in Tokyo; about lives in Brazil made in Grosse Pointe and Milan. The family has effectively ceased to be a barrier against outside events, a haven in a heartless world.

A right-wing version of this analysis calls for a return to the patriarchal family, which is impossible and undesirable. But leaving aside the issues of the politics of the household, we have to wonder how capitalism can survive this new personality type. On one hand, the system, especially its American variant, depends on credit-financed consumption to keep the wheels spinning, but on the other, the financial system can't live indefinitely with its consequences. Policymakers can impose sadomonetarism, but it's not clear that the system can bear it either economically or psychopolitically over the long term. The attempt to evade the sadomonetarist logic produces only a *bizzarria* of hollow prosperity, speculative bubbles, and an atmosphere of generalized irresponsibility. The attempt to conform to it provokes economic stagnation and corrosive popular resentment. This is another way of looking at the Minsky paradox.

Marx

As James Crotty has said, Keynesians have historically emphasized finance at the expense of production, and Marxists production at the expense of finance; many Marxists have treated production as fundamental, and finance as epiphenomenal, a curious replication of orthodoxy.[23] While this is a basically accurate characterization of much of the Marxian tradition, it's not really true of Marx himself. Though Marx's writings on finance are mostly fragmentary and undeveloped, they are richly suggestive, and it's clear he considered it central to his analysis.[24]

Hilferding's curse

One of the reasons for the sorry state of Marxian theories of finance — with the honorable, though recent exception of writers like Crotty, Gerald Epstein, Robert Fitch, Duncan Foley, David Harvey, Robert Pollin, and the editors of *Monthly Review* — is the shadow cast by Rudolf Hilferding and his *Finance Capital*. The book contains something obsolete, misleading, or wrong on almost every page, from minor offenses to major.

Several examples: Hilferding's (1981, p. 137) claim that changes in interest rates can be "predicted with a high degree of probability" would be welcome news to bond traders, were it true.[25] While the relation between the stock market and real activity is far from simple, it is preposterous to argue, as Hilferding did, that production is unaffected by changes in ownership (pp. 135, 141); the M&A boom of the 1980s and 1990s has radically affected the real world. He mocked the notion that interest payments can dampen profits, and thereby investment, or that changes in interest rates have any significant effect on the business cycle (pp. 286–287) — two notions entirely refuted by modern experience. Probably his greatest mistake, however, was his assertion that industry and finance were becoming one, the product of this union being the finance capital of the title, and with it cartels would replace competition and high tariffs would supercede free trade. The "English system" — now known as the Anglo-American system of stock-market centered capitalism — was "outmoded" and "everywhere on the decline" (p. 293); henceforth, banks would control the commanding heights. Speculation and financial crises were relegated to the past, part of the youthful indiscretions of a now-mature capitalism (pp. 292, 294).[26]

Of course it would be wrong to view recent history, which has seen the spread of the Anglo-American system to the Third World, and the undoing of the bank-centered systems of Germany and Japan, and say that the future belongs to stock markets. Social analysts have an unfortunate habit of projecting their own local and recent experience into the universal future. But history has not turned out Hilferding's way, and there is no evidence right now that time is on his side. The relations between financial capital and real, between shareholders and manager, though growing ever closer, are nonetheless extremely complicated; it's hard to say anything about them without wanting to say "but…" immediately afterwards.

Hilferding's errors were more than intellectual — he did real political damage serving as finance minister of the Social Democratic government in Germany in 1923 and in 1928–29. Faced with inflation in his first term, he advocated a return to gold — orthodox, but perhaps understandable, if unimaginative, in the context of the period's hyperinflation. His second term coincided with the great collapse, which drove unemployment from 7% to 30% in a matter of three years. As the collapse unfolded, Hilferding again advocated austerity — budget cuts and tax increases, while resisting all "inflationary" schemes (Darity and Horn 1985). While Hilferding obviously can't be blamed for the collapse, his loyalty to capitalist financial orthodoxy — what Keynes derided in Britain as "the Treasury view" — is inexcusable in a socialist, and further proof that in practical matters, Marxians can be as blinkered as the most austere Chicagoan.

money and power

Several aspects of Marx's theorizing on money and credit are worth savoring: the inseparability of money and commerce, the political nature of money (and the inseparability of market and state), and the role of credit in breaking capital's own barriers to accumulation.

Unlike mainstream economics, which has a hard time joining theories of money to theories of production, the two are inseparable in Marx. Production is always for profit, and exchange is always for money, and the existence of money presupposes and embodies the whole set of capitalist social relations. This is important not only in the strictly "economic" sense but as is always the case in Marx, also the broadly political sense as well. "The individual carries his social power, as well as his bond with society, in his pocket" (Marx 1973, p. 157). Words like "power" and "bond" are not seen in mainstream economics texts.

Behind the illusions of the market as "a very Eden of the innate rights of man...the exclusive realm of Freedom, Equality, Property, and Bentham" (Marx 1977, p. 280) lie harsher realities. Money, far from being the neutral lubricant of classical theory, or the politically neutralizable one of Keynesian theory, is fundamentally about compulsion and command: capitalists who can't turn their products into cash go under (or in these more indulgent days, file for reorganization), and workers who can't turn their labor into cash will starve. As Negri (1991, p. 23) said in one of his less opaque moments, "[M]oney has only one face, that of the boss." Or as Martin Scorsese put it, talking about his movie *Casino,* "The more gold, the more blood. The more you show the money, you have to show the blood" (Weinraub 1995).[27] What is true for Scorsese and Negri is rarely true for orthodox economics; it invents models that hide the blood and the boss.

In this deeply political role, as one of the fundamental mechanisms of social organization under capitalism, money and credit not only drive competition between capitals and force workers to work or die, they also regulate the affairs of whole governments and countries. Marx emphasized that despite the fantasies of libertarians, who dream of stateless monies like gold, money has to be guaranteed by a state, and credit supervised by one. Money is purely conventional; there's nothing intrinsically magic about gold or Federal Reserve notes. The various forms of money are valuable because people agree they are, and some forceful monopolist — a central bank and a national Treasury — has to be the ultimate guarantor of agreement, or convention would dissolve.[28]

Credit, too, is an important form of social coercion; mortgaged workers are more pliable — less likely to strike or make political trouble. And they need money to live; nearly everyone below the upper middle class is just a few paychecks from insolvency. Any state-sponsored action that lessens the sting of starvation's discipline — unemployment insurance, minimum wages, employment guarantees — is possible only when the working class is strong, and in turn strengthens the class politically; capital passionately wants to maximize the naked rule of money. Even a tight labor market is a threat to discipline, which is why industrialists as well as bankers worry when the unemployment rate gets too low. Some loyal Keynesians, even after having lived through the last 20 years, in which the rule of money has been sharpened, still refuse to concede these points.

money and crisis

Just because production and money can't easily be separated doesn't mean they're identical. In fact, Marx anticipated Keynes in seeing the separation of production and sale as the root of possible crisis — and in treating this as an explicit rejection of Say's law. Money brings in time and the possibility of hoarding: time, because a good is usually sold some time after it is made, running the risk that its sale price could fall below the cost of its production, wiping out the capitalist's expected profit, and hoarding because income need not be spent but may merely be kept idle, since money is a uniquely "imperishable commodity" (Marx 1973, pp. 149, 198–200).

Pure paper and bank money did perish in 19th century crises, so for Marx the most imperishable form of money was gold. In a normal, modern crisis, the flight to money is usually to Treasury bills; but even in modern crises, gold, ridiculed by Keynes as a "barbarous relic," usually regains its charms. In the Third World, a panic can take the form of a flight from the domestic currency, not into gold, but into U.S. dollars. Economies with currencies in collapse often have a whole second set of dollar prices, though it's usually the affluent who have access to greenbacks.

The precise meaning of a cash hoard is not as clear as it might seem. For Keynes, capital kept as money rather than being put into long-term instruments like stocks and bonds was hoarded. But most moderns hoard by parking their money in some short-term instrument like a money market fund or Treasury bills. Therefore, what the hoarder means not to spend still finds its way into the financial circulation, which may end up funding GM's working capital or the Pentagon's purchase of infrared binoculars. Conversely, money spent buying stocks or bonds almost exclusively goes to the previous holders rather than their issuing firms. Clearly, though, the more money that enters the financial circulation, the less is spent on actual goods, thereby increasing the risk of commodities going unsold.

Those complications aside, a reluctance on the part of buyers to part with their funds can bring about a contraction in an economy, and it's the existence of money (and developed financial markets) that makes it possible for players to retire easily and safely from goods markets.

Just as money can't be separated from production or exchange, neither can credit be fully severed from the "real" economy, appearances of their independence to the contrary. "A reciprocal effect takes place here. The development of the production process expands credit, while credit in turn leads to an expansion of industrial and commercial operations" (Marx 1981, p. 612). This is true in several senses: businesses borrow to finance capital expenditures or buy other companies; businesses borrow to buy raw materials and parts; businesses extend credit to their customers (trade credit); and individuals borrow to buy consumption goods. All these forms of credit stretch the limits of both production and consumption beyond what current incomes alone could have managed.

Besides these needs from the borrowing side, there is also the need of capitalists and rentiers to deploy their money profitably; these surpluses, which emerge from production, drive the supply of credit. The credit system makes all forms of capital fungible; it lubricates the transition of every form of wealth into its most wonderfully liquid form, money — "the material representative of general wealth" (Marx 1973, p. 233) — and makes it possible for money, sterile in itself, to be transformed into profit-seeking capital. From this point of view, both sides of the argument between neoclassicals and Keynesians about whether savings precedes investment or vice versa seem reciprocally incomplete; the two activities depend on each other.

Marxists and other theorists of underconsumption have long pointed to the limited buying power of the masses as a perpetual flaw of capitalism. "The ultimate reason for all real crises always remains the poverty and restricted consumption of the masses, in the face of the drive of capitalist production to develop the productive forces as if only the absolute consumption capacity of society set a limit to them" (Marx 1973, p. 615). Though it's not often theorized as such, consumer credit can be thought of as a modern instance of credit's assistance to capital in breaking the barriers to its expansion. Where Marx (1973, p. 613) said that credit to producers stretches their capacity "irrespective of the limits of consumption," consumer credit stretches the limits of consumption — and provides lenders with yet another chance to earn interest on cash that might otherwise have gone idle.

Credit does this mighty work of limit-stretching by pushing firms and households into fundamentally unsustainable positions — transforming them into Ponzi units, in Minsky's taxonomy. At some point, a shock to the system makes debts unserviceable, and then, as they say on Wall Street, it's revealed that leverage is as powerful on the downside as it is on the upside. While it's imprecise to say that credit "causes" such a crisis — the "shock" is usually some interruption of incomes for the indebted units — the credit system is at the center of any crisis' onset and propagation. In the 19th century and into the early 20th, crises were typically marked by "panics" — financial crashes that metastasized throughout the economy, leading to extended depressions. The most recent, and quite possibly final, example of this was the 1929 stock market crash, which marked the opening of capitalism's greatest crisis, the Great Depression. Popular explanations sometimes name the crash as the "cause" of the Depression, while allegedly more sophisticated explanations deny the relation. But the crash is best seen as the opening movement of the broader crisis — the unraveling of a monstrously leveraged financial structure. Credit had served to push stocks to unsustainably high levels; it had also allowed production to expand capacity beyond the limits of consumption. The crash exposed these limits, announced the unsustainability of promises to pay, and rendered investments unprofitable and debts unserviceable. A Fisher deflation was underway.

Of course, we don't have Fisher deflations today; we have expensive bailouts, and not just in the U.S. Actually, the recent U.S. bank and S&L bailouts were rather modest in comparison to disasters elsewhere. Estimates are that the combined losses and rescue costs in the U.S. disaster were about 3% of a year's GDP — compared with 4% for Norway's bank crisis, 6% for Sweden's, 8% for Finland's (all from the late 1980s and early 1990s), and, the world champion, 17% for Spain's (which ran from 1977 to 1985). Altogether, about two-thirds of IMF member countries experienced some sort of credit disaster between 1980 and 1996. Such disasters may have been successfully contained, but that doesn't mean they're insignificant or rare. In fact, some analysts argue that the banking disasters of the last quarter-century are historically unprecedented in both frequency and size (Goldstein and Turner 1996).

There is an important exception to the rule that generalized collapses no longer happen. As Penny Ciancanelli (1992) nicely put it, during the debt crisis of the 1980s the First World banks got a Minsky bailout while the Third World suffered a Fisher deflation. Domestic banking crises in Third World countries over the last decade or two have been far more intense than in the First, with losses ranging from 10% to 25% of GDP. Those countries, however, were unable to mount the kinds of rescue operations seen in the North, and their economies have, in many cases, suffered depressions, sparked and propagated in the classic Fisher manner.

But the experience of successful First World bailouts shows that Marx (1981, p. 621) badly underestimated the power of the state when he said that crises could not be avoided by "allowing one bank, e.g. the Bank of England, to give all the swindlers the capital they lack in paper money and to buy all the depreciated commodities at their old nominal values." Central banks and governments need not go that far; prudential supervision (forgotten in the 1980s, but more or less remembered in the 1990s, with the occasional exception) and multibillion dollar rescue packages have done their work.

Still, credit has made it possible for expansions to exceed what would otherwise have been their natural limits, and the threat of crisis arose when those limits became clear. The S&L disaster ripened (leaving aside the pure swindling, the yacht parties with their cocaine and call girls, the thrift presidents stealing money to expand their personal art collections, etc.) when it became clear that the shopping centers and condos that were built on its lines of credit proved economically pointless; the junk bond crisis ripened when the corporate buyouts and restructuring that junk originally financed were revealed as the Ponzi units they were. Money of the mind had an uncomfortable collision with matter. But thanks to the Resolution Trust Corp. and Alan Greenspan, these crises never became generalized, unlike their ancestors 60 years earlier. No one can proclaim that it will work this way forever, but so far, this has to be counted a major innovation in the state management of capitalism. It may be that the slow rot that has characterized the U.S. economy over the last 25 years — low levels of investment and productivity growth and the decline in real wages — is the system's subtle revenge on its political saviors. But it would be wrong, at least by Marx's lights, to call that rot a crisis, since "permanent crises do not exist" (Marx 1968, p. 497).

credit, consciousness, and beyond

What are we to make socially and politically of the facts that the financial markets have so marginal a role in guiding production in advanced economies, and that the stock market's influence on real investment is thankfully minimal? It's that rentiers serve little social role beyond their own enrichment. As Marx (1963, p. 212) said, rentiers, like paupers, live only on the revenue of the country; from an economic point of view they are equally unproductive; rentiers are simply "respectable paupers."[29]

Marx (1981, pp. 483–484) also quoted Ramsay approvingly as saying that as a country gets richer it produces rentiers, and "in old and rich countries, the amount of national capital belonging to those who are unwilling to take the trouble of employing it themselves, bears a larger proportion to the whole productive stock of society, than in newly settled and poorer districts." Marx thought this growing accretion of rentier wealth would depress interest rates over the long term, but this seems not to be the case.

But it has come to dominate the capitalist world-picture. Money, "the god among commodities," becomes *the* principal object of greed — greed in its most general form, for wealth itself, rather than more specific obsessions, "for clothes, weapons, jewels, women, wine, etc."[30] Certainly 19th century magnates loved their money, but they also took pride in the physical capital they owned — steel mills and transcontinental railroads. Such obsessions now seem quaint; modern tycoons love their portfolios most of all. Interest-bearing capital, Marx (1971, pp. 454–539) wrote, is the most fetishistic form of all, capital *par excellence,* with profit (interest) appearing with no more than the mere passage of time, with no apparent engagement with production: money-bearing becomes characteristic of capital "just as growth is characteristic of trees."

While this progression from industrial to rentier dominance seems to prevail on the global level, it's especially visible when one looks at the history of individual countries and the movement of capitalism's center of gravity: from the Netherlands to Britain to the U.S. and towards Asia. The speed of this evolution seems to have accelerated, with Japan evolving from master industrialist to rentier nation in little more than a generation.

In higher rentier consciousness, production disappears from view. This is apparent not only in ruling-class thinking, but even among its supposed critics. Many postmodern cultural theorists, for whom class is an obsolete concept left over from when production mattered most, see the world as one of identities and desires formed and expressed in the sphere of consumption. "Capital," complained Andrew Ross (1988, quoted in Hawkes, 1996, p. 8), "or rather our imaginary of Capital, still belongs for the most part to a demonology of the Other. This is a demonology that inhibits understanding and action as much as it artificially keeps alive older forms of *ressentiment* that have little or no purchase on postmodern consumer society."[31] Capital becomes fictive, a product of imagination rather than a real social relation; all antagonism disappears, and money becomes not a form of coercion, but a realm of desire, even of freedom. This is unsurprising coming from capital's house intellectuals, but it seems to infect even its opponents. Forms meant to disseminate these mystifying temptations — the media, advertising, PR — become the principal objects of study in themselves, overshadowing relations of property and power.

Immateriality simplifies the work of apologists, as it complicates that of critics. Interest-bearing capital is a "godsend" to bourgeois economists, who yearn to represent capital as an independent source of value in production — which therefore *earns* its profit just as workers earn their wages. Interest, especially in its compounded form, "appears as a Moloch demanding the whole world as a sacrifice belonging to it of right, whose legitimate demands, arising from its very nature, are however never met and are always frustrated by a mysterious fate" (Marx 1971, p. 456). But reformers who aim to transform or abolish credit "without touching upon real capitalist production [are] merely attacking one of its consequences." Interest-bearing capital is a distillation of capital as a social form, not some phenomenon above or apart from it. Therefore, abolishing interest and interest-bearing capital, Marx (1971, p. 472) argued, "means the abolition of capital and of capitalist production itself."

Capitalism without interest may be impossible, but credit and interest predated capitalism; usury, and prohibitions against it, are ancient. Usury came to dominate the feudal order, bleeding it of wealth and hastening its demise, but under capitalism, Marx (1971, p. 531) argued, credit is subordinated to production. That looks less true now; the needs of money seem increasingly to take precedence over those of production. This is seen most visibly in the shift of policy-making in the rich countries from the stimulation of growth to its suppression in the name of holding down inflation. Instead of acting as a stimulus to production, the credit system — the preservation of paper values — looks increasingly like a barrier.

It would be wrong, though, to attribute this just to a mood swing among the policy-making class. As economies mature, rentier wealth accumulates; family enterprises become public companies, and fortunes become severed from their roots. On the capital markets:

> All particular forms of capital, arising from its investment in particular spheres of production or circulation, are obliterated…. It exists in the undifferentiated, self-identical form of independent value, of money…. Here capital really does emerge, in the pressure of its demand and supply, as *the common capital of the class….* [It appears] as a concentrated and organized mass, placed under the control of the bankers as representatives of the social capital in a quite different manner to real production (Marx 1981, pp. 490–491; emphasis in original).

The modern owning class is formed in large part through the creation and trading of standardized claims on the wealth and labor of others.

What do such owners contribute? In what Marx knew as a joint-stock company, and we know as the modern large corporation, not much. Unlike classical capitalists, who ran the operation and thus earned something like a wage of superintendence along with a share of the profits, today's managers are paid a (high) wage of superintendence, while the profits go mainly to outsiders. Of course that high managerial wage, even if it takes the form of a paycheck, still has to be considered mainly a share of profits. But the lion's share goes to outside stockholders and creditors.

It's tempting to bemoan this relation as parasitical, which it is, but that's not all. "The social form of capital devolves on interest, but expressed in a neutral or indifferent form; the economic function of capital devolves on profit of enterprise, but with the specifically capitalist character of this function removed" (Marx 1981, pp. 506–507). That is, rentiers receive their share of profits in what feels like interest, even if their literal form is dividends with little trace of its origins (since dividends appear as the return that capital earns simply with the passage of time), and the managers run firms as professional supervisors — as workers (even if more royally paid than in Marx's day) rather than owners.[32] The classic 19th century apology for capital, which held profit to be the wages of superintendence, has long been undermined. In the late 20th century, the social role of functionless owners is rarely investigated, but their case is hardly compelling.

Modern bosses *are* paid monstrous salaries; one study, by Pearl Meyer & Partners Inc., found that CEOs of big firms earned 212 times what the average U.S. worker did in 1995, compared with a mere 44 times in 1965 (Duff 1996). But their role as managers doesn't require these vast sums; they're paid that well just because they can get away with it. And with the growth of professional managers working for distant shareholders, "the capitalist vanishes from the production process as someone superfluous." Cooperatives show, Marx said, that workers could hire managers as easily as do the owners of capital (Marx 1981, pp. 511–512).

The growth of credit allowed entrepreneurs with no capital, whether skilled, unskilled, or felonious, to use the capital of others. Previsioning Donald Trump, whose net worth was held together in the 1980s in part by slick, publicist-generated magazine articles about how rich and successful he was, Marx wrote: "The actual capital that someone possesses, or is taken to possess by public opinion, now becomes simply the basis for a superstructure of credit." Previsioning modern pension fund managers, who appropriate workers' savings and run them largely in their own interest, paying themselves grandly in the process, he wrote: "What the speculating trader risks is social property, not his own. Equally absurd now is the saying that the origin of capital is saving, since what this speculator demands is precisely that *others* should save for him" (Marx 1981, p. 570).

The chain of displaced responsibilities that characterize modern corporate capitalism, Marx argued, was essential both to its development and the development of better possibilities.

> But within the capitalist system itself, this expropriation takes the antithetical form of the appropriation of social property by a few; and credit gives these few ever more the character of simple adventurers. Since ownership now exists in the form of shares, its movement and transfer become simply the result of stock-exchange dealings, where little fishes are gobbled up by the sharks, and sheep by the stock-exchange wolves. In the joint-stock system, there is already a conflict with the old form, in which the means of social production appear as individual property. But the transformation into the form of shares still remains trapped within the capitalist barriers; instead of overcoming the opposition between the character of wealth as something social, and private wealth, this transformation only develops this opposition in a new form.... Without the factory system that arises from the capitalist mode of production, cooperative factories could not develop. Nor could they do so without the credit system that develops from the same

mode of production. This credit system, since it forms the principal basis for the gradual transformation of capitalist private enterprises into capitalist joint-stock companies, presents in the same way the means for the gradual extension of cooperative enterprises on a more or less national scale. Capitalist joint-stock companies as much as cooperative factories should be viewed as transition forms from the capitalist mode of production to the associated one, simply that in the one case the opposition is abolished in a negative way, and in the other in a positive way (Marx 1981, pp. 571–572)

At the beginning of this excerpt, Marx seemed to be writing about the formation of modern corporations in the mid-19th century, a time of Robber Barons, scam artists, and financial panics — a process being repeated today in the so-called emerging markets of the Third World. In the First World, things are a bit more regularized now. But Marx's essential point is that corporations represent proof that the mechanisms of social production are separable from the structure of ownership. In other words, the modern corporation shows that production can be organized on a large scale over time and space, bringing together thousands of workers in phenomenally productive cooperation. But these institutions are nonetheless run by and for a small group of owners and managers whose social role is peripheral or even harmful to the institution's proper running. This contradiction, in Marx's words, constitutes "the latent abolition of capital ownership contained within it" (Marx 1981, p. 572).

Capitalist ownership had thus become socially useless at the same time corporate capitalism had created a powerful organizational form. Indeed, this very separation of ownership and management, made possible by the joint-stock company and stimulated by the development of modern credit markets, had become a powerful motor of growth:

[Credit is] the principal lever of overproduction and excessive speculation…because the reproduction process, which is elastic by nature, is now forced to its most extreme limit; and this is because a great part of the social capital is applied by those who are not its owners, and who therefore proceed quite unlike owners who, when they function themselves, anxiously weigh the limits of their private capital. This only goes to show how the valorization of capital founded on the antithetical character of capitalist production permits actual free development only up to a certain point, which is constantly broken through by the credit system. The credit system hence accelerates the material development of the productive forces and the creation of the world market, which it is the historical task of the capitalist mode of production to bring to a certain level of development, as material foundations for new forms of production. At the same time, credit accelerates the violent outbreaks of this contradiction, crises, and with these the elements of dissolution of the old mode of production.... The credit system has a dual character immanent in it: on the one hand it develops the motive of capitalist production, enrichment by the exploitation of others' labour, into the purest and most colossal system of gambling and swindling, and restricts ever more the already small number of the exploiters of social wealth; on the other hand however it constitutes the form of transition towards a new mode of production. It is this dual character that gives the principal spokesmen for credit, from Law through to Isaac Péreire, their nicely mixed character of swindler and prophet (ibid., pp. 572–573).

Modern anticorporate antiglobalizers — like people in and around the San Francisco-based International Forum on Globalization (Henwood 1996a; 1996b) — seem not to appreciate any of these virtues of capitalist socialization, and have no sense of how to organize social production on any reasonable scale.[33] Big multinationals may be too large on social and political grounds, if not economic ones, but there's no way to sustain an industrial society without something like the corporate form.

Marx's view that corporate capitalism has made possible its own transcendence, by organizing production on a large and sustained scale and simultaneously rendering its owners socially vestigial, has gone somewhat out of fashion, to put it mildly, but is sorely worth recovering. In the light of his interpretation of the corporation as containing the seeds of a postcapitalist future, an analysis of that institutional form is in order — in the interests not only of understanding but also of transformation.

notes

1. References to Keynes, unless otherwise noted, are to the *Collected Works,* abbreviated as *CW,* followed by the volume number and page. *The General Theory* is volume VII, and its pagination matches that of the popular Harcourt Brace paperback edition.
2. Production is measured by expenditures on production during the period covered; incomes are those derived from production. While capital gains on the sale of assets may seem like income to an individual, to the NIPAs they don't exist, since there is no corresponding production to charge the income against. For more on national income accounting conventions, see Young and Tice (1985) and U.S. Department of Commerce, Bureau of Economic Analysis (1992).
3. Post-Keynesianism is a label applied to a varied set of economic theories that are at odds with both centrist Keynesian and right-wing monetarist theories. Post-Keynesians

typically dismiss what Joan Robinson called "bastard Keynesianism" — the revisions of Keynes's thought that gutted its more radical content, reducing it to a mere tool for countering the business cycle — particularly the notion of boosting the budget deficit through tax cuts and/or spending increases to fight a recession. Post-Keynesians place great emphasis on financial instability and the importance of uncertainty in keeping investment below the level that would guarantee full employment. Post-Keynesians don't believe that capitalist economies tend automatically toward optimal outcomes; instead, markets often fail, prices don't necessarily give the right signals to participants, and the best plans are often frustrated by surprises that come with the passage of time. By contrast, mainstream neoclassical economists believe that markets always clear (that is, supply and demand always balance, leaving neither buyers nor sellers unsatisfied), prices give accurate signals, and time is of little theoretical interest except maybe in the short term. Though generally left-of-center, post-Keynesians range from those like Paul Davidson, who are strongly pro-capitalist, through social democrats and, at the extreme, to economists who combine Keynesian theories of finance with a Marxian analysis of production and a hostility to capitalism as a system. The latter trace their pedigree to Michal Kalecki; other ur-figures include Nicholas Kaldor and Joan Robinson. Davidson insists on spelling it "Post Keynesian." He said (personal communication) this was to distinguish his brand of thought from the "brand of neoclassical synthesis Keynesianism" that Paul Samuelson was calling post-Keynesian in the 1970s. The hyphen's absence, said Davidson, is "a matter of product differentiation." Even Davidson, however, is regarded as *outré* by the mainstream of the economics profession. For a brief overview, see Holt (1996).

4. Fixed capital consists mainly of machinery and buildings; working capital, of materials in the process of production; and liquid capital, of inventories (Keynes *CW* V, p. 116).

5. Note that interest rates affect only investment goods markets. Keynes, accurately reflecting the practice of his time, said that borrowing to finance consumption was so "uncommon" that it could be safely neglected (*CW* V, p. 238). But now it reads like a memoir of an innocent time. In the first quarter of 1996, consumer credit in the U.S., excluding mortgages, totaled $1.1 trillion, and home mortgage debt, $3.4 trillion — amounts that could never be ignored, theoretically or practically.

6. When I presented a version of this argument at a *Grant's Interest Rate Observer* conference in 1994, Sir Alan Walters, a Thatcher intimate who was in the audience, objected strenuously to my choice of monetary aggregate — what corresponds to the U.S. M2. "No no no!," he exclaimed; "you should have used Sterling M0!" A medieval theologian could have done no better. A review of some major empirical studies of the relation between money growth and inflation by the Bank for International Settlements (Gerlach 1995) showed that most of the tales of money causing inflation are the result of including countries with very high rates of inflation; when those are eliminated, the relation all but disappears. In most cases, extreme inflation is associated with gigantic budget deficits financed by the central bank's printing money, typically in response to some extreme condition like war or social collapse — in other words, cases of little relevance to normal situations in the rich industrial countries.

7. Of course there are many rates of interest in the real world, dependent on the maturity of a loan and the perceived riskiness of a borrower. Speaking of "the" rate of interest is merely shorthand for the constellation of rates in effect at a given moment. Keynes's use of MEC is rhetorically interesting; one wonders if he preferred the technocratic term because it avoids the unpleasant class associations of "profits."

8. It is almost a law of the social sciences that the virtue of anything called "natural" is that it preserves the status quo. Riffing on Wicksell's concept of the natural interest rate, Milton Friedman introduced the idea of nature to unemployment. In his 1967 presiden-

tial address to the American Economic Association — his presidency was an early sign of the profession's rightward move out of Bastard Keynesianism towards sadomonetarism — he argued that if the authorities pushed unemployment below its natural rate, inflation would be inevitable (Friedman 1968b; Pesaran 1992).

9. Or as they say on Wall Street, during a bull market, cash is trash.

10. The description applies to many markets, not just stocks. What reasonable tales have the gyrations in oil prices over the last 25 years told? Were the long-term prospects of oil any different at $30 a barrel from $3? Do any of these prices tell us that oil is a finite resource that will asphyxiate us if we burn all the crude that lies underground?

11. And of course it would be the worst sort of vulgar Marxism to attribute Bentham's emergence and influence to the needs of the evolving competitive market system.

12. By monetary crank I mean someone who believes that the major problems of capitalism are the result of debt and interest, ignoring the overriding importance of profit, and instead holding that if you fix finance everything else will fall into place.

13. The idea must of been all over Paris in the early 1970s. In *The Mirror of Production*, Baudrillard (1975) made a very similar argument.

14. One of the leading post-Keynesians, Paul Davidson (personal communication) responded to my assertion that the decline in real business investment was caused by the decline in corporate profitability by saying that the decline in profitability was the result of bad monetary policy.

15. Both Freud's and Keynes's theorizing was transformed by bourgeois society into techniques of adjustment: psychoanalysis became a branch of mental hygiene, and Keynesianism part of a toolbox for business cycle management.

16. There was a lively exchange on this topic on the Post Keynesian Thought (PKT) computer network involving Paul Davidson, Randall Wray, and many others including me in the spring of 1995. It's on the PKT archive, <http://csf.colorado.edu/mail/pkt/index.html>. Look for the April–June 1995 files.

17. This paragraph elides the distinction between money and credit, as I've done several times throughout this book. In the narrowest sense, money is the instrument used for the final settlement of debts. In a world where gold is considered the only real money and everything else — from paper money to the most exotic financial instrument — is credit, the distinction is pretty firm. But in a world where gold is a relic and paper and electronic transactions prevail, then the distinction is very hard to preserve. We think of dollar bills as money, but they are an obligation of the Federal Reserve, backed, if you can call it that, by the Fed's assets, which are mainly U.S. Treasury bonds. Currency accounts for only about a third of M1, the narrowest definition of the money supply in U.S. practice; checking accounts are responsible for most of the balance, but checks are fundamentally a credit instrument, since the recipient has to assume they're not made of rubber. Classically, most forms of money in developed capitalist economies represent liabilities of the banking system — some form of deposit or other — or instruments, like money market funds, that are analogous to bank deposits. To hard-money nuts, this is surreal, but their view of gold as the essence of money still depends on a social convention, an act of faith not unlike credit. At a slightly higher level of sophistication, goldbugs love the metal because it's the only form of money that doesn't depend on the creation of debt, but if it weren't for debt, capitalist economies would never have grown as dramatically as they have. Debt is more fundamental to capitalism than gold.

18. As I was making final corrections on this book, Minsky died. This was a great loss. It's hard to think of another economist who contributed as much in the decades after World War II, and with as little recognition.

19. The name "Ponzi" comes from the famous financial con game run by Charles Ponzi,

which promised huge returns to investors — but could pay off the first round of plungers only with money taken in from a second round, the second from the third, and so on. Sooner or later you run out of new suckers, and the whole thing crashes down. Mainstream economists sometimes object to Minsky's use of the term as inappropriate to something as serious as corporate finance, but it seems exactly right to me.

20. Anyone who has observed modern goldbugs knows that behind their faith often lies a deep snobbery, a contempt for "common," debased forms of money like paper, which lack the aristocratic status of the sacred metal. Economically, they love the austere, punishing regime of a gold standard, which makes mass prosperity difficult, and hate loose money, which threatens to make prosperity more widespread than it should be. Though there is an economic point to this, the psychosocial truth is another matter entirely; while gold is certainly rarer than feces, both are undifferentiated substances; an ingot is as characterless as a turd. But, as Fenichel (1945, p. 281) wrote, the anal characters who love money love the kind that *appears* to be "*not* deindividualized; they love gold and shining coins."

21. Or as the Slits put it in their 1979 song "Spend, Spend, Spend": "I need something new/ Something trivial will do/I need to satisfy this empty feeling."

22. Needless to say, the gender contrast alludes to convention, not to timeless essences.

23. Even a Marxist as admirable as Anwar Shaikh (1995) takes a very fundamentalist view of finance. To Shaikh, the volatility of stock returns is not a function of Shiller-like overreaction, but is an accurate reflection of real-sector developments — specifically, the marginal profitability of new corporate investments. When questioned, Shaikh says that the direction of influence is only one way, from the real to the financial, with the financial side having no significant effect on the real at all. Shaikh is unable to provide a mechanism that explains this determination other than a notion of "turbulent arbitrage"; he can estimate marginal profitability, but no real investors compute it the way he does. It's likely that his model is simply capturing the same business cycle and interest rate effects that link stock markets and the real world; in fact, his measure is not unlike Wall Street estimates of the next quarter's profits — though of course the analysts do theirs ahead of the fact, and economists after it. Further, his "discovery" hardly undermines the notion that stock markets overreact to short-term data — quite the contrary, it confirms it in a roundabout way.

24. One example of this centrality: "I exclude Sismondi from my historical survey here because a critique of his views belongs to a part of my work dealing with the real movement of capital (competition and credit) which I can only tackle after I have finished this book" (Marx 1971, p. 53).

25. Not only is this empirical nonsense, it's un-Marxian. Unlike commodity exchange, argued Marx, which is ultimately regulated by the law of value — the relative labor time embodied in commodities — the rate of interest is regulated only by market competition (though broadly conceived, allowing for the influence of tradition, culture, and central bank policy). And, when it is "competition as such that decides, the determination is inherently accidental, purely empirical, and only pedantry or fantasy can seek to present this accident as something necessary" (Marx 1981, p. 485).

26. No list of his most embarrassing moments can omit his prediction, uttered days before Hitler's appointment to the Chancellorship, that the Nazis would never take power (Darity and Horn 1985).

27. This sense of money is snuffed by remarks like those of Duncan Foley, in his introduction to de Brunhoff's (1976, p. viii) *Marx on Money*: "Marx's writings on money remain in a 'pre-model' stage, and it will be necessary for us to bring this theoretical position to the point of exact expression in a series of models." Why ever must we do this? How would it offer any more illumination than the *Grundrisse*'s prose? Would it make it a

"Marxian" model if one included a dummy variable for the boss's face, and another for the spillage of blood?

28. Recall that even during the days of the high gold standard in the 19th century, the ultimate regulator of the system was the Bank of England, with the British Navy always lurking in the background.

29. Marx opposed revenue to capital; capital is a kind of cash flow that returns a profit, but revenue doesn't. From the employers' point of view, a wage paid to a productive worker is a form of capital, since the worker creates more in value for the capitalist than he or she pays out in the wage; from the boss's point of view, a worker is a profitable investment. (If this sounds harsh, blame capitalism, not Marx.) But paupers and rentiers produce nothing in return for their income; they simply consume, without contributing a profit or a product in return.

30. Many postmodernists are skeptical about speaking of capitalism as a system. But in its role as the general form of wealth, and in its "political" role as emphasized by Negri, money is the institution that renders — in its violent, reductive, yet seductive way — all the fragments into exchangeable parts of a single system, be the fragments commodities, services, bits of nature, even lives themselves.

31. Ross seems to have evolved away from this position, with his more recent interest in the sweatshop reality behind the glitz of the fashion industry.

32. Actually, Marx also anticipated the Michael Jensen critique of bloated managements swindling shareholders out of their rightful booty: "over and above the actual managing director, a number of governing and supervisory boards arise, for which management and supervision are in fact a mere pretext for the robbery of shareholders..." (Marx 1981, p. 514).

33. The IFG is funded by foundations sponsored by Doug Tompkins, the co-founder of Esprit Clothing. Tompkins made his fortune in precisely the sorts of Third World and domestic sweatshops his Forum now denounces. Tompkins' Foundation for Deep Ecology — which ironically owns stock in Telefonos de Mexico, Allstate, Citicorp, and Wal-Mart — has the most Malthusian reputation in the green funding world, not a place known for hostility to the Parson.

6 Governance

If money is an instrument of control, then financial markets are a lot more than the institutional matchmakers for saving and investment. You can see that clearly by looking at how an owning class's power is asserted over corporations and governments through financial mechanisms.

governing corporations

> *[T]he modern corporation may be regarded not simply as one form of social organization but potentially (if not yet actually) as the dominant institution of the modern world.... Where its own interests are concerned, it even attempts to dominate the state.*
> — Adolph A. Berle and Gardiner C. Means, *The Modern Corporation and Private Property*

Marx was right; the separation of the unitary capitalist into the rentier and manager was an important innovation in the history of capitalism. Surprisingly few economists since have given the matter much thought.

Given the vast powers of big business, how firms are run is of great interest to almost everyone. But in American public speech, consideration of the firm and how it's run is confined to a fairly narrow circle of specialists in the professional and businesses press.[1] So restricted, the debate takes on the quality of a family fight within capital. For example, writing in the *Harvard Business Review,* a place where academic theory meets real business practice, one of the gurus in the field, John Pound (1995), identified the three "critical constituencies" of a firm: managers, shareholders, and the board of directors. Ordinary workers, customers, suppliers, and communities aren't included.

One reason the governance issue is interesting is that it's an implicit admission that markets do not regulate themselves as perfectly as we're told. If the competitive market system worked as well as its adherents say, then there would be little need for shareholders to worry about how "their" corporations are run; reward and punishment would be administered by "the market," with minimal conscious intervention. The same could be said about the stock market; if it really did discipline ineffective managers and reward good ones, then the governance debate would be pretty small beer. But obviously neither the product nor stock markets work as advertised. That means that capital is admitting that corporations must be subject to some kind of outside oversight. If that's the case, then the question becomes oversight by whom, in what form, and in whose interest.

Few economists pay much attention to corporations, or how they're owned and run. As Eugene Fama (1991) noted, "many of the corporate-control studies appear in finance journals, but the work goes to the heart of issues in industrial organization, law and economics, and labor economics." He might have added politics and culture, since these too shape and are shaped by big business. Corporate governance is too important a matter to be left to finance theorists.

Economists often analyze financial structures, if they look at them at all, in a fairly mechanistic fashion. Changes in corporate investment are treated as almost hydraulically influenced by changes in interest rates or stock prices.[2] They pay much less attention to financial structures as institutions of legal and social control.

Take, for example, the difference between debt and equity. Modigliani and Miller famously said there was none of any significance. But as Oliver E. Williamson (1988; 1993) noted, there are great qualitative differences between them. According to Williamson, the appropriate form of finance varies with the nature of the underlying corporate assets. Debt is appropriate if the proceeds are used to fund "highly redeployable" assets; if the borrower gets in trouble, the debt-financed assets could be sold, and the debts repaid. To finance more specialized investments, which depend on a specific firm or a narrow market for their value, equity is more appropriate, since equity gives the suppliers of funds the right to supervise managers — and replace them, should things go wrong. In practice, however, shareholder supervision isn't as easy as that sounds, as we'll see in a bit.

The relations between financial and governance structures have become clearer in recent years, as increasing attention has been paid to international differences in corporate ownership and control and their possible influence on economic performance. Broadly speaking, the U.S. and Britain share a structure characterized by widely dispersed ownership and loose external controls, while Japan and Germany exhibit much more concentrated ownership and tighter external control. Of course, such an extreme characterization does violence to the particulars, and especially so since the systems in all four countries have been changing in recent years, but it's still a useful place to start.

The fundamental issues are these: stockholders want high stock prices, bondholders and other creditors want their interest paid regularly and their principal eventually returned, and managers want a peaceful life with high salaries and minimal external intrusion. (In most mainstream theories, what workers want is of no matter; the only theoretical problem is how to get the most effort out of them for the least pay and with the least supervisory exertion.) Often these goals collide. High-risk strategies that might pay off in a big gain in a firm's stock price may strike creditors as putting the security of their payment stream at risk. Stockholders may resent the conservative influence of creditors on corporate strategies. Both sets of outside interests may resent managerial perks and complacency, while managers might try to mislead outsiders into thinking the corporation is doing better than it really is. When a firm gets into trouble, stockholders are likely to favor indulgence (that is, some degree of debt forgiveness), while creditors are often happy to see stockholders wiped out and the firm wholly or partly liquidated to satisfy their claims. Further, different classes of creditors — there's usually a hierarchy, with some more senior than others — may have different interests in a bankruptcy. Managers, however, are often tied to a firm, either through habit, or convenience, or what economists call firm-specific human capital (which means that skills honed over the years in a particular corporate environment may be near-worthless in another), and reluctant to see it liquidated.

transactional analysis

In much received economic theory, the firm is a simple black box, with no conflicts among managers, workers, creditors, and owners (stockholders).[3] The firm simply applies raw materials to its stock of machines and labor, creates a product that it costlessly and unproblematically sells, and earns profits for its shareholders. Later, Modigliani and Miller would show that it didn't matter where the capital came from, so external finance too became just another input, like labor and raw materials, of no great theoretical or practical interest.

In a famous paper that was largely responsible for his winning of the 1991 Nobel Prize in Economics, Ronald H. Coase (1937) challenged this orthodoxy. Coase posed the question, largely unasked in classical economics, of why firms exist. Coase quoted this aphorism from Sir Arthur Salter as embodying the classic (and classical) mode of thought — a view that was to become the routine punditry of the 1990s: "The normal economic system works itself." That is, supply and demand, production and consumption, are equilibrated by the self-regulating mechanism of the price system. Of course, individuals plan for themselves within this self-regulating miracle, but no coordinating institution beyond that is required.

But, Coase countered, Salter's view does not obtain within the firm at all. "If a workman moves from department Y to department X, he does not go because of a change in relative prices, but because he is ordered to do so." Firms, in a formulation of D.H. Robertson that Coase quoted approvingly, are "islands of conscious power in this ocean of unconscious cooperation like lumps of butter coagulating in a pail of buttermilk" (as if the butterlumps thought themselves into existence). Not every aspect of economic activity can be encompassed by the price system. The costs of negotiating contracts for everything would be prohibitive; were a boss to take bids and write a contract for every letter she needs typed, nothing would ever get done. In Coasian language, the transaction's costs would exceed its return. Further, contracts cannot be written to cover every eventuality; every spill can't be anticipated, so it pays to have a janitor on hand to deploy whenever an unexpected disaster presents itself. In such cases, the price system hardly enters the picture. Or, in Coase's concise definition, "the distinguishing mark of the firm is the supersession of the price mechanism."

But under capitalism, the scope of conscious planning rarely extends beyond a firm's boundaries; the price system is the normal governor of relations among firms and between firms and final consumers. Conventional economics still treats the market as essentially self-regulating: the system, outside the firm, still works itself. But in reality there are substantial costs of time and money devoted to making the system work. Sellers must seek buyers, and buyers must weigh the competence and honesty of sellers. Transactions costs are far from trivial — as much as half U.S. GDP, according to one estimate cited by Coase (quoted in Williamson and Winter 1993, p. 63).

Though Coase didn't make the point, the transaction cost argument for the existence of the firm can be applied to the provision of capital. Conventional theory assumes that entrepreneurs can raise capital for their projects effortlessly and costlessly, when in fact they cannot; even the most seasoned corporation has to pay commissions to the bankers underwriting its paper, and for less established and virginal ventures, capital can be expensive to raise, if it's available at all. Established firms economize on such costs by tapping their own in-house sources of capital — profits. As the figures cited in Chapter 2 on the cost of finance show, these transaction costs are quite stiff, making internal finance quite attractive.

By introducing the firm as an institution and the transaction as a unit of analysis, Coase did help bring economics into closer engagement with the real world — though as he noted in 1970, the paper was "much cited and little used" (quoted in Williamson and Winter 1993, p. 61). Mainstream economics remained largely indifferent to the costs of the price system, at least until the 1970s — ironically, as the supposedly costless "magic of the marketplace" was about to score great political triumphs.

But in some ways, Coase simply exchanged one black box for another. While his firm was exposed to the competitive price system on the outside, the firm itself was a conflictless hierarchy that "worked itself." The workman told to move from Y to X did as he was told, and there was no conflict between managers and owners, or creditors and stockholders. And aside from the rigors of competition, his model of transactions was also rather pacific. There was no stark conflict between producer and consumer, worker and boss. While his intellectual heirs have introduced some aspects of these conflicts into their analysis, they tend to use the ideologically neutered language of transactions, contracts, and information, rather than the more blooded language of conflict and struggle.[4]

The rediscovery of Coase in the 1970s led to a school of transactions costs economics, Oliver Williamson prominent among its practitioners, who use the theory to explain much of social life. Any organization can be seen as existing to economize on costs. While it's refreshing to see mainstream economists take some notice of institutions, their assumptions are still deeply individualistic. Their basic unit of analysis is the transaction; all the social mechanisms that precede and surround the transaction are elided. The firm — or nonprofit organization, government, or even family — is seen as a web of individual contracts, not a social organism with a life of its own. Politics and power largely disappear in what's called the new institutional economics.

Radical institutionalists look to Veblen for a sharper view (Knoedler 1995). Veblen noted that many transactions are undertaken not for efficiency, but for reasons of power — to undermine competitors or secure monopoly position. He emphasized that businesses wanted to make money, not run the best industrial system imaginable. The difference in emphasis is important, because the Coasian view sees the corporation's role as maximizing efficiency, not profit, which is another matter entirely. Advertising, planned obsolescence, predatory pricing, and spurious innovation are partly or wholly socially useless, even malignant, activities, but they are profit-maximizing. Veblen also argued that an industrial system run for social efficiency rather than maximum profit might see more internalized and fewer market transactions. Sometimes profit-maximizing will lead to socially beneficial combination and coordination, but sometimes it won't. Janet Knoedler (1995) argued, for example, that GM's integration with its suppliers (like Fisher auto body) had less to do with economizing on costs than with simplifying the annual style change, a marketing rather than an industrial consideration. But that is getting political, which is something most economists never do.

theorizing corporations

You have to leave the field of economics to find much interesting thinking about corporations. There's no better starting point than the taxonomy proposed by the César Ayala (1989) in his excellent survey of the field. Ayala, a sociologist, divided the literature on the control of big business into three schools of thought — Robber Baron, Managerial, and Bank-Spheres. As he put it, "The Robber Baron school is committed to the idea that Big Business represents a historical regression which reintroduced 'feudal' elements into the economy; the Managerial school is committed to the idea that managers 'rule' the economy; and the Bank-Spheres school is committed to the idea that banks 'rule' the economy." All three views have a long pedigree, and remain popular today, embedded in populist thought of both left and right.

The Robber Baron school holds that the great empire builders of the late 19th and early 20th century — like Gould, Rockefeller, and Morgan — appropriated through violence and conspiracy the wealth of the nation that was once dispersed in the hands of small producers. Rather than viewing concentration as proceeding from the inner essence of capitalism, as both Marxists and most business historians would, the Robber Baron school sees it as a perversion of a "natural" state of competition. This naturalization of petty capitalism is a dearly held American myth; it forgets the violence that marked the appropriation of the continent in the first place, and it also forgets the earlier violence that marked the establishment of capitalism in Europe — the theft of common land, the criminalization of vagrancy, of even poverty itself, that Marx called primitive accumulation. While the Robber Barons undoubtedly committed many crimes, legal and moral, during the course of their empire building, and businesses today commit crimes, literally and figuratively, every day of their existence, there is little doubt that large firms are far more efficient and formidable competitors than the tiny producers they replaced. It was not crime that made big business what it is today, nor is it crime that keeps it there.

In this regard, an interesting contrast can be made with British capitalism, which was very late in adopting the modern large corporate form. Early joint-stock companies were dissolved after they'd done their work of opening up foreign trade, and the mainstream of business was dominated by small and mid-sized firms of a sort more congenial to the Robber Baron school. The smaller firms were owned by a family or a small group of partners, and run in a highly "personal" style, rather than being professionally managed by a well-structured hierarchy. This organizational backwardness gave U.S. and German firms a critical edge as Britain lost ground to its rivals in the late 19th and early 20th centuries (Arrighi 1994, p. 282; Chandler 1990, chapters 7–9).[5]

These British firms also failed to invest at a sufficiently high level. As Chandler (1990, p. 285) noted, these failures happened despite the fact that "London was the largest and most sophisticated capital market in the world," a market, ironically, that German and U.S. firms tapped for finance. British money capital preferred to wander overseas in search of higher returns than were available at home. Deep capital markets are no substitute for good management, and the presence of the first is no guarantee of the development of the second.

Berle, Means, and managerialism

Typically, the concern with the governance of the modern large corporation, which hinges in the classic formulation on the separation of ownership and control, is traced to Adolph Berle and Gardiner Means's *The Modern Corporation and Private Property* (1932/1967). To Berle and Means, modern capitalism is characterized by the simultaneous concentration of production in the large corporation and the dispersion of ownership among hordes of shareholders. That dual movement marked a profound transformation in the nature of property. The function of the 19th century owner–entrepreneur had been divided in two. Formal ownership was delivered into the hands of thousands, even millions, of dispersed stockholders, rarely capable of organizing themselves to affect the operations of the firms whose titles they held. Actual control, however, fell to managers, who though formally responsible to the stockholders, were in fact largely independent, self-sustaining, and answerable to no one in particular as long as things didn't go badly wrong. In the eyes of jurisprudence, a firm and its owners were entirely distinct, with the corporation itself acquiring the rather mystical status of a person under law.

This arrangement is a surprisingly recent innovation in economic and legal life. In the eighteenth century, the corporate charter was essentially a gift of the state, typically for a very specific purpose, like the right to trade in the Hudson Bay area, or to run a ferry service.[6] This tradition extended into the 19th century, as the early railroads were laid down. Frequently it was a grant of monopoly privileges. Charters typically were specific: the enterprise's mission was tightly defined, and its capital structure and financial practices were closely supervised.

With the growth in the scale of production, these strictures were loosened. In 1837, Connecticut passed the first modern law of incorporation, permitting associations "for any lawful business." Over the next 60 years, most other states fell into line. Step by step with the development of the modern corporation — or maybe just a step or two behind — came the growth of managerial autonomy. For example, in the early 19th century, shareholders weren't allowed to delegate their vote by proxy to management; but by the time of Berle and Means, the proxy had become "one of the principal instruments not by which a stockholder exercises power over the management of the enterprise but by which his power is separated from him" (p. 129). Shareholders typically have had neither the time nor the machinery necessary for scrutinizing management and attending annual meetings, so in normal times they delegate the responsibility of voting their shares to the managers who are formally their hired agents.

In his preface to the 1967 revised edition, Berle described the new system as one of "collective capitalism," an affair that yokes together thousands of corporations, and millions of employees, owners, and customers — too many people to be considered private enterprise in the classic sense; and since the state was now so deeply involved in economic affairs, no redefinition of "private" could ever be broad enough to apply. Research was no longer carried out by lone inventors, but in teams, and no longer within a single enterprise, but in cooperation with university and government researchers — often with subsidies from public and nonprofit sources.

(Despite the individualist ideology of the high-tech world, basic research as well as product development still is highly social.) To the 1967 Berle, these changes had moved us "toward a new phase fundamentally more alien to the tradition of profit even than that forecast" in the first edition of their book, published 35 years earlier.

Reading the updated Berle 27 years later, even more than the 1932 original, it's hard to imagine that anyone could have thought that modern corporate society moves by anything significantly different from the maximization of profit. But the belief that the advent of the large corporation had changed capitalism into a more humane, progressive force was a core belief of American liberalism from the New Deal through the end of the 1960s. Profit maximization, the motor of 19th century entrepreneurial capitalism, had been replaced by growth, and competition by long-term corporate planning and administered prices. In one moving *cri de rentier* (pp. 115–116), Berle and Means denounced the potential for managerial abuse of the poor owner: "out of professional pride," managers may "maintain labor standards above those required by competitive conditions," or "improve quality above the point" that is likely to be maximally profitable to shareholders! This holds the potential for "a new form of absolutism, relegating 'owners' to the position of those who supply the means whereby the new princes may exercise their power." Reversing the usual populist casting, it's not the owner of capital who is the parasite in this model, but the managers who run production.

As Berle and Means put it, historically speaking, shareholders have "surrendered a set of definite rights for a set of indefinite expectations" (p. 244). For example, shareholders have no right to sell corporate property on their own; they delegate such powers to their agents, managers. That alone makes shareholding a different kind of ownership from what the common sense of the word describes. But shareholders have an out: they can sell their shares. As Berle and Means said, stock markets are a means for transforming these expectations into cash, which is why the market is "a focal point in the corporate system of today" (p. 248). If there were no market to let them out of a position quickly and cheaply, absentee owners would think twice about assuming their strange role.

Berle and Means spoke of investors as supplying capital to corporations, and argued that the markets' provision of liquidity allows them to get this money back on a moment's notice at no expense to the corporation. But stock investors rarely supply funds to the corporations they own; with rare exceptions, they're simply buying shares issued long ago from others who bought them in the same manner. So the social division of labor that Berle and Means describe — between the providers of capital who are the real risktakers and the managers who are largely insulated from risk — is too flattering to the rentier.

Their characterization of stockholders as entirely passive is quaint. While Berle and Means did acknowledge a disciplinary role for stock prices in general — firms that want to raise equity capital have to cultivate the markets' favor — they allowed for no direct assertion of shareholder influence on management. Quite the contrary; they described the relation between stockholders and the modern firm as fundamentally casual.

> For property to be easily passed from hand to hand, the individual relation of the owner to it must necessarily play little part. It cannot be dependent for its continued value upon his activity. Consequently, to translate property into liquid form the first requisite is that it demand as little as possible of its owner.... [I]f property is to become a liquid [sic] it must not only be separated from responsibility but it must become impersonal — like Iago's purse: " 'twas mine, 'tis his, and hath been slave to thousands" (p. 250).

Impersonal, alienated property, easily parceled out and passed around: what an alluring model of society.

The Modern Corporation and Private Property offered a rethink of the notion of profit (p. 300). By official definitions, profit is the reward for risk-taking and a spur to efficiency. What then will motivate modern managers? Although they control the pace of innovations in production, any windfall profits they might generate will mostly be passed on to stockholders. If managers do innovate, they aren't properly rewarded; and if they know they won't be properly rewarded, they may shirk at innovation. Bureaucracy, dispersed ownership, and complex and contradictory sets of incentives had replaced the clarity of the owner-manager of yore. Berle and Means (p. 245) rather excessively called this an "approach toward communist modalities."

Ironically, this line of thinking has gone out of fashion with the capitalist triumphalism of recent years, whose preferred mode has been the celebration of the entrepreneur. Of course, right-wing ideologues and publicists have celebrated smaller firms and demeaned dinosaurs like IBM, but the grip of giant firms on the U.S. economy — and increasingly on the global economy — has hardly been loosened.

These ideas didn't originate with Berle and Means. A century and a half earlier, Adam Smith (1976, Book 2, pp. 264–265) had this to say about the joint-stock company (a quote that's a staple of the corporate governance literature, and this chapter will be no exception):

> The directors of such companies, being the managers rather of other people's money than of their own, it cannot be well expected that they should watch over it with the same anxious vigilance with which the partners in a private copartnery frequently watch over their own. Like the stewards of a rich man, they are apt to consider attention to small matters as not for their master's honor, and very easily give themselves a dispensation for having it. Negligence and profusion, therefore, must always prevail, more or less, in the management of the affairs of such a company.

Smith made this sound like the doom of capitalism, something the corporate form has obviously not brought about.

Berle and Means themselves cited Walther Rathenau's observations, drawn from German experience, that ownership had been "depersonalized," and the enterprise itself had been "objectified" into "an independent life, as if it belonged to no one…. [This] leads to a point where the enterprise becomes transformed into an institution which resembles the state in character" (p. 309). This prefigured Berle and Means; Smith's observation reads more like an early version of modern rentier thought.

Writing in 1896, Herbert Spencer (1972) noted that the development of the credit system had allowed production to break beyond the limits of individual owners or small partnerships, a development that also "made available for industrial purposes, numberless savings which otherwise would have been idle…. [S]tagnant capital has almost disappeared." Stagnant capital is no capital at all; Spencer meant that money hoards that might have festered in isolation can, by virtue of the modern system, be transformed into capital. But, as he'd written 30 years earlier in "Railway Morals and Railway Policy," the joint-stock structure is rich with opportunities for mischief. The system reproduces all the faults of political democracy, Spencer argued; just as there are tremendous gaps between voters and their representatives, shareholders have little effective control over a firm's directors and managers, and directors and managers resent any expression of supervisory interest. "Like their prototype, joint-stock companies have their expensive election contests, managed by election committees, employing election agents; they have their canvassing with its sundry illegitimate accompaniments; they have their occasional manufacture of fraudulent votes." While modern law has made outright fraud extremely rare, in both the political and corporate arenas, Spencer's description remains an accurate characterization of the corporate proxy contest. The difficulty of running an electoral challenge to corporate management gives the "small organized party" a great advantage over "the large unorganized one." Shareholders are "diffused throughout the whole kingdom, in towns and country houses; knowing nothing of each other, and too remote to coöperate were they acquainted." They know nothing about business, and are, in most cases, "incompetent to judge of the questions that come before them." Spencer painted this unflattering picture of the typical railway's ultimate owners:

> [E]xecutors who do not like to take steps involving much responsibility; trustees fearful of interfering with the property under their care, lest possible loss should entail a lawsuit; widows who have never in their lives acted for themselves in any affair of moment; maiden ladies, alike nervous and innocent of all business knowledge; clergymen whose daily discipline has been little calculated to make them acute men of the world; retired tradesmen whose retail transactions have given them small ability for grasping large considerations; servants possessed of accumulated savings and cramped notions; with sundry others of like helpless character — all of them rendered more or less conservative by ignorance or timidity, and proportionately inclined to support those in authority. To these should be added the class of temporary shareholders, who, having bought stock on speculation, and knowing that a revolution in the Company is likely to depress prices for a time, have an interest in supporting the board irrespective of the goodness of its policy.

Don't managers and shareholders share an interest in maximizing profits? No, Spencer said; managers may have no long-term interest in the firm, but may bend its affairs to maximize their personal profits rather than the firm's. Spencer joins Smith as a precursor of modern rentier thought.

Berle and Means made the same point about managerial opportunism in their conclusion: "the men in control of a corporation can operate it in their own interests, and can divert a portion of the asset fund or income stream to their own uses," and the shareholders are sociologically and legally powerless to stop this. Had they stopped here, Berle and Means would have fit nicely into the proto-rentier crowd. But, according to them, instead of trying to strengthen the rights of "passive shareholders," "the community" could choose to relax classic notions of property rights. Outright plunder should be prevented, but the community must also assert its rights, and the corporation must be governed in "the larger interests of society. Should the corporate leaders, for example, set forth a program comprising fair wages, security to employees, reasonable service to their public, and stabilization of business," the shareholders should accept the hit to profits guaranteed by this high-minded program. Corporate control, they concluded, "should develop into a purely neutral technocracy, balancing a variety of claims by various groups in the community and assigning to each a portion of the income stream on the basis of public policy rather than private cupidity" (pp. 312–313). Economic government would come to resemble classic American interest-group politics.[7]

Mainstream economics acknowledged the transformations outlined by Berle and Means, but claimed that they didn't matter much. Competitive product markets and the threat of takeover assured the basic classical notions of the firm (insofar as the firm was theorized at all) still applied to large, manager-dominated firms as well as small entrepreneurial units. The firm as black box essentially survived both Coase and Berle and Means.

Outside mainstream economics, however, managerialism held great sway, even on much of the left. As Baran and Sweezy (1966, pp. 15–16) said in *Monopoly Capital*, in the modern giant corporation, "control rests in the hands of management...a self-perpetuating group" with "[r]esponsibility to the body of stockholders...a dead letter." They dismissed fashionable propaganda of the 1950s and 1960s — like Berle's, among others — about how the "soulful corporation" had come to balance social responsibility with profit making, arguing to the contrary that modern firms are if anything better positioned to maximize profits than the smaller ones of yore, because of longer planning horizons. In their model, investment funds are almost entirely internally generated (which they still are), and therefore firms are largely independent of the financial sector (which they still aren't). While Baran and Sweezy rightly noted the incredible expense of intermediation — the army of high-paid brokers, agents, and bankers — its role was largely unexamined; instead, finance was reduced to an "absorber of surplus," and dismissed in less than three pages (Baran and Sweezy 1966, pp. 139–141).

For liberals of the 1960s, the scripture was Galbraith's (1967/1978) *New Industrial State*. To Galbraith, the stockholders were vestigial, a "purely pecuniary association" divorced from management, too numerous and dispersed to have any influence (Galbraith 1967/1978, pp. 71–79, 138). When displeased with "their" corporation, they would sell the stock rather than pick a fight with management. Stockholder rebellion among large corporations was "so rare that it can be ignored," because trouble-free profitability was the norm. Of course, management told Congressional committees that the board and the stockholders were in control, and conducted yearly meetings to flatter the nominal owners, but Galbraith's corporation was run by the technostructure.

Unlike Baran and Sweezy, Galbraith dismissed profit maximization as the goal of the giant firm in favor of the growth in sales and prestige. To thrive, it needed not maximum profits, but "a secure minimum of earnings" that would keep it from having to tap troublesome capital markets or cope with demanding outside stockholders (pp. 151–152). Secure mediocrity was the ideal. The technostructure had little to gain from high profits, which would only be passed along to shareholders, and might even entail higher risk — risk that could disturb managerial autonomy. His technocrats were modestly paid, and managerial compensation was divorced from the stock price. "[T]he case for maximization of personal return by top management is not strong" (p. 108). Growth in revenue, however, was a sure route to growing power, prestige, and employment: "Expansion of output means expansion of the technostructure itself" (p. 157). The totem of sales growth was magnified on the national level in the sanctification of rapid GDP growth as the end of all economic activity.

But, warned Galbraith, any lapse in growth could be catastrophic. His reasoning is illuminating in light of recent middle-management layoffs. "Costs can no longer be reduced simply by laying off blue-collar workers." The technostructure had become a major cost-center, in modern jargon, and could not be reduced piecemeal, but would have to be lopped off in vast swathes. Worse, the technostructure would have to make the decision to attack itself — to fire one's fellow club members. Such actions "would not have the agreeable impersonality which is associated with firing someone at a greater distance or of a different social class" (p. 158).

Like Berle, but unlike Baran and Sweezy, Galbraith argued that the large corporation had become subservient to society and the state. Government stabilized the economy, provided a skilled workforce, and set the strategic tone for the national economy. Planning and administration, a joint venture by large firms and the state, had replaced market relations. Stockholders had become "passive and functionless, remarkable only in his capacity to share, without effort or even without appreciable risk, the gains from the growth by which the technostructure measures its success" (p. 356). The (Keynes-echoing) "euthanasia of stockholder power," along with the supersession of the market mechanism by the state and the technostructure, had become "accepted facts of life" (p. 357). Galbraith lodged aesthetic objections to this new regime — it made ugly cities and vulgar ads — but its political and economic triumph seemed secure.

Edward Herman's 1981 study, financed by the Twentieth Century Fund, was a swan song of managerialism. Based on 1970s data, Herman found U.S. firms to be overwhelmingly under managerial control, with a steady decline in control by families, financial interests, and outside corporations since the 1920s. Citing work by Richard Rumelt, Herman nonetheless rejected Galbraith's claims about the diminished role of profit maximization, arguing that the modern corporation's decentralized "profit centers," individual units responsible for profit and loss to top management, were a form of direct scrutiny that could be even more intense than the less immediate pressures of product markets. Senior managers of U.S. corporations often run them as a sort of hothouse capital market, with divisions competing aggressively for the allocation of capital from headquarters.

Managerialism, liberal and Marxist, shared a belief that competition was a thing of the past. Stable oligopolies and managerial rationality had replaced the anarchy of 19th century *laissez-faire*. In some sense, this was an accurate description of the world, particularly the United States, in the 1950s and 1960s. It ceased to be true by the 1970s. The conglomeratization movement of the late 1960s thrust Wall Street into the remaking of corporate America; neither vestigial nor passive, financial operators played board games with whole companies. The recession of 1973–75, then the worst since the 1930s, shattered confidence and was the first view of a new nastiness in the economic tone that would characterize the next 20 years. U.S. firms would suffer the bite of competition from Japan and Europe, smashing the Galbraithian idyll. The deep bear market of 1973–74, the first act of several years of sluggish-to-awful stock markets, led to massive shareholder disappointment and a fresh wave of takeover activity, the first since the 1960s. Managerialism was under siege.

Aux armes, rentiers!

Early U.S. manifestations of bank or financial control theories were the heartland populism of the middle and late 19th century, which was directed against the railroads and the financiers behind them. This populist tradition was picked up by the muckrakers of the turn of the century, who blasted Standard Oil, Morgan, and the other "spheres of influence" (Ayala's Bank-Spheres school). In 1913, the famed Pujo Committee of the U.S. House of Representatives uncovered a system of interlocking directorates and other forms of influence centered around six major banks: J.P. Morgan & Co.; First National Bank of New York; the National City Bank of New York; Lee, Higginson & Co.; Kidder Peabody; and Kuhn, Loeb. The bankers' control over credit to the giant enterprises in their orbit gave them control over the commanding heights of the U.S. economy, creating significant barriers to entry for those outside the circle. This is the purest form of banker control theory. Later analysts, including Paul Sweezy in the 1930s, made similar influence maps, though not always with the same names and positions. Sweezy's model was not bank-centered, but he did include a bank in each one of his eight major groups. Only a few years later, however, Sweezy decided that financial power had declined during the Depression (Ayala 1989), and by the 1960s, finance largely disappeared from *Monopoly Capital*. It reappeared, though, in the pages of Sweezy's *Monthly Review* starting in the 1970s. This oscillating theoretical role for finance is a reflection of historical trends, rather than confusion or inconsistency; it's refreshing to watch a theorist change with the times rather than catechistically stick to a single model and bend the facts to fit.

Interest in financial control, or at least influence, began to grow across the ideological spectrum. In the mainstream, Baum and Stiles (1965), spied a growing potential for financial power that was as yet unexercised. After the 1968 publication of a report by the House Banking Committee, detailing the ownership of large blocks of stock by the trust departments of the major New York City banks, theories of financial control enjoyed a renaissance on the left, notably the long, book-length series in *Socialist Revolution* by Robert Fitch and Mary Oppenheimer (1970) and the later book by David Kotz (1978) — a book that owes a great deal to Fitch and Oppenheimer. Most Marxists rejected the Fitch/Oppenheimer thesis — that the New York banks were exerting increasing control over industrial America, and that managerialism was dead — with great vehemence.

In a response to Fitch and Oppenheimer, Paul Sweezy (1972) answered the question of their title, "who rules the corporations?" with a simple declaration: "monopoly capital rules the corporations, including not only industrials and utilities but also banks and other profit making institutions." Following Marx's formula that the capitalist is the personification of capital, Sweezy argued that monopoly capital was personified by monopoly capitalists, that is, the inhabitants of "the executive suites and boardrooms of America's giant corporations." According to Sweezy, there was no conflict between financial and industrial interests; faithful to Lenin and Hilferding, he argued instead that monopoly capital was the union of finance and industry into a single entity. The giant corporation, with its dozens of subsidiaries and divisions, was more a financial being, not unlike a stock portfolio, than the simple productive unit run directly by an old-style industrialist. If finance were separate from and dominant over industry, Sweezy asked, why did the lordly financiers allow General Motors to set up a subsidiary to finance vehicle purchases (the General Motors Acceptance Corp., or GMAC)?

There's no question that the large Fortune 500-class industrial corporation is run on financial principles, that its business units are often deeply involved in finance — General Electric has a very active financial arm, GE Capital; the other big auto companies have large units like GMAC; and all the familiar rest. But there's also no question that in recent years purely financial interests have increasingly asserted their influence over these hybridized giant corporations.

Kotz outlined several stages in the evolution of finance's relationship with nonfinancial corporations. The first, between the Civil War and World War I was characterized by first the promotion of railroads and then their subsequent reorganization, with the help of European capital, and then the promotion of the big industrial trusts — all under the guiding hand of bankers. The next period, which ran through the 1929 crash, was marked by a trend towards institutionalization and away from strong individual bankers, and the international transformation of the U.S. from borrower to lender. During the New Deal, the bankers were on the run, blamed for the slump and finding themselves under closer scrutiny and tighter regulation. No one needed the investment bankers either; large corporations financed themselves, either through profits or direct deals with institutions, and the federal Reconstruction Finance Corp. usurped "a great part of the functions of what in an economic sense is investment banking," in the words of a Wall Street partner (quoted in Carosso 1970, p. 395). After World War II, however, Kotz argued, there was a resurgence of banker power, led by insurance companies, mutual funds, and, most important, the trust departments of commercial banks.

Unfortunately, Kotz turned to the old model of groups, though he couldn't decide whether the groups were dominated by their banks, with the industrial members subordinate, or if they represented a fusion of common interests. Kotz's classification scheme was this: a Chase group, consisting of two commercial banks, Chase Manhattan and Chemical, and two insurance companies, Metropolitan Life and the Equitable; a Morgan group, consisting of two commercial banks, Morgan Guaranty and Bankers Trust, the Prudential insurance company, and two investment banks,

Morgan, Stanley and Smith, Barney; a Mellon group, consisting of Pittsburgh's Mellon Bank and the investment bank First Boston; and a Lehman–Goldman, Sachs Group, consisting of those two old-line (predominantly Jewish, in contrast to the WASPy pedigree of the other groups) investment banks (Kotz 1978, p. 85). While the case for such alliances has been difficult to make since the New Deal reforms of the 1930s, the concept looks hopelessly out of date in the 1990s. Long-term relationship banking broke apart beginning in the late 1970s; customers and bankers now shop around for the best deal rather than respecting long-term business ties; portfolio management boutiques have eclipsed bank trust departments in money management; and ownership changes have transformed the supposed interest-group landscape. Prudential bought Bache in the early 1980s to have its own in-house investment bank and distribution network for offloading some of its own financial holdings; Smith Barney is now a subsidiary of the Travelers insurance company; First Boston is owned by a Swiss bank; and Lehman has been bought and sold several times.

Kotz was also unable to argue persuasively that financial control made much difference. He claimed that corporations under financial control were likely to maximize profits, with perhaps a bit more caution than they might otherwise — more like old-line capitalist firms than the "soulful" manager-run corporations of high liberal theory (Kotz 1978, pp. 143–144). He further argued that financial control meant a greater concentration of economic and political power than textbook myths about competitive markets and dispersed power. While this is undeniably true, large manager-run corporations also give the lie to textbook myths — it's hard to reconcile the real GM with the textbook image of the passive, price-taking corporation adapting to market conditions — and Kotz's claims about the exercise of monopoly power by banks were largely speculative and unproved.

Kotz and Fitch and Oppenheimer were virtually alone in the 1970s in arguing for a major financial role in the governance of big business. Managerialism had largely won the theoretical argument and it seemed empirically well-grounded, too.

the financial upsurge

Things in the mid-1990s, however, are another story entirely. Today's corporate world bears little resemblance to that described by Galbraith, Baran and Sweezy, and Herman: shareholders are far less passive, boards less rubber-stampish, and managements less autonomous than at any time since

Berle and Means. Since the early 1980s, influence from the financial sphere has been greater than at any time since the 1920s.

It's not so much that the managerialists were wrong. Their descriptions and analysis were right for their time, but the corporate world has changed enormously over the past 20 years. There was little conflict between managers and stockholders during the Golden Age, and it even seemed possible that wages could increase steadily without eating into profits. Large firms could behave as quasi-monopolies, raising prices when costs rose, controlling the pace of technical change, and blocking entry of competitors. Now that Golden Age is gone. Growth is suppressed through tight monetary and fiscal policy, technical change is rapid, companies as grand as IBM and GM can stumble, wages have been forced down to expand profits, and competition is encouraged worldwide by deregulation and market-opening policies. The owners — stockholders, Wall Street, whatever you want to call them — have encouraged these changes in the interests of controlling inflation and boosting the prices of financial assets. Their control isn't preeminent; managers have resisted stockholder interference, though workers have lost nearly every battle. Managerialism and the vestigial role of the stockholder were historically contingent features of the Golden Age, not the markers of a new phase of capitalism.

"Financial control" is an admittedly imprecise term, encompassing a whole spectrum of influences. Its classic U.S. usage refers to the takeover of industrial firms by banker–operators like J.P. Morgan, buying up an important share of its securities and taking seats on the board. When a firm was "Morganized," there was no question about who controlled it, whatever the formal financial and managerial structures. While that kind of direct bankerly control was banned by the financial reforms of the 1930s, there are some industrial firms that were taken over during the 1980s, brought under the control, if not ownership, of leveraged buyout boutiques like Kohlberg Kravis Roberts and Forstman, Little — though for the most part this treatment was reserved for firms below Fortune 500 size. In many, perhaps most, cases, these were not intended as permanent arrangements; the idea was to take the company public again at a later date at a great profit to the buyout artisans — either because they managed to achieve new efficiencies thanks to their managerial genius and the disciplinary effects of debt, or because an interminable bull market would simply accommodate them profitably through the mere passage of time.

Influence need not be so direct as outright ownership. The classic textbook explanation of the power of finance is that investors and bankers scrutinize firms when they seek outside money, either debt or equity. Certainly this is the case, but influence need not be even this direct. Managers may simply take a cue from the price of their firm's stock, or listen to the advice of analysts and investors about what course they could take to boost it. Also, most large corporations have representatives of banks and insurance companies sitting on their boards, but of course their degree of influence is both debatable and variable.

Such financial boardmembers may only exert their influence at critical moments. As Kevin Delaney (1992, pp. 69–71) pointed out, John Schroeder, a retired vice-chair of J.P. Morgan who served on the Johns–Manville board, was instrumental in pushing the firm to file for bankruptcy when faced by mounting legal claims for exposing its workers and customers to asbestos. (Morgan had served as Manville's lead bank for over 50 years.) Bankruptcy protected the assets of the company against claims of the litigants, allowing the creditors not only to be repaid in full, but also to lend Manville fresh money at high interest rates. Stockholders were nearly wiped out, and the asbestos victims' awards were strictly capped. The moral — the corporate governance moral, that is, leaving aside the stingy treatment of the injured — is that the financier on the board may be quiet when things are going well, but in a crisis, he or she may be a crucial player.

The Johns–Manville example may be a model of the broader upsurge of financial influence; financiers may have been satisfied with corporate performance during the Golden Age, but more recent decades have been the economy-wide equivalent of an asbestos crisis. This might be a good time to take a look at recent theories of corporate governance.

Jensenism

Starting in the mid-1970s, Michael Jensen, Chicago-school fellow traveller now at Harvard, began developing a finance-based theory of corporate governance that would become influential in the 1980s. Though it took some time to evolve to full ripeness, Jensen's argument is, in a phrase, that stockholders can't trust the managers they've hired to run their corporations, and a radical realignment is in order.

In 1976, Jensen and his collaborator William Meckling tried to build a formal model relating financial structure and managerial performance. As with most formal models, their indifference curves and $\delta B(X')$'s were built on a series of simplifying assumptions. Listing those of Jensen and Meckling should remind lay readers just how strange these exercises can get (numbers omitted):

All taxes are zero.

No trade credit is available.

All outside equity shares are non-voting.

No complex financial claims such as convertible bonds or preferred stock or warrants can be issued.

No outside owner ever gains utility from ownership in a firm in any way other than through its effect on his wealth or cash flows.

All dynamic aspects of the multiperiod nature of the problem are ignored by assuming there is only one production–financing decision to be made by the entrepreneur.

The entrepreneur–manager's money wages are held constant throughout the analysis.

There exists a single manager (the peak coordinator) with ownership interest in the firm.

Every one of these assumptions violates reality. Among the more glaring violations: taxes exist prominently; net trade credit to nonfinancial corporations was over $340 billion at the end of 1995; it's a rare corporation that issues nonvoting shares; time is continuous and endlessly complicating, since today's bad decision can haunt managers for years; there are many layers of management beneath the "peak coordinator."

Let's set these reservations aside, however, and explore Jensen's world. No matter what you think of his answers, Jensen and his collaborators — Meckling, here — have asked some important questions about a social institution that is commonly accepted as part of the landscape, the large joint-stock corporation: "How does it happen that millions of individuals are willing to turn over a significant fraction of their wealth to organizations run by managers who have so little interest in their welfare? What is even more remarkable, why are they willing to make these commitments purely as residual claimants, i.e., on the anticipation that managers will operate the firm so that there will be earnings which accrue to the stockholders?" In plainer English, why, in a world that runs on self-interest, do individual and institutional shareholders entrust the management of the corporations that they legally own to strangers? And why do they arrange it so that they, as stockholders, are the last in line to be paid, after suppliers, creditors, and employees?

It's a marriage of convenience, of course, and, the new critique aside, it's been a successful one. For one, it makes sense for individual entrepreneurs who strike it rich to take their companies public, accumulate financial capital, and put their eggs into baskets other than their own.[8] And just because investors have money doesn't mean they have technical and organizational skills; in an economy characterized by the relentless subdivision of labor, it's no surprise they hire help to run the properties. But over time the rentier function has become institutionalized and the help has evolved into the professional managers of the modern transnational corporation. These two groups can be expected to have areas of disagreement. In the trade, this is known as principal–agent conflict.

Jensen and Meckling spent a lot of time laying out the agency costs of the separation of ownership and control for large U.S. corporations. Managers will typically try to pamper themselves before passing along dividends to the legal owners; the Jensen–Meckling model actually formalizes this as "X = $\{x_1, x_2, \ldots, x_n\}$ = a vector of quantities of all factors and activities within the firm from which the manager derives non-pecuniary benefits, such as office space, air conditioning, thickness of the carpets, friendliness of employee relations, etc." — perks. Calling them perks would look unscientific; disguising them as a vector lends the prestige of mathematics to those easily seduced by subscripts. To minimize perk-grabbing, creditors and stockholders require explicit, frequent financial reporting and outside audits, and also tinker endlessly with the ways of paying senior managers so as to provide the right mix of punishment and reward. On the other hand, executives are suspicious that outside stockholders and creditors are always trying to second-guess them, or cramp their managerial style. Managers and claimants inevitably keep a wary eye on each other; the expense of doing so is known as agency costs.

Managers, Jensen and Meckling argued, would manage in the interest of the outside claimants if they held bigger stakes in the companies. (It's assumed that stockholders' interests are paramount.) Executives' debt and stock holdings should be evenly balanced, to assure they never try to reward or screw one class of holders at the expense of the other (like risky ventures that might offer a big stock payoff, but could lead to default on the bonds, or cautious investments that guarantee steady interest payments but could bore stockholders). Jensen's ultimate sympathies are with risk; in what would later become an obsession, he and Meckling argued that stock options should be an important part of a top manager's pay, "which in effect give him [sic] a claim on the upper tail of the outcome distribution" — a big personal payoff if the stock booms. Unspoken is the assumption that stock prices reliably price managerial decisions; Jensenite theories of governance rest on efficient market theory. If the market sets prices inefficiently, then companies will sometimes wrongly get taken over and managers will sometimes be unfairly overpaid (as opposed, I guess, to normal times when they're fairly overpaid).

But Jensen hadn't yet truly warmed to his subject. Despite all the words and formulas devoted to the costs of agency, his collaboration with Meckling ended with this defense of the status quo: "The growth in the use of the corporate form as well as the growth in market value of established corporations suggests that at least, up to the present, creditors and investors have by and large not been disappointed with the results, despite the agency costs inherent in the corporate form."

Earlier in the paper, the authors had dismissed what would later be called leveraged buyouts, a transaction whose primary academic celebrant was the later Jensen. It would be possible, Jensen and Meckling argued, to eliminate agency costs if shareholders sold firms to managers, who financed their purchase of 100% of the firm's stock with debt and personal wealth. Since this rarely happens, they reasoned, there must be some compelling reasons why. Among those reasons, they concluded, were a rational wariness on the part of creditors, who would worry that managers would take big gambles, hoping for big payoffs that, should they not arrive, would greatly increase the risk of default, even bankruptcy. Preventing those risks would greatly increase the creditors' agency costs, since they'd have to keep managers under constant scrutiny to make sure they weren't playing roulette with the creditors' money.

Jensen changed his mind in the 1980s, becoming the scourge of the public corporation and the typical CEO. A paper written just seven years later with Richard Ruback (Jensen and Ruback 1983) celebrated the virtues of the market for corporate control as a market in which "alternative managerial teams compete for the rights to manage corporate resources." This marked a shift, said Jensen and Ruback, from the classic view in which stockholders hired and fired management:

> [T]he managerial competition model instead views competing management teams as the primary activist entities, with stockholders (including institutions) playing a relatively passive...judicial role.... [S]tockholders in this system have relatively little use for detailed knowledge about the firm or the plans of competing management teams beyond that normally used for the market's price setting function. Stockholders have no loyalty to incumbent managers; they simply choose the highest dollar value offer from those presented to them in a well-functioning market for corporate control.

In this world, everything is constantly up for auction. It assumes that the "market" — which it's conceded is populated by players with no special expertise in the businesses they have at their mercy — can value each management slate's cash-generating potential presciently, and that this constant turmoil has no harmful effect on production. Why everyone should turn somersaults to satisfy passive, almost vestigial, stockholders is one of the great unexplored mysteries of Jensenism; the stock market is always axiomatically the ultimate arbiter of social good.

Jensen (1986a) turned up the heat just three years later, arguing then that it wasn't enough to change managers; managers had to be put under a new disciplinary structure. Despite the pressures of competitive product markets, the bosses of big, public corporations waste money on unproductive (that is, unprofitable) expenditures like perks, investment, and R&D — money that should instead be piped to shareholders. "Free cash flow" was the problem, and Jensen's definition is worth quoting:

> Free cash flow is cash flow in excess of that required to fund all projects that have positive net present values when discounted at the relevant cost of capital. Conflicts of interest between shareholders and managers over payout policies are especially severe when the organization generates substantial cash flow. The problem is how to motivate managers to disgorge the cash rather than investing it at below the cost of capital or wasting it on organzation [sic] inefficiencies.

Jensen's definition sounds more precise than it really is. Cash flow and cost of capital are relatively easy to figure — though different analysts will come up with different measures for each.[9] Judging future projects is the really tricky bit; it assumes firms can know how much money a project can earn. Of course they never can. In practice, one can do little but extrapolate from the past, but that's not really the same thing.

Still, quibbles aside, Jensen was really onto something. Many big firms have more money than they know what to do with — or, more strictly speaking, have more money than they can invest in their basic businesses at a reasonable profit — a more colloquial definition of free cash flow.[10] Margaret Blair and Martha Schary (1993a and 1993b) estimated free cash flow for 18 and then 71 industrial sectors. They used historical data on profitability, which isn't pure Jensen, but that's about all you can do, since one can't divine the future. They found a sharp squeeze on firms, with profitability roughly flat but with a sharp increase in the cost of capital from the 1970s into the 1980s, the result mainly of sustained high interest rates. As the cost of capital rose — the rate of return required by investors under orthodox finance theory — firms could justify only the highest-profit (and one might assume quickest payback, though Blair and Schary don't say this) projects. As they put it, "The expected profitability of future investments fell just as the profitability required by the capital markets climbed to unprecedented highs.... [F]rom 1982 through 1989 the U.S. corporate sector was caught up in an epidemic of free cash flow" (Blair and Schary 1993a, p. 128). In the mid-1990s, it looks like they are once again, but they're doing different things with the money now from what they did in the 1980s.

Jensen's (1986a) answer was to load up these firms with debt — a nice irony, since a broad and sustained demand for fresh debt will push interest rates higher than they would otherwise be, thereby making even more cash flow "free." Jensen offered a nice rationale for Wall Street's liberation of ever more cash flow. Unlike stock, which allows managers to pay what they like to shareholders, high debt bills "bond" managers to pay out a steady stream of cash, rather than "wasting resources on low-return projects." Managers should also receive a large share of their compensation in the form of stock, to make them think and act like shareholders.

As the decade wore on, Jensen celebrated the advent of a new form — the LBO (leveraged buyout) association (Jensen 1989a). The large public company was OK, Jensen said, in growing sectors like computers, biotech, and finance. But older industries —tires, steel, chemicals, brewing, broadcasting, tobacco, pulp and paper products now, and aerospace, cars, banking, electric utilities, machinery in the future — need to be transformed through leverage and ownership. In an LBO, a group of investors, often along with a firm's senior management, take a company private by going deep into debt. The stock typically doesn't trade on a public exchange — though occasionally a small "stub" of shares is left over and continues to trade openly — but is held tightly by the circle of investors.[11] The discipline of debt and the potential vast rewards from holding the stock would inspire managers to heroic feats of accumulation.

This is a marked turnabout from the Jensen of 1976, who had said (with Meckling) that the public corporation seemed to be here to stay, arguing even that LBOs were perverse and risky. Asked by email to explain this radical turn in his thinking, Jensen replied: "What happened was that the data began to indicate quite clearly that the system was not working OK. That the inefficiencies were in fact just as we had seen them in theory, but the markets took a while to adjust. That adjustment is still taking place."

Jensen especially celebrated LBOs engineered by boutiques like Kohlberg Kravis Roberts (KKR) and Clayton & Dubalier; "entrepreneurs" like Carl Icahn, Ronald Perelman, Irwin Jacobs, and Warren Buffett; merchant banking arms of Morgan Stanley and Lazard Frères; and families like the Pritzkers and Bronfmans. These fine people — the forgotten stars of the largely forgotten 1980s — should be trusted to run corporate America like a stock portfolio, from their thinly staffed (20 to 60 people) home offices, transforming the industrial cities of yesteryear into ghost towns.

> With all its vast increases in data, talent, and technology, Wall Street can allocate capital among competing businesses and monitor and discipline management more effectively than the CEO and headquarters staff of the typical diversified company. KKR's New York offices and Irwin Jacobs' Minneapolis base are direct substitutes for corporate headquarters in Akron and Peoria.

The ideal arrangement, the LBO Association, was a venture among three "constituencies": the sponsoring boutique; senior management with a large equity stake; and the big institutional investors who fund the deals. Jensen also celebrated the great innovation "pioneered" by Drexel Burnham Lambert, the junk bond — low-rated, high-risk, high-interest-rate debt that powered the celebrity deals of the 1980s. Thanks to Drexel's distribution network, the ceaselessly innovative Michael Milken, sitting at his X-shaped desk in Beverly Hills, could invent a deal and place the bonds necessary to finance it in the Wall Street equivalent of overnight. His network of S&Ls, insurance companies, mutual funds, and rich individuals, supported in no small part by their Ponzi-like propensity for buying each others' paper, was there for his tapping.

KKR was the prototype for Jensen's new corporate form. In the early years after its birth on May Day 1976, KKR did modest deals, focusing on smallish companies (Bartlett 1991).[12] The partners would approach a firm, persuade the managers to borrow a bunch of money, and jointly buy the firm. They made sure there was plenty of daylight between the cash coming in and the interest payments going out. If all went well, the new owners, full of incentive and energy, would revive the company, and prepare it for sale some years down the road at vast profits. The scheme worked like magic. As the years progressed, the partners lusted after bigger and bigger deals. To swing those, they needed big outside backing, and they got it, though it took some time to convince the hypercautious that leverage could be so profitable. As early as five years after KKR's founding, their investors included Prudential, Aetna, GE's pension fund, Metropolitan Life, J.P. Morgan, and Northwest Mutual. Later on, they'd recruit the Oregon, Washington, and Wisconsin state pension funds, among others. So despite its guerrilla-ish image, KKR was backed by the innermost circles of finance joined by the retirement money of public sector workers.

KKR's early years were spectacular. The five major buyout funds, organized over 1978–86, paid annual profits of over 32% to their investors (Bartlett 1991, p. 346). But the 1989 fund, which did the RJR buyout, was a turkey, returning a mere 4% (Sloan 1994). The new corporate form failed the crucial test: delivering sustained profits to its investors. The publication of Sarah Bartlett's (1991) book, which portrayed KKR as putting its own interests far ahead of those of its investors and its stable of companies, to put it gently, did little to further the buyout boutique's reputation.

Back, though, to Jensen and his manifesto. It drew a blizzard of responses, mainly from anti-Jensenites. One, from Peter Róna (1989), head of the IBJ Schroder Bank & Trust in New York, made several points worth quoting — and Róna's position as a financier rather than an industrialist makes his comments especially interesting. First, Róna argued that Jensen grossly overstated the shareholders' case. In return for limits on their liability (they can see the value of their stock wiped out, but the rest of their assets can't be attached), shareholders give up the right to dispose of corporate property on their own; they can sell the shares, but not the firm's assets. By making the shareholder sacrosanct, Jensen preempted any "thoughtful analysis of the very question that is at the heart of the issue — what *should* be the rights and privileges of shareholders?" Second, the LBO is based on the redistribution today of cash flows expected tomorrow and beyond; if these estimates are wrong, then the public shareholders who are bought out in an LBO have the cash and "everyone else is left with a carcass." But shareholders are in the game only to maximize value; having consummated this goal, "they take pretty much the same view of the corporation as the praying mantis does of her mate." Finally, Jensen assumed that shareholders are better judges of capital projects than are managers and corporate boards — an "ideologically inspired assertion that lacks empirical support." As Róna says, it's hard to imagine how one would go about testing this empirically, but "the burden is on Jensen" to take on the task, "since he has already reported the results."

Jensen's (1989b) response to Róna was evasive, offering little to rebut the charges against him. Jensen did, however, helpfully list some forces he viewed as obstacles to economic progress: "striking Eastern Air Lines pilots, Pittston Coal miners, [and] New York Telephone employees, who seem perfectly content to destroy or damage their employer's organization while attempting to serve their own interests. Ralph Nader's consumer activist organization is another example." (It's a nice irony that public employee pension funds were used to smash some of Jensen's impediments to progress.) The only subclass of Jensen's society to have a claim on corporations, it's clear, are shareholders; workers (managers among them) and consumers serve only at the owners' pleasure.

One of the most interesting statements Jensen made on the appropriateness of shareholders to this great social task is actually something he forgot to say. Defending the RJR Nabisco deal — the bloated climax of the 1980s mania, testimony that his hero Henry Kravis was as vainglorious as any cash-burning CEO — Jensen (1991) pointed to the firm's immense waste of money on perks, sports promotions, and "unproductive capital expenditures and organizational inefficiencies." To that phrase is appended footnote 4:

> As revealed in the book [*Barbarians at the Gate* (Burrough and Helyar 1990, pp. 370–371)], John Greeniaus, head of [CEO Ross] Johnson's baking unit, told KKR that if "the earnings of this group go up 15 or 20%...I'd be in trouble." His charter was to spend the excess cash in his Nabisco division to limit earnings in order to produce moderate, but smoothly rising profits — a strategy that would mask the potential profitability of the business....

Sounds like a perfect example of managerial waste — the kind of planned mediocrity evoked in Galbraith's *New Industrial State*. But curiously, Jensen failed to report the reason for this profit-masking, revealed right after the ellipsis: "It was all done, Greeniaus explained, because Wall Street craved predictability." When unpredictable things happen, Wall Street comes unhinged — efficient market theory, which Jensen once famously described as the best-established principle in all the social sciences, to the contrary. *Shareholders* were responsible for planned mediocrity at RJR Nabisco, something it would be very damaging for Jensen to admit.

Three footnotes later, Jensen (1991, p. 15) got worked up over Susan Faludi's (1990) Pulitzer-prize-winning[13] *Wall Street Journal* piece on the LBO of Safeway, the grocery chain, another KKR deal. The deal, regarded as one of the leverage movement's great successes, brought $28 million in stock profits and $100 million in options to top Safeway execs, $65 million to the investment bankers, another $25 million to lawyers, and $60 million in up-front fees for KKR — and pay cuts and unemployment for Safeway workers. Faludi's tales of suicide, heart attack, impoverishment, and despair among workers displaced after the buyout were nothing compared to "long-run efficiency effects" (Jensen 1991, p. 15). To Jude Wanniski (1990), the Faludi piece was "pure and simple propaganda, the work of an ideologue using the *Journal*'s front page to propagate a specific opinion about how corporate America should conduct its affairs." Wanniski, of course, is the supply-side ideologue who once used the *Journal* editorial page to propagate a specific opinion on how America should conduct its fiscal affairs, one that all but a handful of unreconstructed maniacs now regard as a disaster.

A more dispassionate study of a deal Jensen also loved, this one from a business school and not a business newspaper, also showed harsh effects on workers. Wayne Landsman and Douglas Shackelford (1993) reported that of the 2,209 workers who lost their jobs after the RJR buyout, 72% reentered the workforce at 47% of their pre-buyout wages, that women were more badly hurt than men, and older employees hurt more than younger. To the buyout apologist, these are not necessarily bad things; they would probably be taken as evidence that RJR was overstaffed and its workers overpaid, a waste of money that rightly belongs to shareholders. An LBO is a form of class struggle.

Besides labor, nature too suffered from the buyout boom. In one study of 62 hostile takeover bids between 1984 and 1986, for example, an important target was lumber firms who were not cutting enough timber "given the interest rate, the growth rate of trees, and the price path for timber." The infamous Maxxam takeover of Pacific Lumber was inspired by fallow old redwoods that the latter wouldn't cut. Maxxam, powered by junk, took over Pacific Lumber and liquidated the trees. Thinking like economists, Sanjai Bhagat, Andrei Shleifer, and Robert Vishny (1990, p. 54), declared that "we have a case in which cutting the trees raises efficiency." And if trees are not sacrificed at the rate dictated by interest rates, then Wall Street is being cheated of free cash flow.

Rising to a higher theoretical pitch in his early 1990s work, Jensen likened the "new LBO associations" — those with a KKR-like boutique at the center — to Japanese *keiretsu,* which are groups of associated firms with a large bank at their center (Jensen 1991). But there are important differences between *keiretsu* and the fabled constellation of LBOs. As Jensen conceded, Japanese managers don't own stock (and are quite modestly paid by U.S. standards), but in his LBO ideal, stock would be the main form of management compensation.

Actually the ownership structure of *keiretsu* is quite intriguing, and something market socialists as well as social market types should study.[14] There is a bank at the center of each group, but the bank is not the controlling factor; group members are also heavy holders of their fellow groupmembers' shares. There are also extensive board interlocks, with the main bank typically having a board presence as well. Though members do business — even financial business — with firms outside the group, they also do major business with each other. Clearly these are complex organizations with deep financial, personal, and technical ties, not the narrow owner–owned relation characteristic of Jensen's LBO associations.

These cross-holdings and interlocks bind the firms together, each keeping an eye on the others; they check for "timeliness of delivery, product quality, level of investment" — real, telling signs of corporate health that would elude distant shareholders (Berglöf and Perotti 1994) . In a crisis, group members come to the aid of a troubled firm, with the bank coming in only in case of a more serious crisis (typically solved through restructuring or forced merger). The Japanese term for reciprocal shareholdings, *kabushiki mochiai,* has the meaning of "mutual help, shared interdependence, and stability." In the noneconomic literature, the shares are treated as expressions of mutual trust — signs of the relationship, not the relationship itself. Despite the absence of the takeover threat, managers in troubled firms are neatly removed — perhaps more so than the U.S. In the Japanese case, main banks also provide important finance — the opposite emphasis of an LBO matrix, which exists to deliver a fat stream of interest payments to the sponsors. Berglöf and Perotti also theorize that having the bank as the responsible party of last resort is an excellent discipline on the group, because the bank must worry about keeping deposits. If the firms under its eye do badly, then depositors may shift their money elsewhere.[15] These ties are now loosening under the pressure of the long recession that hit Japan after its bubble burst in 1989. It will be interesting to see how an economic recovery combined with Japanese government commitments to further financial deregulation will transform corporate and financial structures in the late 1990s.

In his more recent work, Jensen (1993) has increasingly emphasized "fundamental technological, political, regulatory, and economic forces" as the source of 20 years of intense business and social upheaval: deep reductions in the costs of production, deregulation, "globalization," "reduced growth rates in labor income, excess capacity, and — ultimately — downsizing and exit." Jensen explained the "1895–1904" merger boom as a form of such exit — the destruction of capital through combination, as "capacity was reduced through the consolidation and closure of marginal facilities in merged entities." That's been happening again in the 1980s and 1990s. This is a gloomier message than his tale of the 1980s — more emphasis is placed on shrinkage than revival — but it's probably a more accurate picture of what M&A is all about.

His social message is even harsher. The stress of this New Industrial Revolution will place "strains...on worldwide social and political systems." Luddites or marching armies of the unemployed could threaten the beautiful revolution and might have to be met with same "militia" that "subdued" the Luddites. The harsh medicine must be taken: "We need look no further than central and eastern Europe or Asia to see the effects of policies that protect organizations from foreign and domestic competition" (Jensen 1993, p. 845). Unions must be broken, employment made more tenuous, plants must be closed — and U.S. corporate governance structures are still not up to the task. The crushing of Drexel, the regulatory murder of the junk bond market, the political backlash against the leverage artists left a vacuum in the disciplinary structure.

Despite his fatuous cheerleading and callous subordination of human lives to efficiency, it must be said again that Jensen really is onto something important in modern American capitalism, something that is often denied by his liberal and populist critics. There is constant pressure on older firms — and given the weakened state of large parts of the mainframe computer business, "older" can be defined pretty liberally — coming both from demanding rentiers and product market competition. Given the ownership and management structure of U.S. industry, there's a conflict among stockholders, managers, and workers over how to manage these strains. Wall Street would like to withdraw capital from these industries — slim them down or eliminate them entirely — and pocket the money. In high market theory, Wall Street can be relied upon to redeploy this liberated capital beneficently, and the squeezed industries will either discover a fountain of youth under the discipline of debt or die. Since the last 200 pages of this book have argued that Wall Street isn't up to that task, the whole finance and governance structure is called into serious question.

The great advantage of Jensenism is that, when combined with an uncritical acceptance of the efficient market religion, it amounts to a unified field theory of economic regulation: all-knowing financial markets will guide real investment decisions towards their optimum, and with the proper set of incentives, owner–managers will follow this guidance without reservation. Many of Jensen's critics, whether they know or mention him by name or simply refer to "the 1980s" or downsizing or corporate restructuring, have no coherent response to the problems of overcapacity, obsolescence, or furious competition. In a time when only the brave or foolish dare criticize capitalism itself, critiques only of a certain style of capitalism are all that can be uttered. In the 1990s, the rhetoric has changed; now it's "technology" and "globalization" that are denounced — but the analysis is still narrowly drawn and the tone of critique equally timorous.

On a less grand note, another virtue of Jensen's work is that it challenges the MM theorem. Whether you want to emphasize the positive aspects of debt — its powers to inspire indebted managers — or its negative ones — the power to bankrupt otherwise healthy corporations — financial structure clearly matters, and matters a lot.

mergers and the market for corporate control

Jensenism is a special case of a broader concept known as the liquid market for corporate control. True religionists believe that while the stock market imposes a certain discipline on management — if you believe in efficient market theory, then the stock price is a real-time report card on corporate management — mere market prices are not enough in extreme cases. If the stock price gets low enough and management is unwilling or unable to respond, then the ultimate sanction for incompetence is a takeover, actual or threatened. An LBO can be thought of as one form of this discipline, but it can take many other forms.

A landmark in the evolution of this line of thinking was Henry Manne's (1965) paper "Mergers and the Market for Corporate Control." The second part of that title, often modified with "liquid," was a commonplace of the 1980s popular and academic literature, almost all of it celebratory. The celebration reached an extraordinary pitch as the leverage boom peaked in 1989. One measure of that mania is a speech delivered in January of that year by Roberto Mendoza, then the VP for M&A at the Morgan Bank. The Morgan, once the epitome of white-shoe propriety, turned more aggressive as the 1980s wore on. After praising the liquid market in corporate control, Mendoza (1989) offered this reflection:

> We often read in the press of returns on equity of 800 to 900 percent over a
> two- or three-year period. Somehow the bias has taken hold that this is an
> excessive return, or that someone is being exploited. We believe that finan-

cial buyers are intelligently using the methodology that many strategic corporate buyers do not use, and that the returns are not excessive; in fact, they are very reasonable. The financial buyer is using leverage in a creative and intelligent manner.

Whatever your moral philosophy, returns of 800–900% are not sustainable. But since Mendoza's argument can be traced in part to Manne's article, let's take a look at it.

Traced only in part, though; note Mendoza said that "financial" buyers rather than "strategic corporate" buyers — that is, bankers and dealmakers, rather than firms in related industries. Manne's article was in large measure pitched as an attack on then-prevailing antitrust doctrine, which was inhibiting mergers among competitors. But Manne also had a larger point to make — that an open season on corporate managers was a way of overcoming the problem of the separation of ownership and control.

Manne's argument was based on efficient market theory before it really had that name, and the conflation of market and economic notions of efficiency: "A fundamental premise underlying the market for corporate control is the existence of a high positive correlation between corporate managerial efficiency and the market price of shares of that company." Poor management makes for a depressed stock, which makes for ripeness for takeover. While acknowledging in a footnote that market prices are subject to what later would be called noise, Manne concluded, with the usual theological fervor, that "over some period of time it would seem that the average market price of a company's shares must be the 'correct' one." Those with the wit and capital (or at least a line of credit) to take advantage of this opportunity can make "enormous" returns from "the successful takeover and revitalization of a poorly run company." Antitrust doctrine and other regulations, Manne claimed, were impeding "the mobility of capital," and thereby "a more efficient allocation of resources."

Manne was a professor of law, and most of his citations are of the legal literature, but his reasoning relied on a theory as pure as that of Modigliani and Miller. Markets are efficient, and by God, anything that gets in their way is the enemy of human progress. But do mergers work the magic he was convinced they did?

No, they don't seem to. First, a bit of history. Mergers are often grouped into four major waves — from 1898 to 1904, when the modern giant corporation took shape, often assembled from many smaller firms in the same industry; the 1920s, a period of further consolidation (or monopolization, in some eyes); the 1960s, the period when conglomerates of unrelated businesses were fashionable; and the early 1980s to at least the moment in 1996 when these words were written, a period during which many of the conglomerates were broken apart, and combinations between firms in the same or related industries predominated. Why mergers should occur in waves is listed in Brealy and Myers' (1991, p. 923) finance textbook as one of the 10 great unsolved mysteries of the field. Whatever the answer — the orthodox dismiss explanations based on such woolly concepts as "manias" and "bubbles," but that explanation seems just fine to me — there's no question that mergers do tend to cluster.

For a look at the historical record one could do no better than a special issue of the *International Journal of Industrial Organization* published in 1989. Bad M&A performance goes back a long long way. For example, despite Manne's complaints about post-1929 regulations interfering with the pure market in corporate control, a study of 134 combinations during the 1920s (Borg, Borg, and Leith 1989) found only "modest success," with the average profitability — measured by stock performance of the acquiring firms — little different from mergers during the 1960s and 1970s, despite huge differences in the economic and legal environments, including the effective suspension of antitrust enforcement after 1920. The earlier mergers were hardly a model; Borg & Co. quote a 1921 evaluation of the turn-of-the-century merger wave that showed that in only five of 35 cases did profits meet or exceed the promises of the promoters in the decade following the combination.

Studies of actual operating results in a more contemporary environment show similar disappointments. An examination of Federal Trade Commission records over the period from 1957 to 1977, which allows fairly detailed study of actual lines of business rather than entire firms, and for privately held firms with no publicly traded securities — both exceptions to the rule for most merger studies — showed that profits of acquired firms tended to decline sharply, a point confirmed by the high rate of subsequent divestitures for the gobbled-up units (Ravenscraft and Scherer 1989). That study also shows that profits of acquired units were often uncommonly high before the merger; "thus," the authors conclude, "there is no broad-gauged support for the 'inefficient management displacement' hypothesis that acquired companies were subnormal performers." Ravenscraft and Scherer concluded, in typically understated academic style, that "the evidence mandates considerable skepticism toward the claim that mergers are on average efficiency-enhancing."

One reason mergers turn out badly is that acquiring firms pay too much. An examination of 137 acquisitions done between 1976 and 1984 showed that acquiring firms paid very optimistic prices for their prey; fair prices figured on the basis of prevailing rates of return showed that the performance gains necessary to justify the prices paid in takeovers were impossible to achieve in normal industrial experience (Alberts and Varaiya 1989).

A broader review of the evidence by Richard Caves (1989) strengthens "skepticism toward the claim that mergers are on average efficiency-enhancing." While there's no denying that the stockholders of target firms enjoy fat profits — they gain from the buyers' overpayments — Caves concluded that "acquirers realized little profit, and what they did obtain came mainly in a private but not a social form." That is, there's no serious evidence that mergers are good for the abstraction known as "the economy," though parties to the deal occasionally make out like bandits. Caves also cites British studies showing little productivity gain and frequent losses coming from mergers — something he attributes to "transition costs," including managerial time taken to make the marriage work and the distractions to all employees "while everyone conjectures on the course of the axe's descent."

Whatever their track record, mergers and takeovers do offer windfalls to stockholders of target companies. Where do the gains to stockholders in takeovers come from? The question is not as silly as it may seem at first. If the stock market were rationally valuing the target firm then why should buyers pay significantly more than the prevailing price? If acquirers do overpay, and shareholders of target firms reap a windfall, who, if anyone, loses? Many studies have come to many conclusions, but the study of hostile deals in the mid-1980s by Bhagat, Shleifer, and Vishny (1990) offered a pretty convincing array of possibilities. They attributed some role to layoffs — "important but not...dominant"; more important in their eyes were tax savings (a byproduct of increased indebtedness); less important were losses to shareholders of the buying firm (a penalty of overpayment) and cuts in investment by the target firm. The dismantling of conglomerates and mergers within industries, they argued, also resulted in improved performance that comes with specialization, and possibly even increased "market power" (that is, monopoly pricing power). Importantly, though, the takeover era was

not typically a reflection of a change in the internal organization of the firm. Management buyouts and acquisitions by raiders are often a temporary step in the reallocation of assets; they are not a new permanent organizational form. The eventual holders of assets are large public corporations, which are not about to be eclipsed (Bhagat, Shleifer, and Vishny 1990, p. 57).

The closing words are an allusion to Jensen's (1989a) infamously wrong *Harvard Business Review* article "Eclipse of the Public Corporation."

If mergers have such a dismal record, why do they happen? There are several theories, many of them presented with the usual complexities, but they all can be boiled down into simple English. *Empire-building*. Managers feel richer and more powerful if their firm is growing, and if the business can't grow quickly on its own, then they can gobble up others. Related to this is the idea that while mergers may not result in a higher rate of return (profits divided by invested capital), they may result in a higher quantity of profits, that is more zeroes on the bottom line. *Hubris*. While the average merger may be a dog, every now and then one can be extraordinarily successful, and perpetrators are convinced they can be the lucky ones. *Promoters' interests*. Bankers who act as matchmakers make oodles of money, with fees running around 1% of the value of a large merger (Du Boff and Herman 1989; Truell 1995); for a routine large merger, this means fees in the scores of millions, divided among a handful of bankers and lawyers for several weeks' worth of admittedly intense work.[16] *Theoretical blindness*. Economists repeat the Manne and Jensen mantras because they *must* be true, the market *must* be right, investors *must* be rational — all music to investment bankers' ears, of course.

Or, maybe mergers are ways of managing decline, of withdrawing capital and players from a saggy sector. In this case it should be no surprise that mergers don't do well; even strong firms in a declining industry are still in a declining industry. The mystery is that stock investors still can't figure this out with a century's track record to study.

Far from figuring it out, Anglo-American capital markets seem more willing to fund growth by acquisition than through internal growth by established firms, and they are often shy about financing startups. This preference, which seems characteristic of Anglo-American style markets and governance structures, would, it seems reasonable to conclude, depress investment levels and economic growth rates. In a study of British firms, Manmohan S. Kumar (1984) found that firms financed their internal growth with internal resources, turning to external finance mainly for acquisitions — acquisitions "did not in the majority of cases have a favourable impact on profitability" (p. 178). If the capital markets were exercising their advertised disciplinary function, that finance should not have been available, but it was.

Saying the "capital markets" haven't figured out the flimsiness of most merger rationales obscures the divisions between perpetrators and victims (the rich victims, not those beneath serious consideration, like displaced workers). Specifically, investment bankers do their best to zap the memories of their clients. Most M&A waves are powered by some financial fad: new issues of watered stock at the turn of the century to finance the trustification of whole industries; unsecured debt instruments called debentures ("Chinese paper") used as the currency of conglomeratization in the 1960s; junk bonds used to finance the leveraged recapitalizations in the 1980s. The logic behind this odd and ever-changing flood of paper was explained by an anonymous investment banker quoted in *The Deal Decade* (Blair 1993, p. 298): "Most mergers do not make sense. Therefore you have to use securities that the buyers do not understand and that are different from the last round of bad merger securities."

Some readers may think I've contradicted myself; having defended the growth of the giant corporation against the criminality hypothesis of the Robber Baron school, I now marshal evidence to show that mergers don't work very well. This apparent contradiction is easily resolved. First, merger isn't the only way to grow; it may be a second-best approach for firms that can't grow on their own. The computer industry today is populated by firms that didn't exist 20 years ago — Dell and Compaq, for example. Acquisition had nothing to do with their entry into the Fortune 500; the firms grew like wildfire because they produced good machines and marketed them well. Japan has seen much lower levels of M&A than the U.S. or Britain; Japanese companies have historically relied heavily on internal growth, with "concomitant benefits to the Japanese economy in the form of new investment and growth" (Mueller 1989). Second, the efficiency of the professionally managed large corporation is a separate issue from growth through acquisition; in most cases, small firms are no match for the prowess of larger ones, though of course older giants like General Motors do stumble badly now and then. But most of GM's problems came from other giant firms, like Toyota, and not from plucky startups. And finally, under capitalism, money talks. Small firms don't have the access to capital or internally generated profits that big ones do. Big firms have so much money, in fact, that they can waste it on stupid acquisitions and still live to tell the story. There's nothing criminal about that unless you consider the profit system itself criminal.

LBOs in retrospect

LBOs were a special case of the market for corporate control, and enough time has gone by to pass rigorous judgment on how they worked out. There seems little doubt that LBO and other restructuring targets were in slow-growing industries, or underperformers within their industries (Blair and Schary 1993b, p. 201); most were in low- or mid-tech sectors. Studies that show cutbacks in investment or R&D by leverage targets may be showing the very intention of the restructurings — to shift capital out of the hands of managers of slow-growing firms and into Wall Street's.

William Long and David Ravenscraft (1993a) summarized their own and others' findings on LBOs as follows.[17] First, a firm was more likely to be a target during the 1980s if its free cash flow was high, or if management shareownership was high; it was less likely to be targeted if its valuation was high (price/earnings, Tobin's q), or if did lots of R&D. Second, a good bit of the premiums paid to shareholders in excess of pre-deal market value came from tax savings. And third, LBOs improved operating income, though this largely got sucked away by high interest payments, and reduced capital expenditures and taxes paid. Fourth, employment at leveraged firms grew at a slower rate than the average of their relevant industrial sectors. And finally, LBOs experienced a great deal of "financial distress," and fell deeply out of fashion.

Long and Ravenscraft also showed a deterioration as the decade went on. Early-1980s (1981–84) LBOs showed good improvements in profitability); later deals showed a deterioration in performance, though not at statistically significant levels. Their studies at the plant level, however, showed no great improvements, meaning that overhead reductions were the source of most of the cost savings.[18] Long and Ravenscraft also demonstrated that deals financed with bank debt greatly outperformed those done with junk — a rather interesting finding, and one confirmed by Kaplan and Stein (1993). This is another blow to Jensenmania, and a stroke in favor of bank over market finance. It's true that average R&D spending by LBO targets was low, but that low average hides the fact that almost half the manufacturing LBOs in Long and Ravenscraft's (1993c) universe were considered large R&D performers by the National Science Foundation. In their sample, R&D declined by 40% after an LBO, and capital expenditures by 9%. Again, such cuts are perfectly in line with the Jensen strategy of transferring capital from corporate managers to portfolio managers; whether society is better off is another question.

Elsewhere, Long and Ravenscraft (1993b) reported that while LBOs led to "substantially" improved operating performance, the gains faded after three years, and that four to five years after the buyout the firm was back where it started. But despite the operating improvement, the interest burden took a big bite, leaving net profits after debt service below pre-LBO levels. Again, that's perfectly consistent with the Wall Street-fattening strategy, but has little to do with fostering a social renaissance.

In a study of 124 large buyouts between 1980 and 1989, Steven Kaplan and Jeremy Stein (1993) came to several fundamental conclusions: (1) prices rose relative to underlying profits or cash flow as the decade proceeded; (2) bank principal repayment requirements stiffened, leading to less of a cash cushion for interest payments; (3) bank debt was replaced by junk bonds as the source of outside money; (4) management teams and dealmakers took ever-larger fees up front; and (5) deals struck later in the decade were far more likely to experience "distress" — default or bankrupcy — than those consummated in the early years. Only one of the 41 1980–84 buyouts they studied experienced "distress," but 30 of 83 (36%) of the 1985–89 deals did — many of them despite cost-cutting and improved operating profitability. Too much debt can ruin even the best business, but after 1985, these deals were far from good.

This broad picture of 1980s M&A, drawn mainly from detailed studies of individual deals, is confirmed by economy-wide data as well. Going into the 1980s, corporate America was deeply undervalued. The stock-only version of Tobin's q ratio (the value of equity divided by underlying tangible assets) averaged 34% between 1974, the depth of the post-OPEC bear market, and 1982, the year the great 1980s bull market began, just over half its historical average.[19] As the decade wore on, however, the q rose sharply — to 47% in 1986, and 60% in 1989, when the leverage boom ended (flow of funds data). Mergers have continued since at even higher q's, but with nowhere near the degree of leverage; you'd have to be insane — or have a high tolerance of risk, to put it more coolly — to borrow heavily to pay prices like 1996's. Cash and stock are the currency of 1990s deals; firms still have plenty of free cash flow. The mergers may not work out in the long run, but at least they won't leave any debt tailings that could turn toxic over time; only the stockholders are at risk.

Deals became more overpriced and riskier at the same time the commitments of managers and financiers to the deals were weakening. High up-front fees encourage irresponsible deal making — book the deal now, the hell with long-term prospects. Tighter repayment schedules meant that asset sales — selling off pieces of a company — rather than improvements in profitability were central to the financing strategy — the very definition of Minsky's Ponzi financial structure. The inferior performance of the public junk bond market suggests that bank lenders are better judges of credit than are mutual fund managers and other portfolio jugglers.

The whole picture of bigger, dumber deals as the buyout binge matured is a severe blow to notions of efficient markets; the whole affair with leverage looks in retrospect like one of the great financial bubbles of all time. But it was a bubble with a flossy intellectual pedigree, deep support from the government (both the elected one and the Federal Reserve) and financial establishment, and with damaging consequences to the real U.S. economy. None of the perpetrators — investment bankers, finance academics, or central bankers — have suffered any blow to their prestige. And none of the governance issues raised by Jensen and his comrades have been solved; we know now that the LBO association hasn't become the new model of business organization, but shareholders are still conniving to get a bigger share of corporate cash flow.

detour: on Felix

I said earlier that liberals and populists denounced the buyout mania as an outburst of greed without analyzing any of its underlying mechanisms. One of their favorite voices of outrage was a Wall Streeter, the soulful banker, Felix Rohatyn, whose position presumably gave him some authority, an authority that couldn't survive a serious confrontation with his résumé. Rohatyn — author of tedious, moralizing pieces in the *New York Review of Books*, supplier of sermon-like quotes to press hacks, failed perennial Democratic candidate for Treasury Secretary, and now something of a has-been — was actually the inspiration for one of the 1980s' dashingest figures, Joe Perella. Perella, partner with Bruce "Bid 'em Up" Wasserman in one of the great buyout machines of the time, told *Institutional Investor* in 1984: "I saw Felix knocking off those mergers at $1 million a clip, with no capital. I was impressed not only with his skill but also by the sheer potential of M&A fees" (quoted in Henwood 1990). Felix, together with his mentor André Meyer, put together ITT and other great 1960s conglomerates at Lazard Frères. Rohatyn and Meyer helped turn Steve Ross from a parking-lot operator into the *capo* of Warner Bros.

Lazard was the first to break the $1 million banking fee, but Meyer wanted nothing to do with the mundane business of underwriting securities to finance real companies; he liked playing with whole companies better. In 1963, Meyer, "with his taste for the sure thing," bought a French company operating in Wyoming named, appropriately enough, Franco Wyoming, liquidated it and fired all the employees and practically over-night made a 300% profit. A name-brand investment bank bought a com-pany, busted it up, and got away with a huge profit and its reputation intact; this was a lesson not lost on Wall Street (Reich 1983, pp. 243–247).

Later, Rohatyn would denounce such practices and urge the creation of a Reconstruction Finance Corporation to retool America. A dealmaker who did virtually nothing to fund productive investment, Rohatyn frequently urged the government to take on the mundane business of industrial fi-nance, clearly too demeaning a task for the sophisticates of Wall Street. As the novelist–polemicist Michael Thomas put it (personal communication), Felix pounds the pulpit with one hand and endorses checks with the other.

going bust

As the 1980s faded, it became clear that the LBO association was not about to replace the public corporation. Despite a burst of M&A activity in the mid-1990s after a lull early in the decade, the dominant transaction was a merger between large public corporations, or the absorption of one unit of a public corporation by another public corporation. A new form of rentier assertiveness came forward in the 1990s as the boutiques and lone operators faded — shareholder activism.

Jensen and his ilk blame the collapse of the buyout movement on regu-lators and the media. By jailing Milken, busting Drexel, and reining in the S&Ls, these spoilsports snuffed the only hope for the restructuring of cor-porate America. In fact, the movement did itself in. A wave of defaults in 1988 and 1989 followed by the near implosion of the U.S. economy in the early 1990s scared all but the loopiest away from experiments in leverage.

In an interview, Jensen expressed great regret that Drexel was not around to finance Kirk Kerkorian's spring 1995 attempt to take over Chrysler. Kerkorian said the automaker was sitting on piles of cash, but Chrysler defended itself by saying it was husbanding resources for the next recession. Jensen said that if Kerkorian had succeeded, debt would have sucked away this cash, which has made Chrysler management "fat, bloated, dumb, and happy." With less cash, the firm would shut ineffi-cient plants (which it should do rather than increase capacity, despite ro-bust demand), and drive a harder bargain with labor and suppliers. To Jensen, Chrysler's greatest moments were when it was near death, and was driven by fear to invent great new efficiencies.[20] (Of course, a loan from the U.S. government didn't hurt either.) But, alas, there was no Drexel, and bankers shied away from financing Kerkorian's attack. It was a firm sign that the 1980s were still too fresh in too many minds for a revival. Maybe in five or fifteen years, but not in 1995.

The main reason that the leverage strategy was so discredited is the insolvency boom graphed nearby, one of the greatest in U.S. history, rivaled only by the deflations of the late 19th century and early 1930s. Jensen himself had argued that going bust wouldn't really be much of a problem for leveraged firms; the new structure, he asserted, would give rise to the "privatization" of bankruptcy — out-of-court arrangements among the handful of players in an LBO, a contrast with the usual big, expensive court fight between fragmented groups of creditors and shareholders.

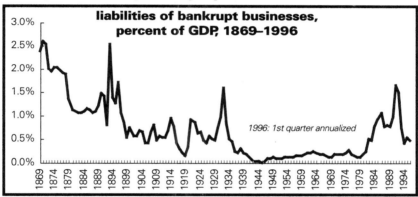

liabilities of bankrupt businesses, percent of GDP, 1869–1996

1996: 1st quarter annualized

A study by the New York Fed made this observation on the insolvency boom: "Evidence suggests that in 1990–92, U.S. corporations found managing their debt in a period of weak cash flows more difficult than anticipated. Perhaps managers took seriously the argument that highly leveraged firms with weak cash flows could generally reorganize their debt without resorting to bankruptcy" (Remolona et al. 1992–93, p. 3). The last sentence is marked by a footnote to congressional testimony by Jensen.

Actually, Jensen seems to have had half, or maybe a quarter, of a point on bankruptcy's privatization. While statistics on the costs of bankruptcy are surprisingly hard to come by, one study of corporate insolvencies between 1986 and 1993 (Betker 1995) showed that the cost of a classic Chapter 11 corporate bankruptcy averaged 3.93% of pre-bankruptcy assets, but an LBO or similar leveraged restructuring of the Jensenite sort generally knocked about 1.3 percentage points off the total. Still, all these restructurings — whether a classic Chapter 11 or an intimate Jensen-style affair — still left leveraged firms under heavy debt. Many 1980s deals went through two bankruptcies. Rajesh Aggharwal (1995) argued that that happened because creditors were unwilling to forgive enough debt to make a firm viable; they feared that if they forgave, someone else (like a nonparticipating creditor) would gain what they lost.

rioting rentiers

The failure of the LBO movement to transform the fundamental nature of the corporate form left shareholders at a bit of a loss. Not satisfied with one of the great long-term bull markets in U.S. history, they continued to whine about "unlocking shareholder value" hidden in the crevices of corporate America. Since leverage turned out to be a very risky way of liberating those hidden dollars, a new strategy was in order.

As the decade turned, that strategy turned out to be shareholder activism. Ironically, one of the early signs of the new activism was the anti-apartheid movement's pressure on universities, churches, public pension funds, and other institutional investors to sell the shares of firms doing business in South Africa. This was a marked departure from the classic passivity of institutional shareholders. But the entirely laudable goal of using financial weapons to end official racism was then quickly eclipsed by more mundane concerns — pressing tired managements to liven up their companies and thereby drive the stock price northwards.

A curious personal tale of the evolution of the new financial assertiveness is the career of T. Boone Pickens, who was one of the *commandantes* of the first wave of the shareholder rebellion. His stab at Gulf was one of the great early moments of the deal decade. During the 1980s, Pickens made relentless fun of CEOs like Andrew Sigler, the boss of Champion International who was managerial America's mouthpiece while the likes of Pickens were wilding their way across the corporate landscape. While Sigler argued that "society" owned firms, not "shareholders," Pickens countered that shareholder value was all. His oil company didn't really drill much — he preferred to explore for oil on the New York Stock Exchange, by buying up other companies with borrowed money (Henwood 1987).

Companies that tried to block takeovers with poison pills and other schemes were Pickens' great enemies.[21] But in 1995, Mesa found itself under attack by hostile suitors including Pickens' former sidekick David Batchelder. Rather than take his own medicine, Pickens had the board adopt a poison pill. Mesa's arguments sound like Sigler's a decade earlier — the outside group was in it just for a quick buck. Pickens' defense: "his days of trying to take over other companies were long gone and that he hated to be called a corporate raider. 'The last time I was involved in a deal was almost 10 years ago,' he said. 'There's no way anybody could characterize me as anything other than a hard working oilman" (Myerson 1995b). Hard work needn't guarantee reward; between 1985 and 1995, Mesa's stock fell 63%, while the overall market rose 171%. By Pickens' own standard, he was a disgrace. He was finally ousted in 1996.

Pickens was behind an attempt to organize small shareholders into a formal pressure group, the United Shareholders Association, cutely abbreviated USA. From its 1986 founding to its 1993 dissolution, USA tracked the performance of large public corporations and compiled a Target 50 list of losers. The USA would try to negotiate with the underperformers, urging them to slim down, undo anti-takeover provisions, and just deliver their shareholders more "value." If satisfaction wasn't forthcoming, USA would ask its 65,000 members to sponsor shareholder resolutions to change governance structures. USA-inspired resolutions were often co-sponsored by groups like the California Public Employees Retirement System (Calpers), the College Retirement Equities Fund (CREF), and the New York City Employees Retirement System (Nycers). In a measure of the smallness of economists' minds, one study discovered that in "the two-day event window [after its announcement]…the average USA-sponsored agreement results in an abnormal stock price reaction of approximately 0.9%. This abnormal return represents a gain in shareholder wealth of approximately $54 million…" (Strickland, Wiles, and Zenner 1994). In tiny steps does progress come.

USA was dissolved by its board because as its president, Ralph Whitworth, put it, it was not USA's goal to stay "around indefinitely as a corporate watchdog activism organization…. Boone Pickens founded USA in the spirit of change — an organization that would set goals, take action, and get things done" (Strickland, Wiles, and Zenner 1994). This suggests that even with visibility, membership, and funding, it's near impossible to get small, dispersed shareholders to act as a unit. It may pay a big-time raider to play this game, but certainly not small holders, and apparently not even small holders banded together.

In 1995, Whitworth joined with Pickens' former associate Batchelder to form Relational Investors, a San Diego-based fund designed to invest in poorly performing companies and act as a "catalyst for change." They were backed by a number of large institutional investors, including Calpers, the most prominent of the shareholder activists. Press reports explain that this move is part of a new phase in Calpers' corporate governance program, a way of pressing underperformers to change their ways of doing business. This, it seems, is the model for the mid-1990s. The heirs of Pickens are now the prowling agents of public pension funds, looking for value, ready to prod more than pounce.[22]

It's surprising how few pension funds have led the rebellion. Most prominent is Calpers, with a handful of other public pension funds at their side. Useem (1996, p. 56) noted that these funds — controlled by elected officials and held in the name of public sector workers — find it easy to adopt an "antimanagement rhetoric, especially when directed against big business." Their agenda, though, looks much less radical than the rhetoric. The strictly governance aspects of this agenda typically include: bringing more outsiders on to the board, in the name of independence; shrinking large boards (15 or more) down to around a dozen, on the theory that large boards are more scattered, and therefore more easily dominated by management; encouraging more scrutiny of management strategy by outside directors; removing obstacles to takeovers in corporate charters; and tying executive and director pay to stock performance, rather than paying flat (and fat) salaries (Salmon 1993; Useem 1996, Chapter 7).

More broadly, these moves have translated into the famed downsizing and investment cutbacks of the first half of the 1990s; the point of the governance agenda, after all, is to increase shareholder wealth by increasing shareholder control. Public justifications for these downsizings have almost always pointed to technological change and global competition, which takes human interest and agency out of the picture, but in fact the proximate cause has more often been pressure for higher stock prices coming from Wall Street portfolio managers.

Institutional investors have made their presence felt most famously through annual hit lists, like Calpers', and another drawn up by the Council of Institutional Investors, a consortium of 100 major pension funds with some $800 billion in assets. Such public humiliations, which have led to boardroom shakeups at household-name firms, have their effects not only on the named targets, but also on the managers of other firms, who get the message and take appropriate action to avoid being on next year's list. As Calpers' general counsel, Richard Koppes, said, "You focus on a few visible ones and make everyone else nervous" (quoted in Berenbeim 1994, p. 29). But aside from these visible struggles, pension fund managers have also worked behind the scenes, pressing their wish lists on often recalcitrant managements, and in some cases, meeting with firms' outside directors, pushing the case for managerial revolution (Lublin 1995b; Useem

1996, p. 108). According to a Conference Board survey, executives from 86% of large U.S. firms were contacted by their institutional shareholders; almost half reported an increase in the number of shareholder calls, with few reporting a decrease (Berenbeim 1994).

Why have the public pension funds, and only a handful of them at that, been prominent in the shareholder rebellion, to the exclusion of other institutional investors? There are several reasons. Private pension funds are inhibited by conflicts of interest, actual or potential; GM's pension fund would have a hard time taking a visible position on a management shakeup at Chrysler. More broadly, since corporate pension funds are ultimately run by CEOs, the chieftains are not eager to stoke challenges to their authority. Mutual funds have also shied away from governance issues; Fidelity, it's said by someone in the know, tried it and withdrew because of bad press, but the company didn't return phone calls asking for comment. Firms like mutual funds with highly visible public images don't want to get caught up in public controversies. But it's highly likely that many of the nonparticipating institutions are happy to have the activist funds in the lead, doing their work for them; they get the benefit of higher share prices without having to take the trouble, or risk their public image by pushing a controversial agenda.

shareholders — who needs them?

Just because Wall Street's short-termism is a cliché doesn't mean it isn't true. In surveys, CEOs and corporate investor relations managers repeatedly complain of pressure from money managers and Wall Street analysts to produce quick profit growth. This is no special pleading coming from a formerly pampered class; money managers themselves confirm to survey-takers that their colleagues are too obsessed with quarter-to-quarter news, and take too little heed of long-term prospects. It can hardly be otherwise, since most big investment managers are graded on their quarterly performance. (Useem 1996). Still, stroking these portfolio jockeys takes a lot of managerial time. CEOs of big U.S. corporations hold six meetings a month with money managers and stock analysts, and chief financial officers (CFOs) hold over twice as many; from that, it's been estimated that CFOs spend 20% of their work time courting Wall Street (Baker et al. 1994). Surely they have something better to do with their time than spending it with people who earn big fees for underperforming the averages.

That set holds CEOs to some strange standards indeed. Confirming Keynes's theorizing of 60 years ago, expectations often matter more than actual results. Perversely, one study cited by Useem (1996, p. 88) shows that "company shortfalls in meeting analyst forecasts are better predictors of [top] executive dismissal than are shortfalls in the actual earnings. Put differently, you are more likely to lose your job if you shock investor sensibilities than if you dock company earnings." And these are the folks who want an even bigger piece of the action.

As Charles Wohlstetter (1993), former chair of Contel, put it, "In sum, we have a group of people with increasing control of the Fortune 500 who have no proven skills in management, no experience at selecting directors, no believable judgment in how much should be spent for research or marketing — in fact, no experience except that which they have accumulated controlling other people's money."

Pension funds are the least regulated of the major institutional investors, which is one reason they've been active in the shareholder rebellion, but this makes them accountable on none but purely financial measures. So rather than solving the agency problem, activist shareholding simply adds another layer of potential irresponsibility.

And what do they really have to contribute? The best periods of U.S. economic growth have occurred when managers ran corporations and shareholders kept their mouths shut. Admittedly there's a chicken–egg problem here; it's no accident that Berle and Means' book came out during the Depression, that governance issues receded during the Golden Age, and that they returned as economic performance deteriorated in the 1970s. But the point is that there's no evidence that shareholder intervention promotes better performance over the long term — better performance, that is, for anyone but shareholders.[23]

Apologists love to finesse this distinction, treating higher share prices as synonymous with a higher social return. But one could argue that by reducing the funds available for real investment, increasing the return to shareholders will depress growth and employment over the long term. It's likely that investment projects or R&D that shareholders might condemn as "uneconomic" would nonetheless leave society as a whole better off.

When I asked Useem what purpose stockholders serve, he answered, wrongly, that they're an important source of capital. I've devoted a good bit of this book to showing that the signals emitted by the stock market are either irrelevant or harmful to real economic activity, and that the stock market itself counts for little or nothing as a source of finance. Shareholders *should* be vestigial; they have no useful role. Instead, they have grown increasingly assertive over the last 15 or 20 years, disguising themselves behind a rhetoric of democracy, independence, and accountability.

Shareholders love to present themselves as the ultimate risk-bearers. But their liabilities are limited by definition to what they paid for the shares, they can always sell their shares in a troubled firm, and if they have diversified portfolios, they can handle an occasional wipeout with hardly a stumble. Employees, and often customers and suppliers, are rarely so well-insulated. Add to this Keynes's argument that the notion of liquidity cannot apply to a community as a whole, and you have a very damaging critique of shareholder-centered governance: what's divine for rentiers is bad news for everyone else.

Apologists for the rentier agenda also argue that "them are us": the portfolio managers demonized as greedy Wall Streeters are really managing all of society's savings for the long-term interest of all.[24] The figures on concentration of stock ownership presented in Chapter 2 make that argument hard to sustain, but apologists also point to the pension benefits that we'll all collect someday if we're lucky enough to make it to 65 or 67. This too is devious. Pension assets, while less concentrated than other forms of financial holdings, are still concentrated; under 40% of the workforce is covered by a pension plan (U.S. Bureau of the Census 1995, p. 383) and the richest 10% control 62% of pension assets (Wolff 1996). It seems odd that workers should be asked to trade a few extra percentage points return on their pension fund, on which they may draw some decades in the future, for 30 or 40 years of falling wages and rising employment insecurity. The point of "shareholder activism" is to increase the profit share of national income, and to claim a larger portion of that profit share for rentiers. Any gains to people of modest means are accidental.

Maybe the present wave of shareholder assertiveness will wane; the temptation to sell a stock rather than take the trouble of lobbying management may eventually triumph over the apparently meager gains to activism. It may be that even with the institutionalization of ownership, shareholding still remains too dispersed to sustain the kind of "relationship investing" advocated by Calpers, the Twentieth Century Fund (1992), or Robert Monks (1995). Professional rentiers and their bankers will no doubt find a new fad designed to unlock shareholder value, and devise a fresh set of arguments for why their enrichment is synonymous with the common good.

Aside from Margaret Blair — though she is far more measured than I — no prominent student of corporate governance has drawn the obvious conclusion from all this research: if outside shareholders serve no useful purpose, then there is no better argument for turning firms over to their workers.[25] Of course, the shareholders don't see this solution as obvious, but that's another story.

governing governments

This chapter and this book have mainly been about the private sector, but it would be incomplete to finish a chapter on "governance" without looking at the relations between Wall Street and government, not only in the U.S., but on a world scale.

One advantage that Wall Street has in public economic debate, aside from its immense wealth and power, is that it's one of the few institutions that look at the economy as a whole. American economic policymaking, like the other kinds, is largely the result of a clash of interest groups, with every trade association pleading its own special case. Wall Streeters presume to care about how all the pieces come together into a macroeconomy. The broadest policy techniques — fiscal and monetary policy — are central Wall Street concerns. For some reason, intellectuals like the editors of the *New York Review of Books* and the *Atlantic* have decided that investment bankers like Felix Rohatyn and Peter Peterson have thoughts worth reading. Not surprisingly, both utter a message of austerity — the first with a liberal, and the second with a conservative, spin — hidden behind a rhetoric of economic necessity. These banker–philosophers, creatures of the most overpaid branch of business enterprise, are miraculously presented as disinterested policy analysts.

Wall Street's power becomes especially visible during fiscal crises, domestic and international. On a world scale, the international debt crisis of the 1980s seemed for a while like it might bring down the global financial system, but as it often does, finance was able to turn a crisis to its own advantage.

While easy access to commercial bank loans in the 1970s and early 1980s allowed countries some freedom in designing their economic policies (much of it misused, some of it not), the outbreak of the debt crisis in 1982 changed everything. In the words of Jerome I. Levinson (1992), a former official of the Inter-American Development Bank:

> [To] the U.S. Treasury staff…the debt crisis afforded an unparalleled opportunity to achieve, in the debtor countries, the structural reforms favored by the Reagan administration. The core of these reforms was a commitment

on the part of the debtor countries to reduce the role of the public sector as a vehicle for economic and social development and rely more on market forces and private enterprise, domestic and foreign.

Levinson's analysis is seconded by Sir William Ryrie (1992), executive vice president of the International Finance Corporation, the World Bank's private sector arm. "The debt crisis could be seen as a blessing in disguise," he said, though admittedly the disguise "was a heavy one." It forced the end to "bankrupt" strategies like import substitution and protectionism, which hoped, by restricting imports, to nurture the development of domestic industries.[26] "Much of the private capital that is once again flowing to Latin America is capital invested abroad during the run-up to the debt crisis. As much as 40–50 cents of every dollar borrowed during the 1970s and early 1980s...may have been invested abroad. This money is now coming back on a significant scale, especially in Mexico and Argentina." In other words, much of the borrowed money was skimmed by ruling elites, parked profitably in the Cayman Islands and Zürich, and Third World governments were left with the bill. When the policy environment changed, some of the money came back home — often to buy newly privatized state assets for a song.

That millions suffered to service these debts seems to matter little to Ryrie. Desperate Southern governments had little choice but to yield to Northern bankers and bureaucrats. Import substitution was dropped, state enterprises were privatized, and borders were made porous to foreign investment. After Ryrie's celebrated capital inflow, Mexico suffered another debt crisis in 1994 and 1995, which was "solved" using U.S. government and IMF guarantees to bail out Wall Street banks and their clients, and creating a deep depression; to make the debts good, Mexicans would have to suffer. Once again, a dire financial/fiscal crisis — the insolvency of an overindebted Mexican government — was used to further a capital-friendly economic agenda.

These fortunate uses of crisis first appeared in their modern form during New York City's bankruptcy workout of 1975. This is no place to review the whole crisis; let it just be said that suddenly the city found its bankers no longer willing to roll over old debt and extend fresh credits. The city, broke, could not pay. In the name of fiscal rectitude, public services were cut and real fiscal power was turned over to two state agencies, the Municipal Assistance Corp. (MAC, chaired by Rohatyn), and the Emergency Financial Control Board, since made permanent with the Emer-

gency dropped from its name. Aside from the most routine municipal functions, the city no longer governed itself; a committee of bankers and their
delegates did, Rohatyn first among them. Rohatyn, who would later criticize Reaganism for being too harsh, was the director of its dress rehearsal
in New York City. Public services were cut, workers were laid off, and the
physical and social infrastructure was left to rot. But the bonds, thank
god, were paid, though not without a little melodrama, gimmickry, and
delay (Lichten 1986, Chapter 6).

The city was admittedly borrowing irresponsibly — though the lenders, it must be said, were lending irresponsibly as well. When a bubble is
building, neither side has an incentive to stop its inflation. But when it
broke, all the pain of adjustment fell on the citizen–debtors. The pattern
would be repeated in the Third World debt crisis, in many U.S. cities over
the next 20 years, and, most recently, with the federal budget.

Obviously the bankers have the advantage in a debt crisis; they hold
the key to the release of the next post-crisis round of finance. Anyone
who wants to borrow again, and that includes nearly everyone, must go
along. But that's not their only advantage. The sources of their power
were cited by Jac Friedgut of Citibank (ibid., p. 192):

> We [the banks] had two advantages [over the unions].... One is that since
> we were dealing on our home turf in terms of finances, we knew basically
> what we were talking about, and we knew and had a better idea what it
> takes to reopen the market or sell this bond or that bond.... The second
> advantage is that we do have a certain noblesse oblige or tight and firm
> discipline. So that we could marshal our forces, and when we spoke to the
> city or the unions we could speak as one voice.... Once a certain basic
> process has been established that's an environment in which our intellec-
> tual leadership...can be tolerated or recognized...we're able to get things
> effected.

It's plain from Friedgut's remarkably candid language that to counter this,
one needs expertise, discipline, and the nerve and organization to challenge the "intellectual leadership" of such supremely self-interested parties. But the city unions had none of this. According to the union boss
Victor Gotbaum (in an interview with Robert Fitch, which Fitch relayed to
me), the unions' main expert at the time, Jack Bigel, didn't understand the
budgetary issues at all, and deferred to Rohatyn, whom he trusted to do
the right thing. For the services rendered to municipal labor, the once-
Communist Bigel was paid some $750,000 a year, enough to buy himself a

posh Fifth Avenue duplex (Zweig 1996). Gotbaum became a close friend of Felix Rohatyn. Politically, the unions were weak, divided, self-protective, unimaginative, and with no political ties to ordinary New Yorkers. Actually they did speak in one voice, that of surrender. It's easy to see why the bankers won.

What was at stake in New York was no mere bond market concern. In a classic 1976 *New York Times* op-ed piece, L.D. Solomon, then publisher of *New York Affairs,* wrote: "Whether or not the promises…of the 1960's can be rolled back…without violent social upheaval is being tested in New York City…. If New York is able to offer reduced social services without civil disorder, it will prove that it can be done in the most difficult environment in the nation." Thankfully, Solomon concluded, "the poor have a great capacity for hardship" (quoted in Henwood 1991).

Behind a "fiscal crisis" lurked an entire class agenda, one that has been quite successfully prosecuted in subsequent crises for the next two decades. But since these are fought on the bankers' terrain, using their language, they instantly win the political advantage, as nonbankers retreat in confusion, despair, or boredom in the face of all those damned numbers.

At the national level, rampant borrowing by the U.S. government throughout the 1980s and early 1990s stimulated a boom for a while, but ended with the austerity packages of the mid-1990s. Tripling the outstanding load of federal debt not only made Wall Street a lot of money — underwriting, trading, and holding the bonds — it greatly increased rentier influence over policy. The opinion of "the markets" — essentially the richest 1–2% of Americans and the professionals who manage their money — is now the final word on economic and social policy. Liberals and populists who are sanguine about deficit financing should recall Friedgut's words: creditors speak with one voice, and they're able to get things effected. Those effects generally involve enriching the creditors at the expense of everyone else.

notes

1. An interesting contrast is Britain, where both politicians and pundits identify bad corporate governance as one of the sources of Britain's limp economic performance.
2. "Hydraulically" is probably too 19th century and industrial. It deserves translation into something more virtual.
3. Though there is a large and growing literature on these topics, the basic issues are concisely summarized by Stephen Prowse (1994), especially pp. 10–15. Tellingly, workers do not appear in Prowse's list of the principal actors in the corporate control drama.
4. Reflecting on his article fifty years later, Coase declared it unfortunate that he used the

employer–employee example so prominently, rather than, say, "the contracts that enable the organizers of the firm to direct the use of capital (equipment or money) by acquiring, leasing, or borrowing it" (Williamson and Winter 1993, p. 65). But the relation of managers and external financiers is a lot more complex; one party is rarely able to tell the other to do something as easily as the boss moves Coase's employee from Y to X. Interestingly, the legal text that Coase quoted from, Batt's *The Law of Master and Servant,* used classical legal language that makes the power relationship much clearer than the modern "employer–employee" dyad. Writing in the 1930s, Coase used both pairs of words; writing in the 1980s, he used only the euphemism.

5. Inefficiently small scale production may be a problem with a long pedigree in Britain. In a case study of a Manchester cotton enterprise from 1798 to 1827, Harvey James (1996) argued that the lack of outside capital (and the reliance entirely on internal funds for expansion) kept the scale of the firm too small for maximum efficiency.

6. This historical sketch follows Berle and Means 1932/1967, Book II, Chapter 1.

7. Of course, interest group models owe as much to myth as fact; some interests, like bondholders and developers, are more poweful than others, like welfare moms.

8. One critique of employee stock ownership plans is that they force workers to put a large portion of their savings into a single asset, and one in which they were already "invested" through their jobs. If the firm fails, they would lose not only their jobs, but all their savings as well.

9. Cost of capital is usually figured as the expected returns on a company's outstanding securities — that is, the average of the stock returns required by investors and the interest rate paid on the firm's debts. Equity return is usually figured using the CAPM or similar models; actual interest rates are used to figure the cost of debt (Brealey and Myers 1991, Chapter 9). Surveys show that firms actually have a "hurdle rate" — a minimum rate of return necessary for an investment project to be undertaken — well above their cost of capital. For example, Poterba and Summers (1991) reported that the firms they surveyed used a hurdle rate of 12.2% *after* inflation — far far above the long-term real return of 7% on stocks and 2% on bonds. The authors observed that "these disparities raise an important question about the link between the variables that financial economists focus on in measuring the cost of capital, and the actual practices of firms." A hurdle rate this high guarantees an epidemic of free cash flow, since the average profitable corporation will throw off much more money than it should reinvest according to this standard.

10. On the other hand, managers, as Jeremy Stein (1989) argues, may deliberately underinvest, leaving themselves a degree of financial slack, in order to insulate themselves from the scrutiny of capital markets. But the overall economy might be better off if the slack funds were fully invested.

11. The typical financial structure of a firm after a leveraged buyout is equity, 5–20%; senior debt, 40–70%; junior debt, 10–30% (Borio 1990, p. 36). In a crisis, first the equity holders would get wiped out, then the junior debtholders; if things went well, the junior debtholders would live to see the high interest payments successfully made, and the stock would rise sharply in value. Of course, those stock gains would merely be on paper, unless the holdings were privately sold or the firm were to go public again.

12. Max Holland's (1989) study *When The Machine Stopped,* paints a highly unflattering portrait of an early KKR deal, the buyout of the machine toolmaker Houdaille Industries — a sad tale of industrial decline and financier rapacity. But investors in the KKR fund that financed the Houdaille buyout did smashingly; too bad the American tool industry hasn't done as well.

13. The modifer "Pulitzer-prize-winning" is there not as testimony to the story's excellence — Faludi's story is quite fine, but lots of crap wins Pulitzers and other prizes — but to

show that a bunch of mainstream worthies took it seriously, an index of the shift of elite opinion against Jensen and Kravis as the decade turned. A similar piece by Bill Adler (1988) in the *Texas Observer* garnered no such notice; Faludi says she didn't learn of Adler's piece until she was well along in her research (Rothmyer 1991).

14. Older financial *keiretsu* include Mitsubishi, Mitsui, and Sumitomo, with ancestors in the pre-World War II *zaibatsu;* the looser, newer groups include Fuyo, Sanwa, and DKB. The *zaibatsu* themselves have roots in 19th century family firms that diversified. It should be emphasized that *keiretsu* are not cartels; they compete quite intensely in the domestic Japanese market.

15. In the mid-1990s, it became very fashionable to denounce Japanese practices and celebrate American ones, because of Japan's lingering recession after its financial bubble burst in 1989. This conveniently overlooks Japan's extraordinary growth in the five decades following World War II — from an average income equal to 11% of the U.S. in 1945 to 86% of the U.S. in 1994 (Maddison 1995, table D-1a).

16. As was pointed out earlier, fees during the recent (post-1980) merger wave have probably totaled between $20 billion and $40 billion. Fees for individual deals can be truly breathtaking; Lazard Frères billed the airline pilots' union $8.25 million for advising them on their *failed* buyout bid for United Airlines — a deal whose collapse brought about a mini-crash in the stock market in October 1989. That sum works out to $41,045 per banker per day — *on a busted deal* (Henwood 1990). Even if they worked around the clock, that's an hourly rate of $1,710.

17. Long and Ravenscraft's study covered several hundred LBOs consummated between 1981 and 1987; the exact number varies from 192 to 821, depending on the data series in question. It uses quite detailed Census data at the firm and plant level. There were 91 1981–84 LBOs, and 107 1985–87 deals.

18. Margaret Blair said in an interview that most of the firm- and economy-wide gains in productivity claimed by buyout partisans were the result of shutting weaker plants, rather than of an improvement in the performance of sites that remained open. Improving productivity at ongoing operations is a very complicated task.

19. Low q's are often associated with mergers. For example, targets of "predatory" acquisitions during the 1960s were disproportionally low-q firms (Barber, Palmer, and Wallace 1994).

20. In the same interview, Jensen claimed that GM was overstaffed by 25–50%. He didn't disclose how he knew this.

21. "Poison pills" are an antitakeover tactic that kick in when a firm is under attack by a hostile suitor. Specifically, they are warrants to buy the firm's stock at a bargain rate that are issued to existing shareholders once a hostile suitor has accumulated a specified amount of stock. The intent is to make a hostile takeover prohibitively expensive.

22. A legal reason for the new institutional assertiveness was a set of important changes in securities regulation in 1992 that made it much easier for shareholders to unite and submit proxy resolutions that force other shareholders to vote on corporate policy or board makeup, and also made it legal for a group of shareholders to lobby their colleagues and present a case to management. Restrictions on communications among shareholders were first imposed to prevent big guys from putting small holders at a disadvantage, but small fry have not yet objected to the new regime, no doubt because the lobbying efforts seem to have led to higher share prices (Blair 1995, pp. 70–73).

23. An announcement that a firm is the target of a governance campaign by institutional shareholders boosts its share price in the short term, but provides little long-term gain in either share price or profitability (Gillian and Starks 1995; Wahal 1995). But of course, shareholder assertiveness takes many more forms than such public finger-pointing.

24. Robert Monks (1995), a former Reaganite who is an eager polemicist on behalf of share-

holder rights, is imaginative enough to argue that since pension funds represent the masses' capital, they are the institutions to which corporations should be accountable. (By pension funds he means their managers, of course.) This accountability represents a check on what Monks admits to be the rather anomalous position of corporations in a professedly democratic society.

25. The Twentieth Century Fund's (1992) most recent take on governance, *Who's Minding the Store?,* is built around an essay by Robert Shiller on excess volatility. Yet the policy conclusions the Fund draws from Shiller's work are the weakest tea imaginable: encouraging patient capital through moral suasion, while taking no tax or regulatory steps towards that goal.

26. In some cases, like Japan and South Korea, the protectionist strategies succeeded; in Latin America, however, they often protected corrupt and incompetent friends of the government. There's no guarantee that protectionism can work as advertised, but it's hard to find an example of a country that industrialized successfully — including the U.S. in the late 19th century — without restricting imports.

7   What is (not) to be done?

After a long critique like this, the author must always be ready for the question, "OK, so what would *you* do?" The temptation is to dismiss it high-mindedly, saying there's a virtue to critique alone, but that would look too cowardly.

Before approximating an answer, though, I have to say that reforms of the financial sphere are nowhere near as easy as is sometimes argued. If you believe that money and finance are somehow epiphenomenal — of secondary importance to the real action of production, or bizarre malignancies that have somehow arisen on the economic body over the years — then the path of action is a lot clearer. But I've spent a lot of time arguing that this isn't the case. While finance is expensive and wasteful, profit always takes the form of money, capital yearns to be liquid and easily mobilized, and financial instruments are the means by which ownership and control are organized. If Negri is right, and he is, that money has the face of the boss, then taking on money means taking on the boss.

It would be much easier if the populists and Proudhonists were right in arguing that money and credit are kept artificially scarce, and the generous provision of both would make life profoundly easier for most of us. But Marx's critique of Proudhon, like that in the *Grundrisse,* should chasten every financial reformer. Marx argued that changes in the instrument of circulation alone do not address the relations of production and distribution, because these relations are embedded in the very notion of money. The need for money makes workers work and capitalists compete; it's not some quantity that comes from outside the economic system, but from deep within it. To be meaningful, any attack on the money system is an attack on the prerogatives of ownership and class power.

Instead of socializing capital through taxation or some other form of expropriation, loose-money dogma simply reduces to a desire for loans on easy terms. "The notion of *crédit gratuit,* incidentally, is only a hypocritical, philistine and anxiety-ridden form of the saying: property is theft. Instead of the workers *taking* the capitalists' capital, the capitalists are supposed to be compelled to *give* it to them" (Marx 1973, p. 123). Or in the case of the American populist, compelled to lend it on easy terms. While it's certainly the case that the working class is better off with a central bank that targets a 5% unemployment rate than one that targets 6%, the differences are not that fundamental.

Recently, we've seen a growth in calls for local moneys — chits representing labor time that circulate in small towns alongside national money — most famously the Ithaca Hours scheme in that town in upstate New York. Prospects for such schemes seem severely limited; at best, they seem applicable to haircuts, but probably not scissors, and certainly not raw steel. As soon as exchange breaks beyond the merely local, capitalist competition is certain to replace egalitarianism as the price-setting principle unless fundamental changes in ownership and the means by which enterprises relate to each other are made. "Labour time cannot directly be money…precisely because in fact labour time always exists only in the form of particular commodities" (Marx 1973, p. 168). The product of a barber can't be exchanged with that of an steelworker; they exchange as haircuts and metal, priced inevitably in money. The form of that money — Ithaca Hours, Federal Reserve notes, or electronic blips — may not be as important as people think.

So any call for financial transformations has to be considered only as a part of a broader attack on the forms of capitalist social power. As this is written, that seems almost unimaginable. What once seemed like mild social reforms — even the bare minimal aspects of a social democratic welfare state we've seen in the U.S. — are viewed by our rulers as an intolerable trespass on their God-given rights. The intensification of the attack on the welfare state in the U.S. and Western Europe since 1989 has made it clear that the boss will grant such concessions only as long as there's a credible threat of total expropriation, which is what the USSR, for all its countless faults, always represented to them. As impossible as expropriation may seem today, it pays to remember the old slogan from Paris 1968: be practical, demand the impossible.

In lieu of a 10-point recipe for social transformation, I offer a montage of critique and suggestion. First a look at a very bad idea; then a review of some mixed ideas; and finally a few more ambitious proposals.

But first, it's important to remember that not all attempts to rein in globalizing finance in the name of the local are politically progressive. Here, for example, is one writer's view:

> Thus, the task of the state toward capital was comparatively simple and clear; it only had to make certain that capital remain the handmaiden of the state and not fancy itself the mistress of the nation. This point of view could then be defined between two restrictive limits: preservation of a solvent, national, and independent economy on the one hand, assistance of the social rights of the workers on the other.... The sharp separation of stock exchange capital from the national economy offered the possibility of opposing the internationalization of the German economy without at the same time menacing the foundations of an independent national self-maintenance by a struggle against all capital. The development of Germany was much too clear in my eyes for me not to know that the hardest battle would have to be fought, not against hostile nations, but against international capital.

That was Hitler (1943, pp. 209, 213), in *Mein Kampf*. One should always be careful of critiques of finance that stop short of being critiques of capital — especially ones that focus on internationalization as an evil in itself.[1]

Social Security privatization: a truly horrible idea

Nothing illustrates the severity of the attack on the welfare state better than the emergence into popular discourse in the U.S. of ideas about privatizing the Social Security system. Until quite recently described as the "third rail" of American politics — touch it and you die — magazines like *Time* and *The New Republic* and even a commission appointed by a Democratic president have signed onto a privatization agenda that was once an obsession of the libertarian right. When Barry Goldwater suggested in 1964 that Social Security be made voluntary, it was considered evidence of his madness; now, the National Bureau of Economic Research publishes how-to papers (Kotlikoff 1995), and the media are doing the important work of selling the plan to the public.

Since the idea probably couldn't be sold on its merits — why destroy a system that is universal, successful, and deeply popular? — it has to be sold deviously. At the core of the deception is the line that the system faces inevitable bankruptcy when the Baby Boomers begin retiring about 10 or 20 years into the next century. The official source of these projections is the annual reports of the Trustees of the Social Security System (Board of Trustees, Federal Old Age and Survivors Insurance and Disability Insurance Trust Funds 1995). As is common with such official efforts, the Trustees present three sets of projections, a gloomy one, an optimistic one, and a supposedly moderate one. Though there are a host of interrelated assumptions involved in each, the salient fact, buried in the report's tables, is that the Trustees assumed an economic growth rate over the next 75 years of 1.4% (down from 1.5% in the 1994 annual report) — half the rate seen in the previous 75 years, and a rate matched in only one decade in this century (1910–1920). Even the 1930s saw a faster growth rate (1.9%).[2] My own simulations, using higher growth rates, show that with more reasonable growth assumptions — even a modest 2.0% growth rate, below the 2.3% average that prevailed between 1973 and 1995 — the system is not facing insolvency. So either the Trustees are using deliberately bearish growth assumptions to promote public doubt of the system (a charge the System's actuary, Steve Goss, strongly denies), or are foreseeing 75 years of depression ahead of us. Big news, either way.

Brokers and insurance companies are taking conscious advantage of this uncertainty surrounding Social Security to try to snag new accounts. Adman Bill Westbrook told the *Village Voice*'s Leslie Savan (1996) that his research found that the growing public distrust of government meant a growing "distrust that institutions like Medicaid or Social Security will be there to take care of people." His research also disclosed "a growing sense of empowerment, the idea that I'm a smart, capable person, and I can make my own decisions." Thus did Westbrook's agency, Fallon McElligott, come up with the "Be Your Own Rock" slogan for its client, Prudential, a company that, even as the new slogan was unleashed on the world, was under investigation in 30 states for "widespread deceptive sales practices, including misleading consumers about the cost of the policies" and "churning" of policies to generate new premiums and commissions (Scism 1996). It's all very surreal: the financial markets, characterized by nothing if not volatility and scandal, are portrayed as rock solid, and government, which has paid its pensioners without interruption and minimal scandal for over 60 years, is seen as wobbly.

The privatizers' model is the Chilean pension system, a creation of General Augusto Pinochet's Chicago-school dictatorship. The model, touted by both the Cato Institute and the World Bank, is centered on a kind of compulsory IRA scheme, in which all covered employees put 10% of their earnings into one of several approved mutual funds, which invest their holdings in the stock and bond markets. (Employers were relieved of having to make a contribution.) The infusion of money has done wonders for the Chilean stock market, but projections are that as many as half of future retirees will draw a poverty-level pension. For those at the low end, there remains a minimal public pension check, which offers recipients the equivalent of under $2 a day (Collins and Lear 1995; Paul and Paul 1995; Frank Solowey, personal communication).

Though proponents love to advertise "efficiencies" of privatized systems, the Chilean system is hardly a model. The competing mutual funds have vast sales forces, and the portfolio managers all have their vast fees. All in all, administrative costs for the Chilean system are almost 30% of revenues, compared to well under 1% for the U.S. Social Security system. Even the 12–14% average administrative costs for the U.S. life insurance industry look efficient by comparison (Diamond 1993).

Finally, the economics of a privatized system, which is inevitably centered on plowing money into the stock market, are pretty dodgy. When questioned, flacks from the libertarian Cato Institute — which is advised by the former Chilean cabinet minister who guided the transformation — make two points: the historical returns on stocks are higher than the implied return on Social Security, and money put into the stock market will promote real investment. As we've already seen, financial theory can't explain stock returns very well (the equity premium puzzle), and virtually no money put into the stock market goes into real investment. When confronted with these details, Cato's flacks sputter and mutter, but they have no solid answer other than to denounce the managerial skills of "government bureaucrats." Flacks also profess great faith in the public's ability to manage its retirement portfolio, but even people with advanced degrees don't really understand the basic arithmetic of interest rates, much less the complexities of modern financial markets.

It's a mystery why the stock market should do any better at solving the demographic problem of Baby Boomer retirement than the public system. Over the long term, the stock market should grow roughly in line with the overall economy; the only way it could greatly exceed the underlying growth rate is if the profit share of GDP were to increase continuously, or valuations were to grow to Ponzi-like levels. Historical return figures — one of the privatizers' favorite arguments — assume that dividends and capital gains are re-invested, when in fact they will be drawn down to finance peoples' retirements; for financing retirement, the stock market is like a giant revolving fund, much like the public system, that finances net sales by one set of parties with fresh purchases by another. Were the Boomers to start selling stocks to finance their retirement, prices would fall unless there was even more coming in from Generations X, Y, and Z. And of course any time between now and then, if one has the bad luck to retire in the midst of a bear market, then he or she may face a fairly miserable retirement.

But the whole notion of private pension funds, either of the sort that prevail now or would prevail under a privatized system, depends on an economic illusion. In one of the more profound passages of the *General Theory*, Keynes (*CW* VII, pp. 104–105) made an argument that has been virtually lost to modern economic thought:

> We cannot, as a community, provide for future consumption by financial expedients but only by current physical output. In so far as our social and business organisation separates financial provision for the future from physical provision for the future so that efforts to secure the former do not necessarily carry the latter with them, financial prudence will be liable to destroy effective demand and thus impair well-being....

Individuals may be able to set aside money for the future, but not a society as a whole; a society guarantees its future only by real physical and social investments. But the financial markets are demanding cutbacks in both public and private investment in the name of "financial prudence." Today, anyone making an argument like Keynes's at an American Economics Association meeting or on *Crossfire* would be regarded as insane.

This is why you won't find anything in this chapter on the "progressive use" of pension funds. Peter Drucker's fears of "pension fund socialism" of the 1970s have realized themselves in the portfolio manager capitalism of the 1990s — which is no surprise, since it's quite natural that capital should appropriate the pooled savings of workers for "management." The whole idea of creating huge pools of financial capital should be the focus of attack, not the uses to which these pools are put. Instead of funding infrastructure development through creative pension-fund-backed financial instruments, finance it with a wealth tax instead.

The lesson of the Swedish wage-earner funds should be chastening to pension-fund reformers (Pontusson 1984; 1987; 1992). The funds were originally conceived by social democratic economists as a scheme for socializing ownership of corporations. In the original mid-1970s proposal, firms would have been required to issue new shares, in amounts equal to 20% of their annual profits, to funds representing wage-earners as a collective. In the space of a decade or two, these funds would acquire dominant, and eventually controlling, interests in corporate Sweden.

This idea scandalized business, which launched a great campaign to discredit it — a task that was greatly simplified by the fact that the funds never attracted broad popular support. The Social Democrats and the unions watered the plan down, and a weak version was adopted in the early 1980s. The funds quickly began behaving like ordinary pension funds; their managers, in a vain attempt at legitimation, began trading stocks in an effort to beat the market averages. Eventually, late in the decade, the wage-earner funds were euthanized.

Why did they fail? For at least two reasons. First, business correctly saw the initial version as a challenge to capitalist ownership, a reminder that finance is central to the constitution of a corporate ruling class. And second, they never attracted popular support — essential to any serious challenge to a corporate ruling class — because they were so abstract. As Pontusson (1992, p. 237) put it, "when collective shareholding funds are reduced to deciding whether to buy shares in Volvo or Saab," it's hard to muster popular enthusiasm. More direct interventions are required — active public industrial policy and greater worker control at the firm level — if ordinary people are to get interested. The stock market, on the other hand, is the home turf of financiers, and any games played on their turf usually end up being played by their rules.

democratizing the Fed

Financial populists often propose to "democratize the Fed," opening up its proceedings to public scrutiny, and making membership on the Board of Governors into an elective office. Fundamentally, this is a fine idea. But, in the spirit of this chapter, its limitations have to be acknowledged.

Congress is an elective office, too, and its proceedings are televised in narcotic detail on C-SPAN, but the body still produces innumerable insults to democracy. The moneyed and powerful enjoy an access to Congress that mere citizens lack, a disparity that is well known; why should applying similar standards to the Fed produce any better results — especially when it comes to the central bank, whose issues are dear to the hearts of rentiers? The spectacles of Congressional tax-writing and budget-making don't offer an inspiring precedent.

Procedure aside, the nature of the central bank may be less important than the broader institutions in which it is embedded. A comparison with other countries demonstrates the point. The most independent of the major central banks is the German Bundesbank (known as "Buba" to its friends);

it does what it pleases with an insouciance that even Alan Greenspan must envy. The least independent of the European central banks is the Bank of England; though it began its life in the seventeenth century as a private institution that served as banker to the state, it was nationalized in 1946 by the Labour government and still takes policy direction from the Chancellor of the Exchequer. Now it must be admitted that Buba has kept interest rates very high over the past several years, out of fear of the inflationary consequences of Bonn's takeover of the former East Germany. Yet over the long term, by any standard — whether by hardheaded ones like growth rates and investment levels, or squishy-humanist ones like poverty rates and income distribution — the German economy has performed far better than the British one for decades.

It would be tempting to conclude from that comparison that maybe an independent central bank is a pretty good thing after all. But the Bank of Japan is largely subordinate to the Japanese Finance Ministry, and by the same standards, tough or soft, Japan's economy has done far better than even Germany's over the long term. So maybe an independent central bank isn't such a good thing after all.

Or maybe the importance of the central bank is exaggerated. Unlike Britain and the United States, which suffer from loosely regulated financial systems and a shoot-from-the-hip stock market mentality, Japan and Germany have rather tightly regulated systems in which stock markets play a relatively unimportant role in both investment finance and corporate governance. Compared with these broader financial structures, the central bank's (in)dependence isn't quite so important.

Populist critiques of the Fed tend to concentrate excessively on its autonomous powers while overlooking the influence of the financial markets on the central bankers: the Fed follows interest rate trends as well as leading them. The 1994 tightening offers a good example. Creditors began selling their bonds, driving up long-term interest rates, several months before the Fed jacked up the short-term rates in February. They reinforced the message with repeated cries urging the Fed to tighten. Even after the Fed began tightening, Wall Street bayed for more. Similarly, Greenspan's urging of deficit-cutting on Clinton was done in the name of pleasing the bond market, a task the new President took to with great public fervor, despite the private reservations reported by Woodward. Were some reconstructed Fed to shift policy into a permanently stimulative mode, it would have to face the prospect of a capital strike on the part of creditors; it might be able to force short-term rates down, but long-term rates could rise toward 20%. Any democratization of the Fed that didn't simultaneously take on the financial elite would quickly face such a disaster.

Sure, the Fed should be opened up — its secrecy ended; its own finances brought into the general federal budget; its personnel made more broadly representative in terms of gender, race, and class; and its narrow, austere criterion of economic management put on permanent furlough. But that kind of transformation could succeed only as part of a broader transformation of financial relations.

investing socially

Over the last decade — essentially since the campaign to purge stock portfolios of companies doing business in South Africa started in the early 1980s — we've seen an explosion in investment funds devoted to goals beyond mere profit-maximization. One can trace the movement's history back further — to the early 1970s, when some Methodist clergy founded the Pax World Fund, and two portfolio managers, Robert Schwartz in New York and Robert Zevin in Boston, started managing money for a few individuals and institutions concerned about where their profits came from (Kinder, Lyndenberg, and Domini 1992).

Besides South Africa, the principal concerns motivating social investors in the early days were nuclear power and weapons-making. That is, the founding impulses were to avoid the noxious. In more recent years, there's been a growth in the desire to do active good with one's investments — to foster development in poor communities, for example, or fund environmentally friendly technologies. The unifying feature of social investing (SI) is the desire to accomplish some social goals along with making a return on one's money.

screens

As might be expected, the field is populated by a full range of people, from cynics looking for a market niche to some fine people looking to transform the world. The mainstream of the SI industry is characterized by some form of social screening. The flavor of that screening can be sampled in an ad in the May–June 1995 issue of the *Utne Reader* for Working Assets, the SI mutual fund giant. Working Assets touted its No-Load Citizens Index Fund thus: "Unlike the S&P 500, however, we have a low concentration in dirty, dying industries like heavy equipment, oil and chemicals, weapons, utilities, alcohol and tobacco. Instead, we've concentrated on clean industries of the future, such as communications, consumer products and services, business equipment, high-tech, finance, healthcare and food production." While every individual company is socially screened, the economic analysis underlying this portfolio selection remains happily unexamined. Forget that the "dying industries" are generally high-wage, and the "clean industries" often less so. And where would communications, business equipment, and other high-tech industries be without the chemicals used in the manufacture of computer hardware, and the low-wage labor exploited in the process? Don't the products of the high-tech industries contribute to the constant cheapening of labor and the much-lamented globalization of the assembly line? Where would any of these glistening industries be without the electricity produced by the nasty oil-powered utilities, or the earth moved and the concrete poured by the products of the heavy equipment industry? Would upper-middle-class Americans, Working Assets' target population, have incomes 50 times the Third World average if it weren't for all those nasty weapons? Doesn't food production profit nicely from the constant cheapening of raw agricultural commodities, a trend that has savaged Third World exporting nations and indigenous producers?[3] Isn't it the cheapest sort of moral bombast to get exercised by tobacco production, one that induces a warm glow in the weed-o-phobe, but involves no significant challenge to the social order? And what service does finance offer except the multiplication of riches for those already blessed with plenty?

But the social investors are, in large measure, part of that financial industry — one that skims the cream, from both the moral and niche marketing points of view, but one that nonetheless never troubles itself with the larger questions of why some have financial assets while most don't, or, more radically, how that translates into the power of creditor over debtor, and why some should profit from the disguised labor of others.

In an interview broadcast on May 9, 1995 on CNBC, the cable TV business news channel, Sophia Collier, the big cheese at Working Assets, said that 40% of the S&P 500 stocks are "socially responsible." That assumes that you have no problem with the giant multinational corporation itself, just some individual malefactors. The leading index of socially responsible stocks, that published by Kinder, Lyndenberg, and Domini, includes about half the S&P 500, presumably the same firms Collier had in mind.

The political thinking of mainstream SI is underdeveloped. In its pragmatic faith in individual action, it's classically American. Social investors also make some odd alliances. An issue of *The Greenmoney Journal* (1995) approvingly quoted mutual fund kingpin (Sir) John Templeton reflecting on ethics, unaware of or indifferent to the fact that his Templeton Prize for Progress in Religion in 1994 went to Michael Novak, famous for his various theological apologias for Reaganomics, nuclear weapons, and Argentina's dirty war against dissidents (Henwood 1994b) — a prize awarded by a board that included distinguished ethicist Margaret Thatcher.

A contradiction no social screen can address is that investment profits originate ultimately, no matter how you dress them up, in the uncompensated labor of workers, and that they depend on a social order in which some people have money to spare and others don't. When asked to comment on this, the former radical academic turned social broker Michael Moffitt conceded, "It's a problem." Moffitt's past makes him aware of "the problem," but most social investors don't even think about it.

With South Africa no longer an issue, the most popular social screens reflect the concerns of upscale liberals: tobacco, women in the boardroom, animal testing, and the grosser environmental crimes. Concerns like women on the assembly line, unionization, and workplace injuries rarely appear. One of the favorite stocks of mainstream SI has been that of the Washington Post Co., a fiercely anti-union firm that publishes the daily journal of record for the DC branch of the status quo.

alternative lending modes

But the SI universe is not all so conventional, and some aspects are experimenting with the actual transformation of property relations. Let's start with the conventional and move gradually away from it. Along with the growth in SI has come an increasing interest in "alternative" financial institutions, like community development banks (CDBs) and loan funds. The most prominent of the CDBs is the South Shore Bank of Chicago, whose promoters say it has revived a declining urban neighborhood while turning in a sterling financial performance. It is touted by some as a model for the free-market era, a private-sector alternative to discredited old social programs, though Lyndon Comstock, founder of Brooklyn's Community Capital Bank, quickly conceded in an interview that a bank, even one with social goals, is still no substitute for public sector spending.

South Shore, founded in 1973, is the oldest and richest of its kind. It has attracted talented bankers and lots of outside depositors. If you read its press, it's done wonderfully well. In what appears to be the first outside effort to audit its claims, Benjamin Esty (1995) of the Harvard Business School found that South Shore's actual record is less impressive than its

PR. When measured against nearby banks of comparable size, its financial performance has been fairly underwhelming. That would be fine if it were accomplishing its social goals, but it appears not to be. When Esty compared social indicators for the South Shore neighborhood with contiguous communities using Census data from 1970, 1980, and 1990, he found the results to be "decidedly mixed at best." While unemployment in the South Shore neighborhood was lower, incomes have fallen more rapidly than in the neighboring communities; overall, concluded Esty, "South Shore's relative performance has been worse than the contiguous neighborhoods." Now there may be all kinds of problems, methodological and conceptual, with this comparison, Esty admits, but these results are nonetheless very damaging to the CDB cause.

Closely related to the South Shore model are various nonbank forms of local lending like community development funds. Though not strictly commercial banks, they too accept money from socially minded investors and then make loans to fund housing rehabilitation, nonprofit housing development, and small businesses. The industry is still quite small. According to the National Association of Community Development Loan Funds (1996), as of the end of 1995, the industry had $108 million in loans outstanding, and $204 million in capital, a third of the capital permanent and the rest borrowed. In the nine years after their 1986 birth, NACDLF member funds financed 56,243 housing units, 73% of them permanently affordable for low-income residents, and created or preserved 11,313 jobs, 59% of them for "low-income people," 51% for women, and 37% for minorities. Their loan loss experience was an impressive 0.92%.

Of course all these numbers are better than nothing. But so far they barely register on the national screen. The total number of jobs "created or preserved" over the entire 10-year history represents less than two days of normal U.S. employment growth; of houses financed, about 10 days of normal U.S. housing production.[4]

And some loans extended under the name of community development look rather odd indeed. In its 1995 annual report, the Northern California Community Loan Fund bragged about a $25,000 loan to establish a Ben & Jerry's ice cream store in San Francisco "that will train and provide employment for low income youth from San Francisco's Tenderloin neighborhood." A sidebar, illustrated with a picture of smiling, freshly employed teens, claims that "the business supports youth programs in several ways: job training takes place in the ice cream parlor, while the profits go towards creating new business enterprises to benefit homeless youth."

Ben & Jerry's is a favorite of the soulful capitalism crowd. Unfortunately, as its own social auditor, the soulful catalog merchant Paul Hawken, admitted in the firm's 1994 annual report, reality didn't support the claims that the Brazil nuts used in B&J's Rainforest Crunch were harvested by indigenous people for their benefit:

> The label on Ben & Jerry's Rainforest Crunch Ice Cream gives the impression that the harvest of the nuts benefits indigenous forest peoples. In fact, the nuts are not harvested or sold by indigenous peoples but by the rubber tappers of Brazilian and Portuguese ancestry who have worked the forests for a century. One might ask what constitutes indigenous status and this might be a minor point if not for the fact that some experts on indigenous peoples believe that the flow of money to these projects has had a damaging effect on tribal cultures. The influx of cash has created inequities, rivalries, and an appetite for western goods while reducing the attention paid to the real issue; land ownership. Quoting Indian Unity: "...Our communities' independence is ... weakened as our well-being is made dependent on western markets.... Selling products is meaningless if we ourselves do not control the marketing projects and the natural resources, if we ourselves do not control our lands and have the right to say what we want...." A second point regarding label accuracy is that the bulk of the nuts used in Rainforest Crunch have been commercially rather than alternatively sourced.[5]

These failings are emblematic of the weakness of SI in general: it too easily becomes just another marketing gimmick, while doing little to address inequities of wealth and power.

In the Third World, similar small-scale lending schemes are proffered as cures for poverty in places where conventional development has failed.[6] The favorite example, the South Shore of the alternative development crowd, is the Grameen Bank of Bangladesh, which offers tiny loans only to women, who supposedly build businesses with the proceeds and exit poverty. Grameen has earned glowing reviews, based mainly on its own testimony and citation of previously published glowing reviews; in fact, hardly a negative word about the bank appeared anywhere in the press until Gina Neff investigated Grameen for *Left Business Observer* (Neff 1996). Despite claims of poverty reduction, over half of Grameen's long-term borrowers can't meet basic nutritional needs. Despite claims of commercial viability, the enterprise is kept going only by philanthropists' subsidies. Despite claims of "empowering" women, Grameen loans formalize women's informal household labor (while blocking their entry into potentially more liberating — with all the appropriate qualifications — waged work), typically without increasing their autonomy within the household (well under half have significant control over the businesses held in their names). By contrast, the Self-Employed Women's Association of India (SEWA) offers credit, but as part of a package of education and political organizing. With Grameen, male lending officers really call the shots.

The appeal of microcredit schemes like Grameen — which have been adopted enthusiastically by the likes of the World Bank, Hillary Clinton, and Citibank — is that they are a low-cost, nonthreatening substitute for real self-organization, like SEWA, and for expensive public programs like education, health care, and infrastructure investment.

It may be that the lesson of the World Bank's experience over the last 50 years is of near-universal applicability: it's very difficult, if not impossible, to borrow your way out of poverty.

rethinking property

More promising than New Age banks are strategies that alter the nature of property relations. For example, community land trusts (CLTs) "are democratically controlled non-profit corporations, with open membership and elected boards. The purpose of a CLT is to acquire land and hold it permanently for the benefit of the community. The land is then made available through long-term leases to individual families, cooperatives, and other organizations who may own buildings on the land. Resale restrictions in the ground lease keep the property available for future purposes" (Community Investment Monitor 1995). CLTs were developed by the founders of the Massachusetts-based Institute for Community Economics (ICE), Ralph Borsodi and Bob Swann, in the 1960s. Lessors on CLT land can be compensated for improvements they make to their building, but they cannot sell it on the open market; the idea is to remove the parcel of land from the property market forever. A similar concept, limited equity co-ops, can be used in cities; residents can buy an apartment from the co-op, and sell it back when they leave — with appropriate compensation for any improvements they might have made and general inflation, but with no possibility of significant trading profits.

A former director of the ICE, Charles Matthei (personal communcation) argues that increases in property values are claimed by individuals, but, aside from improvements made by the occupant, are typically the result of social action like public infrastructure development or general economic growth. It's fundamentally unfair, Matthei says, that these social gains should be captured mainly by private individuals — especially unfair if they contributed little or nothing to their neighborhood's upscaling except having been there at the right time.

Still, CLTs are a speck on the horizon; as of late 1995, there were only 90 of them in the U.S. The ICE, "a leader among leaders," according to the newsletter of the National Association of Community Development Loan Funds (Community Investment Monitor 1995) had equity capital of $531,000 and had lent a total of $26 million between its founding in 1979 and 1995. With the total value of land, buildings, and other tangible assets in the U.S. nearly $20 trillion in 1994, according to the Fed's flow of funds accounts, CLTs have a long, long way to go.

One of the reasons to be skeptical about institutions that don't alter property relations is that institutions and people that start out with noble goals often end up reproducing the ills they were meant to correct. The U.S. is full of community organizations and nonprofit housing developers that now seem indistinguishable, except maybe in matters of style, from conventional real estate developers and banks. It is no accident that the Ford Foundation has embraced community development schemes; no institution in America is better at spotting potential troublemakers and domesticating them (not only in the U.S., but around the world).

taxes: soak the fat boys!

Many of the approaches I've just discussed are attempts to craft market-friendly responses to social problems. They're often represented as fresh approaches to old problems, when in fact they're really convention tarted up as innovation. I'm reminded of Karl Kraus's comment about psycho-analysis — that it's the disease of which it purports to be the cure.

If old thinking can be successfully passed off as new, why not revive some better old ideas than the ones now being re-animated? Capital controls, for example, once a cornerstone of social democratic thinking, are now dismissed as hopelessly obsolete. But why? Why not require government approval of inbound and outbound foreign investment? It worked quite well for Japan and South Korea; why can't capital controls be put in service of an agenda more humane than the rapid growth in GDP and exports? To those who say that modern technology makes it easy to evade such restrictions one can easily reply that it also makes it easier to impose them. The principal obstacles aren't technical, but political (not that the political obstacles are minor).

Perhaps the most unfashionable idea of all is taxing the rich — or soaking the fat boys, as Jack Burden, the journalist turned political consultant, put it to Willie Stark, the Huey Long-ish hero of Robert Penn Warren's *All the King's Men*. Seriously boosting the income tax rate on the richest 1–2% of the population could fund all manner of public programs, from free education and childcare to public jobs programs. And taxation of wealth itself, along with income, would be a wonderful way to raise funds for, say, the upgrading of the public physical and social capital stock — financing urban reconstruction, mass transit, alternative energy research, and environmental repair. Both forms of taxation would also have the lovely side-effect of reducing the wealth and social power of the very rich.

Income taxes are familiar, but wealth taxes aren't. Washington taxes wealth only on the death of the very wealthy, and even then estate taxes are quite porous, and are often referred to as "voluntary," because anyone with time and a clever lawyer can pretty much dodge them.

As of 1990, eleven OECD countries, all in Europe, had some form of wealth taxation in effect, although the burden on the well-off was in general quite light. Simulations by Edward Wolff (1995, chapters 8 and 9) show that adopting the Swiss system of wealth taxation would have raised $34 billion in 1989; the German system, $68 billion, and the Swedish (since repealed by a conservative government), $329 billion — in a year when total revenues from federal income taxes were $446 billion, and the much-bemoaned deficit was $152 billion.

All three models exclude household effects (though not owner-occupied housing) and pensions from wealth taxes, and the German and Swedish versions also spare life insurance. So all three leave the poor and the middle class largely unscathed. Only a Swedish-style tax would bite the upper middle class; those with wealth in the $75,000–100,000 range (in 1989) would face a new tax equal to about 15% of their present income tax; those in the $100,000–250,000 range, 39% of their income tax, and those above $250,000 would take a hit close to or larger than their present income tax liability. Obviously such a tax would have very dramatic economic, fiscal, and distributional effects, unlike the other two national models. A Swiss-style system would be barely noticeable to non-millionaires, and German-style system would hardly touch those with wealth holdings under $250,000. Even so, the amounts of revenue raised would be more than notional in an era where public services are starved for funds.

There are few serious arguments against wealth taxes except the preservation of privilege. Wealth taxes would tend to hit older families harder than younger ones, even though some older families may have lower incomes than their more youthful fellow citizens, but careful design of the tax could mitigate these effects if that were desired.[7] But of course, a wealth tax by definition would hit only those with a lot of commas in their bank balance. Rich folks and their hired pens would no doubt claim very damaging effects on saving and investment, but the U.S., which taxes wealth and income very lightly, has one of the lowest rates of saving and investment in the First World — lower than Sweden in the days of its tax. More generally, "there appears to be no strong evidence that the presence of a wealth tax inhibits savings" (Wolff 1995, p. 54). And, as Wolff points out, the fact that Switzerland taxes wealth makes capital flight arguments a bit hard to sustain, since that country is the target, not the source, of a not insignificant share of the world's flight capital.

Another levy, designed more to change behavior than to raise revenue, would be to tax securities trading. The idea of a transactions tax to cut trading volume goes back at least as far as Keynes (*CW* VII, p. 160), who drew a contrast between Britain, where brokerage commissions and trading taxes were high, and the U.S., where both were low: "The introduction of a substantial Government transfer on all transactions might prove the most serviceable reform available, with a view to mitigating the predominance of speculation over enterprise in the United States." Keynes further argued that the purchase of a security be made "permanent, and indissoluble, like marriage, except by reason of death or other grave cause." Nowadays, of course, marriages are dissolved for reasons other than death or grave cause, and few civilized people would argue that divorce be made as difficult as it was 60 years ago. But if you believe that heavy trading increases the volatility of asset prices and encourages all manner of pointless or malignant financial hyperactivity, then transactions taxes are a simple but potentially powerful remedy. It's not the euthanasia of the rentier exactly, but it's the first prick of the fatal needle.

Stock trading costs in the U.S. for large institutional investors are the lowest of any major market by a considerable margin. According to 1992 data from Frank Russell Securities (cited in Campbell and Froot 1994), U.S. traders paid 0.30% of the value of a transaction in commissions and fees, or 30 basis points (bp) in market jargon; next-cheapest was Britain, at 50 bp; in other markets, the figure was 60 bp or higher. In addition, eight of the 10 countries imposed taxes or other fees on top of the brokers' take. British taxes were equal to another 50 bp, making the cost of moving a share of stock from one set of hands to another more than three times as expensive as the U.S. So, not only does the U.S. have the world's largest capital market, it also has the cheapest.

Transactions taxes are easier to impose than collect, because investors will do everything they can to avoid paying them. They and their bankers will invent new instruments not covered in the tax, or discover loopholes, or move their trading abroad. If they can't evade the tax, they will cut back on trading. That's not necessarily a bad thing; the aim of a transactions tax is to change behavior as much as it is to raise revenue. But achieving both goals requires that the tax be carefully designed.

One thing is clear: a transactions tax must be levied on the traders, not the trade; on the transaction, not the specific security. As Campbell and Froot show, a Swedish tax on brokerage services was easily avoided by doing trades in London and New York. But the U.K.'s transactions tax was levied on changes in ownership, making it very difficult for British investors to avoid. Similarly, local taxes on the New York or Pacific Stock Exchanges, which have been proposed by troublemakers on both coasts, could be very easily evaded, but a national tax on U.S. resident buyers and sellers couldn't be. A tax on stocks alone could be avoided through trading options; a tax on registered securities could be evaded with custom over-the-counter deals; a tax based on legal domicile could be avoided by moving the legal headquarters to a taxless Caribbean isle. For once, clever lawyers could do something socially useful by drafting the transactions tax to foreclose those dodges.

A broad, well-designed tax could raise not insignificant amounts of money. Dean Baker, Robert Pollin, and Marc Schaberg (1994) estimated that, based on 1992 trading figures, a modest tax of 50 bp on stock sales, a 1 bp per year to maturity tax on bonds (so that a 30-year bond would be subject to a 30 bp tax), and comparable rates on derivatives could raise $60 billion a year assuming no decline in trading, or $30 billion if trading fell by half. That would still leave the costs of trading stocks well below British levels, and Britain is not known as a place where the financial sector is underdeveloped. Baker et al. admirably proposed that the proceeds of the tax be used to finance education, military-to-civilian conversion, and environmental research and repair.

More modestly, James Tobin (1995) has proposed a 0.5% tax on international currency transactions, to dampen exchange market volatility. People transacting real-world business would find the tax negligible, but those trying to profit from every quiver of every exchange rate would be inconvenienced. (If 0.5% isn't a high enough rate to do the trick, then it should be whatever's required to accomplish the task.) Tobin would tax only spot market transactions, exempting derivatives, arguing that prices are set in spot markets, and derivatives prices only reflect, they don't shape, the course of spot prices — though he admits that he's not fully sure of this.[8] Aside from dampening volatility, Tobin also would like to restore more national discretion to economic policymaking. "I am not one," said Tobin, "who thinks that the markets are always imposing upon any central bank exactly the discipline it ought to have." Markets, through ignorance, perverseness, or delusion, can impose policies on countries that are inappropriate to national circumstances, and Tobin thinks his tax might reduce this pressure. Attempts to evade the tax, he argued, could be managed by having it administered by the IMF — even making compliance with the tax a condition of membership. Proceeds of the tax could be used for "worthwhile international purposes" — funding the UN, the World Bank, and the IMF, for example. The latter institutions have contributed greatly to creating the borderless world Tobin bemoans, but liberals rarely seem to have problems with contradictions like this.

Tobin has also argued for a similar tax on stock trades. Tobin lodged a dissent from the tame official recommendations of the Twentieth Century Fund's (1992) Task Force on Market Speculation and Corporate Governance. The report's centerpiece was a long essay by Robert Shiller (1992) on markets' excessive volatility, and the dangers of taking guidance on how to run real corporations from movements in their stock prices. But having raised that interesting question, the worthies on the Fund's panel decided against a transactions tax, preferring instead a revolution in the consciousness of institutional investors — the sprouting of a new culture of patience and self-discipline, as incredible as that may sound to any student of the markets. Over half the worthies were from finance, law, or the Fed; the balance were mainly safe academics. Nonfinancial corporations were conspicuously absent. Tobin wrote, politely, that the "Task Force was wrong to give such short shrift to 'sand in the wheels' of the financial markets" (Twentieth Century Fund 1992, p. 23). Tobin never reflects on what social purpose shareholders serve — but if he were the kind to do that, the Twentieth Century Fund would never have had him on their panel.

Few things, aside from the threat of direct appropriation of their property, make Wall Streeters scream more loudly than the assertion that their pursuits are pointless or malignant, and that their activities should be taxed like a noxious effluent. Listening to those screams would be another positive benefit of a transactions tax.

refusing money

More radical than taxation is what Harry Cleaver (1995) has called "the subversion of money-as-command." If, as Marx held (and Negri emphasized), money and credit are forms of social power — and debt and fiscal crises are used to intensify the force of capitalist rule — then the refusal of that relation would strike sharply at the orthodox order. Cleaver argued that Keynesian welfare state policies, through their excessive generosity, reduced the capitalists' power and increased that of the working class; rising wages and benefits during the Golden Age also contributed to this. Among the virtues of this line of analysis are that it politicizes apparently technical aspects of budget-making, and clarifies the importance of the New York fiscal crisis in introducing the era of capitalist counterattack — still in full swing as these words are written more than 20 years later.

Restoring the welfare state is one line of action — a bit boring, perhaps, but essential to any more radical projects, since nothing boosts the freedom of maneuver for nonelites like a hospitable safety net. A more radical version of the subversion of money is the organized, political refusal to pay debts, a technique that was used with great success in South Africa during the final assault on apartheid. It's hard to imagine the American masses, energized with revolt, collectively scrawling "*Non serviam*" across their VISA bills, but stranger things have happened.

transforming corporations

Finally, since most of this book is about the securities of large private corporations, that's where this chapter should conclude. The long-term goal should be to reduce the financial and governance role of the stock market with an eye towards its eventual elimination. Corporations should be placed increasingly under a combination of worker, community, customer, supplier, and public control. Of course, it's easy to say that in a reasonable-sounding sentence or two, but the actual task, technically and politically, would be difficult as hell.[9]

The present fashion for putting more outside directors on boards, in the name of "independent" supervision, rules out union representatives, who are considered insiders (Blair 1995, p. 81). It also rules out firms' significant suppliers and customers. This is the opposite of Japanese governance structure, with their elaborate cross-holdings and monitoring.

That Japanese structure, with its cross-holding and monitoring mechanisms, seems like a promising model for a more socialized mode of ownership of larger firms (smaller ones could be run as cooperatives). Instead of a bank at the center run on profit principles, one could easily imagine a publicly owned one, run on social principles; various socialized groups would be organized around various publicly owned banks, operating under a broad, publicly drawn macroeconomic plan. The banks would collect money from individuals and institutions with spare balances, and lend them at low rates of interest to enterprises in their constituencies. Depositors, then, would be paid interest on the basis of these earnings. Firms would be governed by boards representing all these constituencies, with the bank exercising long-term supervision. The banks themselves would be answerable to a central bank, which would provide funds and direct investment according to democratically agreed on priorities. The need for outside stockholders, who provide little or no capital and less good advice, would be eliminated.

I realize that this prescription — something like market socialism — is at once spotty and grandiose. But the point is not to provide an elaborate blueprint for a future society, in the style of John Roemer. Off-the-shelf utopias may be useful thought experiments, but they're of limited political use, except maybe as long-term inspiration. A future society has to emerge out of this one, on the basis of experimentation and struggle. I've outlined the fundamental principles of where I think we should go. Consider these closing pages fragments of a first draft for a project aiming to end the rule of money, whose tyranny is sometimes a little hard to see.

notes

1. Obviously, capitalist internationalization, as practiced by multinational corporations, is something to be criticized. But purely localist critiques that view cosmopolitanism itself as dangerous are tinged with xenophobia, and frequently sentimentalize pre-existing local hierarchies out of existence.
2. One rationale sometimes offered for the slow growth rates is that the labor force will grow more slowly over the next seven decades than it has over the past seven; this is precisely the reason offered by the Trustees and the System's actuary, Steve Goss. The economic evidence is, however, that a slowdown in labor force growth will be offset by an increase in productivity growth (Cutler, Poterba, Sheiner, and Summers 1990). Cutler et al. also argue that an aging population is a reason for a *lower* savings rate rather than a higher one — the exact opposite of conventional advice.
3. This is not to argue that modernization is necessarily bad and that indigenous production methods should remain unchanged for all time. But those willing to profit off the trend while basking in moral superiority should take some notice of the contradiction.
4. The NACDLF began lending in 1986. Between the end of 1985 and the end of 1995,

there was a net growth of 19.6 million jobs in the U.S., an average of 164,000 per month, or about 8,000 per business day. Over the same period, housing starts averaged 1.4 million a year, or 5,700 per business day.

5. For more on Ben & Jerry's, and the failings of socially responsible business in general, see the fine series of articles by Jon Entine cited in the bibliography. Entine's first claim to fame was his exposure of the fraud behind the Body Shop, another darling of the tender commerce crowd.

6. Failed, that is, if you think the goal of development is the emergence of poor countries from poverty. If the goal of "development" is to extract resources, money, and labor from the world's poor, then development has been quite successful.

7. Social scientists love to speak of the "intergenerational transmission of welfare dependency" — the likelihood of welfare moms having daughters who themselves become welfare moms. They are less interested in studying the intergenerational transmission of privilege, but a sharp wealth tax would go a long way to reducing that elite form of dependency.

8. Since spot and derivatives markets are now so intertwined, it's hard to imagine how they could be treated so differently for tax purposes. And if the aim is to change behavior as well as raise revenue, the exemption makes no sense at all.

9. This is not to say that Hilferding's idea that seizing a few big banks in the name of the people would lead to socialism was right. Relations within enterprises (i.e., genuine worker control) and relations between enterprises (meaning planned linkages that replace market/competitive ones) must also be transformed.

Appendix

interest rates

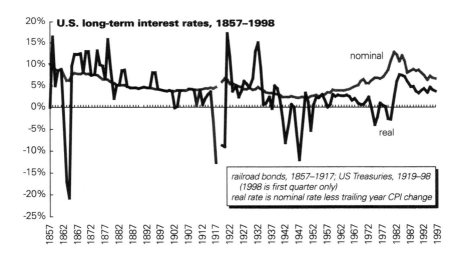

U.S. long-term interest rates, 1857–1998

railroad bonds, 1857–1917; US Treasuries, 1919–98
(1998 is first quarter only)
real rate is nominal rate less trailing year CPI change

interest rates (cont.)

U.S. long-term interest rates
period averages

	real	nominal
decades		
1850s	7.2%	9.5%
1860s	3.1	7.7
1870s	10.6	7.1
1880s	5.3	5.0
1890s	5.1	4.3
1900s	3.2	4.0
1910s	-1.2	4.6
1920s	5.1	5.2
1930s	5.8	3.8
1940s	-3.2	2.4
1950s	1.0	3.0
1960s	2.2	4.5
1970s	-0.2	6.9
1980s	4.8	10.4
1990s	4.1	7.3
periods		
1870–1913	5.7%	5.0%
1914–1949	1.7	4.0
1914–29	2.2	5.1
1930–38	5.9	3.9
1939–44	-1.2	2.6
1945–49	-4.1	2.3
1950–73	1.5	4.1
1974–97	3.1	8.5
1974–81	-0.9	8.5
1982–97	5.0	8.5

As with the graph on the previous page, the long-term rate is that on railroad bonds from1857 to 1917; after 1917, it's the average rate on long-term U.S. Treasury bonds. "Real" rate is computed by subtracting the yearly change in the consumer price index from the nominal rate. Periods are based on Angus Maddison's (1995): the period of high Victorian capitalism — of the gold standard, the British empire, and free trade and free capital flows (1870–1913); the periods of war, troubled recovery, depression, more war, and a less troubled recovery (1914–1949); the postwar Golden Age (1950–73); and the recent Bronze Age. I've divided the recent period into the years of inflation, labor and Third World rebellions, and U.S. imperial erosion (1974–81), and the period since, that of more assertive imperial power, consolidated financier rule, and free trade and free capital flows.

stocks and the economy

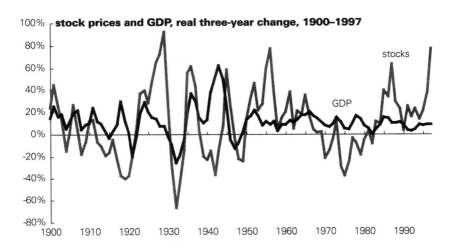

stock prices and GDP, real three-year change, 1900–1997

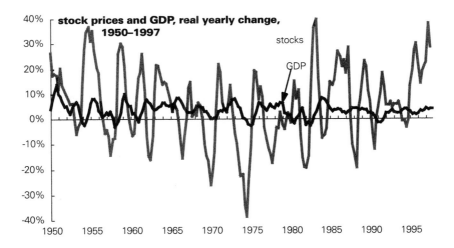

stock prices and GDP, real yearly change, 1950–1997

These charts try to show the relation between the stock market and the real economy. On top is a long-term view, showing three-year real (inflation-adjusted) changes in stocks (the S&P 500 index) and GDP. The stock market more or less follows economic trends — it's hardly infallible as a leading indicator — and often overdoes it in both directions. The tendency to overreact is more visible in the second chart, which plots year to year changes in quarterly averages. For the post-World War II U.S., the market leads the economy by about two quarters, but is still no match for the yield curve as a leading indicator (see p. 122).

financial performance, long-term

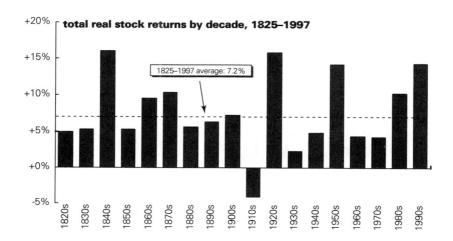

total real stock returns by decade, 1825–1997

1825–1997 average: 7.2%

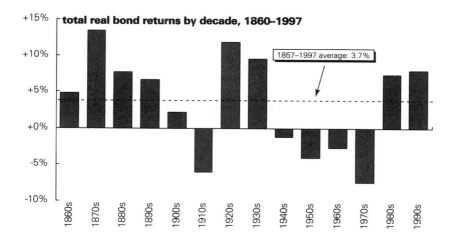

total real bond returns by decade, 1860–1997

1857–1997 average: 3.7%

financial performance, long-term (cont.)

real total returns and change in consumer prices by decade

| | real total returns | | |
	stocks	bonds	CPI
1820s	5.0%		-2.7%
1830s	5.3		-0.6
1840s	16.0		-1.8
1850s	5.3		0.8
1860s	9.6	4.9%	3.5
1870s	10.4	13.5	-2.7
1880s	5.6	7.7	-0.7
1890s	6.4	6.7	-0.8
1900s	7.3	2.2	1.1
1910s	-4.1	-6.0	7.9
1920s	15.9	11.9	-1.8
1930s	2.3	9.6	-1.7
1940s	4.9	-1.1	5.6
1950s	14.2	-4.1	2.1
1960s	4.4	-2.7	2.8
1970s	4.2	-7.4	10.8
1980s	10.2	7.4	4.7
1990s	11.0	9.2	3.0
average	7.0	3.8	2.1
1950–97	7.5	0.1	4.1

Real total returns for stocks and bonds are computed from index numbers representing cumulative real total return (that is, interest and dividends are reinvested). For stocks, the index number is equal to the sum of a year's dividend yield plus price change (expressed as a percent) less the inflation rate (consumer price index) times the prior year's index, or

$$Index_Y = Index_{Y-1} \times (1 + DividendYield_Y + PriceChange_Y + CPI_Y)].$$

For bonds, the index equals a year's average interest payment plus price return (on a bond normalized so that an 8% yield is priced at 100) less the change in CPI. Of course, taxes and transaction costs would make it near-impossible to duplicate these measures; they represent not an actual portfolio's performance, but the comparative tendencies over time. Source: National Bureau of Economic Research web site (http://www.nber.org); *Historical Statistics of the United States,* Bicentennial Edition; Shiller (1991); Goetzmann and Ibbotson (1994); *Economic Report of the President,* various years; standard sources cited in introduction to Bibliography.

owners and issuers of financial instruments, 1997
(billions of dollars and share of total)

credit market debt

total outstanding	$21,118.9	100.0%
debtors		
domestic nonfinancial	15,194.1	71.9
U.S. government	3,804.9	18.0
nonfederal	11,389.3	53.9
households	5,571.5	26.4
nonfinancial corporations	3,282.8	15.5
nonfarm noncorporate business	1,250.1	5.9
farm	156.2	0.7
state and local governments	1,128.7	5.3
rest of world	558.8	2.6
financial	5,366.0	25.4
commercial banks	309.7	1.5
savings institutions	160.3	0.8
life insurance companies	1.8	0.0
government-sponsored enterprises	995.9	4.7
federal-related mortgage pools	1,825.8	8.6
asset-backed security issuers	998.4	4.7
finance companies	554.5	2.6
mortgage companies	36.4	0.2
real-estate investment trusts	73.7	0.3
brokers and dealers	35.3	0.2
funding corporations	373.8	1.8
other	0.6	0.0
creditors		
domestic nonfederal nonfinancial	2,753.7	13.0
households	1,826.9	8.7
nonfinancial corporations	296.3	1.4
nonfarm noncorporate businesses	39.1	0.2
state and local governments	591.5	2.8
U.S. government	201.4	1.0
rest of world	2,270.0	10.7
financial sectors	15,893.8	75.3
monetary authority (Fed)	431.4	2.0
commercial banking	4,031.9	19.1
U.S.-chartered	3,450.8	16.3
foreign banks, U.S. offices	515.4	2.4
bank holding companies	27.4	0.1
banks in U.S.-affiliated areas	38.3	0.2
savings insitutions	925.5	4.4
credit unions	304.2	1.4
bank personal trusts	242.3	1.1
life insurance companies	1,775.4	8.4
other insurance companies	514.4	2.4
private pension funds	831.7	3.9
state and local government retirement funds	577.5	2.7
money market mutual funds	718.8	3.4
mutual funds	894.8	4.2
closed-end funds	99.5	0.5
government-sponsored enterprises	908.6	4.3
federal-related mortgage pools	1,825.8	8.6
asset-backed security issuers	859.5	4.1
finance companies	566.7	2.7
mortgage companies	47.9	0.2
real-estate investment trusts	24.0	0.1
brokers and dealers	183.6	0.9
funding corporations	130.3	0.6

owners and issuers of financial instruments, 1997 (cont.)

U.S. Treasury

total	$3,778.3	100.0%
by type		
savings bonds	186.5	4.9
other	3,591.8	95.1
creditors		
households	304.6	8.1
savings bonds	186.5	4.9
other	118.1	3.1
nonfarm noncorporate business	15.7	0.4
nonfianncial corporations	54.3	1.4
state and local government	279.3	7.4
rest of world	1,265.6	33.5
monetary authority (Fed)	430.7	11.4
commercial banking	269.8	7.1
U.S.-chartered	166.8	4.4
foreign	94.6	2.5
bank holding companies	4.0	0.1
banks in U.S.-affiliated areas	4.4	0.1
savings institutions	14.6	0.4
credit unions	15.7	0.4
bank personal trusts	39.4	1.0
life insurance companies	96.9	2.6
other insurance companies	128.0	3.4
private pension funds	323.9	8.6
state and local government retirement funds	213.6	5.7
money market mutual funds	86.2	2.3
mutual funds	219.0	5.8
closed- end funds	10.6	0.3
government-sponsored enterprises	15.6	0.4
brokers/dealers	-5.0	-0.1

U.S. agency securities

total	$2,848.2	100.0%
by type		
budgetary agencies	26.5	0.9
government-sponsored enterprises	995.9	35.0
federal-related mortgage pools	1,825.8	64.1
creditors		
households	499.8	17.5
nonfinancial corporations	10.0	0.4
state and local governments	95.4	3.4
rest of world	259.2	9.1
monetary authority (Fed)	0.7	0.0
commercial banks	571.0	20.0
U.S.-chartered	497.1	17.5
foreign banks, U.S. branches	62.0	2.2
bank holding companies	5.5	0.2
banks in U.S.-affiliated areas	6.3	0.2
savings institutions	154.8	5.4
credit unions	48.4	1.7
bank personal trusts	38.7	1.4
life insurance companies	252.6	8.9
other insurance companies	51.2	1.8

owners and issuers of financial instruments, 1997 (cont.)

U.S. agency securities (cont.)

private pension funds	159.9	5.6
state and local retirement funds	108.2	3.8
money-market mutual funds	96.3	3.4
mutual funds	122.9	4.3
government-sponsored enterprises	314.6	11.0
asset-backed security issuers	14.1	0.5
brokers and dealers	50.4	1.8
total U.S. Treasury and U.S. agency	*6,626.5*	

corporate and foreign bonds

total outstanding	$3,338.4	100.0%
debtors		
nonfinancial corporations	1,489.5	44.6
U.S. holdings of foreign issues	382.6	11.5
financial sectors	1,466.3	43.9
commercial banks	192.7	5.8
savings institutions	2.8	0.1
asset-backed security issuers	742.2	22.2
finance companies	328.9	9.9
real-estate investment trusts	20.2	0.6
brokers and dealers	35.3	1.1
funding corporations	144.2	4.3
creditors		
households	349.3	10.5
state and local governments	44.5	1.3
foreign holdings of U.S. issues	531.7	15.9
commercial banks	143.1	4.3
savings institutions	58.4	1.8
bank personal trusts	31.4	0.9
life insurance companies	1,025.7	30.7
other insurance companies	148.5	4.4
private pension funds	281.7	8.4
state and local government retirement funds	202.0	6.1
money market mutual funds	33.4	1.0
mutual funds	273.8	8.2
closed-end funds	27.7	0.8
government-sponsored enterprises	33.4	1.0
brokers and dealers	100.7	3.0
funding corporations	53.1	1.6

owners and issuers of financial instruments, 1997 (cont.)

stocks

total market value	$12,958.6	100.0%
issuers		
nonfinancial corporations	7,793.7	60.1
foreign issues held by U.S. residents	1,183.9	9.1
financial corporations	3,981.0	30.7
holders		
households	5,737.6	44.3
state and local governments	79.9	0.6
foreign holdings of U.S. issues	881.7	6.8
commercial banks	2.6	0.0
savings institutions	23.4	0.2
bank personal trusts	259.3	2.0
life insurance companies	582.2	4.5
other insurance companies	176.9	1.4
private pension funds	1,765.4	13.6
state and local government retirement funds	1,295.2	10.0
mutual funds	2,049.4	15.8
closed-end funds	54.2	0.4
brokers and dealers	50.8	0.4

portfolio allocations of households & pension funds, 1997

households

assets	**$27,108.7**	**100.0%**
deposits	3,834.9	14.1
foreign deposits	49.3	0.2
checking deposits and currency	426.1	1.6
time and savings deposits	2,722.8	10.0
money market funds	636.7	2.3
credit market instruments	1,826.9	6.7
open market paper	122.6	0.5
U.S. government securities	804.3	3.0
Treasury	304.6	1.1
savings bonds	186.5	0.7
other	118.1	0.4
agency	499.8	1.8
municipal securities	448.9	1.7
corporate and foreign bonds	349.3	1.3
mortgages	101.8	0.4
stocks	5,737.6	21.2
mutual funds	1,937.5	7.1
security credit	210.7	0.8
life insurance reserves	650.8	2.4
pension fund reserves	7,453.9	27.5
bank personal trusts	1,050.7	3.9
equity in noncorporate businesses	4,087.6	15.1
miscellaneous	318.0	1.2

portfolio allocations, 1997 (cont.)

households (cont.)

liabilities	**5,827.1**	**100.0**
credit market instruments	5,571.5	95.6
home mortgages	3,757.6	64.5
consumer credit	1,265.4	21.7
municipal debt	187.5	3.2
bank loans	61.2	1.0
other loans and advances	193.5	3.3
commercial mortgages	106.4	1.8
security credit	128.8	2.2
trade payables	106.8	1.8
life insurance premiums, deferred and unpaid	20.1	0.3

private pension funds

financial assets	**$3,577.8**	**100.0%**
checking deposits and currency	2.9	0.1
time and savings deposits	25.9	0.7
money market funds	43.1	1.2
security repurchase agreements (repos)	42.0	1.2
credit market instruments	831.7	23.2
open market paper	42.0	1.2
U.S. government securities	483.8	13.5
Treasury	323.9	9.1
agency	159.9	4.5
municipal securities	1.0	0.0
corporate and foreign bonds	281.7	7.9
mortgages	23.3	0.7
stocks	1,765.4	49.3
mutual funds	457.0	12.8
miscellaneous	409.9	11.5
unallocated insurance contracts	241.3	6.7
pension fund contribution receivables	33.4	0.9
other	135.2	3.8

state and local government retirement funds

financial assets	**$2,099.7**	**100.0%**
checking deposits and currency	4.2	0.2
time and savings deposits	2.1	0.1
security repurchase agreements (repos)	35.1	1.7
credit market instruments	577.5	27.5
open market paper	35.1	1.7
U.S. government securities	321.8	15.3
Treasury	213.6	10.2
agency	108.2	5.2
municipal securities	0.9	0.0
corporate and foreign bonds	202.0	9.6
mortgages	17.6	0.8
stocks	1,295.2	61.7
miscellaneous	185.7	8.8

total assets, private and public pension funds   *$5,677.5*

Bibliography

For conciseness' sake, economic and other social statistics derived from standard official sources are not cited in the text. For the U.S., the standard sources for "real sector" data are the national income and product accounts, as published by the Bureau of Economic Analysis (BEA), U.S. Department of Commerce; the BEA's monthly journal, *Survey of Current Business;* the Bureau of Labor Statistics (BLS), U.S. Department of Labor; the BLS's monthly journals, the *Monthly Labor Review* and *Employment and Earnings;* and the Bureau of the Census, U.S. Department of Commerce. U.S. government budget data comes principally from the *Budget of the United States Government, Fiscal Year 1999: Historical Tables.* For U.S. financial sector data, the principal source is the statistical annex to the monthly *Federal Reserve Bulletin* and the *Annual Statistical Digest.* When a source is given as the Federal Reserve's Flow of Funds accounts, this refers to the Fed's periodicals *Balance Sheets for the U.S. Economy* (C.9 series, biannual) and *Flow of Funds: Flows and Outstandings* (Z.1 series, quarterly). International data come principally from the International Monetary Fund's *International Financial Statistics* (yearbook and monthly updates) and *Balance of Payments Statistics* (yearbook); the World Bank's *World Development Report* and *World Tables,* both published annually; and the Organisation for Economic Cooperation and Development's serial *Economic Outlook,* published twice a year, and its companion historical volume. In most cases, data comes from electronic versions of these printed sources: from the Commerce Department's Economic Bulletin Board, various U.S. government web sites (especially those of the Fed and the BLS), and the WEFA database on Dialog. Statistics drawn from other sources are fully referenced. In almost all cases, the data are the latest available as of April 1, 1998.

Aaron, Henry J., and Alicia H. Munnell (1992). "Reassessing the Role for Wealth Transfer Taxes, *National Tax Journal* 45, 119–143.

Abken, Peter A. (1991). "Beyond Plain Vanilla: A Taxonomy of Swaps," Federal Reserve Bank of Atlanta *Economic Review* (March/April), pp. 12–27.

Adler, Bill (1988). "Leveraged Lives," *Texas Observer,* December 23, p. 1.

Aggharwal, Rajesh (1995). "Capital Structure After Debt Restructurings: Why Do Firms Remain Overleveraged?," Dartmouth College mimeo (June).

Aghion, Philippe, Oliver Hart, and John Moore (1992). "The Economics of Bankruptcy Reform," Massachusetts Institute of Technology Economics Department Working Paper 92-11, May.

Akerlof, George (1970). "The Market for Lemons: Quality Uncertainty and the Market Mechanism," *Quarterly Journal of Economics* 84 (August), pp. 488–500.

Alberts, William W., and Nikhil P. Varaiya (1989). "Assessing the Profitability of Growth by Acquisition," *International Journal of Industrial Organization* 7, pp. 133–149.

Ando, Albert, and Franco Modigliani (1963). "The 'Life Cycle Hypothesis of Saving: Aggregate Implications and Tests," *American Economic Review* 53, pp. 55–84.

Aoki, Masahiko, Bo Gustafsson, and Oliver E. Williamson, eds. (1990). *The Firm as a Nexus of Treaties* (London and Newbury Park, Calif.: Sage Publications).

Arestis, Philip, ed. (1988). *Post-Keynesian Monetary Economics: New Approaches to Financial Modeling* (Aldershot, U.K.: Edward Elgar).

Arnon, Arie (1984). "Marx's Theory of Money: The Formative Years," *History of Political Economy* 16, pp. 555–575.

Arrighi, Giovanni (1994). *The Long Twentieth Century* (New York and London: Verso).

Arrow, Kenneth J. (1994). "Methodological Individualism and Social Knowledge," *AEA Papers and Proceedings* 84 (May), pp. 1–9.

Artis, M.J. (1988). "How Accurate is the World Economic Outlook? A Post Mortem on Short-Term Forecasting at the International Monetary Fund," in *Staff Studies for the World Economic Outlook* (Washington: International Monetary Fund, July), pp. 1–49.

ARTnewsletter (1992). "Leggatt Bros. of London Bids Farewell to Changed Art World," (New York: September 29).

Asimakopulos, A. (1983). "Kalecki and Keynes on Finance, Investment and Saving," *Cambridge Journal of Economics* 7, pp. 221–233.

Avery, Robert B., and Gregory E. Elliehausen (1986). "Financial Characteristics of High-Income Families," *Federal Reserve Bulletin* 92 (March), pp.163–177.

Ayala, César J. (1989). "Theories of Big Business in American Society," *Critical Sociology* 16 (Summer–Fall), pp. 91–120.

Bacon, Jeremy (1993). *Corporate Boards and Corporate Governance* (New York: The Conference Board, Report No. 1036).

Baker, Dean, Robert Pollin, and Marc Schaberg (1994). "Taxing the Big Casino: Main Street vs. Wall Street," *Nation* 258 (May 9), pp. 622–625.

Banham, Russ (1993). "On Bermuda's Horizon, 'Acts of God' Bonds," *Global Finance* (September), pp. 82–86.

Bank for International Settlements (1992). "Derivative Financial Instruments and Banks' Involvement in Selected Off-Balance-Sheet Business," *International Banking and Financial Market Developments* (Basel: May).

— (1993). *Central Bank Survey of Foreign Exchange Market Activity in April 1992* (Basel: BIS, March).

— (1998). *International Banking and Financial Market Developments* (Basel: February).

Bank of England (1994). "The External Balance Sheet of the United Kingdom: Recent Developments," *Bank of England Quarterly Bulletin* 34:4 (November), pp. 355–361.

Baran, Paul A. and Paul M. Sweezy (1966). *Monopoly Capital: An Essay on the American Economic and Social Order* (New York: Monthly Review Press).

Barber, Brad M., Donald A. Palmer, and James Wallace (1994). "Determinates of Conglomerate and Predatory Acquisitions: Evidence from the 1960's," University of California–Davis Graduate School of Management Working Paper 10-94 (October).

Barclay, Michael J. (1996). "Bid–Ask Spreads and the Avoidance of Odd-Eighth Quotes on NASDAQ: An Examination of Exchange Listings," Bradley Policy Research Center, Simon School of Business, University of Rochester, Working Paper 96-04 (January).

Barro, Robert (1990). "The Stock Market and Investment," *Review of Financial Studies* 3, pp. 115–131.

Barsky, Robert B., and J. Bradford De Long (1993). "Why Does the Stock Market Fluctuate?," *Quarterly Journal of Economics* 108, pp. 291–311.

Bartlett, Sarah (1991). *The Money Machine: How KKR Manufactured Power & Profits* (New York: Warner Books).

Basel Committee on Banking Supervision (1995). *Planned Supplement to the Capital Accord to Incorporate Market Risks* (Basel: Bank for International Settlements, April).

Baudrillard, Jean (1975). *The Mirror of Production* (St. Louis: Telos Press).

— (1993). *The Tranparency of Evil,* translated by James Benedict (New York and London: Verso).

Baumol, Wiliam J. (1965). *The Stock Market and Economic Efficiency* (New York: Fordham University Press).

Behrens, Rolf (1985). "What Keynes Knew About Marx," *Studi Economici* 26, pp. 3–14.

Bennett, Bruce (1996). "Orange County vs. Merrill Lynch," letter, *Wall Street Journal,* July 1.

Benzie, Richard (1992). "The Development of the International Bond Market," *BIS Economic Papers* No. 32 (Basel: Bank for International Settlements, January).

Berenbeim, Ronald E. (1994). *Company Relations With Institutional Investors* (New York: The Conference Board).

Berglöf, Erik, and Enrico Perotti (1994). "The Governance Structure of the Japanese Financial Keiretsu," *Journal of Financial Economics* 36, pp. 259–284.

Berle, Adolph A., and Gardiner C. Means (1932/1967). *The Modern Corporation and Private Property,* revised edition (New York: Harcourt, Brace & World).

Bernanke, Ben S. (1981). "Bankruptcy, Liquidity, and Recession," *AEA Papers and Proceedings* 71, pp. 155–159.

— (1983). "Nonmonetary Effects of the Financial Crisis in the Propagation of the Great Depression," *American Economic Review* 73, pp. 257–276.

Bernanke, Ben S., and John Y. Campbell (1988). "Is There a Corporate Debt Crisis?" *Brookings Papers on Economic Activity* 1, pp. 83–139.

Bernanke, Ben S., John Y. Campbell, and Toni M. Whited (1990). "U.S. Corporate Leverage: Developments in 1987 and 1988," *Brookings Papers on Economic Activity* 1, pp. 255–286.

Bernard, Henri, and Stefan Gerlach (1996). "Does the Term Structure Predict Recessions? The International Evidence," BIS Working Paper No. 37 (Basel: Bank for International Settlements, September).

Bernstein, Peter L. (1992). *Capital Ideas: The Improbable Origins of Modern Wall Street* (New York: Free Press).

Berthoud, Richard, and Elaine Kempson (1992). *Credit and Debt: The PSI Report* (London: Policy Studies Institute).

Betker, Brian L. (1995). "Administrative Costs of Debt Restructurings," Ohio State University mimeo (May).

Bhagat, Sanjai, Andrei Shleifer, and Robert W. Vishny (1990). "Hostile Takeovers in the 1980s: The Return to Corporate Specialization," *Brookings Papers on Economic Activity: Microeconomics,* pp. 1–85.

Bilello, Suzanne (1992). "Free-Trade Pact Stirs Emotions," *New York Newsday,* August 7.

Black, Fisher (1986). "Noise," *Journal of Finance* 41 (July), pp. 529–543.

Black, Fisher, and Myron Scholes (1973). "The Pricing of Options and Corporate Liabilities," *Journal of Political Economy* 81, pp. 637–654.

Blair, Margaret M, ed. (1993). *The Deal Decade: What Takeovers and Leveraged Buyouts Mean for Corporate Governance* (Washington: Brookings Institution).

— (1995). *Ownership and Control: Rethinking Corporate Governance for the Twenty-First Century* (Washington: Brookings Institution).

Blair, Margaret M., and Martha A. Schary (1993a). "Industry-Level Indicators of Free Cash Flow," in Blair (1993), pp. 99–147.

— (1993b). "Industry-Level Pressures to Restructure," in Blair (1993), pp. 149–203.

Blanchard, Olivier, Changyong Rhee, and Lawrence Summers (1993). "The Stock Market, Profit, and Investment," *Quarterly Journal of Economics* 108, pp. 115–136.

Blaug, Mark (1985). *Economic Theory in Retrospect,* 4th ed. (Cambridge and New York: Cambridge University Press).

Board of Trustees, Federal Old Age and Survivors Insurance and Disability Insurance Trust Funds (1995). *Annual Report, 1995* (Washington: U.S. Government Printing Office).

Bonefeld, Werner, and John Holloway, eds. (1995). *Global Capital, National State and the Politics of Money* (New York: St. Martin's Press).

Borg, J. Rody, Mary O. Borg, and John D. Leeth (1989). "The Success of Mergers in the 1920s: A Stock Market Appraisal of the Second Merger Wave," *International Journal of Industrial Organization* 7, pp. 117–131.

Borio, C.E.V. (1990). "Leverage and Financing of Non-Financial Companies: An International Perspective," *BIS Economic Papers* No. 27 (Basel: Bank for International Settlements, May).

— (1995). "The Structure of Credit to the Non-Government Sector and the Transmission Mechanism of Monetary Policy: A Cross-Country Comparison," BIS Working Paper No. 24 (Basel: Bank for International Settlements, April).

Borneman, Ernest, ed. (1976). *The Psychoanalysis of Money* (New York: Urizen Books).

Bottomore, Tom, Laurence Harris, V.G. Kiernan, and Ralph Miliband (1983). *A Dictionary of Marxist Thought* (Cambridge, Mass.: Harvard University Press).

Bowles, Samuel, Herbert Gintis, and Bo Gustafsson, editors (1993). *Markets and Democracy: Participation, Accountability, and Efficiency* (Cambridge and New York: Cambridge University Press).

Bradley, Michael, and Michael Rosenzweig (1992). "The Untenable Case for Chapter 11," *Yale Law Review* 101 (Spring).

Brealey, Richard A., and Stewart C. Myers (1991). *Principles of Corporate Finance*, 4th ed. (New York: McGraw Hill, Inc.).

Breeden, Douglas T. (1979). "An Intertemporal Asset Pricing Model With Stochastic Consumption and Investment Opportunities," *Journal of Financial Economics* 7, pp. 265–296.

Breeden, Douglas T., Michael R. Gibbons, and Robert H. Litzenberger (1989). "Empirical Tests of the Consumption-Oriented CAPM," *Journal of Finance* 44, pp. 231–262.

Brooks, John (1973). *The Go-Go Years* (New York: Weybright and Talley).

Brown, Norman O. (1985). *Life Against Death* (Middletown, Conn.: Wesleyan University Press).

Bruck, Connie (1988). *The Predators' Ball* (New York: The American Lawyer/Simon and Schuster).

Bulow, Jeremy, and Paul Klemperer (1991). "Rational Frenzies and Crashes," *Centre for Economic Policy Research Discussion Paper* No. 593 (London, CEPR, October).

Burrough, Bryan, and John Helyar (1990). *Barbarians at the Gate* (New York: Harper & Row).

Business International (1992). *Managing the Global Finance Function*, Special Report No. P253 (London: Business International).

Calmes, Jackie (1996). "Federal Mortgage Firm Is Facing New Assault to Privileged Status," *Wall Street Journal*, May 14, p. A1.

Campbell, John (1995). "Goodbye Central: The Blast of Revolution in Telecommunications," Federal Reserve Bank of Boston's *Regional Review* (Winter), pp. 7–10.

Campbell, John Y., and Kenneth A. Froot (1994). "International Experience with Securities Transaction Taxes," Harvard University mimeo.

Cantillo, Miguel. (1995). "The Rise and Fall of Bank Control in the United States: 1890–1920," University of California at Berkeley Walter A. Haas School of Business, Research Program in Finance Working Paper No. 254 (October).

Cantor, Richard (1990). "Effects of Leverage on Corporate Investment and Hiring Decisions," *Federal Reserve Bank of New York Quarterly Review*, Summer, p. 31.

Cantor, Richard, and Frank Packer (1995). "Sovereign Credit Ratings," *Current Issues in Economics and Finance* 1 (Federal Reserve Bank of New York), June.

Card, David, and Alan B. Krueger (1995). *Myth and Measurement: The New Economics of the Minimum Wage* (Princeton: Princeton University Press).

Carosso, Vincent P. (1970). *Investment Banking in America: A History* (Cambridge: Harvard University Press).

— (1987). *The Morgans: Private International Bankers 1854–1913* (Cambridge: Harvard University Press).

Caves, Richard E. (1989). "Mergers, Takeovers, and Economic Efficiency: Foresight vs. Hindsight," *International Journal of Industrial Organization* 7, pp. 151–174.

Chandler, Alfred D. Jr. (1977). *The Visible Hand: The Managerial Revolution in American Business* (Cambridge: Harvard University Press).

— (1990). *Scale and Scope: The Dynamics of Industrial Capitalism* (Cambridge: Harvard University Press).

Cheng, Li-Lan (1996). "Equity Issue Under-Performance and the Timing of Security Issues," unpublished paper, National Economic Research Associates Inc., White Plains, N.Y.

Chen, Nai-Fu. (1991). "Financial Investment Opportunities and the Macroeconomy," *Journal of Finance* 46, pp. 529–554.

Chen, Nai-Fu, Richard Roll, and Stephen A. Ross (1986). "Economic Forces and the Stock Market," *Journal of Business* 59, pp. 383–403.

Cherian, Joseph A., and Robert A. Jarrow (1994). "Options Markets, Self-Fulfilling Prophecies, and Implied Volatilities," mimeo, Boston University School of Management (October).

Chick, Victoria (1976). *Transnational Enterprises and the Evolution of the International Monetary System,* University of Sydney, Transnational Corporations Research Project, Research Monograph No. 5.

— (1983). *Macroeconomics After Keynes: A Reconsideration of the* General Theory (Deddington, U.K.: Philip Allan Publishers).

Chiodi, Guglielmo, and Marcello Messori (1984). "Marx's Analysis of the Relationship Between the Rate of Interest and the Rate of Profits: A Comment," *Cambridge Journal of Economics* 8, pp. 93–97.

Christie, William G., and Paul H. Schultz (1994). "Why Do NASDAQ Market Makers Avoid Odd-Eighth Quotes?," *Journal of Finance* 49 (December), pp. 1813–1840.

Christie, William G., Jeffrey H. Harris, and Paul H. Schultz (1994). "Why Did NASDAQ Market Makers Stop Avoiding Odd-Eighth Quotes?," *Journal of Finance* 49 (December), pp. 1841–1860.

Ciancanelli, Penelope (1992). "The Role of Accounting in the Debt Crisis," paper delivered at the European Institute for Advanced Studies in Management conference, Madrid (University of Manchester mimeo).

Clarke, Simon (1993). *Marx's Theory of Crisis* (London: Macmillan).

Cleaver, Harry (1995). "The Subversion of Money-as-Command In the Current Crisis," in Bonefeld and Holloway 1995, pp. 141–177.

Coakley, Jerry, and Laurence Harris (1983). *City of Capital* (Oxford: Basil Blackwell).

Coase, Ronald H. (1937). "The Nature of the Firm," *Economica* 4, pp. 386–405, reprinted in Williamson and Winter (1993), Chapter 2.

Cochrane, James L. (1991). "The Internationalization of Trading," speech delivered to a *Financial Times* conference, London, April 22.

Cockburn, Alexander (1995). *The Golden Age Is In Us* (New York and London: Verso).

Cohen, Darrel, Kevin Hassett, and Jim Kennedy (1995). "Are U.S. Investment and Capital Stocks at Optimal Levels?," Federal Reserve Board, Finance and Economics Discussion Series No. 95-32 (July).

Cohen, Randolph B., and Christopher K. Polk (1996). "COMPUSTAT Selection Bias in Tests of the Sharpe–Lintner–Black CAPM," unpublished paper, University of Chicago, Graduate School of Business (January).

Collins, Joseph, and John Lear (1995). *Chile's Free Market Miracle: A Second Look* (San Francisco: Food First Books).

Community Investment Monitor (1995). "Member Profile: Institute for Community Economics Revolving Loan Fund," *Community Investment Monitor* (Winter), p. 3.

Corbett, Jenny, and Tim Jenkinson (1993). "The Financing of Industry, 1970–89: An International Comparison," mimeo, Oxford University.

Corbett, Jenny, Jeremy Edwards, and Tim Jenkinson (1994). "Financial Structure and Corporate Governance: An International Comparison," mimeo, Oxford University.

Cosh, A.D., A. Hughes, K. Lee, and A. Singh (1989). "Institutional Investment, Mergers and the Market for Corporate Control," *International Journal of Industrial Organization* 7, pp. 73–100.

Cowles, Alfred (1933). "Can Stock Market Forecasters Forecast," *Econometrica* 1, pp. 309–324.

— (1944). "Stock Market Forecasting," *Econometrica* 13, pp. 206–214.

Crabbe, Leland E., Margaret H. Pickering, and Stephen D. Prowse (1990). "Recent Developments in Corporate Finance," *Federal Reserve Bulletin* 76, pp. 593–603.

Crotty, James (1990). "Owner–Manager Conflict and Financial Theories of Investment Instability: A Critical Assessment of Keynes, Tobin, and Minsky," *Journal of Post Keynesian Economics* 12 (Summer), pp. 519–543.

— (1994). "Are Keynesian Uncertainty and Macrotheory Compatible? Conventional Decision Making, Institutional Structures, and Conditional Stability in Keynesian Macromodels," in Dymski and Pollin 1994, pp. 105–139.

— (1992). "Neoclassical and Keynesian Approaches to the Theory of Investment," *Journal of Post Keynesian Economics* 14, pp. 483–496.

Cutler, David M., and James M. Poterba (1991). "Speculative Dynamics," *Review of Economic Studies* 58, pp. 529–546.

Cutler, David M., James M. Poterba, Louise M. Sheiner, and Lawrence H. Summers (1990).

"An Aging Society: Opportunity or Challenge?," *Brookings Papers on Economic Activity* 1, pp. 1–73.

Cutler, David M., James M. Poterba, and Lawrence H. Summers (1989). "What Moves Stock Prices?," *Journal of Portfolio Management* 15 (Spring), pp. 4–12.

— (1990). "Speculative Dynamics and the Role of Feedback Traders," *AEA Papers and Proceedings* 80 (May), pp. 63–68.

— (1991). "Speculative Dynamics," *Review of Economic Studies* 58, pp. 529–546.

Cutler, David M., and Lawrence H. Summers (1988). "The Costs of Conflict Resolution and Financial Distress: Evidence from the Texaco–Pennzoil Litigation," *RAND Journal of Economics* 19 (Summer), pp. 157–172.

Darity, William A., Jr., and Bobbie L. Horn (1985). "Rudolf Hilferding: The Dominion of Capitalism and the Dominion of Gold," *AEA Papers and Proceedings* 75 (May), pp. 363–368.

Davidson, Paul (1972). *Money and the Real World* (New York: John Wiley & Sons).

Davis, Carolyn D., and Alice P. White (1987), "Stock Market Volatility" (summary of staff study), *Federal Reserve Bulletin,* September, pp. 609–610.

de Bondt, Werner F.M., and Richard Thaler (1985). "Does the Stock Market Overreact?," *Journal of Finance* 40 (July), pp. 793–805.

de Brunhoff, Susanne (1976). *Marx on Money* (New York: Urizen Books).

Debreu, Gerard (1991). "The Mathematization of Economic Theory," *American Economic Review* 81 (March), pp. 1–7.

du Boff, Richard B., and Edward S. Herman (1989). "The Promotional–Financial Dynamic of Merger Movements: A Historical Perspective," *Journal of Economic Issues* 23 (March), pp. 107–133.

De Cecco, Marcello (1992a). "Foreign Exchange Markets: History," in Newman et al. (1992).

— (1992b). "Gold Standard," in Newman et al. (1992).

Delaney, Kevin J. (1992). *Strategic Bankruptcy: How Corporations and Creditors Use Chapter 11 to Their Advantage* (Berkeley and Los Angeles: University of California Press).

De Vroey, Michel (1984). "Inflation: A Non-Monetarist Monetary Interpretation," *Cambridge Journal of Economics* 8, pp. 381–389.

Diamond, Peter (1993). "Privatization of Social Security: Lessons From Chile," paper presented at the 12th Latin American meeting of the Econometric Society, Tucuman, Argentina (August 20).

Dietrich, Michael (1994). *Transaction Cost Economics and Beyond: Towards a New Economics of the Firm* (London and New York: Routledge).

Dillard, Dudley (1987). "Money as an Institution of Capitalism," *Journal of Economic Issues* 21 (December), pp. 1623–1647.

Du Boff, Richard B., and Edward S. Herman (1989). "The Promotional–Financial Dynamic of Merger Movements: A Historical Perspective," *Journal of Economic Issues* 23 (March), pp. 107–133.

Duff, Christina (1996). "Top Executives Ponder High Pay, Decide They're Worth Every Cent," *Wall Street Journal,* May 13, p. B1.

Dymski, Gary (1994). "Asymmetric Information, Uncertainty, and Financial Structure: 'New' versus 'Post'-Keynesian Microfoundations," in Dymski and Pollin (1994), pp. 77–103.

Dymski, Gary, and Robert Pollin (1994). *New Perspectives in Monetary Economics: Explorations in the Tradition of Hyman P. Minsky* (Ann Arbor: University of Michigan Press).

Economist (1991). "Schools Brief: Risk and Return," *Economist,* February 2, p. 72.

— (1992a). "Pollution and the Poor," *Economist,* February 15, p. 18.

— (1992b). "Let Them Eat Pollution," *Economist,* February 8, p. 66.

— (1992c). "Beta Beaten," *Economist,* March 7, p. 87.

— (1996). "Unhappy Families." *Economist,* February 20, pp. 23–25.

Economist Intelligence Unit (1992). *Building the Next-Generation Global Treasury,* Research Report No. F-208 (London and New York: EIU).

Elston, Julie Ann (1994). "Ownership Structure, Investment, and Liquidity Constraints: Evidence from German Manufacturing Firms," mimeo, Wissenschaftzentrum Berlin.

Entine, Jon (1994). "Shattered Image: Is the Body Shop Too Good to be True?," *Business Ethics* (September/October).

— (1995). "When Rainforest Ice Cream Melts: The Messy Reality of 'Socially Responsible Business,'" *Electronic Journal of Radical Organisation Theory* (Internet: http://www.mngt.waikato.ac.nz/leader/journal/dialogue/entine1.htm).

— (1996a). "Let Them Eat Brazil Nuts: The 'Rainforest Harvest' and Other Myths of Green Marketing," *Dollars and Sense* (March/April), pp. 30–35.

Estrella, Arturo, and Frederic S. Mishkin (1996). "The Yield Curve as a Predictor of U.S. Recessions," *Current Issues in Economics and Finance* 2 (Federal Reserve Bank of New York, June).

Esty, Benjamin C. (1995). "South Shore Bank: Is It the Model of Success for Community Development Banks?," Harvard Business School Working Paper 95-072 (February).

Faludi, Susan (1990). "The Reckoning: Safeway LBO Yields Vast Profits but Exacts a Heavy Human Toll," *Wall Street Journal*, May 16, p. A1.

Fama, Eugene F. (1965a). "The Behavior of Stock Prices," *Journal of Business* 37, pp. 34–105.

— (1965b). "Random Walks in Stock Market Prices," *Financial Analysts Journal* (September–October), pp. 55–59.

— (1968). "What 'Random Walk' Really Means," *Institutional Investor* (April), pp. 38–40.

— (1970). "Efficient Capital Markets: A Review of Theory and Empirical Work," *Journal of Finance* 25, pp. 383–423.

— (1980). "Banking in the Theory of Finance," *Journal of Monetary Economics* 6, pp. 39–57.

— (1981). "Stock Returns, Real Activity, Inflation, and Money," *American Economic Review* 71, pp. 545–565.

— (1991). "Efficient Capital Markets: II," *Journal of Finance* 46, pp. 1575–1617.

Fama, Eugene F., and Kenneth R. French (1988). "Permanent and Temporary Components of Stock Prices," *Journal of Political Economy* 96, pp. 246–273.

— (1989). "Business Conditions and Expected Returns on Stocks and Bonds," *Journal of Financial Economics* 25, pp. 23–49.

— (1992). "The Cross-Section of Expected Stock Returns," University of Chicago Center for Research in Security Prices Working Paper 333 (January).

Fama, Eugene F., and Michael C. Jensen (1983), "Separation of Ownership and Control," *Journal of Law and Economics* 26, pp. 301–325.

Farrell, Christopher, and Leah J. Nathans (1989). "The Bills Are Coming Due," *Business Week*, September 11, p. 84.

Fazzari, Steven M., R. Glenn Hubbard, and Bruce C. Petersen (1988). "Financing Constraints and Corporate Investment," *Brookings Papers on Economic Activity* 1, pp. 141–206.

Federal Open Market Committee (1993). "Record of Policy Actions," *Federal Reserve Bulletin* 79 (April), pp. 323–329.

Federal Reserve Bank of New York (1993). *Studies on Excess Capacity in the Financial Sector* (New York: Federal Reserve Bank of New York, June).

— (1994). *Studies on Causes and Consequences of the 1989–92 Credit Slowdown* (New York: Federal Reserve Bank of New York, February).

Federal Reserve Board (1980). *Introduction to the Flow of Funds* (Washington: Board of Governors of the Federal Reserve System).

— (1993). *Guide to the Flow of Funds Accounts* (Washington: Board of Governors of the Federal Reserve System).

Feldman, Robert A., and Manmohan S. Kumar (1994). "Emerging Equity Markets: Growth, Benefits, and Policy Concerns," IMF Paper on Policy Analysis and Assessment PPAA/94/7 (March).

Fenichel, Otto (1945). *The Psychoanalytic Theory of Neurosis* (New York: W.W. Norton & Co.).

Ferenczi, Sándor (1976). "The Ontogenesis of the Interest in Money," in Borneman (1976).

Finance & Treasury (1993). "Time to Confess" (London: Economist Intelligence Unit, June 14).

Financial Times (1993). "The Lex Column: Daimler's New Gloss," October 6.

Finnerty, John D. (1992). "Financial Engineering," in Newman et al. (1992).

Fisher, Irving (1933). "The Debt-Deflation Theory of Great Depressions," *Econometrica* 1, pp. 337–357.

Fisher, Peter R. (1996). "Treasury and Federal Reserve Foreign Exchange Operations, January–March 1996" (New York: Federal Reserve Bank of New York, May).

Fitch, Robert (1971a). "Who Rules the Corporations? Reply," *Socialist Revolution* 2, pp. 150–170.

— (1971b). "Sweezy and Corporate Fetishism," *Socialist Revolution* 2(6), pp. 93–127.

Fitch, Robert, and Mary Oppenheimer (1970). "Who Rules the Corporations?," *Socialist Revolution* 1(1), pp. 73–107; 1(5), pp. 61–114; 1(6), pp. 3–94.

Foley, Duncan K. (1983). "On Marx's Theory of Money," *Social Concept* 1 (May), pp. 5–19.

— (1986). *Understanding Capital: Marx's Economic Theory* (Cambridge, Mass.: Harvard University Press).

Fortune, Peter (1991). "Stock Market Efficiency: An Autopsy?," *New England Economic Review* (March/April).

Foucault, Michel (1973). *The Order of Things: An Archaeology of the Human Sciences* (New York: Vintage Books).

Francke, Hans-Herman, and Michael Hudson (1984). *Banking and Finance in West Germany* (New York: St. Martin's Press).

Frank, Robert H., Thomas Gilovich, and Dennis T. Regan (1993). "Does Studying Economics Inhibit Cooperation?," *Journal of Economic Perspectives* 7 (Spring), pp. 159–171.

Freud, Sigmund (1908). "Character and Anal Erotism," in James Strachey, ed., *The Standard Edition of the Complete Psychological Works of Sigmund Freud,* vol. 9 (London: Hogarth Press), pp. 167–176.

Friedman, Benjamin (1984). Comment on Shiller's "Stock Prices and Social Dynamics," *Brookings Papers on Economic Activity* 2, pp. 504–508.

Friedman, Benjamin M., and David I. Laibson (1989). "Economic Implications of Extraordinary Movements in Stock Prices," *Brookings Papers on Economic Activity* 2, pp. 137–189.

Friedman, Milton (1961). "The Demand for Money," *Proceedings of the American Philosophilcal Society* 105, reprinted in Friedman (1968a).

— (1962). "Should There Be an Independent Monetary Authority," in Leland B. Yeager, ed., *In Search of a Monetary Constitution* (Cambridge, Mass.: Harvard University Press), reprinted in Friedman (1968a).

— (1968a). *Dollars and Deficits: Inflation, Monetary Policy and the Balance of Payments* (Englewood Cliffs, N.J.: Prentice–Hall).

— (1968b). "The Role of Monetary Policy," *American Economic Review* 58 (March), pp. 1–17.

— (1970). "A Theoretical Framework for Monetary Analysis," *Journal of Political Economy* 78, pp. 193–238.

— (1988). "Money and the Stock Market," *Journal of Political Economy* 96, pp. 221–245.

— (1992). "Quantity Theory of Money," in Newman et al. (1992).

— (1993). "End the Fed's Fine-Tuning," *Wall Street Journal,* September 15.

Friedman, Milton, and Anna Jacobson Schwartz (1963). *A Monetary History of the United States, 1867–1960* (Princeton: Princeton University Press).

Fritz, Sara (1995). "Stock Deals Put Lawmakers Under Scrutiny," *Los Angeles Times,* June 27, p. A1.

Fromme, Herbert (1995). "Munich Re Counts the Cost of Chaos," *Lloyd's List,* March 14, 1995.

Fromson, Brett D. (1994). "Whitewater Rumors Push Dow Down 23; Perceptions, Not Specifics, Spook Markets," *Washington Post,* March 11.

Froot, Kenneth A., Michael Kim, and Keneth Rogoff (1995). "The Law of One Price Over 700 Years," mimeo, Harvard Business School.

Froot, Kenneth A., and Andre F. Perold (1990). "New Trading Practices and Short-Run Market Efficiency," National Bureau of Economic Research Working Paper No. 3498.

Fullerton, Howard N. (1992). "Evaluation of Labor Force Projections to 1990," *Monthly Labor Review* 115 (August), pp. 3–14.

Galbraith, John Kenneth (1967/1978). *The New Industrial State,* third edition (New York: Houghton Mifflin Co.).

— (1988). *The Great Crash 1929* (Boston: Houghton Mifflin Co.).

Gale, William G., and John Karl Scholz (1994). "Intergenerational Transfers and the Accumulation of Wealth," *Journal of Economic Perspectives* 8, pp. 145–160.

Gapper, John (1995). "US Shareholder Activists To Launch Campaign Abroad," *Financial Times,* June 8.

Garber, Peter M. (1990). "Famous First Bubbles," *Journal of Economic Perspectives* 4 (Spring), pp. 35–54.

Geisst, Charles R. (1988). *A Guide to Financial Institutions* (London: Macmillan Press).

Gerlach, Stefan (1995). "Testing the Quantity Theory Using Long-Run Averaged Cross-Country Data," Bank for International Settlements Working Paper No. 31 (December).

Gerrard, Bill, and John Hillard (1992). *The Philosophy and Economics of J.M. Keynes* (Aldershot, U.K.: Edward Elgar).

Gertler, Mark (1988). "Financial Structure and Aggregate Activity: An Overview," *Journal of Money, Credit, and Banking* 20 (August), pp. 559–588.

Ghilarducci, Teresa (1992). *Labor's Capital: The Economics and Politics of Private Pensions* (Cambridge: MIT Press).

Gillian, Stuart L., and Laura T. Starks (1995). "Relationship Investing and Shareholder Activism by Institutional Investors," mimeo, Department of Finance, University of Texas (January).

Gilmour, Ian (1992). *Dancing With Dogma: Britain under Thatcherism* (London: Simon & Schuster).

Glasberg, Davita Silfen. (1989a). *The Power of Collective Purse Strings* (Berkeley: University of California Press).

— (1989b). "Bank Hegemony Research and Its Implications for Power Structure Theory," *Critical Sociology* 16 (Summer–Fall), pp. 27–50.

Glassman, James K. (1994). "Big Money Stock Deals for the Favored Few: Maybe 'IPO' Really Means 'Ingratiating Public Offering,'" *Washington Post,* June 22, p. F1.

Goetzmann, William N., and Roger G. Ibbotson (1994). "An Emerging Market: The NYSE from 1815 to 1871," mimeo, Yale School of Management (December 14).

Goldstein, Joshua (1995). *PACs in Profile* (Washington: Center for Responsive Politics).

Goldstein, Morris, David Folkerts-Landau, Mohamed El-Erian, Steven Fries, and Liliana Rojas-Suarez (1992a). *International Capital Markets: Developments, Prospects, and Policy Issues* (Washington: International Monetary Fund).

Goldstein, Morris, Peter Isard, Paul R. Masson, and Mark P. Taylor (1992b). "Policy Issues in the Evolving International Monetary System," *IMF Occasional Paper No. 96* (Washington: International Monetary Fund, June).

Goldstein, Morris, David Folkerts-Landau, and a Staff Team from the International Monetary Fund (1993). *International Capital Markets: Part II. Systemic Issues in International Finance* (Washington: International Monetary Fund, August).

— (1994). *International Capital Markets: Developments, Prospects, and Policy Issues* (Washington: International Monetary Fund, September).

Goldstein, Morris, and Philip Turner (1996). "Banking Crises in Emerging Economies: Origins and Policy Options," BIS Economic Papers, No. 46 (Basel: Bank for International Settlements, October).

Grady, Patrick, ed. (1980). *Peering Under the Inflationary Veil* (Ottawa: Canadian Government Publishing Centre).

Granger, Clive W.J., and Oskar Morgenstern (1970). *Predictability of Stock Market Prices* (Lexington, Mass.: D.C. Heath and Co.).

Grant, James (1992). *Money of the Mind* (New York: Farrar Straus & Giroux).

— (1995). "How Do You Spell Complacency?," *Grant's Interest Rate Observer,* April 14.

— (1996). "Rate of Money Turnover," *Grant's Interest Rate Observer,* June 7.

Green, Francis, and Bob Sutcliffe (1987). *The Profit System: The Economics of Capitalism* (Harmondsworth: Penguin).

Greenspan, Alan (1966). "Gold and Economic Freedom," *The Objectivist* (July), reprinted in Ayn Rand, *Capitalism: The Unknown Ideal* (New York: Signet Boooks).

— (1989). Statement before the Committee on Ways and Means, U.S. House of Representatives, February 2, 1989, reprinted in *Federal Reserve Bulletin* 75 (April), pp. 267–272.

Greeenmoney Journal (1995). "Integrative Investing," *Greenmoney Journal* 3 (Spring/Summer), p. 1.

Greenwald, Bruce C., and Joseph E. Stiglitz (1984). "Informational Imperfections in the Capital Market and Macroeconomic Fluctuations," *AEA Papers and Proceedings* 74, pp. 194–199.

— (1987). "Imperfect Information, Credit Markets, and Unemployment," *European Economic Review* 31, pp. 444–456.

— (1993). "Financial Market Imperfections and Business Cycles," *Quarterly Journal of Economics* (February), pp. 77–114.

Greenwald, Bruce, Joseph E. Stiglitz, and Andrew Weiss (1984). "Informational Imperfections in the Capital Market and Macroeconomic Fluctuations," *American Economic Review* 74, pp. 194–199.

Greenwood, Daphne T., and Edward N. Wolff (1992). "Changes in Wealth in the United States, 1962–1983," *Journal of Population Economics* 5, pp. 261–288.

Greider, William (1987). *Secrets of the Temple* (New York: Simon and Schuster).

Griffith-Jones, Stephany (1981). *The Role of Finance in the Transition to Socialism* (London: Frances Pinter Ltd., and Totowa, N.J.: Allanheld, Osmun & Co.).

Grossman, Sanford J., and Oliver D. Hart (1980). "Takeover Bids, the Free-Rider Problem, and the Theory of the Corporation," *Bell Journal of Economics* 11, pp. 42–64.

Grossman, Sanford J., and Joseph E. Stiglitz (1980). "On the Impossibility of Informationally Efficient Markets," *American Economic Review* 70, pp. 393–408.

Gurley, John, and Edward Shaw (1955). "Financial Aspects of Economic Development," *American Economic Review* 45 (September), pp. 515–538.

Hall, Bronwyn H. (1992). "Investment and Research and Development at the Firm Level: Does the Source of Financing Matter?," NBER Working Paper No. 4096 (Cambridge, Mass.: National Bureau of Economic Research, June).

Hamilton, James D. (1986). "On Testing for Self-Fulfilling Speculative Price Bubbles," *International Economic Review* 27, pp. 545–552.

Hansell, Saul (1994). "Derivatives as the Fall Guy: Excuses, Excuses," *New York Times,* October 2, section 3, p. 1.

Harcourt, G.C. (1972). *Some Cambridge Controversies in the Theory of Capital* (Cambridge: Cambridge University Press).

Hardouvelis, Gikas A. (1988). "Evidence on Stock Market Speculative Bubbles: Japan, the United States, and Great Britain," *Federal Reserve Bank of New York Quarterly Review,* Summer, pp. 4–16.

Hardy, Quentin (1992). "Japanese Companies Need to Raise Cash, But First a Bond Market Must Be Built," *Wall Street Journal,* October 20.

Harris, Laurence (1988). "Alternative Perspectives on the Financial System," in Harris et al. (1988), pp. 7–35.

Harris, Laurence, Jerry Coakley, Martin Crosdale, and Trevor Evans (1988). *New Perspectives on the Financial System* (Beckenham, U.K., and New York: Croom Helm).

Harverson, Patrick (1993). "Daimler Puts on the Style for NY Debut," *Financial Times,* October 6.

Harvey, David (1982). *The Limits to Capital* (Chicago: University of Chicago).

Harwawini, Gabriel, and Donald B. Keim (1993). "On the Predictability of Common-Stock Returns: World-Wide Evidence," mimeo, Rodney L. White Center for Financial Research, Wharton School, University of Pennsylvania (December).

Hawkes, David (1996). *Ideology* (London and New York: Routledge, 1996).

Hayek, Friedrich A. (1932). *Prices and Production* (New York: Macmillan).

Henwood, Doug. (1987). "Old Livernose and the Plungers," *Grand Street* 7 (Autumn), pp. 175–184.

— (1990). "Felix the Fox," *Village Voice,* July 31, pp. 29–32.

— (1991). "The Uses of Crisis," *Left Business Observer* No. 46 (June).

— (1992). "Toxic Banking," *Nation* 254 (March 2), p. 257.

— (1994a). "Mythbusting: Small Not Beautiful, Downsizing Not Productive," *Left Business Observer* No. 66 (October).

— (1994b). "Templeton & Mobius: 6% Inflation and a Killer Bear," *Left Business Observer* No. 67 (December).

— (1995). "The Contract with Mexico," *Left Business Observer* No. 68, March.

— (1996a). "Antiglobalization," *Left Business Observer* No. 71, January.

— (1996b). "Globalization Followup," *Left Business Observer* No. 72, March.

Herman, Edward S. (1981). *Corporate Control, Corporate Power: A Twentieth Century Fund Study* (Cambridge and New York: Cambridge University Press).

Hilferding, Rudolf (1981). *Finance Capital* (London and Boston: Routledge & Kegan Paul).

Hitler, Adolf (1943). *Mein Kampf,* translated by Ralph Manheim (Boston: Houghton Mifflin Co.)

Holland, Max (1989). *When the Machine Stopped: A Cautionary Tale from Industrial America*

(Cambridge: Harvard Business School Press).

Holmes, Alan R. (1969). "Operational Constraints on the Stabilization of Money Supply Growth," in *Controlling Monetary Aggregates* (Boston: Federal Reserve Bank of Boston), pp. 65–77.

Holt, Ric (1996). "What is Post Keynesian Economics." (Internet: gopher:// csf.Colorado.EDU:70/00/econ/authors/Holt.Ric/What_is_Post_Keynesian_Economics).

Hudson, Michael (1996). *Merchants of Misery: How Corporate America Profits from Poverty* (Monroe, Maine: Common Courage Press).

Hulbert, Mark (1994). "Long-Term Performance Rankings," *The Hulbert Financial Digest,* July.

Hviding, Ketil (1995). "Financial Deregulation," *OECD Observer* 194 (June/July), pp. 30–33.

Hymer, Stephen Herbert (1979). *The Multinational Corporation: A Radical Approach* (New York: Cambridge University Press).

Ikenberry, David, Josef Lakonishok, and Theo Vermaelen (1994). "Market Underreaction to Open Market Share Repurchases," *Journal of Financial Economics* 39, pp. 181–208.

International Monetary Fund (1991). *World Economic Outlook* (Washington: IMF, May).

— (1993). *World Economic Outlook* (Washington: IMF, October).

— (1995). *Private Market Financing for Developing Countries,* World Economic and Financial Surveys (Washington: IMF, March).

Jagannathan, Ravi, and Ellen R. McGrattan (1995). "The CAPM Debate," Federal Reserve Bank of Minneapolis *Quarterly Review* 19 (Fall), pp. 2–17.

James, Harvey S. (1996). "British Industrialization and the Profit Constraint Hypothesis: The Case of a Manchester Cotton Enterprise, 1798–1827," University of Hartford economics department (Internet: http://econwpa.wustl.edu/eprints/eh/papers/9612/9612003.abs).

Jameson, Fredric (1991). *Postmodernism, Or the Cultural Logic of Late Capitalism* (Durham: Duke University Press).

Jaroslovsky, Rich (1989). "Washington Wire," *Wall Street Journal,* February 17, p. 1.

Jaspersen, Frederick Z., Anthony H. Aylward, and Mariusz A. Sumlinski (1995). *Trends in Private Investment in Developing Countries: Statistics for 1970–94,* International Finance Corp. Discussion Paper No. 28 (Washington: World Bank).

Jensen, Michael C. (1978) "Some Anomalous Evidence Regarding Market Efficiency," *Journal of Financial Economics* 6, pp. 95–101.

— (1984). "Takeovers: Folklore and Science," *Harvard Businss Review* 62 (November–December), pp. 109–121.

— (1986a). "Agency Costs of Free Cash Flow, Corporate Finance, and Takeovers," *AEA Papers and Proceedings* 76, pp. 323–329.

— (1986b). "The Takeover Controversy: Analysis and Evidence," *Midland Corporate Finance Journal* 4 (Summer), pp. 6–32.

— (1988). "Takeovers: Their Causes and Consequences," *Journal of Economic Perspectives* 2, pp. 21–48.

— (1989a). "Eclipse of the Public Corporation," *Harvard Business Review* 89 (September–October), pp. 61–74.

— (1989b). "The Evidence Speaks Loud and Clear," response to letters criticizing Jensen (1989a), *Harvard Business Review* 89 (November–December), pp. 12–14.

— (1991). "Corporate Control and the Politics of Finance," *Journal of Applied Corporate Finance* 4 (Summer), pp. 13–33.

— (1993). "The Modern Industrial Revolution, Exit, and the Failure of Internal Control Systems," *Journal of Finance* 48 (July), pp. 831–881.

Jensen, Michael C., and William H. Meckling (1976). "Theory of the Firm: Managerial Behavior, Agency Costs and Ownership Structure," *Journal of Financial Economics* 3, pp. 305–360.

Jensen, Michael C., and Kevin J. Murphy (1990). "Performance Pay and Top-Management Incentives," *Journal of Political Economy* 98, pp. 225–264.

Jensen, Michael C., and Richard S. Ruback (1983). "The Market for Corporate Control," *Journal of Financial Economics* 11, pp. 5–50.

Jensen, Michael C., and Jerold B. Warner (1988). "The Distribution of Power Among Corporate Managers, Shareholders, and Directors," *Journal of Financial Economics* 20, pp. 3–24.

Julius, DeAnne (1991). *Foreign Direct Investment: The Neglected Twin of Trade* (Washington, The Group of Thirty, 1991).

Kader, Ahmad A. (1985) "The Stock Market as a Leading Indicator of Economic Activity," *Atlantic Economic Journal,* 13 (March), p. 100.

Kahneman, Daniel, and Amos Tversky (1979). "Prospect Theory: An Analysis of Decision Under Risk," *Econometrica* 47 (March), pp. 263–291.

Kalecki, Michal (1990). *Collected Works,* edited by Jerzy Osiatynski, Vol. 1 (Oxford: Clarendon Press).

Kane, Sara (1993). "Seminar Looks at the Role of Finance in Regional Development," *IMF Survey* 22, July 12.

Kaplan, Steven N., and Jeremy C. Stein (1993). "The Evolution of Buyout Pricing and Financial Structure in the 1980s," *Quarterly Journal of Economics* 108 (May), pp. 313–357.

Katz, Jane (1995). "Going Public," Federal Reserve Bank of Boston's *Regional Review* (Winter), pp. 18–24.

Kaufman, Allen, and Ernest J. Englander (1993). "Kohlberg Kravis Roberts & Co. and the Restructuring of American Capitalism," *Business History Review* 67 (Spring), pp. 52–97.

Kaufman, Henry (1994). "Structural Changes in the Financial Markets: Economic and Policy Significance," Federal Reserve Bank of Kansas City *Economic Review* 79 (Second Quarter), pp. 5–16.

Keeton, William R. (1995). "Multi-Office Bank Lending to Small Businesses: Some New Evidence," Federal Reserve Bank of Kansas City *Economic Review* 80 (Second Quarter), pp. 45–58.

Kennedy, Peter (1987). *A Guide to Econometrics,* 2nd edn. (Cambridge: MIT Press).

Kennickell, Arthur, Douglas A. McManus, and R. Louise Woodburn (1996). "Weighting Design for the 1992 Survey of Consumer Finances," unpublished technical paper, Federal Reserve Board.

Kennickell, Arthur, and Janice Shack-Marquez (1992). "Changes in Family Finances from 1983 to 1989: Evidence from the Survey of Consumer Finances," *Federal Reserve Bulletin* 78 (January), pp. 1–18.

Kennickell, Arthur, and Martha Starr-McCluer (1994). "Changes in Family Finances from 1989 to 1992: Evidence from the Survey of Consumer Finances," *Federal Reserve Bulletin* 80 (October), pp. 861–882.

Kennickell, Arthur, and R. Louise Woodburn (1997). "Consistent Weight Design for the 1989, 1992, and 1995 SCFs, and the Distribution of Wealth," unpublished technical paper, Federal Reserve Board, June 23

Kenway, Peter (1980). "Marx, Keynes and the Possibility of Crisis," *Cambridge Journal of Economics* 4, pp. 23–36.

Keynes, John Maynard (1936/1964). *The General Theory of Employment, Interest, and Money* (New York: Harcourt Brace Jovanovich). Reprinted as vol. VII of Keynes (1973).

— (1973). *The Collected Writings of John Maynard Keynes,* Donald Moggridge, ed. Citations in text of *CW* are to the volume and page of this edition.

— (1988). *The Economic Consequences of the Peace* (New York: Penguin).

Kinder, Peter D., Steven D. Lyndenberg, and Amy L. Domini (1992). *The Social Investment Almanac* (New York: Henry Holt and Co.).

Kindleberger, Charles P. (1978). *Manias, Panics, and Crashes: A History of Financial Crises* (New York: Basic Books).

— (1986). *The World in Depression, 1929–1939* (Berkeley: University of California Press).

Knecht, G. Bruce (1994). "Houston Firms Sold Risky 'Toxic Waste' For Wall Street Giants," *Wall Street Journal,* December 20, p. A1.

Kneeshaw, J.T. (1995). "A Survey of Non-Financial Sector Balance Sheets in Industrialized Countries: Implications for the Monetary Policy Transmission Mechanism," BIS Working Paper No. 25 (Basel: Bank for International Settlements, April).

Knoedler, Janet T. (1995). "Institutionalist Theories of Business Enterprise, from Coase, Williamson, and Veblen: Convergence, Divergence, and Some Evidence," mimeo, Bucknell University.

Kolko, Gabriel (1963). *The Triumph of Conservatism* (New York: Macmillan).

— (1984). *Main Currents in Modern American History* (New York: Pantheon).

Koski, Jennifer Lynch, and Jeffrey Pontiff (1996). "How Are Derivatives Used? Evidence from the Mutual Fund Industry," unpublished paper, University of Washington Business School (January).

Kothari, S.P., Jay Shanken, and Richard G. Sloan (1995). "The CAPM: 'Reports of My Death Have Been Greatly Exaggerated," University of Rochester, Bradley Policy Research Center, Financial Research and Policy Studies working paper FR 95-21 (September).

Kotlikoff, Laurence J. (1995). "Privatization of Social Security: How It Works and Why It Matters," National Bureau of Economic Research Working Paper No. 5330 (October).

Kotlikoff, Laurence, and Lawrence Summers (1981). "The Role of Intergenerational Transfers in Aggregate Capital Accumulation," *Journal of Political Economy* 89, pp. 706–732.

Kotz, David M. (1978). *Bank Control of Large Corporations in the United States* (Berkeley and Los Angeles: University of California Press).

Kovel, Joel (1980). "Narcissism and the Family," *Telos* 44 (Summer), pp. 88–100.

Kripalani, Manjeet (1995). "New Fund Mania," *Worth,* June, pp. 63–64.

Kristov, Lorenzo, and Alan L. Olmstead (1992). "Savings Banks," in Newman et al. (1992).

Kuczynski, Pedro-Pablo (1988). *Latin American Debt* (Baltimore: Johns Hopkins University Press).

Kumar, Manmohan S. (1984). *Growth, Acquisition and Investment* (Cambridge: Cambridge University Press).

Kuntz, Phil, and Glenn R. Simpson (1996). "Lawmakers Keep Earning Quick Profits on IPOs," *Wall Street Journal,* June 18, p. A3.

Kurtz, Howard (1994). "Media Awash in Whitewater, Some Critics Warn," *Washington Post,* March 12.

Lakonishok, Josef, Andrei Shleifer, and Robert W. Vishny (1992). "The Structure and Performance of the Money Management Industry," *Brookings Papers on Economic Activity: Microeconomics,* pp. 339–392.

Landsman, Wayne R., and Douglas A. Shackelford (1993). "Worker Displacement Following the RJR Nabisco Leveraged Buyout," Kenan–Flagler Business School, University of North Carolina mimeo (August).

Lavoie, Don (1983). "Some Strengths in Marx's Disequilibrium Theory of Money," *Cambridge Journal of Economics* 7, pp. 55–68.

— (1986). "Marx, The Quantity Theory, and the Theory of Value," *History of Political Economy* 18, pp. 155–170.

Lavoie, Marc (1984). "The Endogenous Flow of Credit and the Post Keynesian Theory of Money," *Journal of Economic Issues* 18 (September), pp. 771–797.

Layne, Richard (1993). "The World's Safest Banks," *Global Finance,* September, pp. 57–80.

Leijonhufvud, Axel (1992). "Natural Rate and Market Rate," in Newman et al. (1992), vol. 3, pp. 5–7.

Leontief, Wassily (1971). "Theoretical Assumptions and Nonobserved Facts," *American Economic Review* 61, pp. 1–7.

Levinson, Jerome I. (1992). "New Proposals for the Debt Crisis," in Robert C. Effros, ed., Current Legal Issues Affecting Central Banks, Vol. 1 (Washington, D.C.: International Monetary Fund).

Lewontin, R.C. (1995). "Sex, Lies, and Social Science," *New York Review of Books* 42 (April 20), pp. 24–29.

Lexecon Inc. (1995). "Clustering and Competition in Asset Markets," (Chicago: Lexecon Inc., May 23).

— (1996). "The Orange County Bankruptcy and Its Aftermath: Some New Evidence," (Chicago: Lexecon Inc., April 25).

Lewis, Michael (1989a). "How Wall Street Took the S&Ls for a Ride," *Manhattan, inc.,* November, pp. 31–33.

— (1989b). *Liar's Poker* (New York: W.W. Norton).

Lichten, Eric (1986). *Class, Power and Austerity: The New York City Fiscal Crisis* (South Hadley: Bergin and Garvey).

Lichtenberg, Frank R., and Donald Siegel (1990). "The Effects of Leveraged Buyouts on Productivity and Related Aspects of Firm Behavior," *Journal of Financial Economics* 27, pp. 166–194.

Light, Jay O. (1989). "The Privatization of Equity," *Harvard Business Review* 89 (September–October), pp. 62–63.

Lipietz, Alain (1985). *The Enchanted World: Inflation, Credit and the World Crisis* (London: Verso).

Lipin, Steven (1994). "Risk Management Has Become Crucial In a Year When Strategies Proved Wrong," *Wall Street Journal,* September 29, p. C1.

Litan, Robert I. (1992). "Savings and Loan Crisis," in Newman et al. (1992).

Livingston, James (1986). *Origins of the Federal Reserve System: Money, Class, and Corporate Capitalism, 1890–1913* (Ithaca: Cornell University Press).

Lo, Andrew, and A. Craig MacKinlay (1988). "Stock Market Prices Do Not Follow Random Walks: Evidence from a Simple Specification Test," *Review of Financial Studies* 1, pp. 41–66.

— (1990). "When Are Contrarian Profits Due to Stock Market Overreaction?," *Review of Financial Studies* 3, pp. 175–205.

Lomax, John (1991). "Housing Finance — An International Perspective," *Bank of England Quarterly Bulletin* 31 (February).

Long, William F., and David J. Ravenscraft (1993a). "Decade of Debt: Lessons from LBOs in the 1980s," in Blair (1993), pp. 205–238.

— (1993b). "The Financial Performance of Whole Company LBOs," U.S. Census Bureau Center for Economic Studies Discussion Paper CES 93-16 (November).

— (1993c). "LBOs, Debt and R&D Intensity," *Strategic Management Journal* 14, pp. 119–135.

Loughran, Tim, and Jay R. Ritter (1995). "The New Issues Puzzle," *Journal of Finance* 50, pp. 23–52.

Lublin, Joann S. (1995a). "Give the Board Fewer Perks, A Panel Urges," *Wall Street Journal,* June 19, p. B1.

— (1995b). "Pension Funds Take Aim Again at Weak Stocks," *Wall Street Journal,* October 2, p. A4.

— (1996). "Unions Brandish Stock to Force Change," *Wall Street Journal,* May 17, p. B1.

Lucas, Robert E. Jr. (1978). "Asset Prices in an Exchange Economy," *Econometrica* 46, pp. 1429–1445.

Maddison, Angus (1995). *Monitoring the World Economy, 1829–1992* (Paris: Organisation for Economic Cooperation and Development).

Malkiel, Burton G. (1990). *A Random Walk Down Wall Street* (New York: W.W. Norton & Co.).

Mamis, Justin, and Robert Mamis (1977). *When to Sell: Inside Strategies for Stock-Market Profits* (New York: Cornerstone Library).

Mandel, Ernest (1978). *Late Capitalism* (London and New York: Verso Press).

— (1983). "Keynes and Marx," in Bottomore et al. (1983), pp. 249–251.

Mankiw, N. Gregory (1989). "Real Business Cycles: A New Keynesian Perspective," *Journal of Economic Perspectives* 3 (Summer), pp. 79–90.

— (1990). "A Quick Refresher Course in Macroeconomics," *Journal of Economic Literature* 28, pp. 1645–1660.

Manne, Henry G. (1965). "Mergers and the Market for Corporate Control," *Journal of Political Economy* 73 (April), pp. 110–120.

Mansley, Mark (1994). *Long Term Financial Risks to the Carbon Fuel Industry from Climate Change* (London: Delphi Group).

Marglin, Stephen A. (1974). "What Do Bosses Do?: The Origins and Functions of Hierarchy in Capitalist Production," *Review of Radical Political Economics* 6 (Summer), pp. 60–112.

Markowitz, Harry (1952). "Portfolio Selection," *Journal of Finance* 7, pp. 77–91.

— (1991). "Markets and Morality, Or Arbitragers Get No Respect," *Wall Street Journal,* May 14.

Marsh, Terry A., and Robert C. Merton (1986). "Dividend Variability and Variance Bounds Test for the Rationality of Stock Prices," *American Economic Review* (June), pp. 483–498.

Marx, Karl (1963). *Theories of Surplus Value,* vol. 1, translated by Emile Burns (Moscow: Progress Publishers).

— (1968). *Theories of Surplus Value,* vol. 2, translated by S. Ryazanskaya (Moscow: Progress Publishers).

— (1971). *Theories of Surplus Value,* vol. 3, translated by Jack Cohen and S.W. Ryazankaya (Moscow: Progress Publishers).

— (1973). *Grundrisse,* translated by Martin Nicolaus (New York: Penguin).

— (1977). *Capital,* vol. 1, translated by Ben Fowkes (New York, Vintage).

— (1978). *Capital,* vol. 2, translated by David Fernbach (New York: Vintage).

— (1981). *Capital,* vol. 3, translated by David Fernbach (New York: Vintage).

Mattick, Paul (1969). *Marx and Keynes: The Limits of the Mixed Economy* (Boston: Extending Horizons Books).

Mayer, Martin (1990). *The Greatest-Ever Bank Robbery: The Collapse of the Savings and Loan Industry* (New York: Charles Scribner's Sons).

McCoy, Charles, Richard B. Schmitt, and Jeff Bailey (1990). "Behind the S&L Debacle — Hall of Shame: Besides S&L Owners, Host of Professionals Paved Way for Crisis," *Wall Street Journal,* November 2.

McGeehan, Patrick (1996). "One More Record for '96: Best Year for Stock Issues," *Wall Street Journal,* November 19, p. C1.

McGowan, William G. (1992). "Why Nasdaq?," in National Association of Securities Dealers 1992, pp. 19–28.

McKenzie, Colin, and Michael Stutchbury, eds. (1992). *Japanese Financial Markets and the Role of the Yen* (North Sydney, Australia: Allen & Unwin).

Mead, Walter Russell (1990). *The Low-Wage Challenge to Global Growth: The Labor Cost–Productivity Imbalance In Newly Industrialized Countries* (Washington, Economic Policy Institute).

Mehra, Rajnish, and Edward C. Prescott (1985). "The Equity Premium: A Puzzle," *Journal of Monetary Economics* 15, pp. 145–161.

Mehta, Stephanie N. (1996). "Drop in Returns Is Expected for Venture-Capital Firms," *Wall Street Journal,* November 19, p. B2.

Menchik, Paul L., and Martin David (1983). "Income Distribution, Lifetime Savings, and Bequests," *American Economic Review* 73, pp. 672–690.

Mendoza, Roberto G. (1989). "Treasurer's Conference: The Changing International Banking Environment," mimeo, J.P. Morgan, January 30.

Merton, Robert C. (1973). "An Intertemporal Capital Asset Pricing Model," *Econometrica* 41, pp. 867–887.

— (1992). "Options," in Newman et al. (1992).

Meulendyke, Ann-Marie (1989). *U.S. Monetary Policy and Financial Markets* (New York: Federal Reserve Bank of New York).

Mfume, Kweisi (1993). Statement before the Committee on Banking, Finance, and Urban Affairs, U.S. House of Representatives, October 7.

Michie, R.C. (1992). "Development of Stock Markets," in Newman et al. (1992).

Michl, Thomas R. (1991). "Debt, Deficits, and the Distribution of Income," *Journal of Post Keynesian Economics,* pp. 351–365.

Miller, Merton H. (1977). "Debt and Taxes," *Journal of Finance* 32, pp. 261–265.

— (1988). "The Modigliani–Miller Propositions After Thirty Years," *Journal of Economic Perspectives* 2 (Fall), pp. 99–120.

— (1991). "Leverage" (Nobel Memorial Prize Lecture, 1990), *Journal of Finance* 46, pp. 479–488.

Minsky, Hyman P. (1957). "Central Banking and Money Market Changes," *Quarterly Journal of Economics* 71 (May), reprinted in Minsky (1982a), pp. 162–178.

— (1964). "Longer Waves in Financial Relations: Financial Factors in the More Severe Depressions," reprinted in Thomas Mayer, ed., *International Library of Critical Writings in Economics,* 7 (1990) (Aldershot, U.K. and Brookfield, Vt.: Edward Elgar, pp. 352–363.

— (1975). *John Maynard Keynes* (New York: Columbia University Press).

— (1978). "The Financial Instability Hypothesis: A Restatement," *Thames Papers in Political Economy,* reprinted in Minsky (1982a), pp. 90–116.

— (1982a). *Can "It" Happen Again?* (Armonk, N.Y.: M.E. Sharpe, Inc.).

— (1982b). "Debt Deflation Processes in Today's Institutional Environment," *Banca Nazionale del Lavoro Review* 143 (December), pp. 375–393.

— (1986). *Stabilizing an Unstable Economy* (New Haven: Yale University Press).

— (1992). "Consumption Tax Can Bring Back Thrifty American," *Wall Street Journal,* October 7.

Mishel, Lawrence, and Jared Bernstein (1994). *The State of Working America 1994–95* (Armonk: M.E. Sharpe for the Economic Policy Institute).

Mishkin, Frederic S. (1978). "The Household Balance Sheet and the Great Depression," *Journal of Economic History* 38, pp. 918–937.

Modigliani, Franco (1944). "Liquidity Preference and the Theory of Interest and Money," *Econometrica* 12 (January), pp. 45–88.

— (1980). "Inflation-Induced Errors in Stock Market Values: United States," in Grady (1980), pp. 17–19.

— (1988). "The Role of Intergenerational Transfers and Life Cycle Saving in the Accumulation of Wealth," *Journal of Economic Perspectives* 2, pp. 15–40.

Modigliani, Franco, and Merton H. Miller (1958). "The Cost of Capital, Corporation Finance and the Theory of Investment," *American Economic Review* 48 (1958), pp. 261–297.

— (1963). "Corporate Income Taxes and the Cost of Capital: A Correction," *American Economic Review* 53 (1963), pp. 433–443.

Modigliani, Franco and James Poterba. (1989) "A Little Extra Leverage Is No Cause for Alarm: US Corporate Debt," *Financial Times,* February 8, p. 25.

Moffett, George D. III (1991). "Democracy: Today's calls for Liberty Echo the Popular Revolts of the Mid-19th Century," *Los Angeles Times,* June 23, p. A23.

Monks, Robert A.G. (1995). "Corporate Governance in the Twenty-First Century: A Preliminary Outline," mimeo, Lens Inc. (Washington).

Moore, Basil (1988a). "Unpacking the Post-Keynesian Black Box: Wages, Bank Lending and the Money Supply," in Arestis (1988), pp. 122–151.

— (1988b). *Horizontalists and Verticalists: The Macroeconomics of Credit Money* (New York: Cambridge University Press).

Morck, Randall, Andrei Shleifer, and Robert W. Vishny (1990). "The Stock Market and Investment: Is the Market a Sideshow?," *Brookings Papers on Economic Activity* 2, pp. 157–215.

Morgenstern, Oskar. (1950). *On the Accuracy of Economic Observations* (Princeton: Princeton University Press).

Mueller, Dennis C. (1989). "Mergers: Causes, Effects, Policies," *International Journal of Industrial Organizations* 7, pp. 1–10.

Mullin, John (1993). "Emerging Equity Markets and the Global Economy," *Federal Reserve Bank of New York Quarterly Review* 18 (Summer), pp. 54–83.

Mullineux, A.W. (1984) *The Business Cycle After Keynes: A Contemporary Analysis* (Totowa, N.J.: Barnes & Noble Books).

— (1990). *Business Cycles and Financial Crises* (New York and London: Harvester Wheatsheaf).

Munnell, Alicia H., and Nicole Ernsberger (1987). "Pension Contributions and the Stock Market," *New England Economic Review* November/December, pp. 3–14.

Munnell, Alicia H., Geoffrey M.B. Tootell, Lynn E. Browne, and James McEneaney (1996). "Mortgage Lending in Boston: Interpreting HMDA Data," *American Economic Review* 86 (March), pp. 25–53.

Myers, Stewart C. (1984). "The Capital Structure Puzzle," *Journal of Finance* 39, pp. 575–592.

Myers, Stewart C., and N.S. Majluf (1984). "Corporate Financing and Investment Decisions when Firms Have Information that Investors Do Not Have," *Journal of Financial Economics* 13 (June), pp. 187–221.

Myerson, Allen R. (1995a). "Panel Backs Shift in Board Members' Pay," *New York Times,* June 19, p. A2.

— (1995b). "Mesa, at Pickens's Urging, Adopts Takeover Defense," *New York Times,* July 7, p. D3.

Nation (1989). "Tax the Big Casino," *Nation* 249 (August 21), p. 189.

— (1990). "Milken De-Wigged," *Nation* 251 (December 17), pp. 755–756.

National Association of Community Development Loan Funds (1994). "Defining the Industry: NACDLF Stastistical Profile as of December 31, 1993," *Community Investment Monitor* (Summer), p. 12.

— (1996). *Annual Report, 1995* (Philadelphia: NACDLF, June).

National Association of Securities Dealers (1992). *The NASDAQ Handbook* (Chicago: Probus Publishing).

— (1995). *1995 Nasdaq Fact Book & Company Directory* (Washington: NASD).

Neff, Gina (1996). "Microlending, Microresults," *Left Business Observer* No. 74 (September).

Negri, Antonio (1988). "Keynes and the Capitalist Theory of the State in 1929," in *Revolution Retrieved: Selected Writings on Marx, Keynes, Capitalist Crisis and New Social Subjects, 1967-83* (London: Red Notes), pp. 9-42.

— (1991). *Marx Beyond Marx* (Brooklyn: Autnomedia).

Newberry, David M. (1992). "Futures Markets, Hedging and Speculation," in Newman et al. (1992).

Newman, Peter, Murray Milgate, and John Eatwell (1992). *The New Palgrave Dictionary of Money and Finance* (London: Macmillan Press, and New York: Stockton Press), 3 vols.

New York Stock Exchange (1990). *Shareownership 1990* (New York: New York Stock Exchange).

— (1994, 1995). *Fact Book,* yearly (New York: New York Stock Exchange).

Nietzsche, Friedrich (1967). *On the Genealogy of Morals,* translated by Walter Kaufmann and R.J. Hollingdale (New York: Vintage).

Niggle, Christopher J. (1991). "The Endogenous Money Supply Theory: An Institutional Appraisal," *Journal of Economic Issues* 25 (March), pp. 137–151.

Norris, Floyd (1995). "On the Amex, a Bad Idea Is Laid to Rest," *New York Times,* May 12, p. D1.

Northern California Community Loan Fund (1996). *Annual Report, 1994–95* (San Francisco: Northern California Community Loan Fund, June).

O'Callaghan, Gary (1993). *The Structure and Operation of the World Gold Market,* Occasional Paper No. 105 (Washington: International Monetary Fund, September).

O'Connor, James (1987). *The Meaning of Crisis* (New York and Oxford: Basil Blackwell).

— (1988). "Capitalism, Nature, Socialism: A Theoretical Introduction," *Capitalism Nature Socialism* 1 (Fall), pp. 11–38.

O'Hara, Maureen (1992). "Savings and Loan Associations," in Newman et al. (1992).

Organisation for Economic Co-Operation and Development (1993a). *Economic Outlook* 53 (June).

— (1993b). *Employment Outlook* (July).

— (1994). *Financial Statistics Monthly* (June).

Ortega, Bob (1995). "Life Without Sam: What Does Wal-Mart Do if Stock Drop Cuts Into Workers' Morale?," *Wall Street Journal,* January 4, p. A1.

Paltrow, Scot J. (1996). "SEC Comes Down Hard on Parent of Nasdaq," *Los Angeles Times,* August 9, p. D1.

Panico, Carlo (1980). "Marx's Analysis of the Relationship Between the Rate of Interest and the Rate of Profits," *Cambridge Journal of Economics* 4, pp. 363–378.

Parboni, Riccardo (1981). *The Dollar and Its Rivals: Recession, Inflation, and International Finance* (London: NLB/Verso).

Parsons, Wayne (1990). *The Power of the Financial Press: Journalism and Economic Opinion in Britain and America* (New Brunswick: Rutgers University Press).

Passell, Peter (1992). "Economic Scene: Fun, Games, Bankruptcy," *New York Times,* April 29, p. D2.

— (1996a). "Race, Mortgages and Statistics," *New York Times,* May 18, p. D1.

— (1996b). "Success and Sharp Elbows," *New York Times,* July 2, p. D1.

Patinkin, Don (1992). "Neutrality of Money," in Newman et al. (1992).

Paul, Susanne S., and James A. Paul (1995). "The World Bank, Pensions and Income (In)Security in the Global South," *International Journal of Health Services* 25, pp. 697-725.

Peach, Richard (1992–1993). "The Ratio of Net Interest to Cash Flow — Projected Future Values," *Federal Reserve Bank of New York Quarterly Review* 17 (Winter), pp. 24–26.

Perelman, Michael (1989). *Keynes, Investment Theory and the Economic Slowdown: The Role of Replacement Investment and q-Ratios.* (London: Macmillan).

— (1991). "Liquidity Demand and Investment," *Review of Political Economy* 3, pp. 467–496.

Pesaran, M. Hashem (1992). "Natural Rate Hypothesis," in Newman et al. (1992).

Pickering, Margaret Hastings (1991). "A Review of Corporate Restructuring Activity, 1980–90," Staff Study 161 (Washington: Federal Reserve Board, May).

Pitelis, Christos (1987). *Corporate Capital: Control, Ownership, Saving and Crisis* (Cambridge and New York: Cambridge University Press).

—, ed. (1993). *Transaction Costs, Markets and Hierarchies* (Oxford and Cambridge: Blackwell).

Plosser, Charles I. (1984). "Money in a Theory of Finance," *Carnegie–Rochester Conference*

Series on Public Policy 21.

— (1989). "Understanding Real Business Cycles," *Journal of Economic Perspectives* 3 (Summer), pp. 51–77.

Pollin, Robert (1986). "Alternative Perspectives on the Rise of Corporate Debt Dependency: The U.S. Postwar Experience," *Review of Radical Political Economics* 18, pp. 205–235.

— (1990). *Deeper in Debt: The Changing Financial Conditions of U.S. Households* (Washington: Economic Policy Institute).

— (1991). "Two Theories of Money Supply Endogeneity," *Journal of Post Keynesian Economics* 13 (Spring), pp. 366–396.

— (1993). "Marxian and Post Keynesian Developments in the Sphere of Money, Credit and Finance: Building Alternative Perspectives in Monetary Macroeconomics," University of California at Riverside, Department of Economics, Working Paper 93-4 (February).

— (1994). "Borrowing More But Investing Less: Economic Stagnation and the Rise of Corporate Takeovers in the U.S.," mimeo, University of California at Riverside, Department of Economics (December).

— (1995). "Financial Structures and Egalitarian Economic Policy," *New Left Review* 214 (November/December), pp. 26–61.

Pontusson, Jonas (1984). "Behind and Beyond Social Democracy in Sweden," *New Left Review* 143 (January/February), pp. 69–96.

— (1987). "Radicalization and Retreat in Swedish Social Democracy," *New Left Review* 165 (September/October), pp. 5–34.

— (1992). *The Limits of Social Democracy : Investment Politics in Sweden* (Ithaca: Cornell University Press).

Porter, Michael E. (1992). *Capital Choices: Changing the Way America Invests in Industry* (Washington: Council on Competitiveness, and Cambridge, Mass.: Harvard Business School).

Posen, Adam (1995a). "Declarations Are Not Enough: Financial Sector Sources of Central Bank Independence," in Ben Bernanke and J. Rotenberg, eds., *NBER Macroeconomics Annual 1995* (Cambridge: MIT Press).

— (1995b). "Central Bank Independence and Disinflationary Credibility: A Missing Link?," Federal Reserve Bank of New York Staff Report No. 1 (May).

Poterba, James M., and Andrew A. Samwick (1995). "Stock Ownership Patterns, Stock Market Fluctuations, and Consumption," *Brookings Papers on Economic Activity* 2, pp. 295–372.

Poterba, James M., and Lawrence H. Summers (1986). "The Persistence of Volatility and Stock Market Fluctuations," *American Economic Review* 76, pp. 1142–1151.

— (1988). "Mean Reversion in Stock Prices: Evidence and Implications," *Journal of Financial Economics* 22, pp. 27–59.

— (1991). "Time Horizons of American Firms: New Evidence From a Survey of CEOs," unpublished background paper for Porter (1992), Massachusetts Institute of Technology (October).

Pound, John (1995). "The Promise of the Governed Corporation," *Harvard Business Review* 73 (March–April), pp. 89–98.

Prowse, Stephen (1994). "Corporate Governance in an International Perspective," BIS Economic Papers No. 41 (Basel: Bank for International Settlements, July).

Prud'homme, Rémy (1991). "Information Technology and the Future of the City," *OECD Observer*, August/September.

Ravenscraft, David J., and F.M. Scherer (1989). "The Profitability of Mergers," *International Journal of Industrial Organization* 7, pp. 101–116.

Regan, Edward V. (1996). "End the Municipal Bond Subsidy," *Wall Street Journal*, March 21.

Reich, Cary (1983). *Financier: The Biography of André Meyer* (New York: William Morrow & Co.).

Reich, Robert (1989). Letter in response to Jensen (1989a), *Harvard Business Review* 89, p. 10.

— (1991). *The Work of Nations* (New York: Alfred A. Knopf).

Remolona, Eli M. (1990). "Understanding International Differences in Leverage Trends," *Federal Reserve Bank of New York Quarterly Review* 15 (Spring), pp. 31–42.

— (1992–93). "The Recent Growth of Financial Derivative Markets," *Federal Reserve Bank of New York Quarterly Review* 17 (Winter), pp. 28–43.

Remolona, Eli M., Robert N. McCauley, Judith S. Ruud, and Frank Iacono (1992–1993). "Corporate Refinancing in the 1980s," *Federal Reserve Bank of New York Quarterly Review* 17 (Winter), pp. 1–27.

Ricardo, David (1911/1987). *The Principles of Political Economy and Taxation* (London: Everyman's Library).

Rifkin, Jeremy (1996). "Civil Society in the Information Age: Workerless Factories and Virtual Companies," *Nation,* February 26, pp. 11–16.

Rima, Ingrid H., ed. (1991). *The Joan Robinson Legacy* (Armonk, N.Y.: M.E. Sharpe).

Ritter, Jay R. (1991). "The Long-Run Performance of Initial Public Offerings," *Journal of Finance* 46, pp. 3–27.

Robinson, Joan. (1969). *The Accumulation of Capital,* third edition (London: Macmillan).

— (1978). *Contributions to Modern Economics* (Oxford: Basil Blackwell).

— (1980). *Further Contributions to Modern Economics* (Oxford: Basil Blackwell).

Roemer, John E. (1994). *A Future for Socialism* (Cambridge: Harvard University Press).

Rogers, Colin (1989). *Money, Interest and Capital: A Study in the Foundations of Monetary Theory* (Cambridge: Cambridge University Press).

Róna, Peter (1989). Letter in response to Jensen (1989a), *Harvard Business Review* 89, pp. 6–7.

Rosen, Rae D. (1993). "Recent Developments in New York City's Economy," Federal Reserve Bank of New York *Quarterly Review* 18 (Summer), pp. 15–26.

Rosenthal, Neal H. (1992) "Evaluting the 1990 Projections of Occupational Employment," *Monthly Labor Review* 115 (August), pp. 32–48.

Ross, Andrew, ed. (1988). *Universal Abandon? The Politics of Postmodernism* (Minneapolis: University of Minnesota Press).

Ross, Stephen A. (1976). "The Arbitrage Theory of Capital Asset Pricing," *Journal of Economic Theory* 13, pp. 341–360.

— (1987). "The Interrelations of Finance and Economics: Theoretical Perspectives," *AEA Papers and Proceedings* 77 (May), pp. 29–34.

Rotheim, Roy J. (1981). "Keynes' Monetary Theory of Value," *Journal of Post Keynesian Economics* 3 (Summer), pp. 568–585.

— (1991). "Marx, Keynes, and the Theory of a Monetary Economy," in Giovanni Caravale, ed., *Marx and Modern Economic Analysis,* vol. II (Edward Elgar). pp. 240–263.

Rothmyer, Karen (1991). "In From the Cold," *FW* (formerly *Financial World*) 160, June 25, p. 15.

Ryrie, William (1992). "Latin America: A Changing Region," *IFC Investment Review,* Spring, pp. 4–5.

Salmon, Walter J. (1993). "Crisis Prevention: How To Gear Up Your Board," *Harvard Business Review* 71 (January–February), p. 68.

Salwen, Kevin G. (1993). "Labor Letter," *Wall Street Journal,* October 26.

Samuelson, Robert (1990). "Booby Prize: Cancel this Nobel, Please," *New Republic,* December 3, p. 18.

Sardoni, Claudio (1986). "Marx and Keynes on Effective Demand and Unemployment," *History of Political Economy* 18, pp. 419–441.

— (1987). *Marx and Keynes on Economic Recession: The Theory of Unemployment and Effective Demand* (Brighton, U.K.: Wheatsheaf).

Saunders, Norman C. (1992). "BLS Employment Projections for 1990: An Evaluation," *Monthly Labor Review* 115 (August), pp. 15–31.

Savan, Leslie (1996). "The Pause That Refrightens," *Village Voice,* June 11, pp. 16–17.

Schachter, Barry (1992). "Options Markets," in Newman et al. (1992).

Schilder, Paul (1976). "Psychoanalysis of Economics," in Borneman (1976).

Schlesinger, Tom (1995). *Reinvestment Reform in an Era of Financial Change* (Philomont, Virginia: Southern Finance Project, April).

Schumpeter, Joseph A. (1936). Review of Keynes's *General Theory, Journal of the American Statistical Association* 31, pp. 791–795.

— (1939). *Business Cycles: A Theoretical, Historical, and Statistical Analysis of the Capitalist Process* (New York: McGraw-Hill), 2 vols.

Schwert, G. William (1989). "Why Does Stock Market Volatility Change Over Time?" *Journal of Finance* 44, pp. 1115–1153.

— (1990a). "Index of U.S. Stock Prices from 1802 to 1987," *Journal of Business* 63, pp. 399–426.

— (1990b). "Stock Market Volatility," *Financial Analysts Journal* (May–June), pp. 23–34.

Scism, Leslie (1996). "Prudential withheld for months report indicating aides knew of improper sales," *Wall Street Journal,* July 15, p. B9.

Segal, Harvey H. (1992). Review of Peter L. Bernstein, *Capital Ideas. The New Leader,* March 23, p. 17.

Semmler, Willi, ed. (1989). *Financial Dynamics and Business Cycles: New Perspectives* (Armonk: M.E. Sharpe, Inc.).

Shaikh, Anwar M. (1995). "The Stock Market and the Corporate Sector: A Profit-Based Approach," Jerome Levy Economics Institute Working Paper No. 146 (September).

Shamsavari, Ali (1986). "On the Foundations of Marx's Theory of Money," *British Review of Economic Issues* 8 (Spring), pp. 75–98.

Sharpe, Wiliam F. (1964). "Capital Asset Prices: A Theory of Market Equilibrium Under Conditions of Risk," *Journal of Finance* 19, pp. 425–442.

Shell, Adam (1990). "Coping When an Analysts Says 'Sell!,'" *Public Relations Journal* 46 (July), p. 9.

Shiller, Robert J. (1984). "Stock Prices and Social Dynamics," *Brookings Papers on Economic Activity* 2 (1984), pp. 457–510.

— (1988). "Causes of Changing Market Volatility," in Federal Reserve Bank of Kansas City, *Financial Market Volatility* (proceedings of a symposium in Jackson Hole, Wyoming, August 1988), pp. 1–23.

— (1990). "Speculative Prices and Popular Models," *Journal of Economic Perspectives* 4 (Spring), pp. 55–65.

— (1991). *Market Volatility* (Cambridge: MIT Press).

— (1992). "Who's Minding the Store," in Twentieth Century Fund (1992), pp. 25–136.

— (1993). *Macro Markets* (New York and Oxford: Oxford University Press).

Shleifer, Andrei, and Lawrence H. Summers (1990). "The Noise Trader Approach to Finance," *Journal of Economic Perspectives* 4 (Spring), pp. 19–33.

Shleifer, Andrei, and Robert W. Vishny (1986). "Large Shareholders and Corporate Control," *Journal of Political Economy* 94, pp. 461–488.

Shrikhande, Milind M. (1996). "Nonaddictive Habit Formation and the Equity Premium Puzzle," Federal Reserve Bank of Atlanta Working Paper 96-1 (February).

Siegel, Jeremy J. (1992). "The Equity Premium: Stock and Bond Returns Since 1802," *Financial Analysts Journal* (February), pp. 28–38.

Simmel, Georg (1978). *The Philosophy of Money* (Boston: Beacon Press).

Simmons, Jacqueline (1996). "Home Prices Soar in Unexpected Places," *Wall Street Journal,* February 13.

Simons, Katerina, and Stephen Cross (1991). "Do Capital Markets Predict Problems in Large Commercial Banks?," *New England Economic Review* (May–June), pp. 51–56.

Singh, Ajit (1995). "Pension Reform, the Stock Market, Capital Formation, and Economic Growth: A Critical Commentary on the World Bank's Proposals," mimeo, Cambridge University, Economics Department (December).

Sloan, Allan (1994). "KKR Deal Makes a Silk Purse Out of a Cow's Ear," *New York Newsday,* September 18, p. A86.

Smith, Adam (1976). *An Inquiry Into the Nature and Causes of the Wealth of Nations,* edited by R.H. Campbell and A.S. Skinner (Oxford: The Clarendon Press).

Southern Finance Project (1993). "The Wages of Banking" (Charlotte, N.C.: Southern Finance Project, October 1).

Spencer, Herbert (1972). "Joint-Stock Companies," excerpts from *Principles of Sociology* (1896), vol. 3, part 8, and "Railway Morals and Public Policy" (1854), from *Essays,* vol. 2 (1868) reprinted in J.D.Y. Peel, ed., *Herbert Spencer on Social Evolution* (Chicago: University of Chicago Press), pp. 225–233.

Stein, Jeremy C. (1989) "Efficient Capital Markets, Inefficient Firms: A Model of Myopic Corporate Behavior," *Quarterly Journal of Economics,* pp. 655–669.

Steindel, Charles (1992). "Changes in the U.S. Cycle: Shifts in Capital Spending and Balance Sheet Changes," Federal Reserve Bank of New York Research Paper No. 9224 (December).

Steiner, Robert, and Kevin G. Salwen (1992). "Stock Specialists Often Keep Best Quotes to

Themselves," *Wall Street Journal,* May 8.

Sterngold, James (1992). "Fed Chief Says Economy Is Resisting Remedies," *New York Times,* October 15.

Stevens, Wallace (1971). *Opus Posthumous* (New York: Alfred A. Knopf).

Stewart, James B. (1991). *Den of Thieves* (New York: Simon & Schuster).

Stiglitz, Joseph E. (1972). "On the Optimality of the Stock Market Allocation of Investment," *Quarterly Journal of Economics* 86, pp. 25–60.

— (1982). "The Inefficiency of Stock Market Equilibrium," *Review of Economic Studies* 49, pp. 241–261. ·

— (1985). "Credit Markets and the Control of Capital," *Journal of Money, Credit, and Banking* 17, pp. 133–152.

— (1988). "Money, Credit, and Business Fluctuations," *The Economic Record* 64, pp. 307–322.

— (1990). "Symposium on Bubbles," *Journal of Economic Perspectives* 4 (Spring), pp. 13–18.

— (1993). *Economics* (New York: W.W. Norton & Co., Inc.).

Stiglitz, Joseph E. and Andrew Weiss (1981). "Credit Rationing in Markets with Imperfect Information," *American Economic Review* 71, pp. 393–410.

Strickland, Deon, Kenneth W. Wiles, and Marc Zenner (1994). "A Requiem for the USA: Is Small Shareholder Monitoring Effective?," Kenan-Flagler Business School, University of North Carolina at Chapel Hill mimeo (April).

Sullivan, Teresa A., Elizabeth Warren, and Jay Lawrence Westbrook (1989). *As We Forgive Our Debtors: Bankruptcy and Consumer Credit in America* (New York: Oxford University Press).

Summers, Lawrence H. (1981). "Inflation, the Stock Market, and Owner-Occupied Housing," *American Economic Review* 71, pp. 429–434.

— (1985). "On Economics and Finance," *Journal of Finance* 40 (July), pp. 633–635.

— (1986). "Does the Stock Market Rationally Reflect Fundamental Values?," *Journal of Finance* 41, pp. 591–600.

Sweezy, Paul M. (1972). "The Resurgence of Financial Control: Fact or Fancy? (A Response to 'Who Rules the Corporations?,'" *Socialist Revolution* 8 (March–April), pp. 157–192.

— (1986). "The Regime of Capital," *Monthly Review* 37 (January 1986), p. 1–11.

Taylor, Jeffrey (1995). "Curb on Political Gifts by Bond Underwriters Has Lots of Loopholes," *Wall Street Journal,* May 8.

Taylor, Mark P. (1988). "What Do Investment Managers Know? An Empirical Study of Practitioners' Predictions," *Economica* 55, pp. 185–202.

Tegen, Andreas (1994) "Western World Gold Industry: Ownership and Control 1993," *Raw Materials Report* 10:1, p. 17.

Teoh, Siew Hong, Ivo Welch, and T.J. Wong (1995). "Earnings Management and the Post-Issue Underperformance of Seasoned Equity Offerings," mimeo, University of Michigan.

Thackray, John (1989). "Restructured Once? Then Do It Again," *Euromoney,* June 1989, p. 57.

Thomas, Sam (1995). "The Saga of the First Stock Index Futures Contract: Was It a Case of the Market Using the Wrong Model and Not Learning," mimeo, Weatherhead School of Management, Case Western Reserve University, Department of Banking and Finance.

Thurow, Lester C. (1975). *Generating Inequality: Mechanisms of Distribution in the U.S. Economy* (New York: Basic Books).

Tobias, Andrew (1982). *The Invisible Bankers: Everything the Insurance Industry Never Wanted You To Know* (New York: Linden Press/Simon & Schuster).

Tobin, James (1958). "Liquidity Preference as Behavior Towards Risk," *Review of Economic Studies* 25 (February), pp. 65–86.

— (1978). "Monetary Policies and the Economy: The Transmission Mechanism," *Southern Economic Journal* 44, pp. 421–431.

— (1984). "The Efficiency of the Financial System," *Lloyd's Bank Review* (July), pp. 1–15.

— (1995). Remarks to luncheon seminar sponsored by the Canadian Center for Policy Alternatives, Ottawa, May 29 (Ottawa: CCPA).

Tobin, James, and William C. Brainard (1977). "Asset Markets and the Cost of Capital," in Bela Balassa and Richard Nelson, eds., *Economic Progress, Private Values, and Public*

Policy: Essays in Honor of William Fellner (Amsterdam and New York: North-Holland Publishing Co.), pp. 235–262.

Tomlinson, Jim (1990). *Hayek and the Market* (London: Pluto Press).

Toner, Robin (1995). "No Free Rides: Generational Push Has Not Come to Shove," *New York Times,* December 31, sec. 4, p. 1.

Truell, Peter (1995). "Lotus Deal To Generate $35 Million Just in Fees," *New York Times,* June 13, p. D6.

Turner, Philip (1991). *Capital Flows in the 1980s: A Survey of Major Trends,* BIS Economic Papers, No. 30 (Basel: Bank for International Settlements, April).

Twentieth Century Fund (1992). *The Report of the Twentieth Century Fund Task Force on Market Speculation and Corporate Governance* (New York: Twentieth Century Fund Press).

Uchitelle, Louis (1994). "Growth of Jobs May Be Casualty in Inflation Fight," *New York Times,* April 24, p. A1.

United for a Fair Economy (1996). "Born on Third Base," (Boston: United for a Fair Economy, October).

United Nations Centre on Transnational Corporations (1991). *World Investment Report 1991: The Triad in Foreign Direct Investment* (New York: United Nations).

U.S. Bureau of the Census (1975). *Historical Statistics of the United States, Colonial Times to 1970* (Washington: U.S. Government Printing Office).

— (1993). *Money Income of Households, Families, and Persons in the United States: 1992,* Series P60-184 (Washington: U.S. Government Printing Office).

— (1994a). *Statistical Abstract of the United States* (Washington: U.S. Government Printing Office).

— (1994b). *Household Wealth and Asset Ownership: 1991,* Current Population Reports P70-34 (January).

— (1995). *Statistical Abstract of the United States* (Washington: U.S. Government Printing Office).

U.S. Bureau of Labor Statistics (1992). "Consumer Expenditures in 1991," News Release 91-607 (Washington: BLS, November 22, 1991).

U.S. Commodity Futures Trading Commission (1994). *Annual Report* (Washington: CFTC).

U.S. Congressional Budget Office (1993). *Resolving the Thrift Crisis* (April).

— (1996). *Assessing the Public Costs and Benefits of Fannie Mae and Freddie Mac* (May).

U.S. Department of Commerce, Bureau of Economic Analysis (1992). *National Income and Product Accounts of the United States,* Volumes 1 and 2 (Washington: U.S. Government Printing Office).

— (1994). "Foreign Direct Investment in the United States" and "U.S. Direct Investment Abroad," *Survey of Current Business* 74 (August), pp. 98–161.

U.S. Department of the Treasury, Securities and Exchange Commission, and Board of Governors of the Federal Reserve Board (1992). *Joint Report on the Govenment Securities Market* (Washington: U.S. Government Printing Office).

U.S. General Accounting Office (1991). "Leveraged Buyouts: Case Studies of Selected Leveraged Buyouts," GAO/GGD-91-107 (Washington: GAO, September).

— (1994a). "Bank Regulatory Structure: The Federal Republic of Germany," GAO/GGD-94-134BR (Washington: GAO, May).

— (1994b). "American Stock Exchange: More Changes Needed in Screening Emerging Companies for the Marketplace," GAO/GGD-94-72 (Washington: GAO, May).

U.S. House of Representatives, Committee on Ways and Means (1992). *Green Book: Overview of Entitlement Programs* (Washington: U.S. Government Printing Office, May 15).

U.S. Office of Management and Budget (1995). *Budget of the United States Government, Fiscal Year 1996: Analytical Perspectives* (Washington: U.S. Government Printing Office).

Useem, Michael (1989). "Revolt of the Corporate Owners and the Demobilization of Business Political Action," *Critical Sociology* 16 (Summer–Fall), pp. 7–27.

— (1996). *Investor Capitalism: How Money Managers Are Changing the Face of Corporate America* (New York: Basic Books).

Wachtel, Paul, editor (1982). *Crises in the Economic and Financial Structure* (Lexington, Mass.: Lexington Books/D.C. Heath and Co.).

Wadhwani, Sushil B. (1986). "Inflation, Bankruptcy, Default Premia and the Stock Market,"

Economic Journal 96, pp. 120-138.

Wahal, Sunil (1995). "Pension Fund Activism and Firm Performance," mimeo, Kenan–Flagler Business School, University of North Carolina (March).

Waller, David (1992). "Germany Reaches Agreement on a Single Exchange," *Financial Times,* October 7.

Wall Street Journal (1991). "Nobel Lessons in Finance," *Wall Street Journal,* May 14, p. A22.

Wanniski, Jude (1990). "The Inquisition Ax Falls," *FW* (formerly *Financial World*) 159, December 11, pp. 12–13.

Watson, John L. (1992). "Market Makers: Hallmark of the Nasdaq Market," in National Association of Securities Dealers 1992, pp. 223–234.

Webb, Sara, and Tracy Corrigan (1994). "Hedge Fund Muscle Sized Up," *Financial Times,* March 3.

Weicher, John C. (1995). "Changes in the Distribution of Wealth: Increasing Inequality?," Federal Reserve Bank of St. Louis *Review* (January–February), pp. 5–23.

Weinraub, Bernard (1995). "Martin Scorsese, Attracted to Excess, Still Taking Risks," *New York Times,* November 27, p. C11.

Whichard, Obie G., and Jeffrey H. Lowe (1995). "An Ownership-Based Disaggregation of the U.S. Current Account, 1982–93," *Survey of Current Business* 75 (October), pp. 52–73.

Williams, Jeffrey (1986). *The Economic Function of Futures Markets* (Cambridge and New York: Cambridge University Press).

Williams, John C., and Charles I. Jones (1995). "Too Much of a Good Thing? The Economics of Investment in R&D," Finance and Economics Discussion Series (FEDS) No. 95-39 (Washington: Federal Reserve Board, Division of Research and Statistics, August).

Williamson, Oliver E. (1988). "Corporate Finance and Corporate Governance," *Journal of Finance* 43 (July), pp. 567–591.

— (1993). "The Logic of Economic Organization," in Williamson and Winter (1993), pp. 90–116.

Williamson, Oliver E. and Sidney G. Winter, eds. (1993). *The Nature of the Firm: Origins, Evolution, and Development* (New York and Oxford: Oxford University Press).

Wilmsen, Steven (1991). *Silverado: Neil Bush and the Savings & Loan Scandal* (Washington: National Press Books).

Winslow, Ted (1992). "Psychoanalysis and Keynes's Account of the Psychology of the Trade Cycle," in Gerrard and Hillard (1992), pp. 212–230.

Wohlstetter, Charles (1993). "Pension Fund Socialism: Can Bureaucrats Run the Blue Chips?," *Harvard Business Review* 71 (January–February), p. 78.

Wolff, Edward N. (1994). "Trends in Household Wealth in the United States, 1962–83 and 1983–89," *Review of Income and Wealth,* Series 40, No. 2 (June), pp. 143–174.

— (1995). *Top Heavy: A Study of the Increasing Inequality of Wealth in America* (New York: Twentieth Century Fund Press).

— (1996). *Top Heavy: A Study of the Increasing Inequality of Wealth in America,* revised and updated edition (New York: New Press).

Wolfson, Martin H. (1986). *Financial Crises* (Armonk, N.Y.: M.E. Sharpe).

Woodward, Bob (1994). *The Agenda* (New York: Simon and Schuster).

World Bank (1994). *World Debt Tables, 1994–95,* 2 vols. (Washington: World Bank).

— (1996). *Annual Report, 1995* (Washington: World Bank).

Wray, L. Randall (1990). *Money and Credit in Capitalist Economies: The Endogenous Money Approach* (Aldershot, U.K.: Edward Elgar).

— (1993). "The Origin of Money and the Development of the Modern Financial System," Jerome Levy Economics Institute at Bard College, Working Paper No. 86 (March).

Young, Allan H., and Helen Stone Tice (1985). "An Introduction to National Economic Accounting," *Survey of Current Business,* 65 (April), pp. 59–76.

Zizek, Slavoj (1994). *The Metastases of Enjoyment* (London and New York: Verso).

Zweig, Martin E. (1986). *Martin Zweig's Winning on Wall Street* (New York: Warner Books).

Zweig, Phillip L. (1996). *Wriston: Walter Wriston, Citibank, and the Rise and Fall of American Financial Supremacy* (New York: Crown Publishers).

Index